Race, Gender, Class, and Criminal Justice

Race, Gender, Class, and Criminal Justice

Examining Barriers to Justice

SECOND EDITION

Danielle McDonald

Professor of Criminal Justice
Northern Kentucky University

Cherie Dawson-Edwards

Associate Professor of Criminal Justice
University of Louisville

CAROLINA ACADEMIC PRESS
Durham, North Carolina

ISBN   978-1-5310-1893-1
eISBN   978-1-5310-1894-8
LCCN   2022046447

See catalog.loc.gov for
Library of Congress Cataloging-in-Publication Data.

Carolina Academic Press
700 Kent Street
Durham, North Carolina 27701
(919) 489-7486
www.cap-press.com

Printed in the United States of America

This book is dedicated to my partner in crime Charles Scott, and our two young sons — Paul and Cormac. The world is a better place because of the three of you, and I am thankful for it.

— Danielle

This book is dedicated to my kids — Cameron and Campbell. You are the reason I fight for justice. I am a mom first and above all things. Writing this was a labor of love that happened during a global pandemic and in the midst of racial justice protests in our city (#sayhername). I must make this a better world for you. This fight takes me away from you a lot and I am grateful that you both get it. I love you for loving me uncondition- ally and understanding the fight. My pen is a protest.

— Cherie

Contents

Introduction

The second edition of this textbook embraces an intentional focus to include more diverse perspectives on the topics covered in the book. This includes the addition of a co-author as well as more references to the writings and research of those from diverse and often underrepresented backgrounds. A more in-depth examination of race and ethnicity also is included with a chapter now dedicated to each topic, their historical connotations, and how these terms are used today. A new chapter also has been added that examines juveniles and explores how childhood is constructed along with how intersectionality impacts the experiences of youth in the juvenile justice system. You also will notice that when referencing race, Black is capitalized and white is not. The authors chose to use a lower case "w" for all references to white with the exception of proper nouns such as White House or when used in direct quotes. This decision was made because the authors felt it was important to amplify the voices of the racially marginalized, especially in this second edition that attempts to better uplift the contributions of Black criminologists and scholars of color.

The purpose of this book is to examine race, ethnicity, class, and gender in the United States and how those who become involved or interact with the criminal justice system will experience the system differently based on these variables. However, it is important when reading this book to keep in mind that these variables are not necessarily independent of one another and many will experience the negative impact and/or privilege of multiple variables at one time. For example, a Hispanic middle-class woman will experience the criminal justice system differently than a Hispanic working-class woman or a white middle-class man.

Each chapter within this book also includes "In Focus" text boxes to further examine an issue that is relevant to the topic being discussed as well as a "Global Spotlight" text box that discusses the topic from a global perspective as well. Each chapter also includes bolded key terms to help the reader easily identify important terms, legislative acts, and court cases, along with a glossary. Each chapter ends with a series of discussion questions to encourage further engagement and reflection with the topic.

The book is divided into six different sections and covers policing, courts, and corrections. The first segment of the book lays the foundation for the historical and current use of the terms race, ethnicity, gender, sex, socioeconomic status, and crime. Chapters 1–5 provide an overview of the history of these terms and how they have changed and evolved over time based on what is occurring within our society politically, socially, and economically. This foundation provides the reader with a better understanding of the past use of these terms, so one can critically examine the impact of these variables on the criminal justice system today.

The second section of this book examines the role of law enforcement within our communities as well as how communities experience and interact with law enforcement differently based on race, ethnicity, religion, and class. Chapter 6 examines racial profiling and how it occurs within African American communities tied to the issue of illegal drugs, within Hispanic communities due to immigration, and within Muslim communities due to the fear of terrorism. Chapter 7 examines the militarization of local law enforcement and the financial support of the federal government that put this in place, as well as the consequences of creating an "us versus them" attitude between the police and the community. The chapter also explores historical and contemporary perspectives of protest policing in light of the 2020 social unrest following the deaths of Breonna Taylor and George Floyd and the possibility of programs, such as community-oriented policing.

The third section of the book examines the impact of the courts and sentencing on those involved in the criminal justice system and how one's experience is different based on one's race, ethnicity, gender, and/or class. Chapter 8 examines the changing role of judges and prosecutors, how discretion determines who is the most powerful actor within the courtroom, and the consequences of this for offenders based on race, ethnicity, gender, and class. The chapter ends with a discussion regarding indigent defense counsel and the impact of not being able to afford a private attorney for many clients. Chapter 9 examines the history and evolution of the death penalty in the United States as well as how the death sentence is applied based on race, class, and gender.

The fourth section of the book focuses on race, ethnicity, gender, and class issues within corrections. Chapter 10 examines the overuse of incarceration in the United States, the War on Drugs, and drug policy along with possible alternatives to incarceration that could be used such as problem-solving courts and innovative community supervision programs. Chapter 11 discusses the topic of reentry and the many obstacles returning citizens face as they work towards becoming productive members of their community, as well as programs that are attempting to help returning citizens overcome these barriers.

The fifth portion of this book addresses additional issues in the criminal justice system that are impacted by race, ethnicity, gender, and class and deserve special attention, but do not fit into the other sections of this book. For example, Chapter 12 focuses on the impact of race, ethnicity, gender, and class on juveniles as they navigate the juvenile justice system, while chapter 13 examines the problem of domestic violence, as well as the resources that are available and the dire need for more resources to address this problem. Chapter 14 addresses the problem of human trafficking and how this crime occurs within the United States but can be incredibly difficult to investigate and prosecute criminally.

The final and sixth section of the book concludes with Chapter 15, which offers an examination of where we are currently with racism and sexism, both of which overlap with the issue of class, from a criminal justice perspective. This chapter also notes that many improvements have occurred in improving racist and sexist policies and attitudes within the United States, while also acknowledging that we as Americans still have a long way to go to overcome our racist and sexist past.

Defining the Terms

ONE

Defining Race

Learning Objectives

1. Understand and critically examine the evolution of the term "race" using the framework of social construction.
2. Explain how institutions, organizations, and systems influence our understanding and perception of race.

The Social Construction of Race

Barak et al. (2010) define *race* as a "constellation of traits including physical characteristics, national origin language, culture and religion" (p. 78). This constellation is constructed by society and political interests, which determine what constitutes a racial category, the categorical characteristics, and who belongs. The concepts of "race" and "ethnicity" are related but distinct. We'll take a closer look at ethnicity in the next chapter, but first we'll tackle the evolution of the term "race" in the U.S. It has been suggested that race should be viewed as a verb before fully exploring how it is presented as a noun (powell, 1997). It is argued that race is something done to persons, not necessarily what they are. In this sense, race is described as a "function" and serves to challenge the premise that racism can be addressed without understanding the "racing" of America (p. 103). Specifically, powell (1997) argues "before someone can be said to possess a racial characteristic or identity, there must first be a process of 'racing' in which the attributes that differentiate racial classifications are designated and signified" (p. 104). As a social construct, racialized groupings are given meaning through a socio-historical lens that provides the context for the racing process. This is also known as racial formation, a concept defined as the "sociohistorical process by

Figure 1.1. © Adobe Stock/luckybusiness

which racial categories are created, inhabited, transformed and destroyed" (Omi & Winant, 1994, p. 55).

In the United States, a combination of race, national origin, and ethnicity are used to categorize and measure the population. The following racial categories, for example, are identified and tracked through the United States Census: white (76.3%), Black/African American (13.4%), Asian (5.9%), two or more races (2.4%), American Indian/Alaskan Native (1.3%), or Native Hawaiian/Pacific Islander (.2%) (U.S. Census Bureau, 2019). These choices are referred to as racial categories on the census even though most of these groupings are based on region of origin or shared culture, with the exception of the categories white and Black/African American, which directly reference skin color.

Jacobson (1998) outlined three eras of defining race between 1790 to 1965. In the first era, 1790 to 1840, race was defined as either Black or white. From 1840 to 1920, race became more unclear as the country saw a mass influx of immigrants and accompanying prejudice against various immigrant groups. Jacobson refers to "variegated whiteness," which relates to the idea that certain immigrant groups were considered more acceptable based on their perceived degree of whiteness. From 1920 to 1965, after immigration restrictions, "color again triumphed as a badge of race" (Kolchin, 2002, p. 156). This depiction of the chronology of race oversimplifies the racing process and does not adequately consider the many ways that race was regulated, codified, and weaponized in the U.S. It fails to consider the othering that occurs in the racing process. This chapter will focus on how race has been shaped by policy, practices, and perceptions of those othered as non-white.

Racing in the U.S.: Whiteness and Black Bodies

While racial categories in the U.S. expand beyond the Black-white dichotomy, an explanation of race in the U.S. must include the particular constructions of whiteness and Blackness in the U.S. How race is centered in U.S. racial ideology depends on who is describing it. On one hand, whiteness is arguably centered in the racial ideology of the U.S. (Kolchin, 2002). However, Lebron (2017) argues: "The Black body has always been at the center of racial inequality in America—how could it not, given our irrational preoccupation with skin color" (p. 102). The assignment of racial categories occurs through visual observation or self-identification. Often physical characteristics are used for racial classifications, such as skin color, facial features, the shape of one's head, and hair texture (Sue, 2006). The *social construction* of race means that it is an ideological depiction as opposed to a biological fact (Nunnally, 2018).

IN FOCUS

Racializing Asian Bodies

In 1854, the case *People v. Hall* provided an early racial categorization for Chinese immigrants. The California Supreme Court prohibited the testimony of a Chinese witness against a white defendant on the premise that an existing statute made it impermissible for "Blacks," "Mulattos," and "Indians" to testify against "whites." At that time, though the Court realized there was no racial category for Chinese persons, they declared them as "Indians." Just a few decades later, in 1882, the first versions of federal Chinese Exclusion legislation appeared. In early years, Chinese persons were categorized from a lens of national origin; however, Congress ultimately adopted the approach that Chinese referred to "any person of Chinese ancestry—a form of bloodline categorization" (Chang, 2013, p. 953). The "racialized Chinese body" eventually included a wide variety of groups, ultimately leading to the Immigration Act of 1924, which used euphemistic language banning immigration for "aliens ineligible for citizenship." By 2000, the U.S. Census Bureau had separated Asian and Pacific Islander into different racial categories. The US history of racially categorizing the Chinese-Asiatic body is similar to the racialization of Black and white bodies. The concept of "foreignness" as an ascribed label uniquely places Asian bodies in a perpetual state of Otherness. Asians in the U.S. are seen as perpetual foreigners, since their racial identity is directly connected to the "phenotypical Asian ethnic appearance," regardless of Asian immigrant or generational status (Tessler et al., 2020, p. 640).

One lens is to analyze the construction of "Black bodies" as opposed to Black people. This is necessary for understanding the historical construct of Black as a racial category. Kolchin (2002), operating from a lens of Whiteness Studies, suggested that during the period of 1790 to 1840 "Americans saw people as either Black or white" (p. 156). It should be noted that the enslaved that were of African descent did not retain personhood in the U.S. It is inaccurate to refer to their race as having application to people when at the time the enslaved were "commodified and economized" Black bodies that were considered property, not people. As Kendi (2019) stated:

> The White body defines the American body. The White body segregates the Black body from the American body. The White body instructs the Black body to assimilate into the American body. The White body rejects the Black body assimilating into the American body—and history and consciousness duel anew. (p. 33)

A better grasp of the social construction of Black bodies facilitates insight into how race is part of a bigger machine with social, political, and economic moving parts that impact how people interface based on "racially ascribed social norms, social networks, expectations and political preferences" (Nunnally, 2018, p. 2).

Many would argue that these social norms, networks, expectations, and political leanings are rooted in white supremacy culture and that Black bodies and Blackness are relegated to the lower rungs of society due to the centering of whiteness. These arguments are supported by powell's explanation of how racing occurs:

> Racing is largely a top-down process where the more powerful group first denudes the racial Other of its self-definition. This is often done by denying the racial Other its language and culture and then assigning a set of characteristics to this group that are beneath those of the more powerful group.

In 1860, Jefferson Davis proclaimed that America was founded "by white men for white men" (Kendi, 2019, p. 33). "White" was initially defined as those of British heritage, and the benefits of being white only applied to these groups. Irish and German immigrants, for example, were heavily discriminated against. However, Irish and Germans eventually were included under the category of white as new waves of immigrants from other parts of Europe, such as Italy, began to arrive in the United States and the negative attention was turned toward them. Those of Jewish descent also were not viewed by American society as white until after the Holocaust, even though their skin was white and they were of European descent. Therefore, the definition of white broadened over time based on what was happening politically, socially, and economically within society (Painter, 2012).

Scholars acknowledge that whiteness is not necessarily problematic without the accompanying concepts of white privilege and white supremacy. However, the invisibleness of whiteness may lead white people to believe that the way they live their lives is morally neutral, average, or ideal (Sleeter & Bernal, 2004). Whiteness becomes problematic because it is:

a) Predicated on white supremacy
b) Imposed overtly and covertly on People of Color
c) Made invisible to those who benefit from its existence. (Sue, 2006, p. 15)

Whiteness can be viewed as the collection of physical characteristics primarily determined by fair or light skin color/tone, although other physical features may be deemed desirable, such as blond hair, blue eyes, or elongated face. It should be noted that whiteness does not apply negative or positive attributes to these characteristics. However, white supremacy firmly suggests that whiteness is positive and non-white groups represent the negative. *White supremacy* is defined as "a doctrine of white superiority and non-white inferiority that justifies domination and prejudicial treatment of minority groups" (Sue, 2006, p. 17). While many associate this concept only with the racialized history of the U.S., there is much evidence that white supremacy remains embedded in systems, institutions, and structures while also providing advantages based on race.

Race, the Slave Trade, and Colonization

In 1607, Great Britain founded the Virginia colony. Virginia proved to be a fertile place, and soon workers were needed to farm the crops that were being sent back to Great Britain. In the beginning, Irish and poor English laborers were used to fill this shortage of labor. They were sent on ships from England to the new colony, bringing with them hopes and dreams for a brighter future. These impoverished laborers entered into contracts of indentured servitude to pay for their journey, during which they would work for a number of years with the promise they would eventually be granted their freedom to start a new life. Although the majority of laborers during the 1600s were of European descent, there were a few African slaves who had been brought to the colonies via the Caribbean islands. Both European and African slave laborers were treated horrendously and would on occasion band together to fight back against their oppressors, such as in 1676, during Bacon's Rebellion (Breen, 1973).

IN FOCUS

Denmark Vesey

Enslaved Africans are rarely portrayed in history books as fighting back against their oppressors. However, many fought back on an individual level by slowing down their work, pretending to be sick, or escaping and heading North. Others came together to fight back, and there were several large uprisings led by those who were enslaved and many more plans that were discussed, but that did not come to fruition. For example, Denmark Vesey was an enslaved African in Charleston, South Carolina. In 1799, he won the lottery and was able to buy his freedom for $600. He was literate and became a prominent figure within his church, where he preached against slavery by comparing it to the enslavement of the Israelites in the New Testament. He believed that God would punish those who participated in slavery just as had occurred in the Bible. In 1822, Vesey, along with other church leaders from the African Methodist Episcopal Church, began to plot a rebellion where they would take over the city arsenal and kill the men who were slave owners. Their movement grew, and they were able to successfully recruit slaves from the city as well as the rural areas. However, about two weeks prior to the rebellion, several slaves who feared the violence that was to come told their slaveholders of the plot, and the leaders of the rebellion were gathered and hanged. In all, 35 people were executed. Although new restrictions were placed on the enslaved in Charleston, Black Africans memorialized Vesey and continued his teachings regarding slavery. Vesey and his rebellion also inspired others involved in the abolition movement, such as writers Frederick Douglass and Harriet Beecher Stowe (PBS, 2003).

Towards the end of the 1600s, the demand for labor grew as cotton and tobacco production expanded. However, the landowners were finding it increasingly difficult to control their labor force as there were now a number of freed English and Irish laborers who lived in the colony as well. Freed English and Irish laborers were demanding rights and land in exchange for their labor. However, the landowners did not agree. This led to mounting tension between the laborers and the landowners as well as fears among the wealthy that the poor freed English and Irish laborers would band together with the African slaves to fight the wealthy, minority landowning population (Breen, 1973).

However, by the end of the 1600s the labor shortage and unrest was resolved. Due to technological advances in shipping, it was now possible to transport African slaves directly from Africa to the colonies. This created a supply of slave labor that was more abundant and accessible than the white indentured servants. Freed Irish and English servants also were benefiting from the booming economy in the Virginia colony and were not as impoverished. Many freed English and Irish servants were able to afford land in Virginia or in nearby colonies where the land was cheaper. African slaves and freed Europeans no longer had servitude and poverty in common, breaking their bond and motivation to fight together (Breen, 1973).

By the early 1700s, African slaves were well established as the primary source of labor in the Southern colonies. As the awareness of the brutality of the slave trade and the lives of the slaves became better known, people started to speak out against slavery and the anti-slavery movement began. This forced those who were pro-slavery to defend their positions. Earlier conceptions used the term "race" more frequently to refer to three distinct groups of people—Europeans, Indians, and Africans. Now people were no longer being grouped based upon class or whether they were free, but rather physical characteristics such as skin color (Smedley, 1997).

Later, the Great Chain of Being was used to justify the harsh treatment of Africans. *The Great Chain of Being* was an ancient concept used by monarchies in medieval times to keep their subjects in line. It was believed that God was the highest on the chain, followed by the king, people, animals, and plants. Everyone and everything had a place in the hierarchy and were connected, so that for one part of the chain to work, all have to do their task. As long as everyone sticks to their place within the hierarchy, then there will be harmony. However, if one part of the chain is broken, there will be chaos. Monarchies relied on this concept to impart the belief to their subjects that if they offended against the crown, they would be offending directly against God (New World Encyclopedia, 2014).

In the 1700s, the Great Chain of Being was connected to race. It was argued by those who were pro-slavery that there was a hierarchy among the races, with Europeans or white people at the top of the hierarchy and Africans or Black people at the bottom. Social characteristics, such as one's character or intellect, also were believed to be tied to one's race and therefore unchangeable, just as one's skin color was unchangeable. Those who were pro-slavery were able to dehumanize slaves by elevating the status of Europeans on the hierarchy above Africans, which was then used to justify the harsh treatment of the slaves and the idea of owning people (Smedley, 1997).

Race, Biology, and the Scientific Community

Racialized categories have a deep tradition in pseudo-scientific proof that Black people are inferior. The same Black bodies that were considered valuable as property became "biologically and societally repugnant" once freed (Nunnally, 2018, p. 6). In the late 1700s, the theory of *polygenism*, or the belief that humans fall into different species and are not one race, gained further traction, as did the notion of a racial hierarchy supported by the ideological framework of the Great Chain of Being. Now the idea of separate races with distinct differences among them was being discussed in the scientific community, seeming to give it further legitimacy. By the early 1800s, scientific methods were being applied to examine the differences between the races. The pro-slavery physician Samuel Morton, for example, measured skull capacity to examine differences in brain size among races (American Anthropological Association, 2011).

The idea of separate races went widely unchallenged until the publication of Charles Darwin's *On the Origin of Species by Means of Natural Selection* in 1859. Darwin's book had a profound impact on the scientific community as scientists now began to ponder how evolution impacted everything around them. This led to changes in our understanding of race as well and whether there were separate races or just one human race, also known as **monogenism**. This new theory explained the differences between groups of people through evolution; for example, darker skin color reflected how the human body had evolved and was not a result of separate races. One's skin would be darker, for example, if in one's environment one is exposed to more sunlight. The skin's pigmentation in this case evolved to a darker color to serve as a natural barrier to the sun. At this point, there were two distinct theories on race—polygenism, or the belief there are separate races, and monogenism, or the belief that there is only one human race (American Anthropological Association, 2011).

In 2003, the **Human Genome Project**, which was tasked with mapping the human genome, concluded there were not separate species of humans. According to the Human Genome Project, humans share 99.99% of the same genetic makeup, making it impossible for there to be separate human species or races (National Human Genome Research Institute, 2014). However, the notion of separate races is so ingrained in our psyche that some researchers continue to try to identify and understand these incredibly minute differences.

The Human Genome Project has scientifically demonstrated through DNA research that there are not sub-species of humans or different races. Therefore, the differences that had been assumed to exist biologically between the races do not exist. However, it's impossible to deny that race impacts the way we interact with one another on a daily basis and can have very real consequences. Next, we will examine the history of race in America and the impact it has on society politically, socially, and economically.

IN FOCUS

Cesare Lombroso and Biological Determinism

Cesare Lombroso, the "father of criminology," drew from Darwin's evolutionary theory and developed his research based on biological determinism. Theories of biological determinism served to support the idea that white people were superior other races. Lombroso is known for his premise that crime in Southern Italy was the fault of inferior people of African descent. In an 1871 work, "White Man and Colored Man: Lectures on the Origin and Variety of Human Races," he claimed:

> black represented the lowest and most primitive race… the African had changed little for millennia, still displaying infantile and monkey like manner of smiling and gesturing. (Gabbidon, 2007, p. 10)

Lombroso's claims about Black people were based on a belief that they possessed an undeveloped and smaller brain. He also believed that they had dominant foreheads and thus their "passions drown [their] intelligence" (Gabbidon, 2007, p. 10). Lombroso continued to connect race and crime when explaining the criminal behavior of women. He claimed that Black women and Indigenous women were masculine presenting and attributed it to atavism. Atavism was Lombroso's theory that criminals were "atavistic" or throwbacks in evolution. Later Willem Bonger, a Dutch criminologist, discredited Lombroso's work and observed that "criminality is not a characteristic" and that crime was "completely different" from characteristics that one is born possessing (1943, p. 27).

Race, Reconstruction, Politics, and the Courts

On April 12, 1861, the Civil War began, and war was waged between the Northern and Southern states over state's rights and the right to own slaves. On January 1, 1863, the *Emancipation Proclamation* freed slaves living in states fighting against the North. However, the Civil War did not end until May 9, 1865, when the North declared victory over the South (American Anthropological Association, 2011).

The Reconstruction Period that followed the Civil War, from 1865 to 1877, brought political progress for the newly freed slaves. On December 18, 1865, the *Thirteenth Amendment* was passed and officially abolished slavery. The Emancipation Proclamation had only covered those who were enslaved in Southern states fighting against the North, but the Thirteenth Amendment abolished the practice of slavery throughout the United States. The *Civil Rights Act of 1866* stated that one cannot be discriminated against based on race for jobs or housing and all citizens are equally protected by the law (American Anthropological Association, 2011).

Coupled with the Thirteenth Amendment, the Reconstruction Act of 1867 led to drastic political progress for the formerly enslaved. The Equal Justice Initiative (EJI) records that:

> In elections for new state governments, Black voter turnout neared 90 percent in many jurisdictions, and Black voters—who comprised a majority in many districts and a statewide majority in Louisiana—elected both white and Black leaders to represent them. More than six hundred African Americans, most of them formerly enslaved, were elected as state legislators during this period. The

Reconstruction states sent sixteen Black representatives to the United States Congress, and Mississippi voters elected the nation's first Black senators: Hiram Revels and Blanche Bruce. The newly elected and racially integrated Reconstruction governments took bold action at the state level, repealing discriminatory laws, rewriting apprenticeship and vagrancy statutes, outlawing corporal punishment, and sharply reducing the number of capital offenses. African Americans also won election to law enforcement positions like sheriff and chief of police, and were empowered to serve on juries. (2017a, p. 10)

Unfortunately, this change in politics did not translate into a new way of thinking for many Southerners, who continued to feel Black people were not equal to white people and should be treated accordingly. This made life in the South difficult economically for freed Black people, many of whom did not have anywhere to go and were dependent upon white landowners for work. These difficult economic times also were coupled with growing tensions within social spaces, where many white people were fighting back against the new federal laws giving Black men more access to that to which white men were already entitled.

In response, former Confederate soldiers began organizing "social clubs" that grew into massive paramilitary groups who catapulted into a racial terror designed to overthrow Reconstruction. It should be noted that while the KKK has largely been described as a group of white supremacists, the concept of white supremacy culture, as noted earlier in this chapter, is based on a broader concept that includes an acknowledgement that Black life has been regulated and dictated from its onset by the enduring legacy of centering whiteness in policy and practice. The Equal Justice Initiative (2017a) reports that these vigilantes had the "tacit endorsement of the broader White community" (p. 11).

The formation of the Ku Klux Klan (KKK), for example, occurred during the summer of 1866 following the passage of the Thirteenth Amendment. The intention of the KKK was to remove the Republican Party from office, keep Black people relegated to the lower rungs of society, and reinstate white supremacy. Despite the creation of the KKK, political progress continued for racial equality over the next couple of years. In 1868, the *Fourteenth Amendment* was passed, providing due process and equal protection under the law for all men. In 1870, the *Fifteenth Amendment* was passed, which allowed all men to vote despite color, race, or if one had been previously enslaved. And between 1870 and 1871, the *Enforcement Acts* were passed as a direct response to the KKK and proclaimed that if a state failed to recognize a Black man's right to be on a jury, vote, hold office, or experience equal protection under the law then the federal government could step in to address the violation (American Anthropological Association, 2011). For example, in 1871, the Ku Klux Klan Act was passed, which granted access to federal courts if one's civil rights were violated and permitted federal prosecution of civil rights violations (EJI, n.d.).

However, this positive momentum was met with a huge setback in 1873, when the United States Supreme Court heard the *Slaughter House Cases*. These consolidated cases were the first United States Supreme Court case to be heard on the new Fourteenth Amendment. The United States Supreme Court concluded, with a narrow margin of 5–4, that the Fourteenth Amendment only applied to an American citizen's federal rights and not their state rights. Therefore, the amendment could no longer be applied at the state level. This was a major setback for the racial equality movement and the federal government's ability to intervene on the behalf of someone who was being discriminated against at the state level (American Anthropological Association, 2011).

Throughout the 1870s, the KKK remained a powerful force in the South and was able to sway the ballot boxes with their intimidation practices. The KKK attempted to accomplish their mission by holding night raids where they dressed in all white gowns with hooded masks to hide their identity. During these night raids, they terrorized the Black community with violent lynchings and burning crosses (Chalmers, 2014). The Black Codes of post-Civil War times were simply revisions to the old Slave Codes, which dictated and restricted the enslaved's daily experiences. Arguably, Black Codes simply replaced the word "slave" with "Black." These codes were enforced by white people due to implications of legislation like the Reconstruction Act of 1867, which enfranchised Black men while simultaneously restricting the vote for former Confederates. In the South, many state legislatures passed laws creating crimes of moral turpitude that assigned felon status to certain crimes most likely to be committed by freedmen.

This led to a return of Democrats in office across the South (Chalmers, 2014). Another direct reaction to the passage of the Thirteenth, Fourteenth, and Fifteenth Amendments was the start of what later became known as *Jim Crow laws*. Jim Crow laws were used to segregate Black people and white people in public and social spaces within the South by, for example, insisting on separate bathrooms for white people and Black people as well as separate restaurants and stores (PBS, 2002). *Racial terror lynchings*, which were not just carried out by the KKK, became a mechanism to ensure that newly freed Black people were kept in their place and white superiority was maintained. Racial terror lynchings are distinguished as a mechanism to maintain the lower status of Black persons and enforce Jim Crow laws. Racial terror lynchings were extralegal and should not be considered "frontier justice." Instead they usually occurred in locations with operating criminal justice processes by the hands of white citizens who believed the legal process was not punitive enough for Black people. This is evident by the types of "offenses" punishable by lynching. Often the offense was an imaginary or exaggerated interaction between a Black man and a white woman which was deemed a violation of the social code. The Equal Justice Initiative (EJI) (2017a) reports:

Racial terror lynching was a tool used to enforce Jim Crow laws and racial segregation, a tactic for maintaining racial control by victimizing the entire African American community, not merely punishment of an alleged perpetrator for a crime. Our research confirms that many victims of terror lynchings were murdered without being accused of any crime; they were killed for minor social transgressions or for demanding basic rights and fair treatment. (p. 31)

Another distinction between these acts and state-sanctioned capital punishment was the lack of accountability for perpetrators and the absence of justice for lynching victims and the community. In addition, these lynchings distinctly targeted and terrorized entire Black communities as a racial control device. From 1877 to 1950, there were over 4,084 documented racial terror lynchings in the most active lynchings states: Alabama, Arkansas, Florida, Georgia, Kentucky, Louisiana, Mississippi, North Carolina, South Carolina, Tennessee, Texas, and Virginia (EJI, 2017a).

As a direct response to Jim Crow laws, The **Civil Rights Act of 1875** was passed. This United States federal law stated that one cannot discriminate based on race for public accommodations or public transportation. However, this victory was short lived. In 1883, the United States Supreme Court, in the consolidated decision for **The Civil Rights Cases**, declared the Civil Rights Act of 1875 unconstitutional, because you cannot force private individuals to abide by the law, only state agencies. It also was decided that the Thirteenth Amendment eliminated slavery, but does not prohibit one from being discriminated against (PBS, 2002). This decision was followed a few years later, in 1896, by the United States Supreme Court case **Plessey v. Ferguson**, which ruled that separate social and public spaces were constitutional as long as the spaces were equal. *Plessey v. Ferguson* provided legitimacy and solidified the place of Jim Crow laws. Now those who believed Black people and white people should be segregated within social and public spaces had the backing of the greatest court in the land—the United States Supreme Court (PBS, 2002).

Race and Social Movements

In 1909, the **National Association for the Advancement of Colored People** (NAACP) was formed by bringing together Black and white civil rights leaders. By 1910, they had started their own newsletter, *The Crisis*, and were actively creating branches in both the North and the South. Although many Black Southerners were members of the NAACP, they had to be in secret to not risk losing their jobs or worse. The NAACP was active and successful in a variety of arenas, fighting for racial justice through the media, protests, investigating acts of lynching, and advocating for defendants of court cases (PBS, 2002).

Four new United States Supreme Court justices were appointed, between 1937 and 1940, drastically changing the ideological makeup of the court and making it more likely for the federal government to intervene in cases of racial discrimination and segregation. In 1938, the Supreme Court case **Gaines v. Canada** was the first case to start tearing down racial segregation laws. Gaines, a Black student, was denied admission to the all-white Missouri State Law School. Gaines argued that since there was not an equal alternative, he should be allowed to attend the all-white school. The court upheld the *Plessey* decision and concluded the state of Missouri had to pay for Gaines to attend school out of state or build a law school for Black students. Even though *Plessey v. Ferguson* was upheld, *Gaines v. Canada* began the dismantling of separate but equal because it was now more expensive and logistically difficult to uphold segregation (PBS, 2002).

The NAACP, armed with counsel, civil rights leaders, and lawyer Thurgood Marshall (later a Supreme Court justice), began taking on the courts in a series of cases throughout the 1940s that helped to further disassemble segregation laws one by one. These victories led to the landmark 1955 case **Brown v. Board of Education**, where Marshall argued before the Supreme Court that segregation in education was unconstitutional due to the unequal environments of segregated schools. Marshall argued that segregated schools violated the Fourteenth Amendment by denying an entire race equal protection under the law. The Supreme Court agreed and unanimously voted that schools should no longer be segregated (PBS, 2002).

Although progress had occurred through the courts, there was still noticeable segregation in public spaces throughout the South as well as in the schools. All across the country young people, religious organizations, and civil rights leaders came together and demanded equal treatment in public spaces for all, no matter the color of their skin. Martin Luther King, Jr., for example, was an influential leader of the Civil Rights Movement. King was a Baptist preacher and founder of the civil rights group **Southern Christian Leadership Conference** (SCLC), which used nonviolent protest as a mechanism to bring awareness to the issue of segregation in the South. These nonviolent protests were often met with violence; for example, protestors were regularly targeted with police brutality, and leaders were often battered with violence through assassinations and bombings (PBS, 2014).

During the spring of 1963, the SCLC led **The Birmingham Campaigns**, which brought the Civil Rights Movement into the national spotlight. Over the course of a few months, nonviolent civil rights protestors organized and participated in a series of protests, including lunch counter sit-ins as well as marches and targeted store boycotts in Birmingham, Alabama. The protestors, including women and children, were met with police dogs and water hoses; the encounters were documented for a national audience. As these stories were broadcast on television across the country, sympathy spread for the nonviolent Civil Rights Movement. This led to the city of Birmingham backing down and agreeing to desegregate the city. This was a major accomplishment for the Civil Rights Movement, as Birmingham had been known as America's most segregated city (PBS, 2014).

However, integration in the South was not easy and was often met with violence, as was the case in the Sixteenth Street Baptist Church bombing in Birmingham just months after the Birmingham Campaigns. The church had been targeted as a known meeting place for civil rights leaders. The bombing killed four little girls and injured twenty-two others during Sunday services (Barber, 2002).

The Civil Rights Movement and the level of violence that had been used against the nonviolent protestors had resonated with the American public and many were again demanding the federal government intervene. This led to the passage of the *Civil Rights Act of 1964*, which prohibited segregation in public spaces, businesses, and schools, along with the prohibition of discrimination in employment. The Civil Rights Act of 1964 was a major win in the movement towards racial equality and the biggest victory since the legislation of the Reconstruction Era (Our Documents, 2014a).

Since Reconstruction, laws also had been created across the South to make it easy to *disenfranchise* (deny the right to vote through legislation or intimidation). Hate groups such as the KKK intimidated voters at the polling stations and in raids leading up to the vote. Restrictions such as the use of literacy tests were used to keep eligible voters from registering to vote, if they were unable to pass a test. Civil rights protestors turned their attention to removing these barriers to voters and bringing attention to laws and tactics that were disenfranchising many voters throughout the South.

IN FOCUS

Disenfranchisement and the "Menace of Negro Domination"

Voter disenfranchisement has been a pervasive tool for diluting the voting power of racialized minorities in the U.S. Voter disenfranchisement policies such as the poll tax, literacy tests, grandfather clauses, and felony disenfranchisement were all facially race-neutral policies designed to counteract the "menace of negro domination" (Behrens et al., 2003). For example, poll taxes were implemented by Southern states following the Civil War as a way to keep African Americans from voting by imposing a tax that must be paid prior to voting. From 1885 to 1908, all eleven former Confederate states rewrote their constitutions to include provisions restricting voting rights with poll taxes, literacy tests, and felon disenfranchisement. By 1964, most states had removed poll taxes, but there were still five Southern states that implemented the tax to keep minorities and the poor from being able to vote. Poll taxes were eliminated for federal elections with the passage of the Twenty-Fourth Amendment, in January of 1964. However, it was not until the passage of the 1964 Civil Rights Act a few months later that Americans were protected against poll taxes at the state level as well (Bondi, 2015). While poll taxes have been mostly eliminated, a recent Florida law has been deemed a modern-day poll tax. In 2018, Florida, one of the last states to have a lifetime voting ban for convicted felons, passed a state constitutional amendment that restored the voting rights of convicted felons once they complete "all terms of sentence including parole or probation."

At the time of its passage, nearly 1.4 million Floridians (including one out of every five Black adults in the state) were disenfranchised due to felony disenfranchisement. Though the amendment had almost 65 percent of Florida voters' approval, the Florida legislature passed Senate Bill 7066, which now prevents the restoration of felon voting rights until all "legal financial obligations" are met (Grossman & Stern, 2020). Felon voter restrictions date back to the mid-1800s and became more prominent in the South in order to disenfranchise formerly enslaved persons. Public records for the constitutional conventions of Virginia (1901–02), South Carolina (1895), Mississippi (1890), and Alabama (1901) document that the purpose of the nineteenth-century felon disenfranchisement laws in those states was to suppress the Black vote (Dawson-Edwards, 2017). Many of these new constitutions were made to stop the advancement of Black citizens and to uphold segregationist prohibitions against interracial marriage and integrated public education. Florida's felon restoration provisions have been categorized as a modern-day poll tax.

On March 7, 1965, a day that would later become known as "Bloody Sunday," a few hundred protestors marched from Selma, Alabama, with the intention of heading to Montgomery, Alabama. After only a few blocks they were met by local and state police, who brutally attacked the nonviolent protestors with nightsticks and tear gas. This led to a series of protests that drew thousands from across the state to the capitol (National Park Service, 2014). A few months later, the ***Voting Rights Act of 1965*** was passed, making literacy tests illegal and assigning federal monitors to states that had participated in discriminatory practices (Our Documents, 2014b). The attempts to remedy the racial ills of those times and the legacy of slavery is perhaps best summed up by President Lyndon B. Johnson who famously said: "You do not take a person who, for years, has been hobbled by chains and liberate him, bring him up to the starting line of a race and then say, 'You are free to compete with all the others', and still justly believe you have been completely fair."

Race Today

The Civil Rights Movement of the 1950s and 1960s had a direct impact on the opportunities that were opened for many Black Americans. Black upper and middle classes formed as opportunities for education were equalized, and President Barak Obama, a Black man, was elected president of the United States of America in 2008. In 2020, Kamala Harris was elected as the first U.S. vice president who identifies as a Black and Indian American woman. All of this was unimaginable only a few years ago. Some point to these accomplishments of the Civil Rights Movement as an example of how America is now color blind. This may seem true for some Americans who live in homogenous racial communities. It can be easy to believe that people are not treated differently based upon the color of their skin when the majority of those around you resemble you. However, to deny that people are treated differently based upon their race is to deny the experiences of many Americans and to underestimate the power of one's own privilege.

GLOBAL SPOTLIGHT

Global Colorism

In these critical moments of recognizing and celebrating differences while raising issues related to racial justice, more attention is being given to the issue of colorism. Colorism is usually related to the gradation of skin tone and the accompanying ideals of racial hierarchy. Colorism can also be related to secondary racial features such as hair texture, facial features, etc. Ultimately, as Dr. Joy DeGruy stated, "colorism is rooted in proximity to whiteness" (Riley & Yates, 2020). Recent research in the U.S. has shown that school discipline and colorism intersect with evidence that girls with a darker skin tone are two times more likely to be suspended than girls with lighter or white skin tones (Blake et al., 2017). Other research has shown that colorism impacts court proceedings and sentencing (Bahraini et al., 2021) and even the death penalty (Eberhart et al., 2006). In addition to the criminal justice system, other social issues also reflect the impact of colorism. For example, Reece (2021) found that dark-skinned African Americans earn $11.72 compared to light-skinned African Americans at $14.72 and white Americans at $15.94.

Globally, colorism is an issue that must be acknowledged and examined due to its detrimental effects on people of color and the unacknowledged way it contributes to racialized treatment. As such, it is important to note that U.S. conceptualizations do not necessarily comport with how other parts of the world view race and color. Colorism permeates across the globe in different ways and is complicated by how race is conceptualized in different cultures. In Latin America, the term "race" is rarely used, and Latin Americans instead prefer "color" to categorize people by race and ethnicity (Telles & Paschel, 2014). However, similar to the U.S., it is apparent that lighter skin toned individuals in Latin America experience advantages related to a number of issues (i.e., education, health, marriageability, etc.). Colorism in Latin America has even been codified by law. For example, the census in Brazil has used a classification system based on color since 1872. Up until 1991, the census asked the question "what is your color?" with options for white, Black, and mixed. It was then changed to read "what is your color or race?" (Dixon & Telles, 2017).

Jacobs et al. (2016) suggested that even now "pigmentocracy employs hegemonic ideals of beauty, influenced by the privileges of white supremacy established historically." The lasting legacy of colorism across the world is reflected in the modern skin bleaching industry. Skin bleaching is the use of cosmetic products to depigment darker skin. It is used to mitigate the disadvantages of darker skin despite the hazardous materials often used. In India, the skin whitening industry is estimated at $500 million and is often used to improve marriageability (Frayer, 2020). Colorism appears to be fueling the cosmetic industry in certain parts of the world in an exploitative response to disadvantages based on racialized features. Frayer (2020) reports that skin tone is a filter option on some Indian marriage websites. Dixon and Telles (2017) suggest that "Whiteness and light skin are now worldwide commodities that can be obtained for the right price."

Privilege comes in many forms and is often something that is not acknowledged by the group who holds the advantage (McIntosh, 1986). In fact, it can be difficult to notice privilege unless you are the one being excluded. Privilege also can be difficult to see because it is not always clear cut. For example, you can be privileged in one area of your life and not in another (McIntosh, 1986). In the case of race, privilege comes to those who are white. White people, for example, may not face the same challenges Black people often do when navigating the criminal justice system. Laws put in place during the War on Drugs specifically targeted drugs thought to be used more often in the Black community (this is covered in more depth in Chapter 5). White parents also do not have to worry about their sons when they are in public spaces the same way Black parents do (Amber, 2013). Black parents, for example, often instruct their sons to only engage with police in certain ways and to be mindful of their behavior when in public places, such as convenience stores. These lessons are taught due to the history of how the police and public have interacted with young Black men (Amber, 2013).

Today differential treatment based on race is more likely to include one's ability to access goods, services, and opportunities due to one's race, or what is more broadly referred to as *institutional racism* (Ford & Kelly, 2005). This occurs when the policies and procedures of an institution, public or private, treat people differently or provide different services based upon race. This can be seen, for instance, when a police department stops and frisks Black men walking down the street at disproportionate rates or when someone who offends against a white person receives a longer sentence than someone who offends against a Black person (more on this in Chapter 6). According to Miller and Garran (2008), institutional racism is a phenomenon that "leads to exclusion from neighborhoods, jobs, schools, politics, health and mental health care" (p. 32). They also suggest that institutional racism leads to a higher likelihood of contact with the criminal justice system. Institutional racism is de-

Figure 1.2. © iStock / jacoblund

scribed as a widespread social pattern that enforces oppression on minority groups. It includes areas governed by seemingly race-neutral policies such as political racism, residential racism, educational racism, and racism in the criminal justice system, all of which play into the continued disorganization of certain communities (Dawson-Edwards, 2017).

Ibram Kendi has popularly been recognized for amplifying the term anti-racist. An *anti-racist* is "one who is supporting an anti-racist policy through their actions or expressing an anti-racist idea" (p. 13). His work has been prominently displayed and applied in recent years due to the recognition that racism remains in the U.S. and the "marriage" between racist laws, practices, and mindsets creates and institutionalizes racialized inequities. Kendi argues that it is important to use the term "racist policy" instead of using language like "institutional" or "structural" racism. This argument is based on the concrete nature of policy and the need to state specifically what the problem is and where it lies. This approach to understanding the pervasiveness of racism through policymaking encourages a focus on specific policies that not only have oppressive intent but also those whose impact continues to be seen in society. For instance, felony disenfranchisement laws in many Southern states were specifically created to counteract the Black vote and their legacies persist. An example of racialized impact without intent can be found with a look at Kentucky. As a border state, Kentucky's felony disenfranchisement laws existed long before the end of the Civil War, so unlike Southern states there is no evidence that the law was racially motivated. However, its racialized impact continues to be felt centuries later. For instance, as a result of racial disparities in felony convictions, Kentucky has the highest disenfranchisement rate for Black people in the country, with one of every four (26.2 percent) African American adults barred from voting (EJI, 2017b). The challenge of combatting racism is to recognize that as racial reconciliation remains a goal, truth telling must occur. These truths remain difficult for many Americans because the racial curriculum, or how we learn about race and racism, does not adequately prepare them for these difficult topics.

Summary

In 1978, U.S. Supreme Court Justice Harry Blackmun penned: "In order to get beyond racism, we must first take account of race. There is no other way. And in order to treat some persons equally we must treat them differently." In many ways the advancements we have seen over the last 100 years in racial equality are incredible, but in other ways little has changed. Instead, racism has just taken on a different form and is not as easily recognizable as it once was during the days of slavery or the Civil Rights Movement. Although there are individuals or organizations that will discriminate against a person or group due to their skin color, most people do not espouse their negative views of race in person anymore, as it is not seen as politically correct to do so and may be viewed as offensive.

Discussion Questions

1. What does the author mean by the social construction of race? Be sure to provide examples of how this occurs.

2. How has biology been used to connect race to inferiority and crime?

3. How did social movements, such as the Civil Rights Movement, impact the definition of race in the United States? What organizations or social movements are fighting for equality for all ethnicities and races today? How are these organizations similar to and/or different from the organizations of the twentieth century?

Key Terms

race	Human Genome Project
social construction	Emancipation Proclamation
whiteness	Thirteenth Amendment
white supremacy	Civil Rights Act of 1866
Great Chain of Being	Fourteenth Amendment
polygenism	Fifteenth Amendment
monogenism	Enforcement Acts

Slaughter House cases
Jim Crow laws
racial terror lynchings
Civil Rights Act of 1875
The Civil Rights Cases
Plessey v. Ferguson
National Association for the Advancement of Colored People
Gaines v. Canada
Brown v. Board of Education

Southern Christian Leadership Conference
The Birmingham Campaigns
Civil Rights Act of 1964
disenfranchise
Voting Rights Act of 1965
privilege
institutional racism
anti-racist

References

Amber, J. (2013, July 29). The talk: How parents raising black boys try to keep their sons safe. *Time.* http://content.time.com/time/magazine/article/0,9171,2147710,00.html

American Anthropological Association. (2011). Race: Are we so different? http://www.understandingrace.org/home.html.

Bahraini, A., Lueras, M., & Johnson, O. (2021). Colorism, racism, and the criminal justice system: How is an innocent black man in prison for life? *CrimRxiv.* https://scholar.google.com/citations?view_op=view_citation&hl=en&user=B6p7GpwAAAAJ&citation_for_view=B6p7GpwAAAAJ:9yKSN-GCB0IC

Barak, G., Leighton, P., & Flavin, J. (2010). *Class, race, gender & crime: The social realities of justice in America* (3rd ed.). Rowman & Littlefield Publishers, Inc.

Barber, G. (2002). The Birmingham church bombing. PBS NewsHour. http://www.pbs.org/newshour/updates/media-jan-june02-birmingham_04-18/

Behrens, A., Uggen, C., & Manza, J. (2003). Ballot manipulation and the "menace of negro domination": Racial threat and felon disenfranchisement in the United States. *American Journal of Sociology, 109*(3), 559–605.

Blake, J., Keith, V. M., Luo, W., Le, H., & Salter, P. (2017). The role of colorism in explaining African American females' suspension risk. *School Psychology Quarterly, 32*(1), 118–130.

Bondi, C. (2015). Voting rights: A history of poll taxes. Newsmax. http://www.newsmax.com/FastFeatures/voting-rights-poll-taxes-history/2015/12/30/id/707686/

Bonger, W. A. (1943). *Race and crime.* Columbia University Press.

Breen, T. H. (1973). A changing labor force and race relations in Virginia, 1660–1710. *Journal of Social History, 7*, 3–25.

Chalmers, D. (2014). Essay: Ku Klux Klan. Southern Poverty Law Center. http://www.splcenter.org/contact-us

Chang, R. S. (2013). The invention of Asian Americans. *University of California Irvine Law Review, 3*, 947–964.

Dawson-Edwards, C. (2011, 2017). Politics, policy and DMC communities: The cyclical impact of community political disempowerment on DMC. In N. Parsons-Pollard (Ed.), *Disproportionate minority contact* (pp. 235–250). Carolina Academic Press.

Dixon, A. R., & Telles, E. E. (2017). Skin color and colorism: Global research, concepts, and measurement. *Annual Review of Sociology, 43,* 405–424.

Eberhardt, J.L.,Davies, P G.; Purdie-Vaughns, V.J., & Johnson, S.Lynn. (2006). Looking deathworthy: Perceived stereotypicality of black defendants predicts capital-sentencing outcomes. *Cornell Law Faculty Publications.* Paper 41. http://scholarship.law.cornell.edu/lsrp_papers/41

Equal Justice Initiative (nd). Oct. 17: Violence by KKK in South Carolina forces Pres. Grant to declare martial law. A history of racial injustice. https://calendar.eji.org/racial-injustice/oct/17

Equal Justice Initiative (EJI). (2017a). *Lynching in America* (3rd ed.). https://lynchinginamerica.eji.org/report/

Equal Justice Initiative (EJI). (2017b). Felony disenfranchisement up 68 percent in Kentucky. https://eji.org/news/kentucky-felony-disenfranchisement-up-68-percent/

Ford, M. E., & Kelly, P. A. (2005). Conceptualizing and categorizing race and ethnicity in health services. *Health Services Research, 40,* 1658–1675.

Frayer, L. (2020). Black Lives Matter gets Indians talking about skin lightening and colorism. National Public Radio. https://www.npr.org/sections/goatsandsoda/2020/07/09/860912124/black-lives-matter-gets-indians-talking-about-skin-lightening-and-colorism

Gabbidon, S. L. (2007). *Criminological perspectives on race and crime.* Routledge.

Grossman, P., & Stern, M. J. (2020). The decision upholding Florida's Jim Crow–style poll tax is an affront to democracy. *Slate.* https://slate.com/news-and-politics/2020/09/florida-felony-disenfranchisement-pryor-decision.html

Hooton, E. A. (1939). *Crime and the man.* Harvard University Press.

Jacobs, M., Levine, S., Abney, K., & Davids, L. (2016). Fifty shades of African lightness: A bio-psychosocial review of the global phenomenon of skin lightening practices. *Journal of Public Health in Africa, 7*(2), 552. https://doi.org/10.4081/jphia.2016.552

Jacobson, M. F. (1998). *Whiteness of a different color.* Harvard University Press.

Johnson, L.B. (1965, June 4). Commencement address at Howard University: To fulfill these rights. https://www.presidency.ucsb.edu/documents/commencement-address-howard-university-fulfill-these-rights.

Kendi, I. X. (2019). *How to be an anti-racist.* One World.

Kolchin, P. (2002). Whiteness studies: The new history of race in America. *The Journal of American History, 89*(1), 154–173.

Lebron, C. (2017). *The making of Black Lives Matter: The history of an idea.* Oxford University Press.

Manfred, T. (2012). Why is the Internet so racist? *Business Insider.* http://www.businessinsider.com/internet-racism-2012-5.

McIntosh, P. (1986). White privilege and male privilege: A personal account of coming to see correspondences through work in women's studies. Wellesley College, Massachusetts Center for Research on Women. http://files.eric.ed.gov/fulltext/ED335262.pdf

Miller, J., & Garran, A. (2008). *Racism in the United States: Implications for the helping professions*. Brooks/Cole.

Morning, A. (2008). Ethnic classification in global perspective: A cross-national survey of the 2000 census round. *Population Research and Policy Review, 27*, 239–272.

National Human Genome Research Institute. (2014). All about the Human Genome Project. http://www.genome.gov/10001772

National Park Service. (2014). Selma-to-Montgomery march: National Historic Trail and all-American road. http://www.nps.gov/nr/travel/civilrights/al4.htm

New World Encyclopedia. (2014). The Great Chain of Being. http://www.newworldencyclopedia.org/entry/Great_Chain_of_Being

Nunnally, S. C. (2018). (Re)Defining the black body in the era of Black Lives Matter: The politics of blackness, old and new. *Politics, Groups, and Identities, 6*(1), 138–152.

Omi, M., & Winant, H. (1994). *Racial formation in the United States: From the 1960s to the 1990s* (2nd ed.). Routledge.

Our Documents. (2014a). Civil Rights Act (1964). http://www.ourdocuments.gov/doc.php?flash=true&doc=97

Our Documents. (2014b). Voting Rights Act. http://www.ourdocuments.gov/doc.php?flash=true&doc=100

Painter, N. I. (2012). The expanding definition of whiteness. Big Think. Retrieved from https://www.youtube.com/watch?v=fss-ee0kGG4.

PBS. (2002). The rise and fall of Jim Crow: A century of segregation. http://www.pbs.org/wnet/jimcrow/segregation.html

PBS. (2003). Witness to faith: Denmark Vesey. This Far by Faith. http://www.pbs.org/thisfarbyfaith/people/denmark_vesey.html

PBS. (2014). Black culture connection. http://www.pbs.org/black-culture/home/powell, j. a. (1997).

The racing of American society: Race functioning as a verb before signifying as a noun. *Minnesota Journal of Law & Inequality, 15*(1). https://scholarship.law.umn.edu/lawineq/vol15/iss1/5

Reece, R. L. (2021). The gender of colorism: Understanding the intersection of skin tone and gender inequality. *Journal of Economics, Race, and Policy, 4*, 47–55. https://doi.org/10.1007/s41996-020-00054-1

Riley, D., & Yates, J. L. (2020). What is colorism? How people of color can overcome their own insecurities and biases. *Good Morning America*. https://www.goodmorningamerica.com/style/story/colorism-people-color-overcome-insecurities-biases-71875856

Sleeter, C. E., & Bernal, D. D. (2004). Critical pedagogy, critical theory race, and anti-racist education. In J. A. Banks (Ed.), *Handbook of research on multicultural education* (2nd ed., pp. 240–258). Jossey-Bass.

Smedley, A. (1997). Origin of the idea of race. *Anthropology Newsletter*. http://www.pbs.org/race/000_About/002_04-background-02-09.htm

Sue, D. W. (2006). *The invisible whiteness of being: Whiteness, white supremacy, white privilege, and racism.* In M. G. Constantine & D. W. Sue (Eds.), *Addressing racism: Facilitating cultural competence in mental health and educational settings* (pp. 15–30). John Wiley & Sons Inc.

Telles, E., & Paschel, T. (2014). Who is black, white, or mixed race? How skin color, status, and nation shape racial classification in Latin America. *American Journal of Sociology, 120*(3), 864–907.

Tessler, H., Choi, M., & Kaom, G. (2020). The anxiety of being Asian American: Hate crimes and negative biases during the COVID-19 Pandemic. *American Journal of Criminal Justice, 45*, 636–646.

U.S. Census Bureau. (2019). Quick Facts. https://www.census.gov/quickfacts/fact/table/US/PST045219

TWO

Defining Ethnicity

Learning Objectives

1. Understand and critically examine the evolution of the term "ethnicity" using the framework of social construction.
2. Explain how institutions and organizations influence our understanding and perception of ethnicity.
3. Examine the history of Mexican Americans, Puerto Ricans, and Salvadoran Americans to better understand why it is difficult to define what it means to be categorized as Hispanic and/or Latino in the United States.

Let's begin with the definition of the term "ethnicity" as it will be used throughout this text. "*Ethnicity*" is defined as a way to categorize a group of people based on shared cultural meaning, for example, speaking the same language, living in the same country/region, and/or sharing cultural traditions and holidays. This definition at first glance appears simplistic. However, it is anything but as there are real-life consequences that can be positive or negative based on these categorizations. For instance, the United States Census measures ethnicity as one of many variables to help determine where services will be needed, such as schools and hospitals. The more people who complete the census within a community, the more assistance that community will receive based on its numbers. This data also can be used to ensure services are being distributed equally and are not in violation of anti-discrimination laws (United States Census Bureau, 2020). However, ethnicity also can be used to categorize people to determine who can and cannot enter the country or seek asylum, which can have very serious negative consequences for those who are denied entry.

A framework based on the social construction of ethnicity will be used to better understand the complexity and power of the term ethnicity. The social construction of ethnicity recognizes that people are grouped based on shared ancestry, and these categories were created because of what was occurring at the time socially, politically, and economically. However, what is occurring politically, economically, and socially was and is constantly changing. Therefore, in order to truly understand this term, you must first examine its history and how it has been reinforced through the government, courts, economy, and social interactions (Haney López, 1994). This chapter will examine how the United States defines ethnicity along with how this definition is flawed and the impact it has on real people.

Defining and Measuring Ethnicity in the United States

In the United States, we tend to focus on categorizing the population by race rather than ethnicity. However, the majority of Americans or their ancestors immigrated to the United States from all over the world. Therefore, there are multiple ethnicities within the country. However, most of these ethnicities are categorized as a race when measuring the population. For example, those who emigrated from Ireland would respond their race is white, but when asked about one's ethnicity there will not typically be a category to check for Irish. Ethnicity also has become more difficult to measure as people have had children with those from different ethnic backgrounds. This resulted in a population with multiple ethnic backgrounds, which made it easier to categorize people by race instead of ethnicity (Stevens et al., 2015).

It also is difficult to measure ethnicity because, unlike race, ethnicity is something that one has the option to self-define. Race, or skin color, is identifiable and therefore ascribed by others. Ethnicity, however, is not always as easy to identify. One could identify one's race as Black or white and claim Hispanic or non-Hispanic heritage. One also could claim multiple ethnicities; for instance, someone who has a mother who self-identifies as Korean and a father who self-identifies as Irish and German may claim their ethnicity as Korean, Irish, and German.

However, in the United States, ethnicity is narrowly measured as Hispanic/Latino origin or non-Hispanic/Latino origin and is used to identify those who do not easily fit into the racial categories of Black or white (Cole, 2020). Hispanic and Latino are often used interchangeably even though they have different definitions. *Hispanic* is defined as those who can trace their origin to Spain or Spanish-speaking countries, for example, Mexico and most countries within the region of Central America (with the exception of Belize) and the continent of South America (with the exception of Brazil). *Latino* is defined as someone who can trace their roots to Latin America and speak one of the Romance languages, for example, Mexico, Central America, South America, and the Caribbean. This can be confusing as those from Mexico would be considered to be both Hispanic (from a Spanish-speaking country) and Latino (Spanish is a Romance language). However, those from Brazil are not considered Hispanic (Brazil was colonized by Portugal) but Latino (Portuguese is a Romance language), while those from Belize would not be considered to be Hispanic (colonized by British) or Latino (English is not a Romance language) (Cole, 2020).

GLOBAL SPOTLIGHT

Defining Ethnicity Around the World

The Central Intelligence Agency's (2014) report *The World Factbook* examined the breakdown of race and ethnicity in 236 countries. The majority of countries (198) categorized their populations using national origin or ethnicity. A few (28) categorized their population using national origin and ethnicity, along with race categorized as white, Black, or mixed/mulatto/mestizo. Only 10 countries solely used race or the color of one's skin (white, Black, or mixed/mulatto/mestizo) to categorize the population within their country. All 10 of these countries were colonized at one time by a foreign country and relied on the slave labor of Africans (Morning, 2008).

Although most countries categorize their populations by ethnicity, there is no clear-cut way to define ethnicity that will translate from one country to the next. This is due to constantly evolving definitions, which have made it difficult to make comparisons from one country to another. In the United States, for example, we define ethnicity as Hispanic or non-Hispanic, representing a person's country of origin from one of a list of countries. In other countries, ethnicity is measured by the language one speaks or one's customs (Fearon, 2002).

In the United States, approximately 60 million people (18.5% of the total population) identify their ethnicity as Hispanic and/or Latino. (Office of Minority Health, 2019). Currently, there are ten states that each have 1 million or more Hispanic and Latino people residing there. These states are located in the West (California and Colorado), the Southwest (Arizona, New Mexico, and Texas), the South (Florida and Georgia), the Midwest (Illinois), and Northeast (New York and New Jersey) (Office of Minority Health, 2019). Mexican Americans make up the largest segment (two-thirds) of the Hispanic ethnic population, followed by those of Puerto Rican (10%), Salvadoran (4%), Cuban (4%), and Dominican (4%) descent. Americans of Guatemalan, Colombian, and Honduran descent are 2% of the U.S. Hispanic population, while those of Spanish, Ecuadorian, Peruvian, Nicaraguan, Venezuelan, Argentinian, and Panamanian descent comprise 1% or less of the United States Hispanic population

Figure 2.1. Immigration Reform March in Los Angeles, California, May 1, 2013. © iStockphoto.com/ anouchka. © shutterstock.com/Rena Schild.

(Noe-Bustamante et al., 2019). Hispanic and Latino communities tend to be racially diverse, with most stating their race is white (65%), other (26%), two or more races (6%), Black (2%), Asian (less than 1%), or American Indian/Alaskan Native (less than 1%) (Office of Minority Health, 2019).

Hispanic and/or Latino or Latinx?

It gets tricky when attempting to understand how ethnicity is categorized in the United States; for example, ethnicity is measured as Hispanic/Latino origin or non-Hispanic/Latino origin on the census. This question is used to further break down those who state their race is white to determine if they are from a European background or Hispanic/Latino origin. However, this measure is constantly evolving and changing as the Census Bureau comes up with new strategies to capture the Hispanic population (Krogstad & Cohn, 2014).

The first effort to address this issue through the census occurred in 1970, when an attempt was made to measure origin by asking "Where was this person born?"; followed by "Is this person's origin or descent: Mexican, Puerto Rican, Cuban, Central or South America, Other Spanish, or none of these?" This question was only sent to a sample of respondents to determine its validity and was not as successful as first hoped (U.S. Census Bureau, 2014b). The census had expected people would be willing to mark both their race and their ethnicity, but many only answered one question or the other. By 1980, the question used to measure ethnicity on the United States Census was worded, "Is this person of Spanish/Hispanic origin or descent?" One could respond "No; Yes, Mexican/Mexican American/Chicano; Yes, Puerto Rican; Yes, Cuban; Yes, other Spanish/Hispanic." This question did a better job of capturing the Hispanic population in the United States this census and determined there were 14.6 million Hispanic people living in the states. However, the question still did not capture the entire Hispanic population (Cohn, 2010).

The next major change we saw in the census occurred in 2000, when ethnicity was measured as, "Is this person Spanish/Hispanic/Latino?" The response selections included, "No, not Spanish/Hispanic/Latino; Yes, Mexican American; Yes, Puerto Rican; Yes, Cuban; Yes, other Spanish/Hispanic/Latino" (Cohn, 2010). This year, the census was attempting to capture more of the ethnic population by adding the term Latino. This helped to capture a larger portion of the population, but still did not capture everyone (Lopez, 2013).

Preliminary studies show that the best way to capture the Hispanic and Latino population is to include both race and origin as one question. In pilot tests when the question included race and origin, with Hispanic as an option, the majority (81%) of Latino people choose Hispanic only and no other race (Gonzalez-Barrera and Lopez, 2013). Although this change was considered for the 2020 Census, it did not occur. Instead, question 8 on the 2020 Census asked if the person is of Hispanic, Latino, or Spanish origin. The response selections included, "No, not of Hispanic, Latino, or Spanish origin"; "Yes, Mexican, Mexican Am., Chicano"; "Yes, Puerto Rican"; "Yes, Cuban"; "Yes, another Hispanic, Latino, or Spanish origin—Print for example, Salvadoran, Dominican, Colombian, Guatemalan, Spaniard, Ecuadorian, etc." (U.S. Census Bureau, 2020, question 8). In an attempt to separate race and ethnicity, directly before question 8 there is an arrow with "Note: Please answer BOTH Question 8 about Hispanic origin and Question 9 about race. For this census, Hispanic origins are not races." (U.S. Census Bureau, 2020, question 8).

Whether one identifies as Hispanic or Latino also is dependent upon a variety of factors, such as where one lives. For instance, those who live in the Western portion of the United States are more likely to identify as Latino, while those living in the East are more likely to identify as Hispanic (Cole, 2020). People also may identify by their country of origin rather than Hispanic or Latino, for instance as Mexican American or Cuban American, while others may choose to identify their race as Latino or Hispanic. For instance, Gonzalez-Barrera and Lopez (2013) found that two-thirds of Americans who identified as multi-racial and Hispanic reported Hispanic as being part of their race, while 69% of Latinos between 18 and 29 reported Latino as part of their race. Therefore even though the government and other organizations measure Hispanic/Latino based on ethnicity (national origin and language), most who self-identify as Hispanic or Latino do not view this as a separate category of ethnicity. Instead, it is viewed as an expansion of race (Gonzalez-Barrera and Lopez, 2013). This creates quite a problem for government agencies, such as the U.S. Census Bureau, who are measuring ethnicity and race differently than how people self-identify in their daily lives.

Latinx also is a term used to describe those of Hispanic and Latino descent. Latinx was first used in the late 1990s, but became a more commonly used term in 2016 after the Pulse nightclub mass shooting that targeted LGBTQ patrons (Penaloza, 2020). Latinx is used to be more gender and LGBTQ inclusive, as Spanish is a Romance language that is gender based; for example, Spanish uses Latino for male and Latina for female. However, a national survey of 3,000 Latino people conducted by the Pew Research Center found that only 23% of all Latino adults have heard of the term and only 3% use it to describe themselves (Meraji, 2020). Latinx was more commonly used among Latino adults between 18 and 29 years of age, with 42% stating they have heard of the term, but only 7% using it to describe themselves. Overall, those who completed the survey stated they are more likely to identify by their country of origin, followed by Hispanic, and then Latino with only a small percentage using the term Latinx (Meraji, 2020).

Next, we will briefly examine the history of Mexican Americans, Puerto Ricans, and Salvadoran Americans to better understand the diverse cultures that are categorized as Hispanic and/or Latino. Once we examine their histories and cultures it will become easier to understand why the federal government has so much difficulty capturing this population as well as why there is so much diversity within the Hispanic and Latino communities in regards to how one self-identifies. As you read about the histories of these three cultures, be sure to consider the definition of ethnicity along with the social construction of the term ethnicity and how what was happening at the time politically, socially, and economically impacted how people were categorized and how they interacted with one another.

The Mexican–American War and Manifest Destiny

First, we will examine the history of Mexican Americans, who are the largest Hispanic/Latino group in the United States, with 66% of the total Hispanic/Latino population (Noe-Bustamante, Flores, Shah, 2019). As you read about the history of the relationship between the United States and Mexican Americans, be sure to consider how the social construction of ethnicity and what was happening politically, economically, and socially impacted how ethnicity was defined and how people interacted with one another.

The Mexican–American War was fought over the United States' annexation of Texas, after, in 1836, this area declared independence from Mexico. However, Mexico refused to recognize this secession. Mexico had been given what is now Texas after its battle for independence with Spain, but was unable to fully inhabit the land to keep it under its control due to a lack of settlers to occupy the land and political divisions within the government. On June 16, 1845, Texas and the United States signed a treaty annexing Texas, and on July 4, 1845, Congress passed a resolution recognizing the annexation. Mexico had previously stated it would declare war if the United States annexed Texas, however, instead of declaring war they announced that the annex illegal. On May 13, 1846, the United States Congress declared war against Mexico, in what became known as the Mexican–American War. Today the war is often viewed as an unjust war fought against Mexico to fulfill **Manifest Destiny** or the belief that it was the duty of the United States to go west and acquire land to spread its ideas of freedom and democracy. The war lasted until 1848, with the United States ultimately winning the war (PBS, 2014b).

At the end of the war, the **Treaty of Guadalupe Hidalgo** was signed on February 2, 1848. This treaty gave 500,000 square miles of land—approximately half of the country of Mexico—to the United States for what is now known as the state of Texas. The Mexicans who lived on this land were to keep their land and be given American citizenship. The acquisition of this land allowed the United States to emerge as a global leader and further supported its belief in the legitimacy of its plan of Manifest Destiny (PBS, 2014b).

According to the treaty, Mexican Americans were to retain their land and be treated as citizens, although this did not always happen. Many Mexican Americans had their land stolen from them by white settlers who had moved into the area. These settlers also did not accept the Mexican American community as American citizens and treated them as second-class citizens within the community. This transition proved difficult for Mexican Americans, many of whom were now landless and without a way to provide for their families. This situation played out over and over again as the United States continued to acquire land from Mexico through treaties and war for what is now known as the American Southwest and West (Griswold del Castillo, 2014).

Mexicans Are Not White or Black—Or Are They?

Mexican Americans could not be easily categorized by their race due to their Spanish, Mexican, and Indigenous ancestry. Mexican Americans preferred to be referred to as white, not because they identified with white Europeans, but because the alternative was to be categorized as Black. In 1860, Mexican Americans feared being categorized as Black, because there was concern they would be subjected to the same harsh treatment Black people faced. However, race is ascribed by others and not something that one is typically able to choose. The choices for race on the census that year were white, Black, or mulatto, and the question itself was titled "Color," not "Race." Therefore, census workers would have categorized Mexican Americans as Black because they were not of European descent (U.S. Census Bureau, 2014a).

In 1930, Mexican was added as a racial category to the United States Census. However, this also concerned many Mexican Americans who feared that a classification other than White would solidify discrimination. Mexican Americans were able to successfully petition to have this racial category removed from the 1940 Census (U.S. Census Bureau, 2014c). However, how one was categorized on the census did not really matter because Mexican Americans had been treated as second-class citizens within the United States since the Mexican–American War. Mexican Americans, for example, experienced the same type of discrimination faced by Black people in the South after the Civil War. Mexican Americans were segregated from white people within their communities in public social spaces and within schools. These segregated situations kept Mexican Americans from being able to improve their situations by accessing opportunities for better jobs and kept them impoverished. Those who did not abide by the segregation policies were subject to the same harassment and violence Black people in the South faced, such as lynching and assaults (Latino Americans, 2013).

World War II and the Fight for Equality

In the 1940s, Mexican Americans fought in WWII in large numbers and received more Medals of Honor than any other minority population. Mexican Americans received a hero's welcome when they returned home, and their service in the war seemed to improve the quality of life within their community. Veterans, for example, had been trained in skills they could apply in the labor market after the war, and the GI Bill was making it easier for Mexican American veterans to improve their lives through education and home ownership. However, the hero's welcome did not last long, as veterans were immediately subjugated to the same treatment and discrimination they had faced prior to the war. Congressional Medal of Honor recipient Sergeant Marcario Garcia, for example, was refused service in a restaurant because he was Mexican American. The treatment Mexican American veterans received was contradictory to the American Dream they desired (Zoot Suit Discovery Guide, 2014).

In 1948, the *American GI Forum* was founded by veteran Dr. Hector Garcia to advocate for the rights of Mexican American veterans after a patient of his was denied services at a naval hospital due to his Mexican heritage. The American GI Forum was the only veteran organization that accepted Mexican Americans, and it grew quickly as branches were opened across the country. The organization worked tirelessly to address social service needs through back-to-school drives, for example, but also was active in fighting against discrimination at the polls. In the 1940s, *poll taxes* were used to disenfranchise Mexican American voters, many of whom could not afford the tax that had to be paid before one could vote. The American GI Forum raised money to pay the taxes to help more Mexican Americans to be able to register to vote and fought many court battles to help remove this barrier. However, the organization gained national attention when it fought against the discrimination faced by the Longoria family (PBS, 2014a).

Private Felix Longoria had been killed in action during the war, and his body was finally being returned home for burial in 1948. The only funeral home in his hometown in Texas denied him services because of his Mexican heritage. The American GI Forum sprang into action after Longoria's widow asked Garcia to advocate for her husband, which resulted in Private Longoria eventually being buried in Arlington National Cemetery. However, the Longoria burial had been more than just a win against discrimination for the National GI Forum. It also helped to focus nationwide attention on the discrimination faced by Mexican Americans (PBS, 2014a).

Mexican Americans as an Ethnic Group

Since the 1940s, there had been advances against discrimination for Mexican Americans, but they still experienced segregation within their communities. Mexican Americans, for example, were still battling with the issue of race. They were now recognized as white and recorded their race as such, but they did not experience the same privileges of race as white Americans of European descent. Signs on restaurant doors in the Southwest for example, would declare "Whites Only, No Mexicans or Blacks" (Haney López, 1994).

In 1954, the United States Supreme Court case *Hernandez v. Texas* shifted the debate from one of race to ethnicity. The case involved Pete Hernandez, who had murdered Joe Espinoza in Jackson County, Texas. No one disputed that Hernandez had murdered Espinoza, but the defense appealed the conviction, stating Mexican Americans were not allowed to serve on the jury and had not served on a jury in this county for the past 25 years. The jury had consisted of all white people of European descent, which was in direct violation of the *Fourteenth Amendment* that guaranteed equal protection under the law. The Texas Appellate Court denied the appeal and stated that Mexican Americans were in fact white, and Hernandez had therefore been represented by a jury of his peers (Oyez, 2014a).

The defense team then appealed the case to the United States Supreme Court. They argued that Mexican Americans, although categorized as white, were not treated as such and were in fact segregated and discriminated against as though they were a special class, in violation of the Fourteenth Amendment. This legal argument was successful, and the United States Supreme Court voted unanimously that Mexican Americans, as well as other ethnicities and races beyond Black and white, did have the right to be recognized under the Fourteenth Amendment. Now, for the first time, ethnicity was protected under the Fourteenth Amendment along with race (Oyez, 2014a).

Puerto Rico, Spain, and the United States

Next, we will examine the history of Puerto Ricans, who are the second largest Hispanic/Latino group in the United States with 10% of the total Hispanic or Latino population (Noe-Bustamante et al., 2019). Puerto Rico's multicultural background is influenced by the culture of the indigenous Taino along with the Spaniards, Africans, and Americans who all left their mark on the Caribbean island. This infusion of cultures created a richly diverse population on the island, but also made it difficult for the United States' government to classify Puerto Ricans as either Black or white. As you read about the history of the relationship between the United States and Puerto Rico, be sure to consider how the social construction of ethnicity and what was happening politically, economically, and socially impacted how ethnicity was defined and how people interacted with one another.

The United States acquired Puerto Rico after the *Spanish–Cuban–American War*, where the United States invaded Cuba and the Philippines in support of the revolutionaries in both countries who were trying to overthrow their Spanish governments for their independence. (Office of the Historian, n.d.). The Spanish–Cuban–American War officially ended on December 10th of 1898 with the signing of the *Treaty of Paris*. The treaty gave Cuba its independence and the islands of Puerto Rico and Guam to the United States. The treaty also required Spain to sell the Philippines to the United States. In the end, the Spanish–Cuban–American War "ended Spain's colonial empire in the Western Hemisphere and secured the position of the United States as a Pacific power" (Office of the Historian, n.d., para. 1). This allowed the United States to gain dominance in the Caribbean and to move into Asia (Office of the Historian, n.d.).

Operation Bootstrap, Tax Breaks, and the Economy

In 1917, with World War I in full swing and German warships in the Caribbean, the United States agreed to make all Puerto Ricans United States citizens through the passage of the *Jones-Shafroth Act*. Although Puerto Ricans now had United States citizenship, they still did not have the political control they sought, as the governor of the island remained a presidential political appointee (Editors of Encyclopedia Britannica, 2015). It was not until 1946 that a Puerto Rican would be appointed by President Truman to serve as governor of Puerto Rico. Then in 1947, the United States Congress voted to allow Puerto Ricans to elect their own governor with the first elected governor, Luis Muñoz Marín, taking office in 1949 (Editors of Encyclopedia Britannica, 2015).

IN FOCUS

Puerto Rico Statehood

Puerto Rico is an unincorporated territory. This means the residents there pay taxes to the United States, but they do not have a voting representative in Congress and are only able to vote in the United States presidential primary and not the presidential election. This leaves Puerto Rico without any representation in Congress and makes it difficult to get their needs addressed through the federal government (Carlos & Rivera, 2020).

In 1952, Puerto Rico ratified its Constitution. Since that time, Puerto Ricans have voted six different times over the years to make Puerto Rico a state with the three earliest elections ending in an outcome of no and the last three with a yes. The last vote for statehood took place in 2020 with 52% of Puerto Ricans voting to make it the 51st state. However, in order for Puerto Rico to become a state, Congress would have to introduce an Admission Act or a House Resolution that would need a simple majority in the House and Senate to pass. Most Republicans are against statehood, and most Democrats are for it, as the island is primarily Democratic. This means it will take not only Puerto Ricans voting for statehood, but also someone in Congress taking up the cause and getting a simple majority vote in both the House and Senate (Carlos & Rivera, 2020).

The economy also shifted during this time, moving from large-scale agriculture to manufacturing through a program called Operation Bootstrap. **Operation Bootstrap** attracted American manufacturing companies to Puerto Rico by offering them cheap labor and eliminating the Puerto Rican corporate tax. (Toro, 2013). This plan also focused on decreasing unemployment by reducing the rural farming population on the island through emigration to the mainland, where the United States actively recruited Puerto Ricans living on the island to the United States for seasonal and full-time work. This mass exodus is referred to as **The Great Migration**, where 25% of the Puerto Rican population (500,000 people) left for the mainland between 1950 and 1970 (Sanchez Korrol, 2017). However, by the 1960s, the United States' economy began to shift away from manufacturing, those who had emigrated there found themselves without employment, and many headed home. By 1978, the economy on the island was again not doing well and two thirds of Puerto Rico's population were receiving food stamps (Sanchez Korrol, 2017).

In 1976, the United States federal government implemented **tax code Section 936**, which allowed companies doing business in United States' territories tax breaks on income generated there (Rivera, 2020). At the same time, Puerto Rico's tax code provided incentives for United States-based companies to move to Puerto Rico (Greenberg & Elkins, 2015). For instance, a company in Puerto Rico that was more than 80% owned by shareholders outside of Puerto Rico did not have to pay any corporate income tax, if their profits were distributed through dividends defined as quarterly payments to shareholders in the company (Greenberg & Elkins, 2015). Between 1980 and 1996, these tax incentives were used to entice high-tech and finance companies to the island (Rivera, 2020). However, by the 1990s, pressure was mounting in the United States to do away with corporate tax breaks, and in 1996, the United States Congress voted to phase out tax code Section 936 by the year 2006 (Rivera, 2020).

The United States' economy and influence along with the roll back of tax breaks directly impacted the Puerto Rican economy over the next couple of decades (Rivera,

2020). These economic downturns became too much to bear for many, and between mid-2010 and 2013, 144,000 Puerto Ricans left for the United States mainland (Cohn et al., 2014). This was the largest exodus from the island since the Great Migration, with 44% of those who left reporting they were leaving the island to find work (Cohn et al., 2014). From 1996 to 2014, Puerto Rican manufacturing jobs decreased by half as companies that were no longer incentivized by tax breaks made the decision to leave Puerto Rico and go elsewhere (Rivera, 2020). Then, in 2015, the Puerto Rican government announced it was about to default on billions of dollars of debt to the United States as unemployment on the island reached 15% (Rivera, 2020).

Puerto Rican Debt Crisis and PROMESA

By 2006, Puerto Rico was facing an economic crisis as companies were leaving the island due to the roll back in tax breaks (Lind, 2015). Although Puerto Rico already had a sizable debt, the government and publicly held companies such as utilities were allowed to sell bonds to raise funds due to a federal tax loophole that relaxed debt limits for territories. The public continued to buy these bonds even with Puerto Rico's sizable debt because they were viewed as a good deal due to their status as triple-tax-exempt, where one does not pay federal, state, or local taxes when buying these bonds. This allowed the Puerto Rican government and publicly held companies to continue selling bonds to the public and increase their already mounting debt, while using the funds raised by the bonds to pay off their prior debts (Lind, 2015).

However, this level of ever-mounting debt became impossible to climb out of with an economy that was unlikely to pick back up (Lind, 2015). This led to a death spiral, where tax increases to cover the debt, mass emigration, and cuts on social benefits made it nearly impossible for the economy to recover. All of this has left Puerto Rico with over 70 billion dollars of debt owed by the Puerto Rican government, public utility companies, cities, and banks. This bond debt was owned by hedge funds ($15 billion), mutual bond funds ($11 billion), and by individual Americans ($39 billion) (Lind, 2015).

Puerto Rico is a commonwealth with its own governor and constitution, but its official status is an unincorporated territory of the United States. Therefore, Puerto Rico cannot access Chapter 9 bankruptcy laws in order to restructure their debt (Doyle, 2020). In 2016, the United States Congress passed the Puerto Rico Oversight Management and Economic Stability Act, also known as **PROMESA**. This act created an eight-member oversight board tasked with restructuring Puerto Rico's debt, limited debt collection through lawsuits for a period of time, lowered the federal minimum wage on the island for those 24 years of age and younger from $7.75/hour to $4.25/hour, and cut pension payments by 10% (Guadalupe, 2016).

Figure 2.2. Solidarity With Puerto Rico Rally Chicago Illinois in 2018
© Creative Commons / Charles Edward Miller

Under PROMESA, the Puerto Rican government was required to negotiate their debt with their creditors. However, if an agreement could not be reached between Puerto Rico and their debtors, Puerto Rico could utilize Title III of PROMESA to petition a federal court for assistance in a process that is similar to bankruptcy court (Williams Walsh, 2017). On May 3, 2017, the Oversight Board began the Title III process and by May 17, 2017, the Honorable Laura Taylor Swain began hearing arguments in federal court (Williams Walsh, 2017).

Hurricanes, Earthquakes, and Corruption

On September 20, 2017, *Hurricane Maria* landed on the shores of Puerto Rico, bringing with it 155 mile-per-hour winds and leaving over 3,000 people dead. The entire island lost access to power, and most were unable to obtain clean water and food. Hurricane Maria was the third most expensive hurricane in United States' history with 94 billion dollars in damage and 80% of the island's crops destroyed (Mercy Corps, 2020). Over the next couple of years, nearly 200,000 Puerto Ricans would leave the island due to the slow recovery and the lack of power on the island for nearly a year (Acevedo, 2020).

In 2019, protests erupted on the island and abroad, as Puerto Ricans everywhere took to the streets to take a stand against the economy, corruption, Governor Rossello, and La Junta (The Board). These protests led to Governor Rossello stepping down and Puerto Rico's Attorney General Wanda Vasquez serving as governor until the end of his term (Florido, 2020). Then on January 7, 2020, another natural disaster struck the island in the form of a 6.4 magnitude earthquake (Acevedo, 2020). Shortly after the earthquake, a special independent prosecutor announced they were investigating Governor Vasquez for corruption and her handling of disaster relief after the earthquake (Florido, 2020).

Congress allocated 63 billion dollars in aid to assist Puerto Rico with the hurricane and the earthquake. However, only 17.7 billion of this money has been distributed due to concerns about corruption (Transparency Portal, 2020). The economic collapse along with corruption and the secession of natural disasters has left Puerto Rico in dire straits. The island has an unemployment rate of 8.6% and nearly half (44%) of Puerto Ricans on the island live below the poverty line, which is twice the rate of the poorest state in the United States (Rivera, 2020).

El Salvador and the Civil War, 1980–1992

Finally, we will examine the history of Salvadoran Americans, who are in a three-way tie with Cuban Americans and Dominican Americans for third largest Hispanic/Latino group in the United States, each with 4% of the total population (Noe-Busta-mante et al., 2019). As you read about the history of the relationship between the United States and El Salvador, be sure to consider how the social construction of ethnicity and what was happening politically, economically, and socially impacted how ethnicity was defined and how people interacted with one another.

In the early 1970s, an economic downturn led to decreases in salary along with increases in inflation and unemployment for all Salvadorans. This led to groups of people organizing and demanding change from the government, such as students, labor groups, Catholics, and peasants. These protests were violently repressed, and the organizers of these movements were rounded up by *death squads*, which were unmarked security forces that consisted of military and police intelligence agencies that roamed the streets looking for those who led the opposition against the military-backed government. Those who were taken by the death squads were never seen again. This tactic became even more popular throughout the 1970s as the resistance movement grew; for example, from 1973 to 1976, 48 people disappeared and between 1977 and 1980, 611 people disappeared (Alvarez, 2010).

The activists and protestors demanded the military repression stop and attempted to change their situation through political elections. However, in 1972 and 1977, the military-backed National Conciliation Party refused to concede they had lost the election and stayed in power by denying the election results and claiming election fraud. This made it clear to those demanding change that change was not going to come from working within the system (Alvarez, 2010).

In October of 1980, The Farabundo Marti Front for National Liberation was formed better known as *FMLN*. The FMLN consisted of students, farm labor, factory workers, teachers, and those who had been involved in the government. They were inspired by the 1950s Cuban revolutionaries who were able to overthrow their government through armed resistance. This terrified the United States' government, which feared the FMLN would overthrow the Salvadoran government and create a communist government in its place (Isles, 2019).

Then on December 2, 1980, four American women—three nuns and a woman who worked for the same ministry—were abducted from the airport upon arrival in El Salvador. Their abductors, who were members of the National Guard, later raped, shot, and buried them in a shallow grave. These vicious crimes against American women drew criticism in the United States from their families and the Catholic community, who demanded justice. In response, President Carter stopped the flow of nearly 8 million dollars that had been planned for distribution to the Salvadoran government (DeYoung, 1981). However, the fear of a communist takeover by the FMLN was strong, and on January 13, 1981, President Carter allowed for 5 million dollars of the aid to go to the Salvadoran government for nonlethal equipment (DeYoung, 1981). In 1981, things ramped up again as President Ronald Reagan took office in the United States and the FMLN began to actively fight the Salvadoran government through armed resistance (Isles, 2019). This led his administration to significantly increase support for the Salvadoran military government through further military funding, access to United States' military advisers, and assistance with National Guard training exercises (History.com Editors, 2020).

The war crimes continued in El Salvador against the Salvadoran people with the funding and support of the American government and military. One of the worst examples of this is the *El Mozote Massacre* that occurred over four days in December of 1981 and is the largest massacre in modern Latin American history (Malkin, 2018). The *Atlacatl Battalion,* an elite military unit created and trained by the United States military and led by Colonel Domingo Monterossa, bombarded the village of El Mozote from the air with artillery to disperse the FMLN they believed were hiding in the mountain village. The next day the soldiers entered the village to interrogate the villagers and gather intelligence on the guerillas. Men were separated from the women, while the children were taken to a church building. Throughout the day, the soldiers tortured, raped, and executed all of the adults in the village. Once they were done, they fired multiple shots into the building where the children were being kept and set the building on fire. The bodies of 143 children were recovered from that building, where the average age of the children was six years old. The Atlacatl Battalion then moved on from El Mozote to smaller neighboring villages and continued their campaign of death and terror, leaving nearly 1,000 people dead (Malkin, 2018).

The United States continued to fund the Salvadoran government throughout the civil war, even though mass repression and atrocities against human rights were committed by the Salvadoran military-backed government (Alvarez, 2010). However, it also became more difficult for the United States to justify their support of the Salvadoran government after the murders of six Jesuit priests who were internationally known scholars. On November 16, 1989, the Atlacatl Battalion rushed into the sleeping quarters of six Jesuit priests, their cook, and her teenage daughter, killing them all. The priests had been calling for negotiations between the Salvadoran government and the FMLN to end the violence, which upset the Salvadoran government, who considered the priests to be the brains behind the FMLN movement. Their brutal murders gained international attention and led to the eventual negotiations that ended the El Salvador Civil War (Hajek, 2019). The United States, for instance, forced the Salvadoran government to negotiate with the FMLN by threatening to withhold financial aid (Alvarez, 2010).

On April 4, 1990, the United Nations and Costa Rican President Oscar Arias began arbitrating negotiations between the Salvadoran government and the FMLN. At the **Chapultepec Peace Accords** on January 16, 1992, an agreement was reached, and the El Salvador Civil War officially ended. The agreement ended the war, reduced the size of the military, established a civilian police force, overhauled the electoral system, and reformed the judicial system. The agreement also reintegrated FMLN members back into social and political life by making the FMLN a legal political party. A truth commission overseen by ombudsmen also was formed to investigate the most serious abuses of human rights (Alvarez, 2010).

The United Nations also investigated the United States' involvement in the El Salvador Civil War, concluded the American government had been complicit in human rights atrocities committed by the Salvadoran military, and condemned their involvement (History.com Editors, 2020). The investigation concluded the United States' government sent a total of nearly five billion dollars in aid and training to the Salvadoran government throughout the twelve-year civil war—a civil war that killed more than 75,000 Salvadorans, who were mostly civilians, and displaced 1 million more Salvadorans, with many coming to the United States as refugees (McKinney, 2015).

Life after the Civil War

The 1990s saw three successful democratic elections, with the National Republican Alliance (ARENA) political party winning the presidency in 1994 and 1999 and the FMLN winning the mayoral race in San Salvador in 1997 (BBC, 2018). However, the economy was another matter. Twenty percent of the population of El Salvador had been displaced due to the civil war, and infrastructure across the country was in shambles (Calvo-Gonzalez & Lopez, 2015). These factors made it difficult to bounce back. Although inequality in the country had improved, the sluggish economy made it more difficult to reduce poverty, and by 2000, 44% of the population was living below the poverty line (Calvo-Gonzalez & Lopez, 2015).

In the late 1990s and early 2000s, El Salvador also saw a significant spike in violent crime due to gang violence. In the 1980s and 1990s, during the El Salvador Civil War, thousands of Salvadorans immigrated to the United States to avoid the violence and death that was happening in their homeland. Their claims for asylum in the United States were not granted, so they were forced to enter the country illegally. After arriving in the United States, they often lived in impoverished neighborhoods in cities, such as Los Angeles. In these foreign cities, Salvadoran refugees faced a new challenge: gang violence. This led to the creation of Latino gangs, such as *MS-13* and *Barrio 18*, that initially served as a self-defense tool to combat the violence that was occurring around them (Martinez, 2018).

IN FOCUS

Gang Violence in El Salvador

Much of the violence now that takes place in El Salvador is due to turf wars and revenge between the two largest gangs—MS-13 and Barrio 18. However, these turf wars also extend to civilians as well, where crossing into the wrong neighborhood can get one killed. The gangs believe that if you are outside of your neighborhood you are serving as a spy and must be killed. A fifteen-year-old girl, for example, was shot in the head and killed by a gang member because she made tortillas in one neighborhood, but crossed a street into another neighborhood to sell them. Murders are commonplace, and the police and the government seem unable to stop them (Garsd, 2015). However, the majority of murders take place in one of five Salvadoran cities, and the victims are almost always the poor, while the wealthy are able to avoid violent crime by hiring private security and living in gated communities (Martinez, 2018).

In 1990, the United States Congress created *Temporary Protection Status (TPS)* for Salvadorans who had fled the violence of the civil war. This allowed those with TPS to legally live and work in the United States. In 1992, President George H.W. Bush extended TPS for one year; and in 1993, President Clinton extended TPS for one more year, but then let the program expire in December of 1994 (Schmitt, 2001). In the late 1990s, this led to approximately 200,000 Salvadorans who had been living in the United States being deported to El Salvador. El Salvador was still recovering from the civil war, so when they arrived they found a country that was struggling, where not even the civilian police force had been fully implemented (Garsd, 2015).

Those who had been deported from the United States often did not have immediate family they could live with when they returned home because their families had been displaced during the civil war. There also were few job opportunities for the youth who had returned, which led to large numbers of youth roaming the streets with nowhere to go. This created a situation that made it easy to recruit youth into gangs and soon MS-13 and Barrio 18 became the two largest gangs in El Salvador, with both gangs eventually spreading into Honduras and Guatemala as well (Garsd, 2015).

Gangs in El Salvador do not have much money as they are made up of the poorest of the poor, and they tend to prey on the poor. Therefore, youth in El Salvador join gangs for a sense of belonging and identity, not because they believe they will become wealthy (Garsd, 2015). Most El Salvadorans in gangs, for example, joined when they were 15 years old, with 25 years old being the average age of a gang member (Martinez, 2018). Gang members tend to reside in a house in a poor neighborhood or in jail and live off an average of $250 a month (Martinez, 2018). Gangs make their money from extortion, where they force non-gang members to pay the gang for protection. This can occur in a variety of ways, but the most common is the protection racket, where the gang demands money from businesses in exchange for protection and security. Older gang members will collect "rent" weekly from businesses, and those who do not pay risk serious injury or death to not only themselves, but their family as well (Garsd, 2015).

Then in 2001, a series of earthquakes struck El Salvador in January and February that killed 1,200 people and left more than 1 million homeless (BBC, 2018). This led to nearly 150,000 Salvadorans fleeing the country and coming to the United States. The president of El Salvador pleaded for the United States to provide TPS for those in the United States who had fled due to the earthquake. The Salvadoran president stated the economy and recovery in El Salvador was dependent upon their *remittance*, where Salvadorans living in the United States send a portion of their income home to family. In 2001, President George W. Bush enacted TPS for those who had fled due to the earthquake (Spagat, 2020). Since 2001, TPS has been renewed each year for Salvadorans (Martinez, 2018).

Between 2007 and 2017, poverty decreased in El Salvador from 39% to 29% (Chrol, 2020). The murder rate also decreased significantly between 2015 and 2019, for instance in 2015, 104 people were murdered per 100,000, but by 2019, the murder rates had declined to 36 per 100,000, with significant decreases for each of the years in between (Bureau of Diplomatic Security, 2020). However, it is important to note that although the homicide rate in El Salvador has fallen significantly over the last five years, it is still seven times higher than the homicide rate in the United States (Martinez, 2018). Poverty also remains a difficult barrier for many to overcome as the rural population continues to struggle with unemployment and low wages along with the inability to access services. Most services, for example, are still located in the urban areas and, without good roads as well as reliable transportation, it can be difficult to access services for those living in rural areas (Bureau of Diplomatic Security, 2020). Those in urban areas also continue to face economic hardships due to low pay and overly priced housing, with the poorest being forced into makeshift housing within the city that leaves them vulnerable in earthquakes and mudslides (Causey, 2016).

Social Construction of Ethnicity in the United States

Ethnicity is defined as a way to categorize a group of people based on shared cultural meaning, for example, speaking the same language, living in the same country/region, and/or sharing cultural traditions and holidays. However, after examining the three largest Hispanic/Latino groups in the United States it becomes difficult to see how all of these people can be categorized together under one group. For instance, although Mexican Americans, Puerto Ricans, and Salvadorans all share the common language of Spanish they are not from the same countries/regions of the world and have their own unique cultures and traditions. There also are countries, such as Brazil, that speak Portuguese and are considered to be Latino, but not Hispanic.

However once you examine the ever-evolving definition of ethnicity from the perspective of social construction, it becomes much clearer as to why these definitions are constantly changing. If you recall from earlier in this chapter, the social construction of ethnicity is the idea that people are grouped together based on shared ancestry, and these categories were created because of what was occurring at the time socially, politically, and economically. However, what is happening politically, socially, and economically is constantly changing, which means how ethnicity is defined is also constantly changing, both for how the group defines themselves along with how those outside the group define the group. The United States government, for example, has struggled with how to categorize Mexican Americans who may or may not identify as white or Black. Early attempts through the US Census to categorize Mexican Americans, by adding an additional category for race in the 1930s and through a country of origin question in 1970, were later removed following their first attempts (Brown, 2020; Gomez, 1992). Unfortunately, these questions did not capture the population as hoped, and so an additional attempt was made on the 1980 Census. This time the Census Bureau formed an advisory committee made up of educational leaders from a variety of Spanish-speaking groups, mostly Mexican American, to determine how to ask the question (Gomez, 1992).

The Census Bureau advisory committee recognized that beyond Mexican Americans there also were large populations of Puerto Ricans, Salvadorans, and Cubans who were living in the United States, and placing them all under the category of Mexican American no longer made any sense (Gomez, 1992). Ultimately, the term Hispanic was chosen by the Census Bureau advisory committee because it was viewed as a more inclusive term that was mainstream. The advisory committee viewed this as a positive because it would unite a larger group of people together for political purposes, while the government viewed it as a victory because they now had a term to categorize people who did not fit into the categories of Black and white (Gomez, 1992). The term Hispanic became used more widely within the United States in the 1990s after media markets, such as Telemundo and Univision, used the term as a way to have their audiences view themselves as one large demographic for marketing purposes (Simon, 2020).

The term Latino gained popularity in the 1990s as media outlets began to utilize it (Simon, 2020). Some were drawn to the term Latino because one was not categorized into a group based on being from a country that was colonized by Spain, and the term did not include those from Spain. Others were drawn to this term because they felt it was more inclusive than Hispanic by including those from countries such as Brazil that do not speak Spanish. The United States Census Bureau picked up on this and added Latino to the options for ethnicity in the 2000 Census. Today, we see similar changes occurring with the term Latinx, where some people are using this term to self-identify because they believe it is more inclusive of the LGBTQ community, and it is viewed as gender neutral (Simon, 2020). Even though research shows that few people self-identify as Latinx, this term has been picked up by marketing campaigns and is likely to gain more traction as it moves further into the mainstream (Ruiz, 2021).

Regardless of all the categories one can choose from to identify one's ethnicity in the United States, one thing to keep in mind is that ethnicity is self-ascribed, and it is up to each person to define their own ethnicity. However, one's individual definition of ethnicity also can change based on whether people are interacting with a group of people who are from a similar background or not. For instance, if a person is in a conversation with someone who also would be considered to be Hispanic or Latino, then they are more likely to identify themselves by their country of origin. However, if the same person is in a conversation with people who do not identify as Hispanic or Latino then they are more likely to identify by one of the broader categories of Hispanic or Latino (Simon, 2020).

Ethnicity Today: Immigration

Currently, the biggest issue facing the Hispanic community is that of immigration. Immigration is not a new issue. There have been instances in the past when we have opened our borders to welcome in Mexicans, for example, because we needed laborers during WWII. However, there have been just as many instances when we have deported large numbers of immigrants (Zoot Suit Discovery Guide, 2014).

In 2012, the United States Supreme Court ruled in *Arizona v. US* that immigration is a federal issue and one that should not be taken up by the states (Oyez, 2014b). However, politicians have been reluctant to discuss the unpopular issue of immigration and a pathway to legal citizenship, leaving the undocumented to fend for themselves. This situation became impossible to ignore in the fall of 2011 as a spike of *unaccompanied minors*, children without a legal guardian present, crossed the border into the United States from Central America and Mexico (UNHCR, 2015). By 2013, over 21,000 unaccompanied minors from El Salvador, Guatemala, and Honduras were apprehended at the United States' border. Unaccompanied minors also were coming from Mexico, where nearly 19,000 children were apprehended in 2013 (UN-

HCR, 2015). However, the true surge began in 2014, as nearly 70,000 unaccompanied children along with an additional 60,000 people traveling with family were apprehended illegally crossing into the United States (Sakuma, 2015).

IN FOCUS

Unaccompanied Minors

The United Nations Refugee Agency interviewed 400 unaccompanied minors from El Salvador, Honduras, Guatemala, and Mexico to better understand why the children were fleeing their home countries (UNHCR, 2015). They found that children from El Salvador and Honduras primarily were fleeing violence or threats of violence from organized crime, while children from Guatemala were primarily fleeing due to deprivation of opportunities followed by abuse at home. Mexican children also were primarily fleeing violence or the threat of violence from organized crime, while 38% of the kids interviewed had been recruited or forced to work as guides for smugglers. The research team concluded that a large percentage (58%) of the children interviewed were in need of international protection due to threats of violence. Therefore, all migrant children should be screened for international protection after crossing the border (UNHCR, 2015).

Prior to 2014, the policy in the United States had been to allow those seeking asylum to live with a sponsor until their asylum hearing. However, the sheer volume of those coming across the border seeking asylum began to quickly overwhelm the system. Initially the plan had been to immediately deport the women and children who were crossing the border. However, it was determined that the overwhelming majority of the migrants crossing the border had a credible reason to file for asylum. The Obama administration then decided it would utilize *family detention centers* where mothers and children were housed together. The family detention centers would serve two purposes: as a place for women and children to stay while they sought asylum and as a deterrent or a warning of what will happen to those who were considering crossing the border (Sakuma, 2015).

The family detention centers were intended to resemble normal life and included playgrounds and toys for the children. However, they were still detention facilities, and those held there were expected to participate in security checks three times a day. The detained migrants also experienced further mental and physical deterioration as they waited for months for their court hearings for asylum. The adults housed there engaged in hunger strikes and more than one woman tried to commit suicide (Sakuma, 2015). Lawsuits were filed on behalf of the detained, and it was determined that family detention could not be used for deterrence and that it violated the Flores Settlement Agreement of 1997 (Stracqualursi et al., 2019). The *Flores Settlement Agreement* stated migrant children must be released without delay from detention to their parents, relatives, or a licensed program, for instance a foster care program. During detention, children must be provided with food, water, medical assistance, a toilet and sink, a temperature-controlled environment, supervision, and separation from unrelated adults. The Obama administration officials thought they were following the Flores Settlement Agreement because the children were with their families. However, federal judges concluded they were not and could no longer keep migrant children in detention for more than 20 days with or without their parents. (Stracqualursi, et al., 2019).

In 2016, the number of children with a parent or legal guardian crossing the border illegally as part of a family (77,674) outnumbered those who were unaccompanied minors (nearly 60,000) (Krogstad, 2016). Throughout 2017 and 2018, families with children and unaccompanied minors continued to cross into the United States to claim asylum, with 85% of migrants coming from El Salvador, Guatemala, and Honduras and an additional 12% from Mexico (Cheatham, 2020). In 2017, refugees from Central American countries also began to gain attention from the media as they began to travel to the United States' border in groups known as migrant caravans that ranged in size from a few hundred to thousands (Correal & Specia, 2018). *Migrant caravans* were formed to help protect those who were making the dangerous journey north, as it is common for migrants to experience violent crimes along their journey, such as murder, rape, and robbery. Others joined the migrant caravans because they could not afford to pay a smuggler. These migrant caravans continued into 2018 with the largest being organized in Honduras in October of 2018 and involving 7,000 people, including 2,300 children, from Honduras, El Salvador, Guatemala, and Nicaragua (Correal & Specia, 2018).

In April of 2018, then Attorney General Jeff Sessions ordered federal prosecutors on the border to adopt a *zero-tolerance immigration policy*, where children were to be separated from their parents as a deterrent to not cross the border (Office of Public Affairs, 2018). Sessions believed that if parents knew their children would be taken from them, they would not cross the border illegally. However, many parents were not aware of the policy when they crossed, and others had too much to lose if they did not try, such as their lives or the lives of their children. Then, in May of 2018, the Trump administration ordered that parents who were crossing the border with children be prosecuted with crossing the border illegally even if the parent and child were seeking asylum in the United States. The administration then used the charge of illegal border crossing as a reason to separate children from their parents (Williams, 2018).

The Trump administration's child separation policies outraged the American public, and protests erupted across the United States with people from all political affiliations attending. The public outcry eventually led to President Trump signing an executive order to reverse the policy of family separation on June 26, 2018. The Trump administration planned to utilize family detention centers instead, even though the courts had already stated that migrant children could not be held in family detention for more than 20 days (Colvin & Long, 2018).

Shortly after the Trump administration officially ended their child separation policy in June of 2018, a judge ordered they reunite all of the children with their parents within 30 days for those five and over and within two weeks for those under five. However, this proved to be difficult (Pilkington, 2020). In February of 2021, the Biden administration created a task force to reunite all migrant children who had been separated from their parents. The taskforce also was asked to examine approximately 5,600 additional migrant children cases that occurred under the zero-tolerance policy to determine if additional children were separated from their parents or legal guardian. It has been difficult for the taskforce to reunite the parents and children who have been identified, as records were often incomplete, and most of the parents had been deported to Central America with a smaller portion living somewhere within the United States (Treene & Knight, 2021).

Summary

Upon first glance the term ethnicity appears to be a very simple concept. "Check this box if you identify as Hispanic or Latino and this box if you do not." However, these definitions are anything but simple. As demonstrated throughout this chapter, you must also examine the social construction of these terms and the history of how they have been used in social interactions between people or by the economic and political institutions and organizations that surround those people. In the United States, the government, institutions, and organizations continue to define ethnicity very narrowly, lumping people together from different continents, countries, and regions. However, as we examine the political, economic, and social histories of Mexican Americans, Puerto Ricans, and Salvadoran Americans, it is clear that not all identified as Hispanic and Latino have the same histories, experiences, and concerns.

Discussion Questions

1. What does the author mean by the social construction of ethnicity? Be sure to provide examples of how this occurs with Mexican Americans, Puerto Ricans, and Salvadoran Americans.

2. If you could redefine how ethnicity is defined in the United States, what would this term look like? Be sure to be specific in your definition of what would be and would not be included.

3. Should undocumented immigrants be provided a pathway to citizenship by the United States federal government? If yes, who do you think should be eligible for this plan and why? If no, explain why not and what you believe would be a better policy.

Key Terms

ethnicity	Hurricane Maria
Hispanic	death squads
Latino	FMLN
Latinx	El Mozote Massacre
Manifest Destiny	Atlacatl Battalion
Treaty of Guadalupe Hidalgo	Chapultepec Peace Accords
American GI Forum	MS-13
poll taxes	Barrio 18
Hernandez v. Texas	Temporary Protection Status (TPS)
Spanish–Cuban–American War	remittance
Treaty of Paris	*Arizona v. US*
Jones-Shafroth Act	unaccompanied minors
Operation Bootstrap	family detention centers
The Great Migration	Flores Settlement Agreement
tax code Section 936	migrant caravans
PROMESA	zero-tolerance immigration policy

References

Acevedo, N. (2020). Puerto Rico sees more pain and little progress three years after Hurricane Maria. NBC News. https://www.nbcnews.com/news/latino/puerto-rico-sees-more-pain-little-progress-three-years-after-n1240513

Alvarez, A. M. (2010). From revolutionary war to democratic revolution: The Farabundo Marti National Liberation Front (FMLM) in El Salvador. Berghof Conflict Research. https://berghof-foundation.org/files/publications/transitions9_elsalvador.pdf

BBC. (2018). El Salvador profile: Timeline. https://www.bbc.com/news/world-latin-america-19402222

Bondi, C. (2015). Voting rights: A history of poll taxes. Newsmax. http://www.newsmax.com/FastFeatures/voting-rights-poll-taxes-history/2015/12/30/id/707686/

Brown, A. (2020). The changing categories the US Census has used to measure race. Pew Research Center. https://www.pewresearch.org/fact-tank/2020/02/25/the-changing-categories-the-u-s-has-used-to-measure-race/#:~:text=Mexicans%20were%20counted%20as%20their,a%20separate%20question%20from%20race

Bureau of Diplomatic Security. (2020). El Salvador 2020 Crime & Safety Report. Overseas Security Advisory Council, U.S. Department of State. https://www.osac.gov/

Country/ElSalvador/Content/Detail/Report/b4884604-977e-49c7-9e4a-1855725
d032e#:~:text=Since%202015%2C%20the%20per%2Dcapita,in%20El%20Salvador
%20in%202019

Calvo-Gonzalez, O., & Lopez, J. H. (2015). El Salvador: Building on strengths for a
new generation. World Bank Group. http://documents1.worldbank.org/curated/
en/385371467998190389/pdf/97718-CAS-P151397-K8831-Box391451B-white
-cover.pdf

Carlos, R., & Rivera, J. M. (2020). Puerto Rico wants statehood—but only Congress
can make it the 51st state in the United States. The Conversation. https://thecon-
versation.com/puerto-rico-wants-statehood-but-only-congress-can-make-it-the
-51st-state-in-the-united-states-150503

Causey, R. (2016). Things to know about poverty in El Salvador. The Borgen Project.
https://borgenproject.org/poverty-in-el-salvador/

Central Intelligence Agency. (2014). *The world factbook 2013–14*. https://www.cia.gov/
library/publications/the-world-factbook/fields/2075.html

Cheatham, A. (2020). US detention of child migrants. Council on Foreign Relations.
https://www.cfr.org/backgrounder/us-detention-child-migrants

Chrol, J. (2020). 5 facts about poverty in El Salvador. The Borgen Project. https://bor
genproject.org/tag/poverty-in-el-salvador/

Cohn, D. (2010). Census history: Counting Hispanics. Pew Research: Social & Demographic Trends. http://www.pewsocialtrends.org/2010/03/03/census-history-count
ing-hispanics-2/

Cohn, D., Patten, E., & Lopez, M. E. (2014). Puerto Rico population declines on island,
grows on U.S. mainland. Pew Research Center. https://www.pewresearch.org/his
panic/2014/08/11/puerto-rican-population-declines-on-island-grows-on-u-s
-mainland/

Cole, N. L. (2020). The difference between Hispanic and Latino. https://www.thought
co.com/hispanic-vs-latino-4149966

Colvin, J., & Long, C. (2018). In reversal, Trump orders halt to family separation rule.
AP News. https://apnews.com/article/1dafadd6fee4447cadd4a0179553026e

Correal, A., & Specia, M. (2018). The migrant caravan: What to know about the thousands traveling north. *The New York Times*. https://www.nytimes.com/2018/10/26/
world/americas/what-is-migrant-caravan-facts-history.html

DeYoung, K. (1981). Carter decides to resume military aid to El Salvador. *The Washington Post*. https://www.washingtonpost.com/archive/politics/1981/01/14/carter
-decides-to-resume-military-aid-to-el-salvador/16084fe6-8174-49dc-be5f-a5a14
7566f96/

Doyle, D. R. (2020). The Puerto Rico "bankruptcy:" A cheat sheet. American Bankruptcy Institute. https://www.abi.org/feed-item/the-puerto-rico-%E2%80%9C
bankruptcy%E2%80%9D-a-cheat-sheet

Editors of Encyclopedia Britannica. (2015). Puerto Rico. https://www.britannica.com/
place/Puerto-Rico/The-debate-over-political-status

Fearon, J. D. (2002). Why do some civil wars last so much longer than others? *Journal of Peace Research*, *41*, 275–301.

Florido, A. (2020). Puerto Rico's governor loses primary bid for full term. NPR. https://www.npr.org/2020/08/16/903111430/puerto-ricos-governor-loses-primary-bid-for-full-term

Garsd, J. (2015). How El Salvador fell into a web of gang violence. NPR. https://www.npr.org/sections/goatsandsoda/2015/10/05/445382231/how-el-salvador-fell-into-a-web-of-gang-violence

Gomez, L. (1992). The birth of the Hispanic generation: Attitudes of Mexican American political elites toward the Hispanic label. *Latin American Perspectives*, *19*, 45–58.

Gonzalez-Barrera, A., & Lopez, M. H. (2013). A demographic portrait of Mexican-Origin Hispanics in the United States. Pew Research. http://www.pewhispanic.org/2013/05/01/a-demographic-portrait-of-mexican-origin-hispanics-in-the-united-states/

Greenberg, S., & Elkins, G. (2015). Tax policy helped to create Puerto Rico's fiscal crisis. Tax Foundation. https://taxfoundation.org/tax-policy-helped-create-puerto-rico-fiscal-crisis/

Griswold del Castillo, R. (2014). War's end. http://www.pbs.org/kera/usmexicanwar/war/wars_end_guadalupe.html

Guadalupe, P. (2016). Here's how PROMESA aims to tackle Puerto Rico's debt. NBC News. https://www.nbcnews.com/news/latino/here-s-how-promesa-aims-tackle-puerto-rico-s-debt-n601741

Hajek, D. (2019). "I miss them, always": A witness recounts El Salvador's 1989 Jesuit Massacre. NPR. https://www.npr.org/2019/11/16/774176106/i-miss-them-always-a-witness-recounts-el-salvador-s-1989-jesuit-massacre#:~:text=%22Be%20a%20patriot%2C%20kill%20a,top%20scholars%20in%20El%20Salvador

Haney López, I. F. (1994). The social construction of race: Some observations on illusion, fabrication, and choice. *Harvard Civil Rights-Civil Liberties Law Review*, *29*, 1–62.

History.com Editors. (2020). United States calls situation in El Salvador a communist plot. https://www.history.com/this-day-in-history/united-states-calls-situation-in-el-salvador-a-communist-plot

Isles, D. (2019). El Salvador: A brief history. Teaching Central America. https://www.teachingcentralamerica.org/history-of-el-salvador-book

Krogstad, J. M. (2016). US border apprehensions of families and unaccompanied children jump dramatically. Pew Research Center. https://www.pewresearch.org/fact-tank/2016/05/04/u-s-border-apprehensions-of-families-and-unaccompanied-children-jump-dramatically/

Krogstad, J. M., & Cohn, D. (2014). US Census looking at big changes in how it asks about race and ethnicity. Pew Research Center. http://www.pewresearch.org/fact

-tank/2014/03/14/u-s-census-looking-at-big-changes-in-how-it-asks-about-race
-and-ethnicity/

Lind, D. (2015). Puerto Rico's debt crisis, explained in 11 basic facts. Vox. https://www.
vox.com/2015/7/10/8924517/puerto-rico-bankrupt-debt

Lopez, M. H. (2013). Hispanic or Latino?: Many don't care, except in Texas. Pew Research Center. http://www.pewresearch.org/fact-tank/2013/10/28/in-texas-its-his
panic-por-favor/

Malkin, E. (2018). Survivors of massacres ask: "Why did they have to kill those children?" *The New York Times*. https://www.nytimes.com/2018/05/26/world/americas
/el-salvador-el-mazote-massacre.html

Martinez, S. (2018). Life under gang rule in El Salvador. International Crisis Group.
https://www.crisisgroup.org/latin-america-caribbean/central-america/el-salvador/
life-under-gang-rule-el-salvador

McKinney, C. E. (2015). Twelve years a terror: US impact in the 12-year war in El
Salvador. *International ResearchScape Journal*, *2*, Article 5. https://scholarworks.
bgsu.edu/cgi/viewcontent.cgi?article=1020&context=irj

Meraji, S. M. (2020). Hispanic, Latino, or Latinx? Survey Says. NPR: Code Switch.
https://www.npr.org/sections/codeswitch/2020/08/11/901398248/hispanic-latino
-or-latinx-survey-says?fbclid=IwAR3JdHfLMNYMx1KcrSvXAtDQrPVjyrjRIqr7
2rf3rzzXXQr8OfD6zJhWo2A

Mercy Corps. (2020). The facts: Hurricane Maria's effect on Puerto Rico. https://www.
mercycorps.org/blog/quick-facts-hurricane-maria-puerto-rico

Morning, A. (2008). Ethnic classification in global perspective: A cross-national survey of the 2000 Census round. *Population Research and Policy Review*, *27*, 239–272.

Noe-Bustamante, L., Flores, A., & Shah, S. (2019). Facts on Hispanics of Mexican origin, in the United States 2017. https://www.pewresearch.org/hispanic/fact-sheet/
u-s-hispanics-facts-on-mexican-origin-latinos/

Office of Minority Health. (2019). Profile: Hispanic/Latino Americans. Retrieved
from https://minorityhealth.hhs.gov/omh/browse.aspx?lvl=3&lvlid=64

Office of Public Affairs. (2018). Attorney General announces zero tolerance policy for
criminal illegal entry. Department of Justice. https://www.justice.gov/opa/pr/attor
ney-general-announces-zero-tolerance-policy-criminal-illegal-entry

Office of the Historian. (n.d.). The Spanish-American War, 1898. https://history.state.
gov/milestones/1866-1898/spanish-american-war#:~:text=U.S.%20victory%20in
%20the%20war,of%20Hawaii%20during%20the%20conflict

Oyez. (2014a). *Hernandez v. Texas*. https://www.oyez.org/cases/1940-1955/347us475

Oyez. (2014b). *Arizona v. United States*. http://www.oyez.org/cases/2010-2019/2011/
2011_11_182

Padgett, T. (2014). El Salvador's new president faces gangs, poverty and instability.
NPR. https://www.npr.org/sections/parallels/2014/03/19/291428131/el-salvadors
-new-president-faces-gangs-poverty-and-instability

Passel, J. S., & Cohn, D. (2019). Mexicans decline to less than half the U.S. unautho-
rized immigrant population for the first time. Pew Research Center. https://www.

pewresearch.org/fact-tank/2019/06/12/us-unauthorized-immigrant-population
-2017/

PBS. (2014a). The border. (2014). http://www.pbs.org/kpbs/theborder/history/index.
html

PBS. (2014b). U.S.-Mexican War: 1846–1848. http://www.pbs.org/kera/usmexicanwar
/index_flash.html

Penaloza, M. (2020). Latinx is a term many still cannot embrace. NPR. https://www.
npr.org/2020/10/01/916441659/latinx-is-a-term-many-still-cant-embrace

Pilkington, E. (2020). Parents of 545 children still not found after Trump separation
policy. *The Guardian.* https://www.theguardian.com/us-news/2020/oct/21/trump
-separation-policy-545-children-parents-still-not-found

Rivera, M. (2020). Economy. https://welcome.topuertorico.org/economy.shtml

Ruiz, J. (2021, March 22). Latinx—to use or not to use? Mintel Blog. https://www.
mintel.com/blog/consumer-market-news/latinx-to-use-or-not-to-use

Sakuma, A. (2015). The failed experiment of immigrant family detention. NBC News.
https://www.nbcnews.com/news/latino/failed-experiment-immigrant-family-de
tention-n403126

Sanchez Korrol, V. (2017). History of Puerto Ricans in the US. Center for Puerto Rican
Studies at the City University of New York. https://centropr.hunter.cuny.edu/edu
cation/story-us-puerto-ricans-part-one

Schmitt, E. (2001). Salvadorans illegally in the US are given protected status. *The New
York Times.* https://www.nytimes.com/2001/03/03/us/salvadorans-illegally-in-us
-are-given-protected-status.html

Simon, Y. (2020). Latino, Hispanic, Latinx, Chicano: The history behind the terms.
History Stories. https://www.history.com/news/hispanic-latino-latinx-chicano-back
ground

Spagat, E. (2020). Court: Trump can end temporary legal status for four countries. AP
News. https://apnews.com/article/el-salvador-immigration-pasadena-courts-don
ald-trump-c903626adf3fcdb1d7805f560c37d1be

Stevens, G., Ishizawa, H., & Grbic, D. (2015). Measuring race and ethnicity in the
censuses of Australia, Canada and the United States: Parallels and paradoxes. *Ca-
nadian Studies in Population, 42,* 13–34. https://ejournals.library.ualberta.ca/index.
php/csp/article/viewFile/20439/17947

Stracqualursi, V., Sands, G., Elkin, E., & Rocha, V. (2019). What is the Flores Settlement that the Trump administration has moved to end? CNN. https://www.cnn.
com/2019/08/21/politics/what-is-flores-settlement/index.html

Toro, J. R. (2013). Puerto Rico's Operation Bootstrap. https://library.brown.edu/create/
modernlatinamerica/chapters/chapter-12-strategies-for-economic-developmen/
puerto-ricos-operation-bootstrap/

Transparency Portal. (2020). Portal de Transparencia de COR 3. https://recovery.pr/es

Treene, A., & Knight, S. (2021). Biden has yet to reunite any of the migrant families
separated under Trump. https://www.axios.com/family-separation-migrants-re
unification-biden-4d251d63-c774-4c22-9839-3970a8d5c2ae.html

UNHCR. (2015). Children on the run. The UN Refugee Agency. https://www.unhcr.org/56fc266f4.html

U.S. Census Bureau. (2014a). 1860. https://www.census.gov/history/www/through_the_decades/index_of_questions/1860_1.html

U.S. Census Bureau. (2014b). 1970 (Population). https://www.census.gov/history/www/through_the_decades/index_of_questions/1970_population.html

U.S. Census Bureau. (2014c). State and county quick facts. http://quickfacts.census.gov/qfd/states/00000.html

U.S. Census Bureau. (2020). Research to improve data on race and ethnicity. https://www.census.gov/about/our-research/race-ethnicity.html

Williams, P. (2018). Sessions: Parents, children entering US illegally will be separated. NBC News. https://www.nbcnews.com/politics/justice-department/sessions-parents-children-entering-us-illegally-will-be-separated-n872081

Williams Walsh, M. (2017). Puerto Rico declares a form of bankruptcy. *The New York Times*. https://www.nytimes.com/2017/05/03/business/dealbook/puerto-rico-debt.html

Zoot Suit Discovery Guide. (2014). Mexican Americans in World War II. http://research.pomona.edu/zootsuit/en/zoot-suit-la/world-war-ii/

THREE

Defining Sex and Gender

Learning Objectives

1. Understand and critically examine the evolution of the terms "sex" and "gender" using the framework of social construction.
2. Explain how others as well as institutions and organizations influence our understanding and perception of sex and gender.

We will begin with a basic definition of the terms "sex" and "gender," but as discussed throughout this chapter, the definitions of these two words are anything but simple. *Sex* is typically categorized into the two categories of male and female and is determined by one's biological makeup, such as chromosomes and hormones, along with external and internal sex organs. However, *gender* is defined by how one identifies within society as either masculine or feminine. Gender is not determined by biological differences, but rather by how we identify ourselves within the world and the how we interact with others based on this self-identity (Nobelius, 2004). At first glance these definitions appear very basic, but not all people fit into the neat categories of male/female or feminine/masculine. In order to better understand the terms sex and gender as well as how they have evolved over the years, we will examine them from a social construction framework. This will allow us to better understand how these terms have evolved through time, due to what is going on socially, politically, and economically within our world.

Defining Sex in the United States

Sex, male or female, is typically assigned upon birth by the doctor who delivers the baby. This is done with a quick observation of whether the baby has a penis (male) or a vagina (female). The majority of the time the parent is told immediately after birth that the child is a girl or boy. However, for approximately 1 in 2,000 births, the sex of the child cannot be determined at first glance. There is a list of 60 different medical diagnoses that these children could fall into, but as a group they are referred to generically by the medical community as *Difference of Sex Development* (DSD). These diagnoses could occur for a variety of reasons and are typically genetic or related to chromosomal or hormonal production in utero. The end result could be over- or underdeveloped sex organs as well as the absence of the sex organ, depending upon the diagnosis (American Academy of Pediatrics, 2015).

In the past, children who were born with a DSD were referred to as "hermaphrodites" and were treated poorly by the medical community. Parents often were not given all of the information needed about their child's diagnosis, and doctors were quick to strongly encourage parents to have the infant undergo surgery to create more typical female or male sex organs. This created an atmosphere of shame and secrecy, making it difficult for parents and their children to seek support outside of their doctor's office. Children who underwent these surgeries typically were not told of their situation and grew up without knowledge of their full medical history. Doctors made the decision of whether the child should be surgically given the anatomy of a male or female, and the outcomes were often crude, with the sex organs only resembling typical male and female sex anatomy (Intersex Society of North America, 2008).

In the 1990s, there was more recognition of the child's as well as the parents' rights, and most doctors now do a better job of informing the patient as well as their families about their diagnosis as well as their options. There also were nonprofits forming at this same time to provide information and support to those who had been through this process as well as for parents who were faced with these decisions for their newborn (for example, the Intersex Society of North America and Advocates for Informed Choice) (Intersex Society of North America, 2008). Activists also were able to lobby for doctors to no longer use the term hermaphrodite and to replace it with *"intersex."* Today, the medical community has replaced the term intersex with difference of sex development (DSD) (American Academy of Pediatrics, 2015). This decision was based on the term intersex referring to being between sexes. It was determined this term was not inclusive as some with DSD strongly identify as male or female and not in between sexes (American Academy of Pediatrics, 2015).

IN FOCUS

Infants and Sex Assignment Surgery

Even though we have come a long way in regards to the rights of the family and child with a difference of sex development, there are still challenges. In South Carolina, for example, there was a lawsuit filed by parents who adopted a child who was born with both male and female sex organs. The child was in state custody, when at 16 months of age the Greenville Hospital System recommended the child be considered for genital surgery. Later, at the Medical University of South Carolina, the child's penis was removed in favor of the vagina even though the child had high testosterone levels and the surgery had been deemed medically unnecessary (Ghorayshi, 2017).

By the time the child was eight years old, it was clear that he strongly identified as a boy. The parents then sued the Greenville Hospital System and the Medical University of South Carolina for medical bills and psychological damage as well as for the pain and suffering their child had experienced as a result of the surgery. The case remained in court for four years, with the Greenville Hospital System settling for $20,000 and the Medical University of South Carolina settling for $440,000 over the next sixteen years. Neither hospitals admitted any wrongdoing (Ghorayshi, 2017). However, the cost of the lawsuit may impact the number of surgeries performed on infants in similar situations in the future.

Currently, there is more public awareness and support for those with DSD. DSD advocates often recommend surgery be performed later in the child's life, when it is believed the child can make a more informed decision. However, even with these recommendations, many doctors still endorse surgical procedures at infancy, believing this will give the child a better opportunity to connect with the assigned sex, and it will be a less traumatic experience overall for the child and the parents as the child grows up (Behrens, 2020).

In the United States, sex is still recorded as male or female on birth certificates in most states. If a person decides to change their sex at a later point in life, they have the ability to change these designations to their preferred sex. However, this is not an easy task due to the paperwork involved. Fortunately, this is starting to change. In 2020, for example, there were 19 states that allowed one to choose M for male, F for female, or X for non-binary on their driver license. Two other states also have approved this change, but it has not been implemented. There also were 13 states that allowed one to choose M, F, or X on their birth certificate and 24 states along with Puerto Rico and

Figure 3.1. People fly symbolic flags and hold signs protesting North Carolina's HB2 law that restricts the rights of those who are transgender. © iStockphoto.com/AwakenedEye.

D.C. that allowed one to change their sex on their birth certificate without proof of surgical reassignment surgery or a court order (MAP, 2020).

Other countries also are changing their paperwork process in order to recognize a third sex when one's sex cannot be determined at birth. In Australia, for example, a child's sex can be recorded as X at birth if the sex cannot be determined in order to avoid paperwork issues later in life (Staff, 2011). Other countries, such as New Zealand and Germany, allow for the parents to leave the box for sex blank at birth, so parents do not feel pressured to make an immediate decision (BBC News, 2013). Although this shows progress on some levels, many DSD advocates fear that creating a third category or leaving the box blank sets people up for discrimination later in life. There also is a concern that this removes attention from the larger issue of unnecessary surgical intervention in infancy (Intersex Society of North America, 2008).

Defining Gender in the United States

The assignment of sex at birth is viewed as so important because this designation determines gender and how the child will be socialized when growing up to take on what is considered by society as a male or female role. Gender socialization begins very early on in life; for example, even though infants cannot express their gender identity at birth, it is done for them by their parents and caretakers. You cannot tell the gender, masculine or feminine, of a baby by looking at the child, because there are not obvious identifiers. Therefore, caretakers will pierce infant girls' ears or put headband bows on their heads to identify the babies as girls. Parents of infant boys will dress boys in clothes that are identified by society to be masculine, for example, those with trucks or dinosaurs on them. This then makes it easier for those who do not know the baby to identify its gender based on outward appearance. Girl infants could certainly wear blue shirts with trucks and one could pierce a baby boy's ears, but parents rarely defy what are viewed as traditional gender roles.

Gender socialization continues throughout the toddler years as parents and others buy toys for the child that further reinforce these gender stereotypes by, for example, buying trucks and blocks for boys and dolls and cooking sets for girls. Children then learn these are their roles in society and that boys build things, while girls take care of babies and the household chores (Lorber, 1994). Even if a parent defies these stereotypes and buys blocks and dolls for a boy, the child will pick up on the notions of what it means to be a boy as he starts school. My husband and I, for example, bought our son what would be considered traditional boy toys, but he also was given a baby doll that he named Baby Billy. When he was younger, Baby Billy went everywhere with us. He went to the playground, the store, and the zoo and sat on his lap while he ate his meals. However, when our son started preschool, he quickly learned that boys do not play with dolls and came home and announced that Baby Billy was really for girls. We discussed with him that it was okay for boys and girls to play with dolls, but Baby Billy no longer went to the store or the playground with us.

This type of pressure to conform to traditional gender roles also comes from other adults. When our son was three years old, for example, we took him to the bike store to pick out a pedal-free bike to learn how to ride. He chose a bike that was hot pink, and the salesman was beside himself explaining to our son and us that he had plenty of red and blue bikes in the back, and he would be happy to get one of those for him. We asked our son if he wanted a red, blue, or the pink bike, and he said he wanted the pink bike. The salesman was visibly upset and said several times to our son that he did not have to get a pink bike until we eventually intervened and asked the salesman to stop. We reminded the salesman that it was his choice, and honestly, the hot pink bike was the coolest looking one of the three.

This type of gender socialization continues well into childhood and is often reinforced by others, as it remains difficult to tell the difference between young boys and girls because they have not started to physically mature. When we see a young child with short hair, for example, we often make the assumption that the child is a boy, while if we see a young child wearing a princess shirt we make the assumption that the child is a girl. However, these assumptions are not always accurate. As children enter into adolescence and later young adulthood, their bodies physically mature and people are able to identify their gender beyond their clothing and hair. However, this is also the time when they will delve further into the gender role they were socialized with as a child or perhaps decide they identify as something else entirely.

In the United States, only two categories of gender, male and female, are legally recognized. However, more recently we have begun to recognize that gender cannot be neatly defined into the categories of masculine or feminine for many, and our definitions of gender outside of the legal realm now reflect this. One category of gender, *cis-gender*, refers to those whose biological makeup matches their gender identity. A person born with a penis and testes (male sex), for example, who self-identifies as a man through his social interactions in the world, his dress, and the roles he takes on in his everyday life (gender) would be categorized as cis-gender. A second category of gender is *transgender*, where someone's biological sex does not match their gender identity or how they present themselves to the world. A person who was born with a vagina and ovaries (female sex), for example, who self-identifies as a man through his social interactions in the world, his dress, and the roles he takes on in his everyday life (gender) would be considered to be transgender. Being transgender is not the same for everyone; for some this may mean changing their clothes and/or name to match the gender they self-identify with, while for others this may include hormone therapy or surgery to look physically more like the gender with which they identify (Zevallos, 2015).

The *third gender* refers to those who do not identify with a specific gender or take on multiple gender identities, as well as cultures that recognize three or more gender categories. Since the United States only recognizes the gender categories of male and female, third gender is typically only used in the United States to describe gender in other cultures or countries. However, prior to the introduction of Christianity and colonization, numerous Native American tribes did not define gender into the two categories of masculine and feminine; instead they believed humans and animals possessed both masculine and feminine traits (Zevallos, 2013).

Gender within the Native American community was viewed on a continuum that was dependent upon the community, as well as one's status and history. The Navajo, for example, defined gender using four different categories. They used the categories of male and female, where those who were born male, for example, fulfilled masculine roles within the community, but they also had two additional categories they referred to as "*two spirit.*" The two spirit feminine man is a biological male who fulfills traditional feminine roles within the community, while a two spirit masculine woman is a biological female who fulfills traditional male roles within the community. However, the Navajo would not consider the two spirit person to be transgender, because this is not something the two spirit person decides, but it is rather a decision made by the elders within the community. The two spirit person is believed to have special connections to their ancestors, and once their gender is reassigned by their elders they are expected to conform to those gender roles. The two spirit person is highly revered within the community and holds a special status, as it is their role to perform cultural and religious ceremonies and practices, due to a spiritual connection to their ancestors. The tradition of the two spirit person was deemed illegal after Westerners invaded and took over Navajo communities, because they were viewed by the colonists as homosexuals. However, there has been some resurrection of this tradition in more recent history (Zevallos, 2013).

GLOBAL SPOTLIGHT

Hijra

An example of third gender is the Hijra of India. The Hijra are composed of eunuchs (castrated males) as well as those who self-identify as transgender or intersex. Prior to British colonization in the 1860s, the Hijra experienced an elevated status and were a celebrated culture within ancient texts. The Hijras were paid to bless marriages and births and performed fertility rituals (Khaleeli, 2014). However, in 1871, under British rule, the Criminal Tribes Act was passed, criminalizing the Hijras' way of life (Scobey-Thal, 2014). After this law, the Hijras were heavily discriminated against and had a difficult time obtaining an education and employment, leaving many within this community to turn to prostitution in order to survive. Recently, in 2014, the Supreme Court of India created a third gender category to protect the Hijra population and require quotas for employers and colleges to improve their education and employment opportunities. However, not all Hijra are happy with the new ruling and would rather categorize their gender based on the gender with which they self-identify. Others fear this ruling takes the focus off of what they view as the more important issue, the law that criminalizes homosexual acts (Khaleeli, 2014).

In the United States, there is growing social acceptance that gender is not binary. For instance, *nonbinary*, also known as *gender queer*, is an umbrella term used to describe those who do not fit into the traditional categories of male and female (Boskey, 2020). There are many categories that fall under nonbinary, as people get to choose how they self-identify. *Agender,* for example, is when one does not identify with a specific gender identity, while *bigender* occurs when one has two distinct gender identities that can occur at the same time or independently. Some also categorize themselves as *gender fluid* or one who moves between two gender identities (Boskey, 2020). It also is important to keep in mind that some who identify as transgender or nonbinary prefer to be called by "they," "them," and "their" pronouns, instead of the traditional male pronouns of "he," "him," and "his" or traditional female pronouns of "she," "her," and "hers." If you are not sure which pronouns someone may prefer, "they," "them," and "their" should be used (Purcell, 2020).

Figure 3.2. The White House lit in rainbow colors. © iStockphoto.com/renaschild.

Defining Sexuality and How It Differs from Gender and Sex

Sexuality is defined as who you are attracted to sexually, who you choose to engage in sexual activity with, and how you identify your behavior. Therefore, one's *sexual orientation* is defined as the sexual attraction one feels towards others. There are many types of sexual orientations. *Heterosexual* is defined as being attracted only to those of the opposite sex, for example males who are sexually attracted to females and females who are sexually attracted to males. The term "*homosexual*" has the clinical definition of being attracted to members of the same sex and is viewed by many to have a negative connotation. A person identifies as *gay* when he or she is sexually attracted to members of the same sex, for example, males who are sexually attracted to males or females who are sexually attracted to females, although this term is more commonly used to refer to men who are sexually attracted to other men. One also can self-identify as a *lesbian*, where women are sexually attracted to other women, while *pansexual* refers to one who self-identifies as being attracted to members of all gender identities, and *bisexual* is defined by those who are sexually attracted to those of their own gender as well as those of another gender (International Spectrum, 2015).

Asexual, also known as *Ace*, is an umbrella term for those who do not feel sexually attracted to others, while *aromantic* or *aro* is a person who does not experience romantic attraction to others. However, most asexuals and aromantics fall on a spectrum. For instance, a *grey-asexual* is someone who is somewhere between asexual and sexual who may experience sexual attraction sometimes. A grey-asexual also may experience sexual attraction, but have a low sex drive or engage in sex with others only in certain circumstances. A *greyromantic* is one who falls between aromatic and romantic and experiences romantic attraction in some circumstances and none in others. A *demisexual* and a *demiromatic* are those who are only sexually attracted to or interested in forming a romantic relationship with others after a bond has been developed over time. Those who identify as *reciprosexual* or *recripromantic* are not attracted to a person sexually or romantically until they know that person is attracted to them, while an *akoisexual* or *akoiromantic* may experience sexual or romantic attraction to another person, but loses interest once the person reciprocates the sexual or romantic feelings (Pasquier, 2018).

The terms homosexual and heterosexual are relatively new. However, the concepts of sexuality and sexual attraction between people of the same sex are not new ideas and have been discussed for centuries. Throughout history, for example, those who engaged in sodomy (anal or oral sex between those of the same or opposite sex) were tolerated, ostracized, killed, or tortured based on who was in control of the government and/or the predominant religious beliefs of the time (*Merriam-Webster*, 2015). This discrimination was often targeted against men who engaged in sodomy, but there are examples of women who engaged in sodomy facing a similar fate. Class also played a part in determining who was discriminated against. Those who were from higher class backgrounds, for example, were given more discretion to participate in sodomy as long as their behavior was not viewed to be excessive by others. However, this notion changed in the nineteenth century, when Queen Victoria of Great Britain began to suspect that aristocratic men were engaging in sodomy with those of the same sex. She then ordered medical doctors to go to the homes of these men and perform physical checks to see if they were engaging in sodomy. This undertaking led to the idea of men who engaged in sodomy as being medically and psychologically defective. Interestingly enough, Queen Victoria did not examine women for similar acts as she did not believe women engaged in what we now refer to as lesbian sex or sodomy (Stanford Encyclopedia of Philosophy, 2015).

Later, in 1869, Karl Maria Benkert, a Hungarian journalist, defined the terms homosexuality and heterosexuality in an attempt to medicalize sexuality. Benkert stated there was evidence one's sexuality was biologically driven and could not be changed. Benkert's desire to medicalize sexuality was driven by an experience he had as a young man, where his close friend was blackmailed due to his sexual orientation and later committed suicide. This incident led to Benkert's interest in the subject of homosexuality and his desire to seek social justice for those who identified as homosexual. At the time, sodomy was illegal, and those who participated in this sexual act were defined using incredibly derogatory terms that did not recognize the biological aspects of sexuality (LGBT History Project, 2012). This changed the debate of homosexual behavior from one that centered on law and religion to now include biology that continued into the early twentieth century. The medicalization of sexuality also led some to believe that those who engaged in same-sex relationships were ill and could be cured, while others had more tolerant viewpoints and believed homosexuality was just a natural part of sexual development. Sigmund Freud, for example, wrote that all humans were innately bisexual and chose either heterosexuality or homosexuality based on their social interactions with their parents and others (Herek, 2012).

By the mid-twentieth century, there were many studies on the topic of same-sex relationships with contradicting conclusions. Some social science studies found those in same-sex relationships to be well adjusted and without any pathology, while others found the opposite. However, many have noted there were several methodological issues with the studies that concluded homosexuality was an illness; for example, some only examined populations that were already seeking psychiatric care (Herek, 2012).

By the 1950s, the American Psychological Association (APA) published their first edition of the Diagnostic and Statistical Manual, more commonly known as the DSM. In the DSM, homosexuality was defined as an illness. This directly impacted how those who identified as homosexual were treated within society and the idea that if homosexuality was an illness it could be cured (Pappas, 2013). Those who were diagnosed as homosexual were subjected to "treatment and rehabilitation" that included lobotomies, shock therapy, and other treatments aimed at convincing the person they were in fact heterosexual (Pappas, 2013). However, by the 1970s, gay activists were starting to sway public opinion toward viewing homosexuality as a sexual orientation and not as an illness. This led to the membership of the APA voting by a slim margin to remove homosexuality from the DSM, in 1974 (Hickey, 2013).

IN FOCUS

"Don't Say Gay" Bill

In 2022, Florida Governor Ron DeSantis signed into law the Parental Rights in Education bill, more commonly known as the "Don't Say Gay" bill (Diaz, 2022). This bill states that kindergarten through third grade school personnel and outside third parties are not allowed to teach on the topics of sexual orientation or gender identity unless the instruction is age or developmentally appropriate. The bill also includes a parental notification requirement, where parents must be notified of any health or support services offered to their kids in school, providing the parents with the opportunity to accept or deny services on behalf of their children. If a parent believes the policy has been violated, they are able to sue the school district (Diaz, 2022).

Supporters of the bill argue this allows parents and guardians to introduce the concepts of sexual orientation and gender identity to their children when they feel it is appropriate (Diaz, 2022). However, opponents of the bill are concerned about the impact this bill will have on LGBTQ youth in Florida. For instance, there are serious concerns regarding LGBTQ youth being outed to their parents or guardians through the parental notification requirements. LGBTQ youth also experience higher rates of depression and suicide than those youth who identify as straight or cisgender. Opponents fear this bill erases LBTQ youth along with their identity, history, and culture, making it that much more difficult for them to find safe spaces which are crucial in decreasing suicide rates (Diaz, 2022).

Even after homosexuality was removed from the DSM, there were many consequences legally and socially for those who openly identified as homosexual. Those who identified as openly gay and lesbian, for example, faced discrimination in the workplace, in their ability to adopt children, and in having their marriages and other civil benefits recognized, and gay consensual sex was illegal in many states. It has only been in recent years that we have started to see many of these barriers removed through United States Supreme Court decisions.

Many Western countries are becoming more accepting of same-sex relationships, and we are seeing a slow shift in laws and policies that no longer condemn people for their sexual orientation. Today, in 65% of the countries recognized by the United Nations, it is legal for people to be in a same-sex relationship. However, this is not true everywhere around the world. Currently, there are 70 countries where it is illegal to be gay, lesbian, bisexual, or transgender, and there are still 12 countries where one can be punished by death for engaging in consensual sexual relations between two adults of the same sex. For example, in Iran, Saudi Arabia, Yemen, and Sudan, along with parts of Somalia and Nigeria, those who engage in consensual sexual acts with a person of the same sex are routinely executed. An additional six countries, including Afghanistan, Brunei, Mauritania, Pakistan, Qatar, and the United Arab Emirates, have laws or religious rules prescribing death for consensual sexual acts between adults of the same sex, but the death penalty is rarely carried out there for this offense (Wareham, 2020).

Changes in Gender Roles

The definition of gender and what is acceptable as gender roles within society is constantly evolving. In order to understand this definition at a particular point in time, one must examine what is occurring within the society politically, socially, and economically. We will start with an example of how cis-gender roles have changed for heterosexual couples. In the early 1700s, with the advancement of technology and the start of the industrial age, men began to leave the farm to look for work outside of the home. This directly impacted gender roles, as the male's role became focused on earning money outside of the home to support the household financially, while women stayed home to care for the children and the household (Wilber, 2000).

Figure 3.3. © Adobe Stock/Ruth

However, as World War II approached and the men left for war there was a dire need for women to engage in work outside of the home. The U.S. government intervened and created the idea of Rosie the Riveter to encourage women to shift their work from the home to the factory, where they were desperately needed for the war effort. Later, when the war ended, women were encouraged to go back to working within the home to make room in the workforce for the men who were returning from war. This changed how traditional gender roles were viewed, and it was once again less socially acceptable for women to work outside of the home. After the war, the economy allowed for the existence of a household where one parent worked and the other stayed home and took care of the house and the children. Jobs at this time, even with only a high school education, often provided a livable wage, health insurance, and retirement benefits that were high enough to support a family on one income (Wilber, 2000).

However, by the 1990s, the economy shifted towards a global economy, where goods were less likely to be made in the United States due to cheaper labor abroad. During this time period, American companies were able to move their factories to countries such as Mexico, Bangladesh, and China, where labor was cheaper and there was not an expectation to provide factory workers with benefits, such as health insurance or retirement. This change in the economy meant there were fewer jobs available in the United States with which one could support a family with only a high school diploma. Therefore, the economy directly impacted gender roles as the need for dual incomes within a household became necessary for many, making it more socially acceptable for women to again work outside of the home. This has had a direct impact on who is responsible for earning the wage that will support the household, which in turn affected who was responsible for taking care of the household and the children (Wilber, 2000).

In 1965, the majority of fathers spent most of their time earning money outside of the home, while today's fathers are working outside of the home and are spending more time taking care of their children and the house as well. Today's working father, for example, is spending twice as much time completing household chores and triple the amount of time with their children, in comparison to fathers in 1965. However, even today a woman working outside of the home still reports doing the bulk of household chores and childcare, but with each generation there does appear to be a more egalitarian split in who takes care of the house and the children. Millennial fathers, for instance, report taking a more hands-on approach both in household work and time spent with children than previous generations (Parker, 2015).

More engagement between fathers and their children also has had a positive effect on their children. The Center for Disease Control found that men who spent more time with their children had children who were more likely to succeed academically and were less likely to be engaged in delinquency and substance use (Jones & Mosher, 2013). However, one cannot forget that class or one's social economic status often plays a part in how much time both women and men are able to spend with their families. Those from higher income brackets are able to take time off for vacations and paid sick time, which directly affects the amount of time one can spend with their children, while parents who are working jobs where they are making less than a living wage are not as likely to experience these same privileges.

Although women are more accepted in the workplace, even in what had been considered nontraditional female jobs, women still face discrimination. Women still earn less money than men; for instance, women earn just .82 cents for every one dollar a man earns (Bleiweis, 2020). This has long-term consequences, making it more difficult for women to save money for needed expenses and for retirement. These numbers also are compounded over a lifetime of working because raises are often based on a percentage of one's base salary, meaning that over the course of one's career the wage gap only continues to grow between men and women (The White House, 2015). However, when one adds race and ethnicity into these statistics the gap only grows, as Black and Hispanic women earn even less money on the dollar than men. In 2019, Asian women earned .90, white women earned .79, Black women earned .62, American Indian or Alaskan Native women earned .57, and Hispanic women earned .54 for every one dollar a white man earned (Bleiweis, 2020).

Earning less money due to one's gender and/or race or ethnicity not only impacts long-term goals, such as savings and retirement, but there are short-term consequences as well. In order to work full time, women must be able to afford childcare, and how much money one has directly determines the quality of that childcare. The pandemic of 2020 further publicly exposed the lack of affordable quality childcare in the United States, when six months into the pandemic one in five childcare centers remained closed. The childcare system had already been strained, but due to government closures and Covid-19 restrictions many childcare centers were forced to close temporarily and in some instances permanently. At the same time, schools were deciding whether to go online or have school in person, with most bouncing back and forth between these models as infection rates increased and decreased in the community throughout the school year. All of this came together and forced many women to leave the workforce to care for family. For instance, in August and September of 2020, 865,000 working women left the workforce—a rate that was four times that of men. This exodus of working women from the workforce coincided with the traditional start of the school year, and many women have stated they made the decision to leave their job to care for their children who would be completing school from home (Covert, 2020).

The amount of time one can take to care for sick children and spend with a child who was recently born or adopted also is directly impacted by class. Women working minimum wage jobs, for instance, are not likely to receive paid days off from work to care for sick children and must make the decision whether to send their children to day care/school or keep them home and face the possible penalties at work for doing so. However, this may not be a choice, as most schools and childcare centers will demand a parent pick up a child who has a fever, because this means the child is contagious. These examples illustrate that although there have been advances in women's rights in the workplace, many women are still not experiencing the same benefits as men, and the impact of this is only further compounded when taking into consideration the race, ethnicity, and class background of the woman (Associated Press, 2015).

Although we are seeing more acceptance of women working outside of the household, the United States primarily engages in traditional notions of gender roles. More women are working outside of the household; however, most women still report being responsible for the majority of household chores and childcare. This is changing as more men take part in the care of their children and performing duties around the house, but overall this is still primarily considered to be women's work (Jones & Mosher, 2013). This is not necessarily true in other Western countries; for example, in Sweden, men are expected and it is socially accepted for them to take care of their children. This can be seen when walking down the street. You are likely to see just as many men taking care of their children as women while, for example, playing with them in the park or walking them from one destination to the next. You also will notice in the designated walking lanes on the sidewalk a picture of a man walking with children to indicate children are in the area, while signs such as this still depict a woman and a child in the United States. These notions also are reinforced through the laws; for example, parents are encouraged to take 16 months of paid leave from work to care for their newly born or adopted children. Two of these 16 months are specifically reserved for the fathers to care for their children (Sweden, 2015). In the United States, this does not occur. The *Family Medical Leave Act* entitles caretakers to take 90 days off from work without losing their jobs upon return, but it is up to the employer to decide whether this time is paid or not and most employers do not provide paid leave (United States Department of Labor, 2015). During the COVID-19 pandemic,, Congress passed the *Families First Coronavirus Response Act*, which gave working parents with children who were at home due to childcare or school closure 12 weeks of guaranteed paid leave. However, there were a lot of restrictions placed on this paid leave, such as working at a company that employed fewer than 500 employees. Due to these restrictions, only 20% of working parents with children at home due to school or childcare closures were able to receive the 12 weeks of paid leave (Covert, 2020).

We also have seen an evolution in the acceptance of gender outside of what had been considered traditional cis-gender roles. Those who self-identify as transgender, for example, are gaining more acceptance within society. This has occurred primarily due to the levels of awareness created by activists and their persistence to reduce the stigma associated with those who identify as transgender. Since 1999, for example, November 20th has been acknowledged as the Transgender Day of Remembrance in order to recognize and remember those who have lost their lives in violent hate crimes, due to their gender identity (GLAAD, 2015). This awareness has directly impacted how many view those who self-identify as transgender. The United States Department of Justice, for example, now offers trainings to police officers to help them be more aware and reduce discrimination when encountering a transgender person who is an offender or victim of a crime. The federal government also allows those who identify as transgender to change their sex designation on passports and social security cards to match their gender identity (Valente, 2014). Medically we have seen improvements as well. There are now several hospital clinics who work specifically with children and adults who are transgender. The Children's Hospital in Cincinnati, for example, has the Transgender Health Clinic that works with patients between the ages of 15 and 24 as well as their families. This clinic offers everything from medical to social services, including working with the youth's family and community during the transition (Cincinnati Children's Hospital and Medical Center, 2015).

However, it should be noted that advances in rights are never guaranteed. For instance, in 2018 there were 21 different anti-transgender bills introduced by 10 states, and 16 states came together to ask the United States Supreme Court to deny transgender people employment protection under the 1964 Civil Rights Act (Human Rights Campaign, 2018). The Civil Rights Act of 1964 passed by the federal government states that one cannot be discriminated against based on one's race, color, sex, or national origin (U.S. Department of Labor, n.d.). The states who brought the case *Bostock v. Clayton County, Georgia* to the Supreme Court argued that those who identify as transgender did not fall under the category sex and were therefore not protected under the 1964 Civil Rights Act (Liptak, 2020). However on June 15, 2020, the United States Supreme Court, in a 6–3 decision, concluded that sexual orientation and transgender were included under the Civil Rights Act and that someone cannot be fired from their job because they are gay or transgender. Prior to this ruling, over half of the states had laws that allowed for someone to be fired for being gay, bisexual, or transgender (Liptak, 2020).

IN FOCUS

Transgender Athletes

In 2020, state legislators began to focus on transgender youth by creating legislation that banned trans youth from being able to play sports (Strangio & Arkles, 2022). As of 2022, there were 15 states that had some sort of ban in place to not allow trans youth to play sports. These bans were often put in place under the guise they were helping female athletes. However, critics of these bills note these laws only harm trans youth, who are already incredibly vulnerable, along with cis-gender female athletes who do not fit the stereotypical ideal of what a female athlete should look like. Biological diversity is a part of sports, with some athletes being larger or faster than others, and these differences are celebrated in male sports. However, things such as muscle mass and height are often called into question when the athlete is female, with this being particularly true if the athlete is a person of color. This harms both cisgender and transgender women, as many of the states with bans in place also have invasive genital tests and body exams if an athlete is suspected to be transgender. It also should be noted that not allowing transgender athletes to participate in sports reinforces the negative beliefs cisgender people often hold about the trans community, further putting those who identify as transgender in harm's way (Strangio & Arkles, 2022).

Although there have been advances in awareness, support services, and legal cases for transgender people, we still have a long way to go before we see true equality. Transgender people still face a lot of discrimination in the workplace, housing, and medical care. For example, those who identify as transgender experience unemployment at a rate three times higher than the general population, with those who are Black and transgender unemployed at a rate that is four times higher than the general population. Socially many are left out by their families either by being kicked out of their home or excluded from social support, with the majority of transgender youth (75%) reporting their families make negative comments about those who identify as LGBT. This lack of family support leads to higher rates of homelessness, with 20% of those who identify as transgender being homeless at some point and 40% of homeless youth identifying as LGBT. Transgender youth also report that they are less likely to get medical care because they fear how the health care workers will treat them due to their gender identity (Human Rights Campaign, 2018).

In the United States between 2013 and 2020, more than 200 transgender people were murdered, and 2020 saw the highest rates of murders yet, with 37 homicides (Roberts, 2020). The majority (66%) of those who were killed were Black women. However, the number of transgender people who have been murdered is viewed as a conservative estimate because police officers often record the victim's sex at birth from their identification rather than the gender one identifies with at the time of their death (Roberts, 2020). In order to understand why the number of transgender people being murdered continues to increase, we must first examine the stigma that surrounds what it means to be transgender (Human Rights Campaign, 2018). Transgender people face stigma from family members who no longer support them, politicians who try to pass legislation that harms the transgender community, and from society at large which does not accept their presence. This lack of inclusion and support leads to those who identify as transgender to be dehumanized by others who do not understand what it means to be a transgender person. This dehumanization, when combined with a lack of opportunities through the legal economy, leads to higher rates of mental and physical health problems, homelessness, domestic violence, and participation in sex work—all of which leaves this population more vulnerable to experiencing violence. These risk factors are even higher for those who are from communities of color and/or strongly religious backgrounds, where few resources and support services are available to support the transgender community (Human Rights Campaign, 2018).

Transgender people also experience discrimination in making decisions that most of us take for granted on a daily basis, such as which bathroom to use in a public space. If one identifies as female, then it would seem the obvious choice would be to use the bathroom labeled for women, but this is not always an easy choice to make as others using the same restroom may get upset. In Missouri, for example, a teenager was beginning to self-identify as female and began using the women's locker room at school. This led to a school board meeting where the issue was discussed by parents and other children who felt uncomfortable with this teen's decision to use the facility for girls (Grinberg, 2015). Unfortunately, this situation is not unique. The overwhelming majority of transgender youth (84%) report they do not always feel safe at school, and over half state they can never use the bathroom they identify with at school (Human Rights Campaign, 2018). To avoid these types of situations, many restaurants and college campuses are beginning to offer unisex bathrooms, so one is not forced to choose between the male and female bathrooms and face discrimination by others who do not understand their choices (Steinmetz, 2015).

The Bathroom Bill

In 2016, North Carolina passed House Bill 2 (HB2), also known as the Bathroom Bill, which included a provision that prohibits those who identify as transgender from using the bathroom that matches their gender identity. This bill was passed after the city of Charlotte implemented a policy allowing people to use the bathroom that matched their gender identity. After the passage of the bill, the state of North Carolina faced an economic boycott; the NCAA basketball tournament championships and the NBA's All Star Game were relocated outside the state (Hersher, 2016). It was estimated that the state over twelve years would lose more than 3.76 billion dollars and nearly 3,000 jobs (Avery, 2020).

The United States Attorney General and the ACLU brought forth lawsuits claiming discrimination due to violations of Title IX and the Civil Rights Act (Hersher, 2016). This led to repeal of HB 2 and the passage of what is referred to as the compromise bill or House Bill 142 (HB 142), in 2017. This bill stated that state agencies could not change their multiple occupancy bathroom without the consent of the General Assembly and that for a period of three and a half years, no city could implement any anti-discrimination laws (Avery, 2020).

A transgender person is also likely to experience discrimination in the criminal justice system when incarcerated. Transgender inmates often face physical and sexual abuse at the hands of other inmates; 16% report experiencing physical abuse, while 15% report sexual abuse during their incarceration. Staff that work within the correctional facilities typically do not receive training on how to work with transgender inmates, which has led to lawsuits. Recently, a transgender woman in Maryland successfully sued the correctional facility where she was being held due to the emotional abuse she experienced from correctional officers who repeatedly taunted her and who placed her in solitary confinement for 66 days because they were not sure whether she should be housed with male or female inmates. The correctional officers who testified in the hearings repeatedly stated they had not been trained on how to work with transgender inmates as an explanation for their behavior and were later found by the court to be in violation of the Prison Rape Elimination Act (Mathias, 2015).

Just as class and race directly impact those who self-identify as cis-gender, these issues also directly impact transgender people. This can be seen in the highly publicized transition of Caitlynn Jenner, who gained popularity in the 1970s as an Olympic athlete and later as a reality TV star on "Keeping up with the Kardashians." After Caitlyn openly identified as transgender, she was given her own reality TV show and has been recognized in numerous venues, including receiving *Glamour* Magazine's award for Woman of the Year. Many have recognized her as a courageous woman for being so public about her personal life and have cited her experience as giving them courage in their own life journey. However, not all of the publicity has been positive; for example, some have insisted that she should not have been recognized as *Glamour*'s Woman of the Year or have made derogatory remarks about her appearance (Celona, 2015).

However, this type of positive attention is not afforded to the majority of those within the transgender community. This is particularly true for women of color and for those who do not have access to the same monetary resources as Caitlynn Jenner. The majority of transgender people who have been murdered in the United States, for example, have been women of color, and most of their stories have received very little media attention or recognition. Transgender people also experience discrimination in the workplace, which directly impacts their earning potential. For instance, 64% of transgender people make less than $25,000 a year, even though they tend to have similar education backgrounds as their cis-gender counterparts who make significantly more. If a transgender person wants to fight against discrimination experienced in the workplace, it can be incredibly difficult to do so, as employment termination due to one's gender identity is still legal in 39 states (American Psychological Association, 2015).

Summary

The definitions of sex and gender are changing. However, these changes cannot be understood without examining them within the social, political, and economic context in which they occur. There have been positive advances in recognizing that sex is more than male and female and that gender must be understood and accepted beyond what had been considered traditional male and female roles, but we still have a long way to go as a society before we see true equality for those who identify outside of these original narrow boxes. It is also important to remember that in order to examine the whole picture when discussing sex and gender, the conversation must include race and class.

Discussion Questions

1. Define and explain the differences between the terms sex, gender, and sexuality. Think back on conversations you have had with others where these terms were used. Can you think of instances where these terms were used incorrectly? Why do you think this happens?

2. How does one's race and class further complicate the barriers faced by women and those who self-identify as transgender?

3. In this chapter it was stated that Sweden provides 16 months of paid leave for those who have recently birthed or adopted a child. What do you think? Should the United States adopt a similar policy?

Key Terms

sex	lesbian
gender	pansexual
Difference of Sex Development (DSD)	bisexual
intersex	asexual
cis-gender	ace
transgender	aromantic
third gender	aro
two spirit	grey-asexual
nonbinary	greyromantic
gender queer	demisexual
agender	demiromatic
bigender	reciprosexual
gender fluid	recripromantic
sexuality	akoisexual
sexual orientation	akoiromantic
heterosexual	Family Medical Leave Act
homosexual	Families First Coronavirus Response Act
gay	*Bostock v. Clayton County, Georgia*

References

Advocates for Informed Choice. (2015). Frequently asked questions. http://aiclegal.org/who-we-are/faqs/

American Academy of Pediatrics. (2015). Explaining disorders of sex development and intersexuality. https://www.healthychildren.org/English/health-issues/conditions/genitourinary-tract/Pages/Explaining-Disorders-of-Sex-Development-Intersexuality.aspx

American Psychological Association. (2015). Lesbian, gay, bisexual and transgender persons and socioeconomic status. http://www.apa.org/pi/ses/resources/publications/factsheet-lgbt.aspx

Associated Press. (2015). Paid sick leave: Calling in sick a luxury for many low-income US workers. http://www.oregonlive.com/business/index.ssf/2015/05/paid_sick_leave_calling_in_sic.html

Avery, D. (2020). LGBTQ rights fight reignited 4 years after N.C.'s bathroom bill controversy. NBC News. https://www.nbcnews.com/feature/nbc-out/lgbtq-rights-fight-reignited-4-years-after-n-c-s-n1250390

BBC News. (2013). Germany allows "indeterminate" gender at birth. http://www.bbc.com/news/world-europe-24767225

Behrens, K.G. (2020). A principled and ethical approach to pediatric intersex surgeries. BNC Med Ethics, 21. Retrieved from https://doi.org/10.1186/s12910-020-00550-x

Bleiweis, R. (2020). Quick facts about the gender wage gap. Center for American Progress. https://www.americanprogress.org/issues/women/reports/2020/03/24/482141/quick-facts-gender-wage-gap/

Boskey, E. (2020). What does it mean to be nonbinary. Very Well Mind. https://www.verywellmind.com/what-does-it-mean-to-be-non-binary-or-have-non-binary-gender-4172702

Celona, L. (2015). Husband of 9/11 hero sends award back over Caitlyn Jenner. *New York Post.* http://nypost.com/2015/11/15/family-of-911-hero-refuses-award-over-caitlyn-jenner/

Cincinnati Children's Hospital and Medical Center. (2015). Adolescent and transition medicine. http://www.cincinnatichildrens.org/service/a/adolescent-medicine/programs/transgender/default/

Covert. B. (2020). The economy could lose a generation of working mothers. Vox news. https://www.vox.com/21536100/economy-pandemic-lose-generation-working-mothers

Diaz, J. (2022, March 28). Florida's governor signs controversial law opponents dubbed 'Don't Say Gay'. NPR. https://www.npr.org/2022/03/28/1089221657/dont-say-gay-florida-desantis

Gender Equity Center. (2013). Definition of terms. University of California Berkeley. http://geneq.berkeley.edu/lgbt_resources_definiton_of_terms#gender_queer

Ghorayshi, A. (2017). A landmark lawsuit about an intersex baby's genital surgery just settled for $440,000. Buzzfeed Science. https://www.buzzfeednews.com/article/azeenghorayshi/intersex-surgery-lawsuit-settles

GLAAD. (2015). Transgender Day of Remembrance #TDOR—November 20. http://www.glaad.org/tdor

Grinberg, E. (2015). Bathroom access for transgender teen divides Missouri town. CNN. http://www.cnn.com/2015/09/03/living/missouri-transgender-teen-feat/

Herek, G. M. (2012). Facts about homosexuality and mental health. University of California Davis. http://psc.dss.ucdavis.edu/rainbow/html/facts_mental_health.html

Hersher, R. (2016, September 19). North Carolina governor drops "bathroom bill" lawsuit against U.S. NPR. http://www.npr.org/sections/thetwo-way/2016/09/19/494573314/north-carolina-governor-drops-bathroom-bill-lawsuit-against-u-s

Hickey, P. (2013). Homosexuality: The mental illness that went away. Behaviorism and Mental Health. http://www.behaviorismandmentalhealth.com/2011/10/08/homosexuality-the-mental-illness-that-went-away/

Human Rights Campaign. (2018). Dismantling a culture of violence: Understanding anti-transgender violence and ending the crisis. https://assets2.hrc.org/files/assets/

resources/2018AntiTransViolenceReportSHORTENED.pdf?ga=2.134244599.784
086800.1608245436-1183287231.1608245436

International Spectrum. (2015). LGBT terms and definitions. https://international
spectrum.umich.edu/life/definitions

Intersex Society of North America. (2008). What is intersex? http://www.isna.org/faq/
what_is_intersex

Jones, J., & Mosher, W. D. (2013). Fathers' involvement with their children: United
States, 2006–2010. *National Health Statistics Reports*, *71*, 1–22. National Center for
Health Statistics, U.S. Centers for Disease Control and Prevention, U.S. Department of Health and Human Services. https://www.cdc.gov/nchs/data/nhsr/nhsr
071.pdf

Khaleeli, H. (2014). Hijra: India's third gender claims its place in law. *The Guardian*.
http://www.theguardian.com/society/2014/apr/16/india-third-gender-claims
-place-in-law

LGBT History Project. (2012, May 12). How male same-sex desire became 'homosexuality.' http://lgbthistoryproject.blogspot.com/2012/05/how-male-same-sex-desire
-got-its-name.html

Liptak, A. (2020). Civil rights law protects gay and transgender workers, Supreme
Court rules. *New York Times*. https://www.nytimes.com/2020/06/15/us/gay-trans
gender-workers-supreme-court.html

Lorber, J. (1994). "Night to his day": The social construction of gender. In J. Lorber
(Ed.), *Paradoxes of Gender* (pp. 13–15, 32–36). Yale University Press.

MAP. (2020). Identity document laws and policies. Movement Advancement Project.
https://www.lgbtmap.org/equality-maps/identity_document_laws

Mathias, C. (2015). Woman who spent 2 months in solitary confinement for being
transgender scores legal victory. *Huffington Post*. http://www.huffingtonpost.com/
entry/sandy-brown-transgender-inmate-legal-victory_5603160be4b0fde8b0d1
2518

Merriam-Webster. (2015). Definition of sodomy. http://www.merriam-webster.com/
dictionary/sodomy

Nobelius, A.-M. (2004). What is the difference between sex and gender? Monash University. http://www.med.monash.edu.au/gendermed/sexandgender.html

Pappas, S. (2013). The history of sex in the DSM. Live Science. http://www.livescience.
com/28380-history-of-sex-dsm.html

Parker, K. (2015). 5 facts about today's fathers. Pew Research Center. http://www.pew
research.org/fact-tank/2015/06/18/5-facts-about-todays-fathers/

Pasquier, M. (2018). Explore the spectrum: Guide to finding your ace community.
GLADD. https://www.glaad.org/amp/ace-guide-finding-your-community

Purcell, C. (2020). What do all the letters mean? Vanderbilt Faculty & Staff Health and
Wellness. https://www.vumc.org/health-wellness/news-resource-articles/lgbtqi
-what-do-all-letters-mean

Reis, E. (2007). Divergence or disorder?: The politics of naming intersex. *Perspectives in Biology and Medicine, 50*, 535–543.

Roberts, M. (2020). Making the deadliest year on record, HRC releases report on violence against transgender and gender non-conforming people. Human Rights Campaign. https://www.hrc.org/press-releases/marking-the-deadliest-year-on-record-hrc-releases-report-on-violence-against-transgender-and-gender-non-conforming-people

Scobey-Thal, J. (2014). Third gender: A short history. *Foreign Policy*. http://foreignpolicy.com/2014/06/30/third-gender-a-short-history/

Staff. (2011). Australian passports to have third gender option. *The Guardian*. http://www.theguardian.com/world/2011/sep/15/australian-passports-third-gender-option

Stanford Encyclopedia of Philosophy. (2015). Homosexuality. http://plato.stanford.edu/entries/homosexuality/

Steinmetz, K. (2015). Everything you need to know about the debate over transgender people and bathrooms. *Time*. http://time.com/3974186/transgender-bathroom-debate/#3974186/transgender-bathroom-debate/

Strangio, C., & Arkles, G. (2022). Four myths about trans athletes, debunked. American Civil Liberties Union (ACLU). https://www.aclu.org/news/lgbtq-rights/four-myths-about-trans-athletes-debunked

Sweden. (2015). Childcare, equality. https://sweden.se/quickfact/parental-leave/

U.S. Department of Labor. (n.d.). Legal highlight: The Civil Rights Act of 1964. https://www.dol.gov/agencies/oasam/civil-rights-center/statutes/civil-rights-act-of-1964

United States Department of Labor. (2015). Family and Medical Leave Act. http://www.dol.gov/whd/fmla/

Valente, J. (2014). Transgender people push for greater acceptance. *USA Today*. http://www.usatoday.com/story/news/nation/2014/11/19/transgender-day-of-remembrance-speak-out/19184225/

The White House. (2015). Your right to equal pay. https://www.whitehouse.gov/equal-pay/career

Wareham, J. (2020). Map shows where it's illegal to be gay 30 years since WHO declassified homosexuality as disease. Forbes. Retrieved from https://www.forbes.com/sites/jamiewareham/2020/05/17/map-shows-where-its-illegal-to-be-gay--30-years-since-who-declassified-homosexuality-as-disease/?sh=beab6a2578aa

Wilber, K. (2000). *Sex, ecology, spirituality: The spirit of evolution*. Shambhala.

Zevallos, Z. (2013). Rethinking gender and sexuality: Case study of the Native American "two spirit" people. Other Sociologist. http://othersociologist.com/2013/09/09/two-spirit-people/

Zevallos, Z. (2015). Sociology of gender. Other Sociologist. http://othersociologist.com/sociology-of-gender/

FOUR

Socioeconomic Status, the American Dream, and Colonialism

Learning Objectives

1. To define socioeconomic status and understand how one's social class status directly impacts one's opportunities in life.

2. Understand and critically examine how the definition of the American Dream has changed and how one's access to this dream is dependent upon socioeconomic status as well as race and gender.

3. Examine the concept of the colonial model and how this directly impacts the opportunities that are available for different populations of Americans.

Socioeconomic status (SES), also known as social class, is determined by measuring an individual's or group's education, income, and employment. One's SES directly impacts one's quality of life, including development across the lifespan as well as physical and mental health. SES also is a powerful measurement because it provides insight into inequalities regarding access to resources, while also examining how privilege, power, and control impact these opportunities (American Psychological Association, 2017).

If you ask about social classes in the United States, more than half of Americans (59%) will tell you they are in the middle class, while an additional 30% will state they are a member of the working class, with only 2% claiming membership in the upper class (Newport, 2018). Americans seem to have a general understanding of social class standing, but how is this defined and how does one's social status impact one's opportunities in life? In this chapter, we will examine how SES or social class impacts

Figure 4.1. © Adobe/Prostock-studio

one's access to resources, which in turn directly affects the opportunities one has in life. We also will examine how these resources and opportunities directly impact one's contact with the criminal justice system as well as one's experience in moving through the criminal justice system.

Social Class and the American Dream

There are a variety of ways to categorize social class in the United States. The majority of Americans tend to recognize three social classes—upper, middle, and lower. However, we will be examining social class using six different categories to help us further break down and understand how one's social class standing can directly impact one's opportunities. The *upper-upper class* is categorized as those earning hundreds of millions up to billions of dollars per year, while the lower-upper class is defined as making millions of dollars per year. The middle class is broken down into two categories, including the *upper-middle class* or those grossing $76,000 or more, and the *lower-middle class*, which is defined as those making between $46,000 and $75,000 per year. The *working class* consists of those making between $19,000 and $45,000 per year, while those grossing $9,000 to $18,000 per year are categorized as the *working poor*. The final category, the *underclass*, consists of those making less than $9,000 per year (Boundless, 2016).

In most cases, there is a direct link between the amount of money one grosses per year and one's education level. Professionals, such as lawyers, tend to have a graduate degree and fall into the upper-middle social class, while those with some college (for example service sector and clerical employees) tend to fall into the working class. However, it is important to remember that these are generalizations, as there are millions of Americans who fall into each of the six social class categories and some will always be outside of the norm (Boundless, 2016).

In the United States, social class is viewed as something that one can control and improve, if one chooses to work hard enough to achieve one's goals in life. However, people are often not able to control the circumstances around them that dictate educational and job opportunities, which are the primary means for improving one's social status. The decline in middle-class jobs that required little to no education beyond high school began prior to the Great Recession of 2008–2009, but the recession certainly helped to speed it along (Cooper, 2015). For example, during the Great Recession most of the jobs (60%) that were lost paid a middle-class wage, but were later replaced during the recovery with low-wage jobs (Pew Research Center, 2015). In 2020, Covid-19 again dramatically impacted the economy as some businesses were forced to close to stop the spread of the virus. Between February and November of 2020, for example, there was a 6% decrease in jobs in the United States (Center on Budget and Policy Priorities, 2020). However, those who were the lowest earners were hit the hardest by the economic downturn, and made up 55% of all jobs lost during this time period (Center on Budget and Policy Priorities, 2020).

Today, the *American Dream*, or the idea that if one works hard enough one can achieve success, is still alive for many (Cooper, 2015). However, how this dream is defined has changed as the number of Americans who fall into the social class category of middle class has decreased in recent years, while the number of those in the working class and working poor has increased. For example, in 1970, 62% of Americans were categorized as middle class, but in 2015 only 40% of Americans made up the middle class, with an additional 43% of Americans categorized as working class (30%) or working poor (13%) (Cooper 2015). Although the percentage of those in the middle class increased to 51% in 2016, the overall median income of those in the middle class stayed the same, while the median income decreased for lower-income workers and increased for upper-class workers (Kochhar, 2018).

In the past, central tenets of the American Dream for the middle and working classes have been home ownership, having a family, and the ability to move up economically through hard work. Although owning a home is still a part of the American Dream for many, it is often not one's top priority. For example, one survey found that only 26% of respondents selected home ownership as a priority, while 37% selected financial security and an additional 36% chose being debt-free as their priorities. Another poll found that when asking Americans to define the American Dream, 54% chose the option of stable employment, where one could pay one's bills and not take on too much debt and only 43% chose the category of increasing income, buying a home, and the ability to save money (Cooper, 2015). In 2019, 70% of Americans believed they could achieve their American Dream, but this response varied depending upon who was asked the question. For instance, 42% of women between the ages of 18 and 49 did not believe they would achieve the American Dream compared to 25% of men in the same age group; and only 39% of all adults surveyed believed the youth will have a better life than their parents (Younis, 2019).

IN FOCUS

Home Ownership, Banks, and Redlining

In the 1930s the federal agency, the Home Owner's Loan Corporation, began working with banks and local real estate agents to determine which neighborhoods were good investments and which neighborhoods should be deemed risky. The neighborhoods that were viewed as risky were literally color-coded red on the map. These maps were made for cities across the United States of 40,000 or more people, and redlined communities were primarily in urban communities with mostly Black and Latino residents. Therefore, those who applied for a mortgage or a home renovation loan on homes in redlined communities were denied, even when they had good credit (Brooks, 2020).

In 1968, the Fair Housing Act was passed, banning discrimination in buying, renting, and applying for a mortgage based on one's race, color, national origin, religion, disability, or family status, effectively ending redlining as an official practice. In 1977, this was followed by the Community Reinvestment Act, which required lenders to submit data on how many loans they deny or accept from those in low-income neighborhoods. These acts have made a positive impact, but there are still lawsuits brought forth today based on redlining practices, and there is now concern about reverse redlining, where people in previously redlined communities are being offered risky subprime loans (Brooks, 2020).

Redlining had once been viewed by the federal government as a best practice for lending. However, we now know this policy had a major impact on the wealth that Black and Latino families have been able to accumulate. In 2018, for example, a study found that Black families lost an estimated $212,000 in wealth over the last four decades because their homes were redlined (Brooks, 2020).

It is difficult to know for sure how Covid-19 will impact the definition of the American Dream, but studies conducted with young adults after the Great Recession provide some insight. Researchers found in interviews with working-class young adults (24–34 years old) that many were not focused on buying a home or a relationship with a significant other due to job insecurity. Instead, they were worried about maintaining consistent employment and not accruing too much debt as it had become increasingly difficult to obtain and keep stable employment. In another survey conducted with middle-class Americans, respondents reported they were not concerned about increasing their income and wealth, but instead were focused on holding on to what they had already accumulated (Cooper, 2015).

Wealth Inequality within the United States

When examining economic inequality most discussions focus on *income inequality*, or the variety of ways one has money coming into one's home and how these resources are distributed within a population. This conversation is important because income inequality has increased significantly over the last 30 years. This is particularly true when comparing the top earners within the United States to rest of the population. For example, the top 10% of earners in the United States make nine times more than the remaining 90% of Americans, and this becomes even more skewed when examining the top 1% of earners, who make over 39 times more than 90% of Americans. However, the discussion of *wealth inequality*, or the unequal distribution of assets within a country, is an even bigger problem within the United States (inequality.org, n.d.).

Wealth is measured by taking one's assets or what one owns (for example, house, stock, retirement, and savings) and subtracting one's liabilities or debt (for example, mortgage, credit card balance, or student loans). Wealth inequality tends to create a bigger divide within a population because wealth, once accumulated, continues to grow; for example, a house as well as retirement funds will continue to increase in value over time. Therefore, it is not surprising that the top 1% of wealthiest Americans own more than half of all stocks within the country and hold only 5% of the total debt, while 37% of Black Americans, 33% of Latino Americans, and 15% of White Americans do not have any wealth or have negative wealth because their debt is higher than their assets (inequality.org, n.d.).

Some of those at the bottom of the wealth distribution are there because they have taken on new debt, such as a mortgage for a house or student loans. Some of these folks will eventually be able to pay this debt down and increase their wealth due to their education and job prospects. However, many will not be able to dig out of their debt and will remain without any wealth because they do not have the same opportunities to earn income and accumulate wealth. This is problematic for all within a society because when you have high rates of wealth inequality there will be less economic growth within the country. For example, if a large portion of the population has more debt than assets they will not have savings or the ability to access credit to make bigger purchases, such as a home, car, or refrigerator, which directly impacts the overall economy as well as how much those at the top are able to accumulate (Ingraham, 2015).

GLOBAL SPOTLIGHT

Global Poverty

The United States is the seventh wealthiest country in the world when measuring wealth per capita or the amount of wealth each person has accumulated (Ventura, 2021). Although many Americans experience poverty, there are many more around the world that experience what is referred to as extreme poverty; for example, 10% of the world's population lives on less than $2.00 per day (Ventura, 2021). Overall, the majority of those living in poverty reside in rural areas, have little to no education, primarily work in the agriculture industry, and over half are children or under the age of 18 (Howton, 2021). Many also lack access to safely managed sanitation (4.2 billion people) and to safely managed clean water (4.2 billion people), while others have no access to basic handwashing stations (3 billion people). Unfortunately, this can have a dire impact. For example, it is estimated that 297,000 children under the age of five die each year due to diarrhea because of their inability to access basic handwashing at home (Osseiran, 2019).

In 2000, world leaders came together to attend the Millennium Summit to address global poverty. Together they created the Millennium Development Goals, with one of their goals being to decrease global poverty rates by 50% from what they were in 1990 by the year 2015. Due to this effort, global poverty had been improving. For example, in 1990, 35% of the world's population lived on less than $1.90 per day, but by 2013 this number had decreased to 10.7% (The World Bank, 2016). However, global extreme poverty is now on the rise again for the first time in 20 years due to the Covid pandemic, and it is estimated that 150 million more people will be living in poverty globally by the end of 2021 (Howton, 2021).

Wealth inequality becomes even more pronounced when one examines the issue and how it impacts those from different races, ethnicities, and genders. White Americans, for example, have significantly more wealth than both Black Americans and Latino Americans. We will use the median when examining wealth as the median is a way to examine the middle point of the data without it being affected by extreme outliers. In 2016, the median amount of accumulated wealth for all households in the United States was $81,704. However, this number is very misleading and must be broken down by race and ethnicity. In 2016, white households had an accumulated median wealth of $146,934, while Latino households had accumulated $6,591 and Black households had accumulated $3,356 in wealth (Collins et al., 2019).

The wealth gap between the races and ethnicities can be partially explained by examining homeownership data and college graduation rates. For example, the main way most Americans accumulate wealth is through home ownership. However, white Americans are much more likely to own their own home (72%) than Black Americans (44%) and Latino Americans (45%). White homeowners also are more likely to see a bigger return on their investment of home ownership than both Black homeowners and Latino homeowners. For example, white households accumulated $1.34 for every $1 a Black household accrued and $1.54 for every $1 a Latino household accrued (Collins et al., 2019). White Americans also are more likely to graduate from college with an associate, bachelors, or graduate degree (47.1% of white Americans; 30.8% of Black Americans, and 22.6% of Latino Americans) (Nichols & Schack, 2020).

Having an associate degree or higher allows one to access better paying jobs with benefits, such as health care and retirement, which directly impact earning potential and one's ability to accumulate wealth. For hundreds of years, Black and Latino families had been either legally not allowed to seek higher education or faced tremendous obstacles in doing so. Today, children of color and those living in rural areas still face barriers that make it difficult for them to do well in the job market and in higher education. For instance, children of color and children who attend rural schools are more likely to attend public schools that are underfunded in comparison to white students living in urban and suburban communities. This further disadvantages kids from underfunded school districts, as they are less likely to be prepared for the rigors of the job market and higher education (Campbell, 2019).

Women also are more likely than men to be directly impacted by the wealth gap. Although more women are working today than ever before, most of this increase has occurred in low-wage jobs, such as housecleaning or childcare. This has had a large impact on Black and Latina women, as they are more likely than white women to be working a low-wage job. Those working low-wage jobs also are less likely to receive fringe benefits, such as health insurance and retirement plans, creating an even further divide in wealth. This all comes together to create a situation where those who are paid low wages are unable to save and accumulate wealth because there is little to nothing left over once they have paid their bills (Mahathey, 2016).

Family obligations also directly impact women and add to the wealth gap between women and men. Mothers, for example, are more likely than fathers to take time off from work to care for family members, including children and extended family, and women on average take a total of 12 years off from work to care for family members. This time off leads to inconsistent income over the course of one's working life, which directly impacts one's ability to save for everyday life needs as well as retirement. Therefore, it is not surprising that women are 80 percent more likely to experience poverty than men after the age of 65 (Mahathey, 2016).

The wealth gap between women and men is likely to continue to grow as working women with children have taken the brunt of the job losses during the Covid-19 pandemic. In the past, working women tended to fair better than working men in times of economic recession because men were more likely to work in jobs that were impacted by economic downturns, such as manufacturing and construction. However-er, the pandemic has drastically changed this economic trend as service sector jobs were hit the hardest with retail stores, restaurants, government buildings, and hospi-tality businesses closed for periods of time to reduce the spread of the virus. Those hit the hardest by this massive change in the economy were women, particularly women of color, as women were 40% more likely to work in the service sector than men (20%) (Karageorge, 2020). However, the biggest reduction in working women came when the fall 2020 school year began, and nearly half of all schools started the school year with remote instruction. This change in education meant that children would be com-pleting their online schoolwork from home and forced working mothers to make difficult decisions about how to balance their work and family life. In August and September of 2020, 865,000 working women left the work force, mostly due to child-care concerns, which was four times the rate of working men (Hsu, 2020). Since the fall, schools have continued to bounce back and forth between online and face-to-face instruction, making it difficult to maintain a consistent schedule for childcare and employment.

The Colonial Model: External Colonialism

In order to fully understand why our society tends to criminalize the poor and not examine the root issues of problems within these communities we need to examine crime from a historical, political, and social perspective. One way to do this is to apply Frantz Fanon's *colonial model*, which examines the colonization of an area and the impact this experience has on the population and their identity as well as their oppor-tunities (Nicholls, 2015). We will be examining how the colonial model is implement-ed through external colonialism and how it continues through internal colonialism by examining how colonialism has impacted the Indigenous population along with Appalachia and African Americans.

The colonial model begins with the concept of *external colonialism*, where one group invades the land of another and sets up a colony in order to maintain their presence. This first portion of the model can be broken down into four phases. The first phase involves a minority population coming in to take over an already estab-lished majority population. The colonizers are typically there looking for land or oth-er resources and in the beginning appear to the native population to be friendly and there to trade goods. These trade negotiations eventually break down as it becomes clear the colonizers are there to steal resources and/or land from the native popula-tion (Staples, 1975). An example of this phase would be when Dutch colonizers came to what is now known as Manhattan Island to acquire land. When they first met with the Indigenous population they participated in amicable trading by trading tools and other items. However, negotiations soon broke down after the Dutch were unable to negotiate the sale of the land, which led to the Dutch using force to acquire the prop-erty (Piecuch, 2011).

The second phase of external colonization occurs when the colonizers begin the process of establishing the colony. In order for the colonizers to successfully establish the colony, they must break down the native customs and culture and recreate it in their own image. This happens in three steps that occur simultaneously. The first step involves *cultural imposition*, or the notion that the colonizer's culture and values are superior to those of the indigenous population. The second step is *cultural disintegration* and occurs when the native populations are no longer allowed to express their identity and culture and are punished for doing so. The third step is *cultural recreation*, where the colonizers replace the culture and values of the native population with their own (Staples, 1975). Indigenous Americans, for example, were referred to as "savages" by the colonizers, and it was believed by the colonizers the Indigenous people's culture was not as sophisticated or modern as their own. The colonizers would point to how Indigenous Americans dressed in animal furs, while the colonizers were dressed in clothes made of fabric, as one example of their superiority. Cultural disintegration and cultural recreation occurred with the Indigenous Americans when their children were taken from them and placed into boarding schools because it was believed the Indigenous Americans were unfit to raise their own children. In these boarding schools the children faced abusive punishments if they spoke their own language or participated in their own cultural traditions, while at the same time they were taught about Christianity and how to behave and dress like those of European descent (American Indian Relief Council, 2015).

The third phase of external colonization occurs when the colonizers attempt to maintain their power over the colony by creating a power structure run by the colonizers. However, if there is ever a threat to this power structure, the military and/or the police will be brought in to squash it (Staples, 1975). An example of this would be the *Wounded Knee Massacre* in 1890. The Lakota tribe had been placed on reservations by the United States government and signed away large portions of their land, including their hunting and farming lands, in exchange for food and assistance from the government. However, the crops that had been planted by the Lakota as well as the white people in the area did not produce due to drought, and everyone was living on half rations, which caused the elderly and small children to die daily of starvation. This led to the Lakota and other Indigenous tribes across the plains to participate in what they called the *Ghost Dance*. The dancers would dance in a circle for hours on end as a form of prayer and meditation, asking for help from their ancestors. After dancing for hours, sometimes they would fall over and die from exhaustion and starvation. The Ghost Dance did not harm anyone, but it scared the white people who were living in the area, and they called for help from the United States government. The United States Army was sent in and rounded up members of Chief Big Foot's band and took away their weapons. The soldiers lined up above the encampment and after a lot of tension and confusion began to shoot the Lakota below with rifles and a rapid fire Hotchkiss gun, killing over 300 people—mostly women, children, and elderly (Wishart, 2011).

The fourth phase of external colonization occurs when a hierarchy is created to keep the colonized from rising up against the colonizers. This hierarchy is created along the lines of race/ethnicity and/or social class, giving privileges and opportunities to a small group of the colonized and not to the rest. These privileges and opportunities given to the few help to create a divide within the colonized population, making it difficult for them to come together as one to fight back against their oppressors (Staples, 1975). The Pine Ridge Reservation in South Dakota is the home of the descendants of the Lakota who were the victims of the 1890 massacre at Wounded Knee. Here social class divides people, as those who want better opportunities for themselves often leave the reservation for education and employment. Indigenous Americans who live off of the reservation, for example, have poverty and education rates that are similar to other minority groups in the United States. However, the rates of poverty are significantly higher on the reservations (Friends of Pine Ridge Reservation, 2019).

Pine Ridge Reservation, for example, is the poorest county in the United States, with 97% of the population living below the federal poverty line and 90% unemployed. The reservation itself is massive, but it is difficult to bring work there because the area is isolated from the rest of the country due to the lack of roads coming in and out as well as the topography of the land. There also are few jobs on the reservation, and most employment is based around basic services that must exist, such as grocery clerk, mail carrier, police officers, teachers, etc. The isolation of the reservation also makes it difficult to travel for work, with the nearest large town (Rapid City, South Dakota) 120 miles from Pine Ridge and the nearest large city (Denver, Colorado) 350 miles away (Friends of Pine Ridge Reservation, 2019).

After the four phases of external colonization are complete, the colonized are left with a feeling of alienation. *Alienation* occurs when the colonized begin to dislike themselves and those who look like them, due to their experiences with the colonizers. This results in people attempting to distance themselves from their own cultural traditions and values and from the larger group. At this point in the colonial model, the colonized will attempt to adapt to their circumstances in one of three ways. Most will assimilate with the colonizer's culture and values, while attempting to the best of their ability to fit in with the society the colonizers have created. Some will attempt to regroup and fight the colonizers in an effort to take back their culture and identity. For example, the *American Indian Movement* or *AIM* started their own schools to educate Indigenous children about their traditional customs and beliefs. However, others will succumb to participating in criminal (for example, theft or drug sales) and/or deviant (for example, drug abuse or suicide) activity in order to cope with their environment (Staples, 1975).

Standing Rock Sioux Tribe and the Dakota Access Pipeline

Today, Native Americans are still fighting for their rights. For example, the Sioux protested the Dakota Access Pipeline, which carries crude oil 1,100 miles from the Dakotas to Illinois (Meyer, 2016). The pipeline was originally supposed to go through the primarily white city of Bismarck, North Dakota. However, the residents of Bismarck complained the pipeline could contaminate their water, so the pipeline was rerouted through the Standing Rock Sioux reservation. The Dakota Access pipeline was approved by the Army Corp of Engineers, but the Sioux were not contacted about the project until the end of the planning process, which violates their right to be consulted. Since 1992, the federal government has agreed to consult native tribes when planning construction projects on their land in order to understand the impact of the project on sacred sites. The Sioux filed a complaint against the Army Corp of Engineers in federal court to stop the pipeline, where they argued the pipeline would cross the Missouri River, creating a significant risk of contamination for their only source of drinking water. The pipeline also crossed sacred burial grounds, and part of the complaint requested that construction be halted immediately to avoid destruction of these sacred sites. The Sioux, along with members from over 200 additional tribes, peacefully protested the Army Corp of Engineers decision and were subjected to police dressed in riot gear, tear gas, and police dogs that bit several protestors, including a child. After months of protesting at the site of the proposed pipeline on the reservation, the Army Corp of Engineers agreed to temporarily halt the construction in order to review the project and to consult the Sioux regarding sacred sites as well as possible water contamination (Meyer, 2016). In January 2017, President Trump signed an executive order to speed up the construction of the pipeline and the approval of the Army Corps of Engineers permits. Then in June of 2017, after the oil had already begun to flow through the pipeline, a federal judge ruled the permits were pushed through too quickly and did not fully consider the environmental impact on the tribe (Barajas, 2017). However, subsequent court rulings decided the pipeline could continue to flow with oil as the case worked its way through the courts and the Army Corps of Engineers completed its environmental impact study (Boland, 2021).

The traditional colonial model has been applied to those situations where one population invades the land of another, where the invader is often white and the invaded are minorities. However, the model also can be applied to other situations and has been expanded over the years. African Americans, for example, were not colonized in the same way as Indigenous Americans. However, the colonial model also applies to this group because the Black community is often viewed as an "underdeveloped colony whose economics and politics are controlled by leaders of the racially dominant group" (Staples, 1975, p. 14). One's race in this situation then determines how one is treated within the society and has a direct impact on how one views oneself as well as the opportunities one has available to improve one's situation (Staples, 1975). The colonial model also can be applied to the Appalachian region within the United States. In this instance, those who came into the region looking for resources were white, and the majority of those living within the region also were white. However, those living within the region were colonized by the landowners who lived outside of the region. In order to understand how the Appalachian region was colonized, we will examine Central Appalachia, focusing on West Virginia.

The first phase of external colonialism occurs when those from outside the region come into the region looking for resources. In West Virginia, they came looking for coal just after the Civil War ended. The colonizers came into the region and purchased from farmers the mineral rights underneath their farms for very little money. Farmers were willing to sell their mineral rights to these outsiders because they needed the money and were unaware of the true value of what they had. Eventually the owners of the mineral rights would send coal operators onto the farmer's land to dig for the coal, which destroyed the farms that sat on the surface. The landowners went to court in an attempt to stop this, but the courts found in favor of the mineral rights owners. This led to people being displaced from their land, which also was their wealth, and forced most of them into the mines for work. Some of the descendants of those who once owned these farms still mine on what was once their families' property today (Guilford, 2017).

The second phase of external colonialism consists of building the colonial society through cultural imposition, disintegration, and recreation, with all three parts happening simultaneously. Cultural imposition occurred as those from outside the region used slurs such as "hillbilly" to enforce that their culture was superior to those who lived in the Appalachia region. In the media, for instance, those in the region were often referred to as peculiar, violent, or lazy to defend the inhumane way those who lived in the region were treated by the coal industry. Cultural disintegration and recreation occurred through the company towns where the miners lived. The company owned everything that existed within the town, such as the houses the miners lived in, the schools their children attended, the doctors they saw when they were sick, and the company store where they shopped for everything from clothing to food. The miners also were paid in *scrip*, which is money from the coal company that can only be spent in the coal town. In other words, it was fake money that was only accepted within the town where you lived and nowhere else. The prices of items in the company store also were incredibly high, so the company stores provided miners with credit and their paycheck would go directly back to the company store to pay off their debt. Scrip made it impossible for people to save money or accumulate any type of wealth and had a long-term impact on the region, as scrip was used as payment by coal operators until 1967, when it was outlawed by Congress. Those who mined were never able to save enough to pass on any wealth to their children, leaving an entire region impoverished for generations (Guilford, 2017).

The third phase of external colonialism occurs when the colonizers govern the native population through those who have been appointed by the colonizers, where their main role is to report back anything that suggests there could be a rebellion. If there is concern of an uprising, the colonizers will use the power of the military and/or police to squash it. In the early 1900s in West Virginia, for example, coal miners attempted to unionize themselves in the southern part of the state. The miners wanted to unionize to address the horrible safety conditions they worked in, low pay, and constant debt to the company store. However, every time they attempted to organize private police detectives were brought in to infiltrate and stop the miners from unionizing. The private police detectives violently harassed miners who were believed to be organizing along with their families, for example, by throwing miners and their families out of their company-owned homes. By 1920, the miners had decided they had had enough and began organizing to form a union in Mingo County. The coal companies again sent in private police detectives to remove the miners and their families from company-owned housing. However, this time, on May 19, 1920, the private police detectives were met at the train station by the mayor of Matewan, the Sheriff Sid Hatfield, and those the pair had gathered. A gun fight ensued between the two parties, and in the end the *Matewan Massacre* left seven private police detectives along with the mayor and two miners dead. Later on August 1, 1921, Sheriff Sid Hatfield was assassinated by private police detectives on the steps of the McDowell County Courthouse by private police detectives in broad daylight (Andrews, 2018).

Sheriff Sid Hatfield had been viewed as a hero among the miners for confronting the coal company's private police detectives in the Matewan Massacre. After Hatfield's death, hundreds of coal miners gathered outside of Charleston with the goal of heading to Mingo County to free the miners there who had been arrested and jailed under martial law for attempting to unionize. However to get to Mingo County, the miners had to first cross through Logan County, where the union had not been able to infiltrate due to their pro-coal company sheriff, Don Chafin. In preparation of the miners' arrival in Logan County, the sheriff had gathered 3,000 men and placed machine guns around Blair Mountain as well as up and down the path to Logan to prevent the miners from getting to Mingo County (MacLowry, 2016).

Eventually 8,000 armed miners, identifying themselves by the red bandanas tied around their necks, gathered at the border of Logan County. On August 31, 1921, the miners entered the town of Logan, setting off the *Battle of Blair Mountain*. However, even though the armed miners significantly outnumbered the Logan County Sheriff's men, the miners were unable to make it past the machine guns, leaving them entrenched in the hills. The Logan County Sheriff also brought in biplanes and dropped pipe bombs filled with shrapnel on the miners. On September 1, the federal government eventually sent Army aircraft and 2,100 soldiers to stop the Battle of Blair Mountain, which had become the largest armed insurrection in the United States since the Civil War. The miners surrendered their weapons to the federal troops, ending the battle on September 2, 1921. The miners had hoped the federal government would intervene on their behalf, since the state police and state government in West Virginia were controlled by the coal companies. However, after the miners had been disarmed, the federal government turned the situation back over to the state and walked away (MacLowry, 2016).

In phase four of external colonialism, the colonizers use a caste system to create a hierarchy based off of race, ethnicity, and/or social class to keep the colonized fighting amongst themselves and not coming together to revolt against the colonizers. The miners in Appalachia were natives of the region itself, but many also were recent immigrants to the United States. There also were many Black families who were coming north looking for work. The coal company towns attempted to exploit the multi-racial and ethnic identities of the miners to divide and conquer the population to keep them from coming together to fight back. Coal company housing was segregated by race and ethnicity, so that there were Black, Italian, Irish, and English sections that were segregated from one another (Boissoneault, 2017).

The Colonial Model: Internal Colonialism

At this point in the colonial model, the colony is well established, and those who have been colonized are kept in their place through the process of internal colonialism. *Internal colonialism* ensues when the colonized are subjected to a subordinate position within the larger community and occurs through political, economic, and social subordination. *Political subordination* occurs when one is kept from being able to participate in the political process. This is incredibly detrimental because if someone wants to make change within their community, the way to do this is through the political system (Staples, 1975). However, the colonized are not allowed to participate in the political process. One example of this would be disenfranchisement, which occurs when people are kept from participating in the election process by law or intimidation. The War on Drugs, for instance, had the biggest impact on poorer, primarily African American communities. One way to change this impact would be to vote for politicians who do not support the draconian laws that were put in place during this time period. However, the largest group directly impacted by disenfranchisement is African American men, many of whom are not allowed to vote because of either their current or past involvement with the criminal justice system.

There are 6.1 million Americans who have been disenfranchised or are unable to vote due to a felony conviction (Chung, 2019). These laws have had the most impact

Figure 4.2. March on Washington for Voting Rights © Creative Commons / Elvert Barnes

on African American communities, where 1 in 13 Black Americans are disenfranchised. Disenfranchisement laws vary from one state to the next, with 18 states not allowing those in prison to vote and 3 states denying those in prison or on parole the right to vote. There also are 17 states that do not allow those in prison or under probation or parole supervision to vote, while an additional 11 states have restrictions in place that keep those who have served their sentence from voting. However, when surveyed, 80% of Americans stated they believed those who have completed their sentence should have their voting rights restored and nearly 66% supported restoring the right to vote for those who are under parole or probation supervision (Chung, 2019). This in turn makes it difficult for the community to come together and create change through the political system.

IN FOCUS

Voter Suppression

Voter suppression occurs when strategies are implemented that reduce voting and/or voter registration, while targeting a specific community. Voter suppression in the United States has primarily impacted the Black community (Duignan, n.d.). However, voter suppression also is a major problem in states with higher Indigenous populations, such as South Dakota and North Dakota. In 2017, a study conducted in

South Dakota found that 32% of the Indigenous population reported the distance needed to travel from their homes to the polls was too far, with some reporting traveling more than 150 miles one way (DeRienzo, 2020). In North Dakota, a law was passed shortly before the 2018 mid-term election that stated one needed to present an ID at the polls when voting that showed a residential street address. The law was challenged by Native American voters in North Dakota who were concerned that those who lived in rural areas and on the reservation would not be able to obtain an ID with a street address due to the use of post office boxes. However, the Supreme Court of the United States refused to intervene as the majority of the court felt reversing the law would cause further confusion (Howe, 2018).

Economic subordination occurs when the colonized are not provided the same opportunities to improve their economic conditions, such as through lack of employment within one's community or failing schools (Staples, 1975). This can be seen in the city of Cincinnati, where 40% of the children residing in the city live below the poverty line (May, 2019). This is the fifth highest rate of childhood poverty in the United States for cities with 250,000 people. This high rate of poverty is primarily due to the lack of jobs that pay a living wage, where someone can support themselves and their family, as well as the high unemployment rates, particularly for African American families. In Cincinnati in 2017, for example, 4.5% of the white population was unemployed in comparison to 11.7% of the Black population, while white families ($62,217) made slightly more than twice as much money as Black families ($29,989) living in the city. This placed Cincinnati, when compared to similarly sized cities, 54th out of 71 for unemployment equality and 60th out of 71 for income equality between Black and white people (Curnutte, 2017).

Social subordination occurs when people are segregated from the larger society (Staples, 1975). This can be seen when people within the urban core are segregated from wealthier populations. It is difficult to separate race and poverty when discussing social subordination, as both of these factors lead to higher rates of segregation within a city. Unfortunately, much of the racial segregation that occurred across the United States was intentional and due to federal housing programs put in place nearly 60 years ago. During the migration to the suburbs, for instance, Black families were intentionally left out of the opportunity to purchase a home, due to their race (Kent & Frolich, 2015). In 1938, for example, the Federal Housing Authority (FHA) made home ownership possible for many, but favored loans to those who lived on the outskirts of the city and not those within the urban core, causing the middle class to move from the inner city. The FHA also redlined communities based on race and did not approve home loans for those in predominately minority communities (The Fair Housing Center of Greater Boston, n.d.). This had a huge impact on the Black population within cities, as home ownership is the primary way many families are able to accumulate wealth. Those who were unable to purchase their own home remained in the center of the city, creating a segregated society based on race and economics. In Cincinnati, for example, the majority of those who live in the city center are African American, resulting in Cincinnati being the fifth most segregated city within the United States (Kent & Frolich, 2015).

If we use the colonial model to examine the impact colonization has had on the colonized population, we can begin to understand why certain communities are thriving and others are not. However, the application of the colonial model requires us to examine the root causes of behavior within a community and specifically how some of us have access to the political and economic system that others simply do not. For instance, it is easy to look at an inner-city neighborhood and say people are poor because they do not work hard enough. But if one were to look closer, they would see those living within these communities do not have access to the same resources to succeed. Public schools, for example, are funded by property taxes, so if people within your neighborhood own their own home and are paying property taxes more money will be funneled into your school system in comparison to a community with lower property values and/or a high percentage of people renting. Money isn't everything in public education, but it certainly can dictate opportunities, such as how many kids are in a class per teacher and whether you can afford to teach foreign languages, art, and music as well as advanced placement classes. All of these "extras" create opportunities that later impact a student after high school and one's ability to gain entrance to college or obtain a job. We also tend to overlook how segregated we are as a society until we take the time to look around our schools and neighborhoods and notice the majority of the faces we see resemble our own. All of these factors when taken together directly impact our opportunities in life and our ability to support ourselves.

The impact of internal colonization also can be felt within the criminal justice system, where there is a two-tiered system based upon class. The resources someone has access to can impact them in a variety of ways as they move through the criminal justice system. For those who have the money to hire a private attorney to represent them in court, the attorney will have more time and financial resources available to them to fight for their release or a lesser sentence. However, someone who is reliant on the public defender system will not necessarily be given the same opportunities because the public defender is provided with a limited amount of money from the state to fight the case and is often overburdened with more clients than they can handle effectively. Another example of class directly impacting individuals in the criminal justice system is the issue of bail. Bail is the amount of money one pays to be released from jail while one waits for the court process to take place. Bail is set by a judge to ensure that someone will later show up for their court hearings, with the idea being that the suspected offender will lose a significant sum of money if they were to skip the hearing. If someone is unable to afford the bail amount, then they will wait in jail until the sentence is decided by the court. This directly impacts the suspected offenders, who will lose their job and become disconnected from their family and friends due to the time spent in jail waiting for the court process to take place (Tafoya, 2013).

People of color are more likely to be affected by these disadvantages than white people because they are more likely to experience living in poverty. For instance, in the United States, Black families earn only 60% of what white families earn, making it more difficult to have the resources to pay for a private attorney or to post bail (Urban League, 2015). These class disparities play a large role in the overrepresentation of minorities within the correctional system, where African Americans are significantly overrepresented in comparison to white people even though white people are two times more likely to be arrested and charged for most crimes than Black people (Sentencing Project, 2018).

Summary

In the United States, wealth inequality continues to increase as the middle class continues to decrease. These changes in the economy have directly impacted the opportunities available to the majority of Americans and have redefined the American Dream for many. The colonial model is one way to examine how one's access to opportunities varies by race, ethnicity, and class as well as a framework to better understand the historical nature of how and why we interact with one another the way that we do.

Discussion Questions

1. How does one's SES or social class status impact the opportunities one has in life?

2. Should we attempt to eliminate wealth inequality in the United States? If no, why not? If yes, how could this be addressed?

3. How does internal colonialism impact suspected offenders as they move through the criminal justice system? What could be done to help alleviate these problems?

Key Terms

socioeconomic status (SES)
upper-upper class
upper-middle class
lower-middle class
working class

working poor
underclass
American Dream
income inequality
wealth inequality

wealth

colonial model

external colonialism

cultural imposition

cultural disintegration

cultural recreation

Wounded Knee Massacre

Ghost Dance

alienation

American Indian Movement (AIM)

scrip

Matewan Massacre

Battle of Blair Mountain

internal colonialism

political subordination

economic subordination

social subordination

References

American Indian Relief Council. (2015). History and culture: Boarding schools. http://www.nrcprograms.org/site/PageServer?pagename=airc_hist_boarding schools

American Psychological Association. (2017). Socioeconomic status. http://www.apa.org/topics/socioeconomic-status/

Andrews, E. (2018, September 1). The battle of Blair Mountain. History Channel. https://www.history.com/news/americas-largest-labor-uprising-the-battle-of-blair-mountain

Barajas, J. (2017). Judge questions Dakota Access Pipeline permits, prompting review. PBS Newshour. http://www.pbs.org/newshour/rundown/judge-questions-dakota-access-pipeline-permits-prompting-review/

Boissoneault, L. (2017). The coal mining massacre America forgot. *Smithsonian Magazine.* https://www.smithsonianmag.com/history/forgotten-matewan-massacre-was-epicenter-20th-century-mine-wars-180963026/

Boland, H. (2021). Dakota Access Pipeline Lawsuit dismissed, tribal and oil industry leaders react. Dakota West NBC. https://www.kfyrtv.com/2021/06/23/dakota-access-pipeline-lawsuit-dismissed-tribal-oil-industry-leaders-react/

Boundless. (2016). Class structure in the U.S. https://www.boundless.com/sociology/textbooks/boundless-sociology-textbook/stratification-inequality-and-social-class-in-the-u-s-9/the-class-structure-in-the-u-s-75/class-structure-in-the-u-s-442-10206/

Brooks, K. J. (2020). Redlining's legacy: Maps are gone but the problem hasn't disappeared. CBS News. https://www.cbsnews.com/news/redlining-what-is-history-mike-bloomberg-comments/

Campbell, N. (2019). A quality education for every child. The Center for American progress. Retrieved from https://www.americanprogress.org/article/quality-education-every-child/

Center on Budget and Policy Priorities. (2020). Tracking the Covid-19 Recession's effect on food housing and employment hardships. https://www.cbpp.org/research/poverty-and-inequality/tracking-the-covid-19-recessions-effects-on-food-housing-and

Chung, J. (2019). Felony disenfranchisement: A primer. The Sentencing Project. https://www.sentencingproject.org/publications/felony-disenfranchisement-a-primer/

Collins, C, Asante-Muhammed, D., Hoxie, J., & Terry, S. (2019). Dreams deferred: How enriching the 1% widens the racial wealth gap. Institute for Policy Studies. https://inequality.org/wp-content/uploads/2019/01/IPS_RWD-Report_FINAL-1.15.19.pdf

Cooper, M. (2015). The downsizing of the American Dream. *The Atlantic*. http://www.theatlantic.com/business/archive/2015/10/american-dreams/408535/

Curnutte, M. (2017). Cincinnati region ranks low in racial equality: Report. The Enquirer. https://www.cincinnati.com/story/news/2017/05/02/greater-cincinnati-low-racial-equality-rankings-report/101198310/

DeRienzo, M. (2020). In South Dakota, Native Americans face numerous obstacles to voting. The Center for Public Integrity. https://publicintegrity.org/politics/elections/us-polling-places/in-south-dakota-native-americans-face-numerous-obstacles-to-voting/

Duignan, B. (n.d.). Voter suppression. Encyclopaedia Britannica. https://www.britannica.com/topic/voter-suppression

The Fair Housing Center of Greater Boston. (n.d.). The historical shift from explicit to implicit policies affecting housing segregation in Eastern Massachusetts. http://www.bostonfairhousing.org/timeline/1934-1968-FHA-Redlining.html

Friends of Pine Ridge Reservation. (2019). Statistics about Pine Ridge Reservation. https://friendsofpineridgereservation.org/about-pine-ridge-reservation-and-foprr/statistics-about-pine-ridge-reservation/

Guilford, G. (2017). The 100-year capitalist experiment that keeps Appalachia poor, sick, and stuck on coal. Quartz. https://qz.com/1167671/the-100-year-capitalist-experiment-that-keeps-appalachia-poor-sick-and-stuck-on-coal/

History Channel. (2015). Wounded Knee. http://www.history.com/topics/native-american-history/wounded-knee

Howe, A. (2018). Court stays out of North Dakota voting dispute. SCOTUS Blog. https://www.scotusblog.com/2018/10/court-stays-out-of-north-dakota-voting-dispute/

Howton, E. (2021). Poverty. The World Bank. https://www.worldbank.org/en/topic/poverty/overview#1

Hsu, A. (2020). "This is too much": Working moms are reaching a breaking point during the pandemic. NPR. https://www.npr.org/2020/09/29/918127776/this-is-too-much-working-moms-are-reaching-the-breaking-point-during-the-pandemi

Inequality.org. (n.d.). Wealth inequality. http://inequality.org/wealthinequality/

Ingraham, C. (2015). If you thought income inequality was bad, get a load of wealth inequality. *The Washington Post*. https://www.washingtonpost.com/news/wonk/wp/2015/05/21/the-top-10-of-americans-own-76-of-the-stuff-and-its-dragging-our-economy-down/

Kane, L. (2015). The wealth gap between black, white and Latino families in the US is astounding. *Business Insider*. http://www.businessinsider.com/racial-wealth-gap-in -the-us-is-astounding-2015-3

Karageorge, E. I. (2020). Covid-19 Recession is harder on women. U.S. Bureau of Labor Statistics. https://www.bls.gov/opub/mlr/2020/beyond-bls/pdf/covid-19-re cession-is-tougher-on-women.pdf

Kent, A., & Frolich, T. C. (2015). The nine most segregated cities. *Huffpost Business*. http://www.huffingtonpost.com/entry/the-9-most-segregated-cities-in-america _55df53e9e4b0e7117ba92d7f

Kochhar, R. (2018, September 6). The American middle class is stable in size, but is losing ground financially compared to upper-income families. Pew Research Center. https://www.pewresearch.org/fact-tank/2018/09/06/the-american-middle-class-is -stable-in-size-but-losing-ground-financially-to-upper-income-families/

MacLowry, R. (2016). *The Mine Wars*. [film] American Experience.

Mahathey, A. (2016). We need to talk about the gender wealth gap. *The Huffington Post*. http://www.huffingtonpost.com/entry/closing-the-gender-wage-gap-isnt -enough_us_57eacf4fe4b07f20daa0fcf7

May, L. (2019). Child poverty rates in Cincinnati, Hamilton County still higher than U.S.as whole. Channel 9 WCPO. https://www.wcpo.com/news/our-community/ child-poverty-rates-in-cincinnati-hamilton-county-still-higher-than-the-u-s-as-a -whole

Meyer, R. (2016). The legal case for blocking the Dakota Access Pipeline. *The Atlantic*. http://www.theatlantic.com/technology/archive/2016/09/dapl-dakota-sitting-rock -sioux/499178/

Newport, F. (2018). Looking into what Americans mean by "working class." Pew Research Center. https://news.gallup.com/opinion/polling-matters/239195/looking -americans-mean-working-class.aspx

Nicholls, T. (2015). Frantz Fanon. Internet Encyclopedia of Philosophy. http://www. iep.utm.edu/fanon/

Nichols, A. H., & Schak, J. O. (2020). Degree attainment for Black and Latino adults. The Education Trust. https://edtrust.org/wp-content/uploads/2014/09/Black-De gree-Attainment_FINAL.pdf

Osseiran, N. (2019). 1 in 3 people globally do not have access to safe drinking water, UNICEF/WHO. World Health Organization. https://www.who.int/news/item/18 -06-2019-1-in-3-people-globally-do-not-have-access-to-safe-drinking-water -unicef-who

Pew Research Center. (2015). The American middle class is losing ground: No longer the majority and falling behind financially. Social and Demographic Trends. http:// www.pewsocialtrends.org/2015/12/09/the-american-middle-class-is-losing-ground/

Piecuch, J. (2011). Dutch-Indian Wars. In S. Tucker, J. R. Arnold, & R. Weiner (Eds.), *The Encyclopedia of American Indian Wars, 1607–1890: A Political, Social and Military History*. ABC-CLIO.

Sentencing Project. (2018). Report to the United Nations on racial disparities in the U.S. criminal justice system. Retrieved from https://www.sentencingproject.org/publications/un-report-on-racial-disparities/

Staples, R. (1975). White racism, Black crime, and American justice: An application of the colonial model to explain crime and race. *Phylon*, *36*, 14–22.

Tafoya, S. M. (2013). Assessing the impact of bail on California's jail population. Public Policy Institute of California. http://www.ppic.org/content/pubs/report/R_613 STR.pdf

Urban League. (2015). The state of Black Cincinnati 2015—Two cities. http://www.cincyfairhousing.com/wp-content/uploads/2015/09/The-State-of-Black-Cincinnati-2015_Two-Cities.pdf

Ventura, L. (2021). Richest countries in the world 2021. *Global Finance*. https://www.gfmag.com/global-data/economic-data/richest-countries-in-the-world

Wishart, D. J. (2011). Wounded Knee Massacre. The Great Plains Encyclopedia. http://plainshumanities.unl.edu/encyclopedia/doc/egp.war.056

The World Bank. (2016). Poverty overview. http://www.worldbank.org/en/topic/poverty/overview

Younis, M. (2019). Most Americans see American Dream as achievable. Gallup. https://news.gallup.com/poll/260741/americans-american-dream-achievable.aspx

FIVE

The Ever-Evolving Definition
of Crime

Learning Objectives

1. The differences between street crimes and corporate crimes.
2. The impact of the media and lawmakers on our understanding of crime.

A *crime* is a behavior that is deemed to be illegal or against the law by the majority of the population. In order for a behavior to be legally considered a crime, there must be an act that causes harm, also known as the ***actus reus***, as well as the intent to commit a crime, or the ***mens rea***. However, the *actus reus* and the *mens rea* must occur together, which is referred to as ***concurrence*** (Legal Information Institute, 2015). Upon first glance, this definition appears to be very clear-cut and straightforward. However, it is anything but simple.

The definition of what a crime is changes from one place to the next as well as from one time period to another. The legal definition of what constitutes an illegal drug, for example, is constantly changing. In the United States, many states have adopted laws declaring that patients with medical ailments can legally possess and use marijuana, while other states have taken the next step and legalized the use of recreational marijuana, while regulating it in a similar manner to alcohol. Over ten years ago, it was unthinkable that states would be willing to legalize recreational marijuana. However, changes in the economy spurred the movement, as states needed to devise a way to bring in more tax revenue to fund state programs, such as roads and schools (Wight & Runyon, 2016). It is important to note that marijuana can be legal for recreational use in one state and still illegal in the neighboring state, while federal laws continue to criminalize marijuana for recreational use (White House, 2015). Therefore, the laws regarding recreational marijuana vary from place to place even within one country.

IN FOCUS

Marijuana Laws

Although marijuana is still illegal at the federal level, states began to legalize recreational marijuana usage after the Great Recession as a way to recover economically.

By the end of 2020, there were 15 states that had enacted or passed laws making it legal to use marijuana for medicinal and recreational purposes with an additional 21 states that allow the purchase of marijuana for medicinal purposes (Gomez, 2020). What are the laws regarding marijuana in your state?

The definition of illegal drugs also changes from one country to the next. Portugal, for example, has decriminalized what were once considered to be illegal drugs in their country, including everything from marijuana to cocaine. This means if one is found to be in possession of drugs they will receive a fine and possibly be referred to a drug treatment facility, rather than face punishment through the criminal justice system. Portugal made this change, in 2001, to reduce the use and cost of the criminal justice system for those who possessed illegal drugs. This change in drug laws freed up money to fund their treatment programs for those who were deemed to be drug addicted (Ingraham, 2015).

As can be seen in the examples above, what is a crime often changes over time and depends on the place where the act occurred and/or who is making the laws as well as their agenda. Therefore, in order to truly understand the definition of crime, we will be examining it from a social construction framework. This framework will allow us to delve into what is occurring within a society politically, socially, and economically that directly impacts what is or is not considered to be criminal behavior.

Defining Street Crime and Corporate Crime

For the purpose of this chapter, we will be separating criminal behavior into two broad categories—street crime and corporate crime. *Street crime* is what we typically think of when the term "crime" is used; for example, assault (physically harming another), robbery (taking property by force or the threat of force), murder (taking the life of another with the intent to cause harm), drug sales (selling illegal drugs), and theft (taking the property of another) would all be categorized as street crimes. The definition of corporate crime, however, is less well known and will require some explanation.

Figure 5.1. An Occupy Austin demonstrator holds a sign calling for the reinstatement of the Glass-Steagall Act. The act restricted affiliations between banks and securities firms. © iStockphoto.com/vichinterlang.

Corporate crime is defined as crime committed by a corporation or their executives in an attempt to meet the goals of the corporation. However, their actions often do not benefit the public, consumers, and/or other employees. These crimes also can be harmful to the public financially and/or physically (Kramer, 2013). There are a wide variety of crimes that can fall into the category of corporate crime, so in order to better understand this term we will examine some examples.

Corporate crimes can include environmental crimes, such as dumping chemicals into a river due to the cost or difficulties of storage. For instance, the Dupont Plant in Parkersburg, West Virginia, manufactures a chemical known as C8 that is used in Teflon to make nonstick cookware. Since 1961, Dupont has been discharging water from their manufacturing plant back into the Ohio River that contained the C8 chemical—even though they were aware the chemical was toxic and being dumped in the river at toxic levels, since 1984. This impacted all who lived within the Mid-Ohio River Valley, as their drinking water came directly from the Ohio River and contained the C8 chemical. In 2005, Dupont paid a $16.5-million-dollar settlement to the federal government for hiding the health information from the public and was ordered to conduct a health study, which found there was a connection between C8 contamination and a variety of illnesses. Due to Dupont's actions, many in the area have been diagnosed with or died from cancer and some are now successfully suing the company for wrongful death and personal injury (Rinehart, 2015).

Securities fraud or manipulating the stock market also can fall under the category of corporate crime. An example of this would be the corporation Enron, where several executives worked together to inflate the price of their stock by hiding their debt in other companies the corporation created. The executives were well aware their stock was not worth what they were telling the public. However, the more people bought the stock at the inflated price, the more money the company as well as the individuals involved were able to make. Eventually, the public became aware of the debt and the inflated stock, but not until after the executives had sold their shares and made millions of dollars. These criminal actions cost the remaining stockholders millions, leaving them with stock that was now only worth pennies, but had once been valued at $90 a share (NPR, 2015a).

Another example of corporate crime is mortgage fraud, or offering corrupt loans that encourage the public to borrow money they cannot afford to pay back. For instance, Bank of America and its subsidiary companies, Countrywide and Merrill Lynch, issued bank loans to people to buy homes who were not likely to be able to pay the loans back based on their credit scores and current income. These loans also often included variable interest rates, which raised the monthly mortgage bill for the customer. The companies then packaged these high-risk loans that people were likely to default on and sold them off to other companies without letting them know the history of the loans. As people began to default on their mortgages and were evicted from their homes, the companies who had bought the bundled loans and their shareholders were left with a huge loss. However, the companies who made the original loans grossed millions of dollars in lending fees and through the sale of the bad loans to other companies. Bank of America was later sued by the U.S. Department of Justice for fraudulent behavior because they did not provide investors with key information regarding their investments and recklessly provided loans to those who could not afford them. Bank of America eventually settled with the Department of Justice for $16.65 billion (Doyle-McClatchy, 2014).

Corporate crime also can be violent, and people can lose their lives. A corporation may continue selling faulty products when it is known that there is a possible danger to the public, but the corporation decides through a cost-benefit analysis that it is in the company's best interest to not address the possible danger and to sell the products anyway. General Motors (GM), for example, knew that many of its cars had a faulty ignition switch that could cause the air bags, steering wheel, and brakes to stop working as the car was in motion. However, GM made the decision to keep the automobiles on the road due to the cost of recalling them. GM was aware of the faulty ignition switches for over a decade, but it wasn't until they were faced with lawsuits that they

Figure 5.2. © Kovalenko I/Fotolia.

began to recall the cars and take responsibility for their actions. Due to accidents that occurred because of the faulty ignition switches, there have been 125 families who sought compensation for the deaths of their loved ones and an additional 62 complainants who were seeking financial damages due to injuries (NBC News, 2014).

Loss of life caused by corporate crime also can occur through unsafe working conditions. An example of this would be the Massey Energy disaster in West Virginia, in 2010. Mine inspectors cited the mine for numerous safety violations over the years, but they were unaware of some of the most detrimental violations. This is because when the inspector arrived at the mine, a call would be made to the supervisors underground to put up roof supports, enact ventilation systems, and remove excess coal dust before the inspector was able to get into the mine. These safety measures were then removed after the inspector left. This illegal behavior occurred because the mine was more efficient and made more money when these safety regulations were not in place. However, the lack of these basic safety regulations also led to an explosion within the mine that took the lives of 29 miners, causing the worst mine disaster in the United States in 40 years (Sullivan, 2014).

The Cost of Street Crime and Corporate Crime

Another difference between street crime and corporate crime is the cost associated with each type of crime. In the United States, street crime costs approximately $2.6 trillion each year, with 85% of this cost associated with violent crimes (Miller et al., 2021). Although federal, state, and local governments do a decent job of tracking street crime, it is difficult to get an accurate cost for corporate crime. This is because the government does not measure the cost of corporate crime as efficiently and effectively as street crime. However, based on research that has been conducted we have a better understanding of the total cost of some corporate crimes. For instance, occupational theft and employee fraud costs the United States approximately $800 billion dollars annually, while computer security and viruses cost approximately $53 billion a year. However, we do not have any cost estimates for other types of corporate crimes such as financial, securities, and mortgage fraud (Cohen, 2016).

Even though it is difficult to get an accurate estimate of costs for corporate crime, we can examine specific cases to gain a better understanding. For instance, in 2008, Fannie Mae and Freddie Mac cost United States taxpayers $200 billion after they had to be bailed out by the federal government, due to their involvement in mortgage fraud (Denning, 2011). Both of these companies are still under the control and oversight of the federal government as they attempt to pay back their loss. This means the total cost to United States taxpayers for the companies' corporate crimes continues to increase (NPR, 2015b).

Understanding the Differences between Criminal and Civil Punishments for Crime

There are differences between who and what can be punished in a criminal versus a civil court. These differences also directly impact where street criminals and corporate criminals are processed and punished as well. We will start by defining and examining the basic differences between criminal and civil cases.

In a *criminal case*, the prosecutor must demonstrate that a person committed a crime *beyond a reasonable doubt*. This is because one is facing the potential of imprisonment and the loss of their freedom. Therefore, the government wants to make sure the person who is being accused of the crime did in fact commit the crime. The jury and/or the judge are then asked to determine if they believe, beyond a reasonable doubt, that this person committed the crime before finding them guilty. If the judge or jury does not have a reasonable doubt, they are supposed to convict the offender, due to the seriousness of the punishment (The Mississippi Bar, 2015).

In *civil cases*, the plaintiff is a person who brings a complaint against another person or organization because they believe the person or organization wronged them. The punishment in a civil case is a fine, where if the person is believed to have committed the act they are required to pay the complainant an amount of money decided by the court to compensate them for the wrong. In a civil case, the burden of proof is lower than in a criminal case, and the court only has to determine the person or organization more likely than not committed the act against the complainant, or by what is referred to as the *preponderance of the evidence*. The burden of proof is not as high in a civil case because the punishment is not as serious as in a criminal case (The Mississippi Bar, 2015).

GLOBAL SPOTLIGHT

Chinese Executions

In China, one can be executed for committing corporate crimes, such as fraud or corruption. Luo Laping, for example, was executed in 2013 after being convicted of corruption after she embezzled $5.14 million from public funds during her career as an urban planner and land developer. However, whether one receives the death penalty is heavily dependent upon one's position within society and political connections. Therefore, not everyone found guilty of these crimes receives the death penalty (Badkar, 2013). For instance, others who received similar sentences had their death sentences overturned after Chinese heads of state intervened (Stevenson, 2021).

Public disapproval of a sentence of death for corporate crimes also has led to fewer executions for economic crimes and corruption. However, in 2021, Lai Xiaomin, the former CEO of a large Chinese state lender, was sentenced to death for bribery, corruption, and bigamy. Although Lai Xiaomin held a position of high status within the business community, his sentence was widely believed to be a message to other elites that corruption will not be tolerated in China (Stevenson, 2021).

When a street crime is committed it can often be tried in both criminal and civil court. If a person murders someone, for example, they can be found guilty of this act in a criminal court and face time in prison. Whether a case is brought to trial in a criminal court is determined by whether there is enough evidence against the suspected offender to convince a jury or judge the suspect did indeed commit the crime beyond a reasonable doubt. Even if the suspect is brought to court because the prosecutor believes there is enough evidence to win a conviction, there is no guarantee the person will be found guilty. The socioeconomic status or class background of the suspect also plays a part. If the suspect has money, they can hire expensive attorneys who will go to great lengths to convince the judge or jury that their client is not guilty by attempting to create reasonable doubt. However, those without means are appointed an attorney who is often overburdened and not provided with the same finances to investigate and bring in witnesses to bolster their client's defense. The family of the victim also can file a complaint against the suspected or convicted offender in civil court, demanding money or a fine for the loss of their loved one.

Corporate crimes are typically tried in a civil court, where the burden of proof is lower. It is difficult for prosecutors in a criminal court to prove beyond a reasonable doubt that one person or a group of people committed a crime. This is because even though the prosecutor can illustrate a crime did occur or people were harmed by the corporation's actions, (for example, chemicals dumped in the river caused cancer deaths or those who drove a faulty car died), it can be difficult to demonstrate one person or a group of people intended for these actions to result in the death or illness of the victim. This is important because in order for there to be a crime one has to demonstrate the criminal act (*actus reus*) and the intent to cause harm (*mens rea*) occurred together (concurrence). Corporate crime offenders do receive hefty fines when tried in civil court, but these fines do not outweigh the financial benefit of committing the crime. In 2014, the federal government fined GM $900 million for not recalling their vehicles that were known to have a faulty ignition switch in civil court (NBC News, 2014). However, GM made a gross profit of $14.77 billion in the same year (Market Watch, 2015).

Also, those who are charged criminally in these cases have millions of dollars at their disposal to hire the best defense team to fight these charges in court and to create a reasonable doubt. For instance, Don Blakenship, the CEO of Massey Energy, was indicted in criminal federal court for the crimes of conspiracy, securities fraud, and making false statements after the explosion in the Upper Big Branch mine killed 29 miners. However, despite the evidence, he was only found guilty on one misdemeanor count of conspiracy and not guilty on the other two charges (Associated Press, 2015).

The Media and Its Impact on Our Understanding of Crime

There are multiple channels on cable television and streaming services for you to select from as well as multiple outlets for news and entertainment on the internet. These numerous selections help to provide the illusion of choice for the consumer. For instance, you can select to watch Fox News or CNBC News to better understand what is going on in the world, and you can decide which radio station to listen to in your car. But, do you really have as much choice and variety in information and entertainment as it appears? In 1983, for example, there were 50 companies that controlled the media in the United States, but today there are only six companies who control 90% of what you watch, listen to, or read. These six companies are AT&T, CBS, Comcast, Disney, News Corp, and Viacom (Louise, 2020).

Even though corporate crime costs our society more financially and in some instances even causes physical harm, most of us are unaware of the dangers of corporate crime. This is in large part because of the focus on street crime in the media. The six companies mentioned earlier earn approximately $430 billion per year, and much of this revenue comes in the form of advertisement (Louise, 2020). Therefore, media corporations are motivated to put stories on the news, radio, and in print that will get people to tune in or read their product, which creates greater exposure for the advertisers and in turn brings in more advertisement revenue (Lutz, 2012).

News stories where the victim is white and young tend to get the most attention because they attract the most viewers, particularly when the victim is a young, white female. The opposite is true for coverage of offenders committing crime, where offenses committed by people of color tend to get the most coverage even though white people are arrested and charged with most crimes twice as often as Black people. This image of white individuals as the victims of crimes and Black individuals as the perpetrators, even though inaccurate, directly impacts the American media consumer, who then buys into the myth of the Black criminal. This becomes problematic for minority communities, as political agendas are often based on the demands of the people, and those who vote are basing their understanding of crime off of what they see on the news. If media consumers believe poor people of color are the threat, they will in turn demand their elected officials do something about those who are viewed as the problem. This then leads to harsh laws and punishments that directly impact poorer, often minority communities (Benson, 2014).

The opposite is true for coverage of corporate crime, where it is rare for corporate crime to be covered on the local or evening news. If corporate crime is covered in the news at all, it is usually on a cable news channel that is discussing business news. It is difficult for many to understand the nuances of corporate crime based on a brief news clip, which doesn't make for exciting news coverage. If people do not tune in or read the story, there is less advertising exposure. This means advertisers are not as likely to buy time or space in the media, which in turn means less profit for the large media corporations. This also is why you rarely see corporate crime as the topic of a popular television crime show. *Law and Order,* for example, has many spin offs, but one of them is not *Law & Order: Corporate Criminals* (Serani, 2011).

Popular culture also directly impacts our understanding of street crime. There are many shows on television that depict the criminal justice system fighting street crime, which further misguides many Americans' understanding of the criminal justice system. *Law and Order* episodes, for example, typically show violent criminals being investigated and sentenced within the period of an hour, portraying an effective and just system. However, the reality is that only 10% of offenders ever make it to the trial phase, because most suspected offenders utilize the plea bargain system and the majority of crimes go unsolved (Devers, 2011).

Other shows, such as *CSI*, portrayed lab technicians who also act as chemists and simultaneously perform investigations at the crime scene. These technicians/investigators then solve the crime by running tests right then and there on DNA collected at the crime scene. However, these crime shows also portray an unrealistic image of the criminal justice system, where there is DNA at all crime scenes, and technicians have the ability to run tests immediately and determine the results. Unfortunately, there isn't DNA at all crime scenes, and crime labs are often backlogged.

IN FOCUS

Crime Labs

Forensic labs across the country have been experiencing backlogs, causing delays in processing criminal cases. One reason for this spike is the increase in forensic samples being taken at crime scenes as DNA evidence becomes more common in criminal cases. Another reason for the increase in DNA samples is due to state and federal laws requiring those who have been arrested (21 states) or convicted of a felony (47 states) to provide a DNA sample that is stored in an offender profile database (National Institute of Justice, 2016).

In North Carolina, for example, the state crime lab was having a difficult time running tests on everything from fingerprints to blood, due to the number of samples they were expected to test. In one case a man ran over and killed a pedestrian. The driver was suspected of driving under the influence, and his blood was taken at the crime scene. The prosecutor put in a rush order for the test results but still weeks later had not heard back from the lab. Later, it was discovered this same driver had been suspected of driving under the influence in another car-related crime, and the results of the blood test for this now two-year-old crime had never been tested. Unfortunately, this also was the case for crimes ranging from murder to sexual assault. This backup in lab results and testing causes multiple problems, because the longer it takes to get the test results back, the less chance the prosecutor has to successfully prosecute the case. This is because witnesses become difficult to find and/or their memories become less clear (Abernethy, 2013).

In an effort to reduce the backlogs found in forensic labs across the country, the National Institute of Justice created the DNA Backlog Reduction Program. This program assists state and local governments by offering grants to crime labs. The purpose of these grants is to provide financial assistance, so forensic labs so can process more cases to decrease their backlog (National Institute of Justice, 2016). However, grants are a temporary solution for what appears to be a growing problem.

State governments also have become involved in the effort to reduce the backlog. For instance, in 2019, state legislators in North Carolina passed the Survivor's Act, which provided six million dollars to test 16,190 backlogged sexual assault kits. As of 2021, 2,965 sexual assault kits had been tested with an additional 5,404 sexual assault kits being processed for testing. The kits that have been cleared resulted in the arrests of 40 offenders who were responsible for 58 sexual assault cases. However, there are not enough funds to address the remaining backlog of sexual assault kits, so the North Carolina Attorney General has asked the state legislators for an additional nine million dollars to clear the remaining backlog of kits by 2023 (Duncan, 2021).

Even though these popular crime shows are not based in reality, the public has bought into the notion that crimes should be resolved quickly and there is always DNA at the scene that can be tested to verify that the suspected offender committed the crime. This misunderstanding is referred to as the *CSI effect*. To test this theory, a study was conducted with 1,000 potential jurors who were surveyed on their TV-viewing habits as well as their expectations for scientific proof to be entered as evidence in a trial. The results showed the two most popular criminal justice-related television shows watched by those surveyed were *Law and Order* and *CSI*. Out of the 1,000 people surveyed, 46% expected there to be scientific evidence in all criminal cases, and 22% expected there to be DNA evidence in all criminal cases. It also should be noted that the more a person watched these criminal justice related-television shows, the more accurate they believed the scientific evidence in the shows to be (Shelton, 2008).

Law Makers and Law Breakers

Most of our laws relating to criminal justice are based on *deterrence theory*, the idea that if you make the punishment outweigh any benefit one would receive from committing the crime, people will rationally choose not to commit the crime (National Institute of Justice, 2016). Although many laws have been passed to deter offenders from committing street crimes, very few laws have been passed or enforced when it comes to those who commit corporate crimes. We have discussed how there is little media coverage of corporate crimes, which keeps the public uninformed and unmotivated to demand change. However, there also is another factor that plays a large part in why these crimes continue to fly under the radar—conflict theory.

Conflict theory is the idea that those in power make the laws the rest of us abide by. The conflict occurs because those in power are not likely to make laws that will negatively impact them or those who help them to get elected to office, such as campaign contributors (Investopedia, 2015). If the coal industry, for example, is a large contributor to your campaign, you are not likely to endorse laws that would help to regulate the coal industry and/or punish those who break these laws within the coal industry. If you were to do this, the coal industry would not support your election campaign the next time around and would likely endorse and support a candidate running against you, who would not support the laws you had previously endorsed to regulate and punish the coal industry. However, passing laws that punish street crimes is a win-win situation for a candidate, because the voting public supports them in this effort, and those who are the most likely to be impacted by these laws, the poor, are not likely to garner enough support to derail their next election campaign.

An example of conflict theory at work is legislation passed only three years after stricter regulations had been put in place by Congress for the banking industry, due to the mortgage crisis of 2008. The more recent 2013 legislation protected large trades conducted by the banking industry from the previously enacted regulations and was

Figure 5.3. © Adobe Stock/R Scott James

written with the help of lobbyists, primarily from Citigroup. The legislation contained 85 lines with more than 70 of the lines taken word for word from information provided by the bank's lobbyists. It was later determined that those who supported the banking-backed legislation had been provided with twice as much money in campaign contributions from banking interests for their most recent election, in comparison with those who voted against the bill (Lipton & Protess, 2013).

The Media, Conflict Theory, and the War on Drugs

The news coverage of street crimes and the popularity of television shows based on street crimes directly impact our understanding of what crime is and who we are likely to be harmed by. Therefore, when the voting public demands there be changes in crime laws these typically revolve around what they know and are seeing on the news and in popular television programs. In the mid-1980s, for example, there was a lot of news coverage surrounding the drug crack cocaine. At the time, many viewed this drug as being the most addictive drug available and one that would destroy our communities. The TV news coverage at the time heavily focused on crimes committed in poor communities, where the offender and victim were Black and the root of the crime was blamed on the addictiveness of crack cocaine. Popular TV shows also covered the issue, and nearly every major network televised a show on the topic of crack cocaine, portraying a drug that made people violent and made them do things they otherwise would not do. The voters tuned in to these programs and became afraid that if they did not demand their politicians act these problems would eventually come to their neighborhoods and children at suburban malls would be smoking the highly addictive drug. However, little attention was paid to the problems occurring within these poorer communities, such as lack of employment, failing schools, and families living below the poverty line, nor the issue of powder cocaine and how this drug was just as addictive as crack cocaine and primarily being consumed by those with money who were often white. Instead, voters, motivated by fear, demanded their politicians react, and weeks before the next election season the Anti-Drug Abuse Act of 1986 was passed (Cobbina, 2008).

Although President Nixon originally declared a War on Drugs in the 1970s, the focus of his war was on stopping illegal substances from entering the United States and getting addicts into drug treatment. In the 1980s, President Reagan again declared a War on Drugs, but with an emphasis on the prohibition and elimination of all illegal drugs in the United States. President Reagan's war officially began, in 1986, with the passage of the *Anti-Drug Abuse Act*, which was the foundation for the War on Drugs we continue to fight today (Brown, 2004). One of the most notable provisions of the Anti-Drug Abuse Act was mandatory minimum sentences. *Mandatory minimum sentences* are enacted by legislators and declare that if a suspect is convicted (found guilty) of a particular crime then they will serve the entire required sentence set forth by the legislation. It was believed that mandatory sentences would serve as a deterrent for those who possessed and sold illegal drugs, because someone would rationally choose not to participate in this behavior, if they were aware of the harsh sentences. In the case of drugs, the idea was to target those who were considered to be kingpin and mid-level drug dealers. For instance, kingpins or those who were caught in possession of 1,000 grams of heroin or 5,000 grams of powder cocaine were to be sentenced to a mandatory minimum of 10 years in prison, while mid-level dealers or those selling 100 grams of heroin or 500 grams of powder cocaine were sentenced to a mandatory minimum of five years in prison (Brown, 2004).

IN FOCUS

Presidential Clemency

The president of the United States has the power to grant clemency to those who have been convicted of a federal crime through commuting sentences or pardoning those who have been convicted of a crime. A commutation occurs when the conviction remains, but the sentence is removed or reduced because it is believed to be too harsh for the crime. A pardon is when a person was convicted of the crime, but the crime is forgiven and the conviction is removed. A pardon can occur after someone has completed their sentence as well as during or before incarceration. Pardons are granted to those who are now believed to be innocent of the crime or when the punishment is viewed as not fitting the crime (ABC News, 2007).

Between 2009 and 2016, President Barack Obama pardoned 70 people and commuted the sentences of just under 1,000 people, with more commutations during his eight years in office than the last eleven presidents combined (White

House, 2016). The majority of those who had their sentences commuted were serving time for a nonviolent drug offense, and slightly more than one third of all those who had their sentences commuted were serving life sentences for a nonviolent drug offense. Ramona Brant, for example, was serving 99 years in prison for conspiracy to sell illegal drugs after her boyfriend and the father of her children was arrested for selling illegal drugs. Ramona was not involved in the sale, use, or possession of the drugs, but she was aware of her boyfriend's behavior. After serving 20 years of her sentence, Ramona's sentence was commuted by President Obama, and she was released from prison (White House, 2016).

These pardons and commutations were part of Clemency Project 2014, where federal inmates who had been convicted of nonviolent, low-level drug offenses, served ten years of their sentence, and maintained good behavior in prison were encouraged to apply for clemency. The Clemency Project ended when President Trump took office. However, President Trump also provided clemency to some nonviolent drug offenders during his presidential term (U.S. Department of Justice, 2018).

Due to the media coverage at the time of what was termed the "crack epidemic," crack cocaine was believed to be the most dangerous and addictive drug of all. Therefore, the sentence for this drug was even harsher. The sentence for possessing crack cocaine became known as the *100:1 ratio*, where the penalty for possession crack cocaine would be 100 times harsher than possession of powder cocaine to reflect the dangerousness of the drug. Therefore, if one were caught in possession of 50 grams of crack cocaine they would be sentenced to a 10-year mandatory minimum, while those in possession of five grams of crack cocaine would be sentenced to a mandatory minimum of five years in prison. However, those in possession of 50 grams of powder cocaine did not trigger a mandatory minimum sentence (Brown, 2004).

The sentencing disparities for powder cocaine and crack cocaine had serious racial implications. Powder cocaine was more likely to be sold in wealthier neighborhoods behind closed doors, in suburban homes, and in college dormitories, making it much more difficult to catch those who were participating in this behavior. However, crack cocaine, a distilled and cheaper form of powder cocaine, was more likely to be sold in an open-air drug market within urban communities. *Open-air drug markets* occur when one sells drugs outside on street corners, waiting for customers to approach. Open-air drug markets leave the dealer exposed, as anyone can sit and watch their behavior to determine what is occurring. This is good for business in that anyone can enter the neighborhood and know where they can purchase drugs, but it is also risky because one is more likely to get caught by the police (Langan, 1995).

Since law enforcement can easily pull into an urban neighborhood in an unmarked van and watch people sell drugs, those who sold drugs in the open-air drug market became a priority. The police would sit in their unmarked van and take pictures of those selling the drugs, and within a couple of days they would have proof beyond a reasonable doubt the person was indeed selling the drug, which would lead to an arrest and an eventual conviction. Once arrested, the person selling the drug was often in possession of five grams of crack cocaine, which triggered the mandatory minimum sentence of five years in prison. This in turn gives the appearance that law enforcement was winning the War on Drugs, with high numbers of arrests for what was considered the most vile drug—crack cocaine (Langan, 1995).

One problem with this drug enforcement strategy is that those who are arrested and removed from the street corners are easily replaced by another drug dealer waiting to take their place, or what is referred to as the *replacement effect*. The open-air drug market was occurring within incredibly poor neighborhoods with high unemployment rates, particularly for young men. The threat of going to prison for five years, even though it appeared to be certain, was not enough to deter those without another source of viable income from participating in the illegal behavior of drug sales. This then creates a vicious cycle, where police surveille an area and make arrests, and another person is back out on the street selling the drugs within a few hours. Although this is an effective strategy for creating high numbers of arrests and the illusion the battle is being won, it does very little for truly eliminating drug use and sales (Langan, 1995). Another issue with focusing law enforcement efforts on low-income urban neighborhoods is that those who are primarily punished for the sale of drugs are young African American men. African Americans constitute approximately 15% of the total United States population and 13% of those who admit to using illegal drugs. However, 37% of those arrested for drug sales, 55% of those convicted of drug offenses, and 74% of those being sentenced to prison for selling illegal drugs are Black. Meanwhile, the majority of people who sell and use illegal drugs are white (Harris, 1999).

Even though Black people were less likely to report drug use or sales than white people, the number of African Americans arrested and sentenced for drug violations was incredibly high (Langan, 1995). These high numbers gave the public the impression the majority of people who used and sold drugs were Black, even though this was factually not true. The police also bought into the notion that the majority of people who sold drugs were people of color, because this was what they were experiencing at work, due to the law enforcement policies that targeted open-air drug markets.

The War on Drugs has been declared a global failure by the United Nations, and their report concluded that illegal drugs are now cheaper and more easily accessible than prior to the start of the war (Global Commission on Drug Policy, 2011). Criminal justice research also has repeatedly noted that the policies implemented during the War on Drugs have disproportionately targeted poorer communities and in particular young African American men. Yet, in spite of all of this, the United States continues to invest billions of dollars to fight the War on Drugs, with the federal

government spending $36 billion dollars on federal, state, and local government ef-
forts in 2020 alone (Elflein, 2020).

However, when one begins to examine the War on Drugs from a conflict theory
perspective it begins to make more sense. Legislators are aware that those who voted
them into office are not directly impacted by the laws and punishments associated
with the War on Drugs, which gives them little incentive to speak out against the war
for fear of appearing soft on crime. The War on Drugs also has become a very profitable endeavor, with private corporations making money off of housing and treating
offenders in private prisons along with privately run residential treatment centers
(Cohen, 2015). Many jobs in law enforcement and corrections also were created in
order to fight the war, including the federal Drug Enforcement Agency (DEA), in
1973, shortly after President Nixon declared the first War on Drugs (DEA, 2017).
Therefore, legislators are not motivated to change the laws regarding the War on
Drugs due to the pressure they receive from their constituents as well as lobbyists
representing private companies and unions representing law enforcement and corrections officers.

Summary

The definition of crime at first glance appears to be very simple, and most Americans believe they have a decent understanding of what crime is and how it occurs.
However, most of us gain our knowledge about the criminal justice system based on
what we see, read, or listen to in the media. We also have a misunderstanding of who
victims and offenders are based on our media consumption, and this directly impacts
our laws. How crime is defined also depends on what is happening around us politically, socially, and economically and can change from one place or time period to the
next. Therefore, it is important to examine our history as well as to dig into the root
causes of crime to gain a broader understanding of what is considered to be criminal
behavior.

Discussion Questions

1. List and explain three main differences between street crime and corporate
   crime. How do these differences impact our understanding of what is crime?

2. You have been assigned to a task force to make the public as well as legislators
   more aware of corporate crime. What pieces of information do you believe
   would be the most important for your audience to become familiar with to
   help educate them on this subject?

3. Can the War on Drugs be implemented so that race and class biases do not
   occur?

Key Terms

crime	preponderance of the evidence
actus reus	*CSI* effect
mens rea	deterrence theory
concurrence	conflict theory
street crime	Anti-Drug Abuse Act
corporate crime	mandatory minimum sentence
criminal case	100:1 ratio
beyond a reasonable doubt	open-air drug market
civil case	replacement effect

References

ABC News. (2007). Commutation? Clemency? Pardon? Sorting out the legalese in the Libby case. http://abcnews.go.com/TheLaw/story?id=3339765&page=1

Abernethy, M. D. (2013). State crime lab backups delaying cases. *The Times News*. http://www.thetimesnews.com/article/20130126/News/301269879

Associated Press. (2015). Ex-Massey Energy CEO guilty of misdemeanor count in coal mine disaster. NBC Business News. http://www.nbcnews.com/business/business-news/ex-massey-energy-ceo-guilty-misdemeanor-count-coal-mine-disaster-n473636

Badkar, M. (2013). 22 Chinese people who were handed the death sentence for white collar crime. *Business Insider*. http://www.businessinsider.com/chinese-white-collar-criminals-death-sentence-2013-7

Benson, C. (2014). Crime coverage in media perpetuates racial stereotypes. *Chicago Reporter*. http://chicagoreporter.com/crime-coverage-media-perpetuates-racial-stereotypes/

Brown, D. K. (2004). Anti-Drug Abuse Act (1986). National Institute of Justice. http://www.nij.gov/topics/law-enforcement/legitimacy/pages/racial-profiling.aspx

Carter, Z. (2015). Lawmakers sneak help for white-collar criminals into justice reform bill. *Huffington Post Politics*. http://www.huffingtonpost.com/entry/corporate-crime-criminal-justice-reform_564cc371e4b031745cef33d4

Cobbina, J. E. (2008). Race and class differences in print media portrayals of crack cocaine and methamphetamine. *Journal of Criminal Justice and Popular Culture*, *15*, 145–167. http://www.nij.gov/journals/259/pages/csi-effect.aspx

Cohen, M. (2015). How for-profit prisons have become the biggest lobby no one is talking about. *The Washington Post*. https://www.washingtonpost.com/posteverything/wp/2015/04/28/how-for-profit-prisons-have-become-the-biggest-lobby-no-one-is-talking-about/

Cohen, M. A. (2016). The cost of white collar crime. In S. Van Slyke, F. Cullen, & M. Benson (Ed.), *Oxford Handbook of White Collar Crime*, p. 78–100. Oxford University Press.

Denning, S. (2011). Lest we forget: Why we had a financial crisis. *Forbes*. http://www.forbes.com/sites/stevedenning/2011/11/22/5086/

Devers, L. (2011). Plea and charge bargaining: Research summary. Bureau of Justice Assistance. https://www.bja.gov/Publications/PleaBargainingResearchSummary.pdf

Doyle-McClatchy, M. (2014). Bank of America settles mortgage fraud case for 16.5 billion. *The News and Observer*. http://www.newsobserver.com/news/business/real-estate-news/article10036964.html

Drug Enforcement Agency (DEA). (2017). DEA history. https://www.dea.gov/about/history.shtml

Duncan, C. (2021). N.C. working to clear massive backlog of sexual assault cases, AG wants funds for DNA tests. Spectrum News 1. https://spectrumlocalnews.com/nc/charlotte/public-safety/2021/05/20/north-carolina-continues-to-test-backlog-of-sexual-assault-kits--40-arrests-made-after-thousands-tested

Elflein, J. (2020). Total federal drug control spending in the United States from FY 2012 to FY 2021. Statista. https://www.statista.com/statistics/618857/total-federal-drug-control-spending-in-us/#:~:text=The%20largest%20amount%20of%20federal,some%2036.8%20billion%20U.S.%20dollars

Global Commission on Drug Policy. (2011). War on drugs: Report of the Global Commission on Drug Policy. United Nations. https://www.globalcommissionondrugs.org/wp-content/themes/gcdp_v1/pdf/Global_Commission_Report_English.pdf

Gomez, S. (2020). All the states that legalized marijuana. Addiction Center. https://www.addictioncenter.com/news/2020/11/states-legalized-marijuana/

Harris, D. A. (1999). Driving while Black: Racial profiling on our nation's highways. American Civil Liberties Union. https://www.aclu.org/report/driving-while-black-racial-profiling-our-nations-highways

Ingraham, C. (2015). Why hardly anyone dies from a drug overdose in Portugal. *The Washington Post*. https://www.washingtonpost.com/news/wonk/wp/2015/06/05/why-hardly-anyone-dies-from-a-drug-overdose-in-portugal/

Investopedia. (2015). Conflict theory. http://www.investopedia.com/terms/c/conflict-theory.asp

Kramer, R. C. (2013). Expanding the core: Blameworthy harms, international law, and state-corporate crimes. https://asc41.com/Annual_Meeting/2013/Presidential%20Papers/Kramer,%20Ronald.pdf

Langan, P. A. (1995). The racial disparity in US drug arrests. National Institute of Justice. http://www.nij.gov/topics/law-enforcement/legitimacy/pages/racial-profiling.aspx

Legal Information Institute. (2015). Criminal law. https://www.law.cornell.edu/wex/criminal_law

Lipton, E., & Protess, B. (2013). Banks' lobbyists help in drafting financial bills. *The New York Times*. http://dealbook.nytimes.com/2013/05/23/banks-lobbyists-help-in-drafting-financial-bills/?_r=2

Louise, N. (2020, September 18). These 6 corporations control 90% of the media outlets in America. The illusion of choice and objectivity. Tech Start Ups. https://techstartups.com/2020/09/18/6-corporations-control-90-media-america-illusion-choice-objectivity-2020/

Lutz, A. (2012). These six corporations control 90% of the media in America. *Business Insider*. http://www.businessinsider.com/these-6-corporations-control-90-of-the-media-in-america-2012-6

Market Watch. (2015). General Motors Company. http://www.marketwatch.com/investing/stock/gm/financials

Miller, T. R., Cohen, M. A., Swedler, D. I., Ali, B., & Hendrie, D. V. (2021). Incidence and costs of personal and property crimes in the USA, 2017. *Journal of Benefit Cost Analysis*, *12*, 24–54.

The Mississippi Bar. (2015). The difference between a criminal and civil case. http://www.msbar.org/for-the-public/consumer-information/the-difference-between-a-civil-and-criminal-case.aspx

National Institute of Justice. (2016). DNA Backlog Reduction Program. http://www.nij.gov/topics/forensics/lab-operations/evidence-backlogs/Pages/backlog-reduction-program.aspx

National Institute of Justice. (2016). Five things about deterrence. Retrieved from https://nij.ojp.gov/topics/articles/five-things-about-deterrence

NBC News. (2014). GM recall. http://www.nbcnews.com/storyline/gm-recall

NPR. (2015a). The fall of Enron: Collapse felt from workers' homes to halls of government. http://www.npr.org/news/specials/enron/

NPR. (2015b). Who owns Fannie Mae and Freddie Mac? http://www.npr.org/sections/money/2015/04/21/401259676/who-owns-fannie-mae-and-freddie-mac

Rinehart, E. (2015). Dupont negligent in C8 case, owes woman 1.6 million. *The Columbus Dispatch*. http://www.dispatch.com/content/stories/local/2015/10/07/Dupont-ordered-to-pay-damages.html

Serani, D. (2011). If it bleeds, it leads: Understanding fear-based media. *Psychology Today*. https://www.psychologytoday.com/blog/two-takes-depression/201106/if-it-bleeds-it-leads-understanding-fear-based-media

Shelton, D. E. (2008). The *CSI* effect: Does it really exist? National Institute of Justice. http://www.nij.gov/journals/259/pages/csi-effect.aspx

Stevenson, A. (2021). China sentences former bank chief to death in rare move. *The New York Times*. https://www.nytimes.com/2021/01/05/business/china-huarong-death-penalty.html

Sullivan, G. (2014). Ex-Massey CEO Don Blankenship indicted for coal mine disaster that killed 29. *The Washington Post*. https://www.washingtonpost.com/news/morning-mix/wp/2014/11/14/ex-massey-ceo-don-blankenship-indicted-for-coal-mine-disaster-than-killed-29/

U.S. Department of Justice. (2018). Clemency initiative. https://www.justice.gov/pardon/clemency-initiative

The White House. (2015). Marijuana resource center. https://www.whitehouse.gov/ondcp/state-laws-related-to-marijuana

The White House. (2016). A nation of second chances: President Obama's record on clemency. https://www.whitehouse.gov/issues/clemency

Wight, P., & Runyon, L. (2016). Marijuana pays for schools in Colorado—kind of—but how will it help Maine? Weekend Edition: NPR. http://www.npr.org/2016/09/10/492118493/marijuana-pays-for-schools-in-colorado-kind-of-but-how-will-it-help-maine

Policing

SIX

Race-Based Policing in Communities of Color

Learning Objectives

1. Understand the differences between the terms "profiling" and "racial profiling" as well as how racial profiling directly impacts Black, Hispanic, and Muslim people.
2. Critically examine how the media, lawsuits, investigations, and data collection directly impact our level of awareness as well as changes in the law regarding racial profiling.
3. Understand how race-based policing has damaged police–community relations within many communities and how utilizing community-oriented policing strategies could help to repair this damage.

Policing strategies based on race have long been scrutinized, rationalized, and studied. In order to come to a shared understanding about a path forward for public safety in communities of color, it is important to understand the evolution of how proposed reform strategies came to be. While these strategies are contemplated, there is a continuing trend of police violence against Black bodies that seems to indicate change may not be on the horizon. Today's issue of racial disparities in police violence, notably those encounters that lead to death, are just further confirmation that Black lives either still don't matter or they matter differently. In Ferguson, Missouri, Black motorists were almost twice as likely to be searched after a traffic stop than whites. In addition, a DOJ report on the practices of the Baltimore Police Department (BDP) revealed that during a five-year period, officers documented 300,000

125

Figure 6.1. San Francisco Police Department officers performing a search of a suspect.
© iStockphoto.com/chameleonseye.

pedestrian stops that were often not prompted by rational circumstances and largely concentrated in Black neighborhoods (Cobbina, 2019). These disparities remain despite decades of research that has shown that a significant difference between Black and white criminality does not exist empirically. More information about the 2020 racial justice protests and calls to divest from the police are covered in subsequent chapters (Chapters 7 and 15). This chapter covers the socio-historical underpinnings of policing strategies which disproportionately impact those who are Black, Indigenous, and People of Color (BIPOC).

Research related to racial profiling has changed over time. Most racial profiling research has examined its incidence, community attitudes regarding police legitimacy and/or utilization of race-based policing tactics, law and policy issues, and methodological and/or theoretical dilemmas (Rice et al., 2005). There are still competing perspectives about the practice and reality of racial profiling. For some, there is a belief that evidence is anecdotal, or the bias is related to differential offending by people of color. Those who believe that tend to view racial profiling as valid and an efficient mechanism for public safety. Others would contend that targeting certain groups leads to blind spots and a self-fulfilling prophecy. As the concept has evolved, it has become increasingly important to not only understand how it has developed but also the implications of race-based policing on communities. This chapter will explore socio-historical, legal, and contemporary perspectives on the topic. It explores how the politicization of issues leads to a focus on them as well increased funding that supports proactive policing but also damages police–community relations in communities of color.

At times those strategies are rooted in race-neutral profiles that alert the police to suspicious behavior. Historically, the broader concept of profiling has been acceptably used in efforts to combat crime. *Profiling* is a practical tool used by law enforcement to help an officer narrow down potential suspects, where an officer uses observed behavior to determine if there is reasonable suspicion the person may be committing a crime (*Merriam-Webster*, 2015). However, the use of profiling that included racialized components appears to be attributed to Special Agent Paul Markonni, who created the drug courier profile as a strategy to assist in drug interdiction efforts by the Drug Enforcement Agency (DEA). The list included characteristics that might pertain to a drug courier but varied by location. The common characteristic was a "source city," which is a location where perpetrators were likely to receive drug shipments and ship out drugs (Conley, 1982). By 1979, the profile was quickly adopted by 20 airports, and a broader expansion occurred by 1985 that included airports from Florida to Southern California (Kadish, 1997). In the **U.S. v. Sokolow** case, the Court ruled that "any one factor set forth in the DEA's profile, by itself, is not dispositive proof of illegal conduct but may amount to reasonable suspicion when considered together with other indicia of criminal activity" (Cogan, 1992, p. 958). The *Sokolow* decision therefore opened the door for officers to use the totality of circumstances coupled with their own experiences. Therefore, if the officer's experience confirmed that most drug couriers are of a certain racial or ethnic background, then it is permissible for that to be a characteristic of the stop (Dey, 1998).

Racial profiling, also known as race-based policing, is different from profiling and is an offshoot of drug courier profiles. **Racial profiling** refers to "the use of race or ethnicity, or proxies thereof, by law enforcement officials as a basis for judgement of criminal suspicion" (Cobbina, 2019). Racial profiling has evolved as a concept through the years. Yet there are still disagreements on whether or not one is referring to officers using race as the sole criteria for targeting a citizen or if race is part of the totality of the circumstances or the "whole picture." It is a more comprehensive concept that includes a range of police discretionary interactions. As established in cases like *U.S. v. Brignoni-Ponce* (1975), it is a clear legal violation for police officers to use race as the sole criteria for targeting an individual. This principle was established in the 1990s after cases such as *U.S. v. Sokolow* mandated that law enforcement consider "the whole picture." In this case, federal agents' suspicions were ignited by Sokolow's circumstances, which included:

(1) he paid $2,100 for two airplane tickets from a roll of $20 bills; (2) he traveled under a name that did not match the name under which the telephone number was listed (although it was later discovered the telephone number was his roommate's); (3) his original destination, Miami, was a source city for illegal

drugs; (4) he stayed in Miami for 48 hours, despite the fact that a round-trip flight from Honolulu to Miami takes 20 hours; (5) he appeared nervous; (6) he checked none of his luggage; and (7) he was wearing a black jumpsuit and gold jewelry. (*U.S. v. Sokolow*, 1989)

The court upheld the decision of the lower court and concluded the officer had the right to stop and frisk a person for illegal drugs based on reasonable suspicion (The Free Dictionary, n.d.).

As Americans, our Fourth Amendment rights protect us against unreasonable searches and seizures. In order for a police officer to fully search a person and seize their property, the officer needs a warrant issued by a court. However, police officers also can search a person and seize their property, if they have *probable cause* or the belief a crime has been or is about to be committed. For example, the officer sees someone climbing through a window and infers a burglary (breaking into a house to steal property) is about to take place. The officer using probable cause has the right to stop this person and fully search them to see if there is any evidence the person committed the crime as well as to take them into custody for further questioning. In another example, if an officer perceives illegal drugs are being exchanged between two parties this can lead to probable cause, because the officer can conclude the crime of selling illegal drugs is taking place. In this example, the officer has the right to search the parties, seize their property as evidence, and take them into custody for further questioning (Hill & Hill, n.d.).

Police officers also use a technique called *stop and frisk* when they are unable to form probable cause but have a reasonable suspicion a crime is about to take place. For example, the officer sees a known drug dealer or someone who fits the profile of a drug dealer in a community where drugs are known to be sold. The officer in this situation has the right to stop the person, question them, and frisk or pat them down on the outer layers of their clothing in order to look for guns or drugs. If the officer believes they have detected a gun or drugs based on the frisk, the officer can conduct a more invasive search of the person and their property. In this instance, if the officer finds a gun or drugs, they have the right to take this person into custody for further questioning. During the frisk, the officer also has the right to use police dogs to sniff out drugs and run a background check on the person to see if they have any outstanding warrants for their arrest (Legal Information Institute, n.d.b).

Stop-and-frisk policies have been upheld and found to be constitutional by the United States Supreme Court. In 1968, the case *Terry v. Ohio* involved an officer who witnessed three men who were walking by a store and repeatedly looking into the window. Their behavior was deemed to be reasonably suspicious by the officer, who did not see them commit a crime, but believed they were checking out the store to

Table 1. Level of Suspicion Needed to Search and/or
Seize Person/Property or Make an Arrest

	Level of Suspicion	Result
Warrant Acquired	Probable Cause	Can arrest as well as fully search and seize person and/or property.
No Warrant	Probable Cause	If crime is a felony, can arrest if person is in public. If crime is a misdemeanor, can arrest if person committed crime in front of police officer. If under arrest, can search person and area within immediate reach, and items near person can be seized.
Traffic Violation	Reasonable Suspicion and/ or Probable Cause	Once stopped for traffic violation, driver and passenger have been seized. Police can search the driver and passenger by frisking them, if officer has reasonable suspicion, they are armed, or they are involved in criminal behavior. Can only fully search the car without a warrant if consent is given, an arrest is made and the car is impounded, or there is probable cause that items in the car were connected to a crime or potential crime.
Stop and Frisk	Reasonable Suspicion	Once stopped, can frisk or pat down outer layer of clothes to look for guns or drugs. If detect guns or drugs, can conduct more thorough search, and if guns or drugs are found can make arrest and seize property.
Exigent Circumstances	Serious Emergency Occurring at Time	Emergency situation, for example gun shots or a building on fire, can be used to justify search, seizure, and arrest without a warrant.

Source: Find Law. (2016). The Fourth Amendment reasonableness requirement. http://criminal.findlaw.com/criminal-rights/the-fourth-amendment-reasonableness-requirement.html.

commit a robbery (take property by force) at a later date. The officer stopped the three men and questioned them. He then frisked the three subjects and found two of the men to have weapons. Terry was already on parole for another crime, so carrying an illegal weapon was a violation of his parole, and he was sent back to prison for a number of years. Terry appealed his case and stated that his Fourth Amendment rights were violated since the officer searched him without probable cause, because it is not illegal to look into a store window. The court upheld the verdict and stated the officer could use reasonable suspicion in a case such as this, where the officer had a reasonable belief that either he or the community was in danger (The Free Dictionary, n.d.).

IN FOCUS

NYC Stop and Frisk

In the early 2000s, the New York City Police Department (NYPD) implemented a stop-and-frisk policy they officially called *stop, question, and frisk*. This policy was enacted as a proactive policing strategy to curb drug crime and gun violence on the streets of New York City. Officers were encouraged to stop, question, and frisk those who they had reasonable suspicion to believe had or could possibly commit a crime. The police justified the stop, question, and frisk policy by stating that because of this strategy crime rates were declining in New York City. Meanwhile, the data collected by the police did not show the policy as being an effective crime prevention tool. For instance, from 2009 to 2012, 2.4 million people were stopped by the police, but only 6% of these stops (150,000) resulted in an arrest and only half of these arrests led to a conviction. In regards to violent crime, when examining the same time period, only 2% of all arrests or .1% of all those stopped were convicted of a violent crime (Gabbatt, 2013).

However, the data collected on the policy did illustrate that the majority of people being stopped were male and either Black or Latino. This led to a lawsuit in 2013 being   filed in federal court stating that the NYPD's stop, question, and frisk policy was unconstitutional because it violated the Fourteenth Amendment, which provides for equal protection under the law. The judge ruled the policy itself was not unconstitutional, but the way the NYPD was implementing the policy was unfairly targeting non-whites and therefore was unconstitutional under the Fourteenth Amendment.

In the fall of 2015, under the newly elected mayor, the NYPD implemented a receipt policy where anyone who was stopped due to reasonable suspicion, but was not arrested, would be given a receipt. This receipt explains the law and includes the name of the officer making the stop along with a box checked on the receipt giving the reason why the person was stopped. Other changes were made to the policy as well; for example, one can no longer be stopped simply because they are in a high-crime neighborhood. These changes in the policy have had a direct impact on the number of people stopped and questioned by the police. In 2011, at the height of the old stop, question, and frisk policy, the police stopped 900,000 people, but in 2015 after the policy had been changed, only 42,000 people were stopped (Parascandola, 2015).

The increased attention on Black deaths at the hands of the police connects to the concept of racial profiling. A reported 25% of police killings of Black people start with a traffic stop. One of the best ways to measure if racial profiling is occurring is through the analysis of traffic stop data. Traffic stop data can be broken down into two categories: safety stops and investigatory stops. **Safety stops** are those related to the safety of motorists and ensuring the roadways are safe to navigate. If an officer sees someone on the highway at two in the morning who is swerving, for instance, the officer is likely to use their experience and judgement to determine this person could possibly be under the influence. After the officer pulls the driver over, they may find the person was indeed drunk on alcohol or just very tired after driving all night. In either case, the officer removed someone from the road who was a danger to themselves and others by using observed behavior to infer the person may be committing a crime. As this example illustrates, profiling itself is not illegal or unethical and can help the officer to make sound decisions using observed behavior and past experience. However, this behavior does become problematic if the officer uses the person's race, ethnicity, national origin, or religion as the reason why the officer believes the driver is committing a crime.

Investigatory stops occur when safety stops shift towards a focus on decreasing the incidence of violent crime and drug trafficking. A way to better facilitate investigatory stops was solidified in the U.S. Supreme Court case *Whren v. U.S.* (1996). Law enforcement targeted traffic stops in an attempt to enforce drug policies. The police, for example, were pulling motorists over for minor traffic violations with the belief they also would find the person was engaged in other illegal activity, in particular selling or possessing illegal drugs. In 1996, the Supreme Court case **Whren v. United States** questioned whether it violated one's **Fourth Amendment** right against unreasonable search and seizure to have their car searched after a traffic stop for a minor traffic violation when there was no probable cause or suspicion of a crime. Ultimately, the Supreme Court ruled the law enforcement strategy did not violate one's Fourth Amendment rights because the Fourth Amendment only applies to unusually harmful searches and seizures (Oyez, n.d.).

Today, traffic stops are recorded, and most police departments readily provide traffic stop data to better monitor their own behavior and to help avoid potential lawsuits. This has resulted in different races and ethnicities being pulled over at similar rates. For instance, in 2008, 8.4% of all white drivers, 8.8% of all Black drivers, and 9.1% of all Hispanic drivers were stopped by police for a traffic violation throughout the United States. The majority of those surveyed believed they were stopped for a legitimate reason, including 86% of white drivers, 74% of Black drivers, and 86% of Hispanic drivers. However, there are still differences in how drivers are treated, after they are stopped. For instance, even though only 5% of all traffic stops resulted in the driver, car, or both being searched, Black drivers were three times more likely than white drivers and two times more likely than Hispanic drivers to be searched (Bureau of Justice Statistics, 2009). There also are differences based on gender, ethnicity, and race. Briggs examined the Police Public Contact Survey from 2005 and found women were 23% less likely to be ticketed and 76% less likely to have their vehicles searched than men. However, if one examined the data and included race, ethnicity, and gender, a different pattern emerged: Black and Hispanic women were just as likely as white men to be ticketed and searched, while white women who were stopped were typically released with a warning (Tidball, 2012).

Wilkins v. Maryland State Police

In 1993, in the case **Wilkins v. Maryland State Police**, Wilkins was pulled over, and his car was searched by the Maryland State Police. The police did not find any drugs on Wilkins or in his car, and he was not issued a ticket for any traffic violations. After this incident, Wilkins sued the Maryland State Police, stating that he was targeted by the police solely because of the color of his skin. The Maryland State Police settled the case and as part of the settlement were ordered to keep records on the demographics of those pulled over and searched in an effort to determine if there were larger racial patterns (Harris, 1999).

As newspapers and popular media began to cover the issue of racial disparities in traffic stops and searches, the public became more aware of what was occurring. This media coverage also led to the term "***driving while Black***," which was used to describe the phenomena of Black drivers being pulled over by the police and searched for suspicion of a crime based solely upon the color of their skin. Driving while Black (DWB) became a familiar term describing a phenomenon where Black people were also just seen as suspicious doing every day, mundane activities (Baumgartner et al., 2017). DWB expanded to "shopping while Black," and "flying while Black," among other activities (Meeks, 2000). As more awareness was created, citizens began to demand that the problem gain more attention and be resolved. In many states, for example, forums were created as a way for Black motorists to tell their stories of being stopped and searched, even though they had not committed a crime. Those who participated in the forums were demanding databases be created to keep track of racial profiling in traffic stops in order to officially document what they already knew to be a problem (Harris, 1999). Now this type of data is readily accessible. In a recent study using North Carolina data, Baumgartner and colleagues (2018) found:

- Black drivers were 63 percent more likely to be stopped even though, as a whole, they drive 16 percent less. Taking into account less time on the road, Black drivers were about 95 percent more likely to be stopped.
- Black motorists were 115 percent more likely than white motorists to be searched in a traffic stop (5.05 percent of Black drivers, 2.35 percent of white drivers).
- Contraband was more likely to be found in searches of white drivers. (Horn, 2020)

A Culture of Crimmigration and Citizenship Profiling

The *Immigration and Nationality Act of 1952* solidified the federal government's control over immigration regulations. It accomplished this by allowing the United States Congress to define immigration policy and the White House to enforce immigration laws while creating limits to the immigration enforcement powers of the states (Seghetti, 2009). In 2008, under President George W. Bush, and later expanded under President Barak Obama, the *Secure Communities* program was created in an effort to manage the issue of immigration at the federal level. Secure Communities was created to remove those who were violent and/or felony offenders who also were undocumented and in the United States illegally with an ultimate goal of removing up to 400,000 people per year. By 2011, the program had been implemented in 44 states (Kohli et al., 2011). Secure Communities was based on direct cooperation between local law enforcement and Immigrations and Customs Enforcement (ICE), which is under the Department of Homeland Security (DHS). ICE checks the provided fingerprints against their own databases to determine if the person should be deported. If ICE wants to question the person in custody, they will contact local law enforcement and ask them to hold the detainee for 48 additional hours, so they can take custody of the person and investigate further (Kohli et al., 2011). Even though the program was intended to target those who had committed felonies, many who were detained and deported had only committed a misdemeanor offense (29%). The program ended in 2014 and was replaced by the *Priority Enforcement Program* or PEP, which was officially implemented in July of 2015. This program still entails local law enforcement working together with Department of Homeland Security and ICE, but with a different focus. For instance, if someone is arrested, their fingerprints are still sent to the FBI who then forwards them on to ICE. However, now ICE has to determine if this person fits one of the priorities set forth by the DHS for removal.

In recent years, there has been a change in how the US addresses immigration, reflecting a culture of *crimmigration*, where criminal and immigration law merge and encourage local law enforcement to address immigration issues. Furthering this culture, it has been noted that within their first 100 days, the deportation policies of the Trump administration changed the way the criminal justice system has interacted with immigration enforcement. During the first three months of 2017, there were 11,000 more ICE arrests than in 2016 in the same time frame (Chawla, 2018). Under both the Obama and Trump administrations there were increasing calls to supplant crimmigration enforcement with local law enforcement. Arguably, these collective local, state, and federal strategies have heightened the likelihood that immigration status serves as a proxy for criminality, which leads to what is referred to as *citizenship profiling*.

Citizenship profiling occurs when stops, searches, and inquiries by the police are related to immigration status. The resulting mass deportation has been called a "gender racial removal program" which targets Hispanic men (Golash-Boza & Hondagneu-Sotelo, 2013, p. 272). While race is not the primary indicator for these interactions, char-

Figure 6.2. © Creative Commons / U.S. Customs and Border Control

acteristics related to race (i.e., phenotypical traits) tend to play a role in the decision to stop, search, or question. Perceptions of foreignness and illegality can be associated with other racialized or ethnic characteristics such as speaking Spanish. Morales et al. (2021) argue that race and ethnicity can "signal" illegality and lead law enforcement officials to suspect an individual is violating federal immigration law. It is clear that racialized signals have significantly impacted a rise in deportations. According to Chawla (2018), the majority of US deportees are from Mexico, with Guatemala, Honduras, El Salvador, and the Dominican Republic following suit. Golash-Boza and Hondagneu-Sotelo (2013) state that "the criminalization of immigrants constitutes a new form of legal violence in Latino communities, legally sanctioned social suffering resulting from the convergence of immigration law and criminal law" (p. 276).

GLOBAL SPOTLIGHT

Racial Targeting in France

In France, 13 men who were Black or of Arab descent brought forth a lawsuit stating the police were specifically targeting and stopping them due to their ethnicity. The men stated they were being stopped, sometimes multiple times a day, and asked for their identity papers when attempting to complete daily tasks, such as going to school or work, even though none of the men had a criminal record. This case gained a lot of attention in France because it was the first time the problem had been specifically dealt with in court. Although many within the visible minority community stated they had been targeted and harassed by police on a regular basis for decades, the government had never addressed the issue because it did not keep data on stops by police to validate these claims. However, a recent study conducted by France's National Center for Scientific Research did find support for these claims and concluded that those who were Black were 12 times more likely and those who were Arab were 15 times more likely to be stopped by the police than those who were white (Sotto, 2016).

The court ruled that three of the 13 men had been stopped illegally based solely on their appearance. However, prior to this case there was not a way for citizens to prove they were being discriminated against by the police, making it incredibly difficult for someone to bring their case to court. The court attempted to remedy this by allowing those who feel they have been discriminated against to bring their case forward as long as there is some type of proof, for example, a witness to the incident. In these cases, the police officer will then have the opportunity to show they stopped the person based on an objective measure and not solely based on one's ethnicity (Sotto, 2016).

Citizenship profiling is best illustrated through *"show me your papers"* laws. For example, Arizona did not believe the federal government was doing enough in regards to immigration and decided to create their own laws. *Senate Bill 1070* has been recognized as the toughest state immigration law and was an attempt to make coming into the state of Arizona illegally so difficult that one would be deterred from doing so (Howe, 2012). Once the Arizona bill was passed there was concern that racial profiling would be used to determine who was undocumented, and the bill was initially stopped from being enacted by the federal courts and later partially by the United States Supreme Court. Section 2B of the bill is often referred to as "show me your papers," which refers to the police in Arizona having the power to stop and question, arrest, or detain anyone they believe to be undocumented. Section 3 of the bill states it is a crime to be in the state of Arizona without proper immigration documentation, while section 5C states it is a crime to be employed or apply for a job without proper immigration documentation. Section 6 states the Arizona police have the power to arrest those they have probable cause to believe have committed a crime that would warrant deportation (Howe, 2012).

In *Arizona v. United States*, the Supreme Court ruled that Sections 3, 5C, and 6 of Senate Bill 1070 were invalid because they violated the Tenth Amendment and the Supremacy Clause. For instance, Section 3, which stated it was a crime to be in Arizona without proper documentation, was invalid because the federal government already had laws regarding being in the United States illegally, and the state law was tougher than the federal law. The Court also ruled Section 5C was invalid because the federal government already had a system in place to work with employers and employees regarding immigration status, and the federal government had used its discretion and chosen not to criminalize this behavior on the part of the employees. Finally, the United States Supreme Court ruled that Section 6 was invalid, because only the federal government can arrest and possibly deport someone due to a warrant or the belief the person may attempt to escape, and the state law cannot be broader than the federal law (Howe, 2012).

However, the United States Supreme Court did not find Section 2B, "show me your papers," to be invalid. The federal government had argued there were concerns this law could lead to racial profiling. However, the Supreme Court disagreed, because the law stated the Arizona police must contact the federal government to determine whether someone is in the United States illegally, and this is something the United States Congress has already encouraged state governments to do. The Supreme Court also stated the issue of racial profiling could not be proven at this point and noted Senate Bill 1070 had provisions in the bill to prevent this, such as stating the police could not use one's race or ethnicity to determine immigration status. However, the court also noted that if racial profiling later became a problem this section of the bill could be challenged again in court (Howe, 2012). Since *Arizona v. US*, several copycat "show me your papers" laws have been passed in states such as Texas, Alabama, Georgia, Indiana, and Utah (Chawla, 2018).

The Effect of Racial Profiling on Community–Police Relations

It is important to understand racial profiling and how it occurs, because the research conducted on this topic has illustrated that this behavior damages police and community relations as well as the public's perception of the police. In one research study, both white and Black individuals completed surveys to better understand attitudes towards police and to examine if there were differences based on race. The study concluded that although the overwhelming majority of both Black and white survey takers agreed racial profiling was wrong, Black people were much more likely (81.6%) to state the issue was widespread in comparison to white people (60.2%). However, Black individuals also were more likely to state they had been profiled by police because of their race (40%), and this number increased dramatically (72.7%) when examining the responses of African American men between the ages of 18 and 34. The overwhelming majority of white people (95%), on the other hand, stated they had not been profiled based on their race (Weitzer & Tuch, 2002).

These experiences with the police directly impact our perception of the police and whether they are fair. For instance, 70% of Black survey takers reported that within their community they were treated less fairly than white people. However, only 33% of white survey takers agreed that Black people within their neighborhood were treated less fairly than white people. The study concluded by stating that race and personal experience were the strongest indicators of one's attitude towards police and their belief of whether the police treated people differently based on one's race (Weitzer & Tuch, 2002). These perceptions of fairness are incredibly important and directly impact the working relationship between the police and the community. If the community does not perceive the police treating people equally, for example, they are less likely to want to work with the police, which can make it extremely difficult for the police to do their jobs effectively.

Unwarranted suspicion based on demographics leads to heightened levels of scrutiny for certain racial and ethnic groups and less trust in the police. The lack of trust leads to concerns about procedural justice, which states that the way individuals perceive the police depends on whether or not they feel like they received fair treatment (Jackson et al., 2012). More recently, research has revealed that every year over 50 million Americans interact with the police. Half of those interactions are initiated by the officer. Police interactions do not just directly impact the individual but also may vicariously affect others in the community. There is increasing evidence that shows that Black Americans in particular are fearful of the police (Graham et al., 2020; Harrel et al., 2020). They fear for themselves as well as for their loved ones. This shows that racialized policing and profiling have a profound effect on Black lives. It is now more obvious than ever that race is a determinant for understanding police–community relations. In a recent nationwide study, Pickett et al. (2022) found that while white Americans feel protected by the police, Black Americans feared the police more than they feared being a victim of a crime. They found that these fears were mediated by lived experiences of negative interactions with the police.

Not only do Black people in America fear the police, they might also directly or vicariously experience racial trauma as a by-product of police interactions. Some suggest that police violence should be viewed as a public health crisis. There is evidence that shows police interactions have mental health implications, such as psychological distress, suicidal thoughts or attempts, and psychotic episodes (Devylder et al., 2018). Pickett et al. (2022) conclude that "Blacks and Whites live in a different world" as it relates to experiences, perceptions, and fear of the police. They call for a focused approach to reducing this fear as central to addressing "the police legitimacy crisis in the U.S." (Pickett et al., 2022).

Community-Oriented Policing as an Alternative to Race-Based Policing

Peyton et al. (2019) found that one positive interaction with the police can increase positive perceptions toward them. The positive perception relates to improved attitudes about police legitimacy, trust, and cooperation. One type of policing that has been regaining traction due to recent events is ***community-oriented policing***. Com-

Figure 6.3. © Adobe / Studio615.

munity-oriented policing allows law enforcement to work together with the community to create an atmosphere of trust, where the community also has a stake in their own safety. By working with the community, the police can better understand the needs of the community and enforce the laws in a preventative manner by working together (COPS, 2014).

There are three parts of community policing that must come together and occur simultaneously in order for this strategy to be successful. First, a ***community partnership*** must occur, where the police work with stakeholders within the community to determine their needs and to create solutions. The police working with the community helps to build a sense of trust within the community, where everyone is working together to prevent crime and reduce fear of crime instead of coming into the community only when there are problems occurring. Community partnerships can take on many forms, for example, working with government agencies, such as parole, probation, schools, legislators, other police departments, and social services. Community leaders or groups also are a powerful way to reach out to the community at large and to gain their support. If law enforcement is able to work with those who are viewed as leaders within the community and gain their trust; these stakeholders can then reach out to the larger community to garner their buy in and support. Nonprofits within the community also make excellent community partners and because they often offer services within the community, they tend to have a handle on what the needs of the community are based on their services and how often they are used (COPS, 2014).

The second element of community-oriented policing that must occur is the ***organizational component***, where within the law enforcement agency, the management, police officers, and technology must come together to support the mission of community-oriented policing. In order for the shift from reactive to proactive policing to be effective, community-oriented policing must be recognized at all levels within the organization. Management, for instance, must create an atmosphere that supports prevention strategies and community partnerships to achieve those proactive tactics. Those in positions of leadership also must be role models for working with community partners and be willing to try new and innovative strategies to prevent crime. Police unions also must be included in the discussion and feel as though they have a stake in the process, which will help their membership to also buy into the new strategies. Police officers need to feel they have discretion or the decision to act or not act when working with the community on a daily basis. If officers working directly with the community are given discretion to make decisions they will feel as though they have more at stake in the initiative and feel more invested in their role in the community (COPS, 2014).

Policies and mission statements should reflect the goals of community-oriented policing and become institutionalized within the agency. The policies also should be transparent, easily understandable, and communicated effectively to the community. Transparency is incredibly important in order to create a foundation of trust between the police and the community. It also is important to take into consideration where police officers are assigned within the community and to provide long-term assignments within the same part of the community. This allows the police officers to have more contact with the same people on a daily basis, so they can build a rapport with those they see every day within the neighborhood. Police officers need to be able to respond to multiple needs within the community and work effectively as part of a team to problem solve. Therefore, it is important that management keep these needs in mind when recruiting, hiring, and training new officers. Technology also plays an important part by providing effective communication between the police and the community as well as internally within the agency. Technology also can be used to help police who are working within the community keep up to date with what is going on in the community, so they can make better informed decisions on the spot (COPS, 2014).

The third element of community-oriented policing that must occur is **problem solving**. Community-oriented policing is a proactive policing strategy that focuses on prevention. Therefore, problem solving must be actively examined in all decision making. To assist police officers in becoming problem-solving oriented the SARA model (Scan, Analyze, Respond, and Assess) can be utilized to create solutions. First, law enforcement must scan or identify the problems within the community that are directly impacting the police and the community, while determining who the stakeholders are and whether the problem is a priority for both the police and the community. Second, law enforcement needs to analyze or better understand the problem by examining the research as well as the offender, victim, and location of the problem. Third, law enforcement and community stakeholders respond by using what was learned through the analysis phase to create strategies to reduce or eliminate the problem. Finally, assessment by all involved must occur to determine what about the response is working and what is not in an attempt to continuously improve the problem-solving strategy (COPS, 2014).

Critiques of Community-Oriented Policing

The majority of the criticisms of community-oriented policing programs focus on how the programs are implemented and in particular how some within the neighborhood feel targeted by the police (Jones-Brown, 2015). Therefore, it is important that when community-oriented policing programs are put into place the police officers are viewed as a resource within the community and not as a threat. Community policing programs are often touted by political leaders as the answer to poor police and community relations, but they also tend to emphasize there should be additional police officers placed within the community when the program is implemented (Starr, 2015). However, an increase in the number of law enforcement officers within a community that already has a negative view of the police based on past experience will be viewed as an occupying force rather than a resource. This is especially true if once the program is implemented policies such as stop and frisk become more widely used and community members have more negative interactions with the police than prior to program implementation. Therefore, community-oriented policing programs should not increase the number of police officers within a community, but instead examine how the number of officers already in place can potentially be reassigned to implement this program. It is important also to remember that police and community relations are sometimes adversarial by nature and that those police officers working within this capacity will need to receive extensive training to ensure the program is being implemented as intended (Starr, 2015).

However, it should be noted that community-oriented policing is not a panacea. Even a carefully implemented and evaluated community policing program does not resolve the issue of racialized police violence, which is an underlying cause of police and community mistrust and something that must be addressed before a community-oriented policing program can be successful. For example, there is genuine fear in many communities, particularly communities of color, that law enforcement officers can harm or kill a person suspected of a crime without losing their job or facing any penalty from the criminal justice system for their behavior. This concern cannot be addressed until those police officers who harm community members without justification or provocation are held accountable for their actions; so far this has not happened in the overwhelming majority of cases (Starr, 2015). Targeting community members based on their race or ethnicity reinforces the belief within some communities that the police can abuse and even unjustly kill members of their community with little to no penalty. Unfortunately, this only deepens an already wide divide between the police and the community. In this environment, it can be nearly impossible to implement a program that seeks to improve and increase trust between the police and the community without addressing the cause of the mistrust.

Summary

Due to media coverage and lawsuits as well as internal and external law enforcement investigations, the awareness of racial profiling based on race, ethnicity, national origin, and religion is growing. Some changes have taken place to stop the use of racial profiling, but the problem still exists. It is imperative that we continue to collect data on current policies and analyze them to better understand their strengths and weakness, so we can attempt to address the problem. Some of this has been done and is occurring, but this process cannot stop if we want to ensure Fourteenth Amendment rights (or equal protection) under the law for all.

Discussion Questions

1. How are the terms profiling and racial profiling similar and different? Be sure to provide examples.

2. What are stop-and-frisk policies? Provide examples. In your opinion, should the police be allowed to use stop-and-frisk policies? Be sure to support your answer using information from the chapter.

3. How does crimmigration and citizenship profiling impact communities and their relationships to the police?

Key Terms

Profiling	Priority Enforcement Program
United States v. Sokolow	Crimmigration
racial profiling	citizenship profiling
Whren v. United States	Immigration and Nationality Act
Secure Communities	Senate Bill 1070
Wilkins v. Maryland State Police	show me your papers
"driving while Black"	community-oriented policing
probable cause	community partnership
stop and frisk	organizational component
Terry v. Ohio	problem solving
stop, question, and frisk	

References

American Civil Liberties Union (ACLU). (n.d.). Arizona's SB 1070. https://www.aclu.org/feature/arizonas-sb-1070

Associated Press. (2013). Federal appeals court upholds rulings that stop-and-frisk is unconstitutional. *The Guardian*. http://www.theguardian.com/world/2013/nov/22/federal-appeals-court-upholds-rulings-stop-frisk-unconstitutional

Associated Press. (2015). U.S. judge dismisses challenge of Arizona's SB 1070 immigration law. *Los Angeles Times*. http://www.latimes.com/nation/immigration/la-na-nn-arizona-immigration-law-20150905-story.html

Baumgartner, F.A., Epp, D.A., & Shoub, K. (2017). Racial disparities in routine traffic stops. *Duke Forum for Law & Social Change*, 9(21), 21–53.

Baumgartner, F.A., Epp, D.A., & Shoub, K. (2018). *Suspect citizens: What 20 million traffic stops tell ss about policing and race*. Cambridge University Press.

Bureau of Justice Statistics. (2009). Traffic stops. http://www.bjs.gov/index.cfm?ty=tp&tid=702

Chawla, M. (2018). "Show me your papers": An equal protection violation of the rights of Latino men in Trump's America. *Touro Law Review*, *34*(4). https://digitalcommons.tourolaw.edu/lawreview/vol34/iss4/15

Cobbina, J. E. (2019). *Hands up don't shoot: Why the protests in Ferguson and Baltimore matter, and how they changed America*. New York University Press.

Cogan, M. R. (1992). The Drug Enforcement Agency's use of drug courier profiles: One size fits all. *Catholic University Law Review*, *41*(4), 943.https://scholarship.law.edu/lawreview/vol41/iss4/6

Conley, W. V. (1982). Mendenhall and Reid: The drug courier profile and investigative stops. *University of Pittsburgh Law Review*, *42*, 835.

COPS. (2014). Community policing defined. US Department of Justice. Retrieved from http://www.cops.usdoj.gov/pdf/vets-to-cops/e030917193-CP-Defined.pdf.

Davis, E., Whyde, A., & Langton, L. (2018). *Contacts between police and the public, 2015*. U.S. Department of Justice, Bureau of Justice Statistics. https://www.bjs.gov/content/pub/pdf/cpp15.pdf

DeVylder J. E., Jun H.-J., Fedina L., Coleman, D., Anglin, D., Cogburn, C., Link, B., & Barth, R. P. (2018). Association of exposure to police violence with prevalence of mental health symptoms among urban residents in the United States. *JAMA Network Open*, *1*(7). https://jamanetwork.com/journals/jamanetworkopen/fullarticle/2715611

Dey, I. (1998). Drug courier profiles: An infringement on Fourth Amendment rights. *University of Baltimore Law Forum*, *28*(2).

Dwyer, C. (2017). Of courts and confusion: Here's the reaction to Trump's immigration freeze. NPR. http://www.npr.org/sections/thetwo-way/2017/01/29/512272524/of-courts-and-confusion-heres-the-reaction-to-trumps-immigration-freeze

Find Law. (n.d.). Federal vs. state immigration laws. http://immigration.findlaw.com/immigration-laws-and-resources/federal-vs-state-immigration-laws.html

The Free Dictionary. (n.d.). Stop and frisk. http://legal-dictionary.thefreedictionary.com/Stop+and+Frisk

Gabbatt, A. (2013). Stop-and-frisk: Only 3% of 2.4m stops result in conviction, study finds. *The Guardian*. http://www.theguardian.com/world/2013/nov/14/stop-and-frisk-new-york-conviction-rate

Gamboa, S. (2015). Obama ends Secure Communities Program that helped hike deportations. NBC News. http://www.nbcnews.com/storyline/immigration-reform/obama-ends-secure-communities-program-helped-hike-deportations-n253541

Golash-Boza, T., & Hondagneu-Sotelo, P. (2013). Latino immigrant men and the deportation crisis: A gendered racial removal program. *Latino Studies*, 11(3), 271–292.

Graham, A., Cullen, F. T., Pickett, J. T., Jonson, C. L., Haner, M., & Sloan, M. M. (2020). Faith in Trump, moral foundations, and social distancing defiance during the coronavirus pandemic. *Socius*, 6, 1–23.

Harris, D. A. (1999). Driving while Black: Racial profiling on our nation's highways. American Civil Liberties Union. https://www.aclu.org/report/driving-while-black-racial-profiling-our-nations-highways

Harris, D. A. (2020). Racial profiling: Past, present, and future? https://www.americanbar.org/groups/criminal_justice/publications/criminal-justice-magazine/2020/winter/racial-profiling-past-present-and-future/

Harris, A., & Amutah-Onukagha, N. (2019). Under the radar: Strategies used by Black mothers to prepare their sons for potential police interactions. *Journal of Black Psychology*, **45**(6–7), 439–453.

Hawley, C., Goldman, A., Sullivan, E., & Apuzzo, A. (2015). Highlights of AP's Pulitzer Prize-winning probe into NYPD intelligence operations. Associated Press. https://www.ap.org/about/awards-and-recognition/highlights-of-aps-pulitzer-prize-winning-probe-into-nypd-intelligence-operations

Hill, G., & Hill, K. (n.d.) Probable cause. http://dictionary.law.com/Default.aspx?selected=1618

Homeland Security. (2015). Fixing our broken immigration system through executive action—Key facts. http://www.dhs.gov/immigration-action

Horn, C. (2020, June 12). Racial disparities revealed in massive traffic stop dataset. https://www.sc.edu/uofsc/posts/2020/06/racial_disparities_traffic_stops.php#.YIh1OJNKhQI

Howe, A. (2012). SB 1070: In plain English. SCOTUS blog. http://www.scotusblog.com/2012/06/s-b-1070-in-plain-english/

Jackson, J., Bradford, B., Hough, M., Myhill, A., Quinton, P., & Tyler, T. R. (2012) Why do people comply with the law? Legitimacy and the influence of legal institutions, *British Journal of Criminology*, 52, 6, 1051–1071.

Johnson, J. C. (2014). The Secure Communities Program, as we know it, will be discontinued. U.S. Department of Homeland Security. https://www.dhs.gov/sites/default/files/publications/14_1120_memo_secure_communities.pdf

Jones-Brown, D. (2015). Neighborhood policing: A safe, respectful, and effective community policing strategy. US Department of Justice. Retrieved from https://cops.usdoj.gov/pdf/taskforce/submissions/Jones_Brown_Delores_Testimony.pdf.

Kadish, M. J. (1997). The drug courier profile: In planes, train and automobiles and now in the jury box. *American University Law Review, 46*(3), 747.

Kocieniewski, D. (2002). Study suggests racial gap in speeding in New Jersey. *New York Times*. http://www.nytimes.com/2002/03/21/nyregion/study-suggests-racial-gap-in-speeding-in-new-jersey.html?pagewanted=all

Kohli, A., Markowitz, P. A., & Chavez, L. (2011). Secure Communities by the numbers: An analysis of demographics and due process. The Chief Justice Earl Warren Institute on Law and Social Policy. https://www.law.berkeley.edu/files/Secure_Communities_by_the_Numbers.pdf

Legal Information Institute. (n.d.a). 10th Amendment. https://www.law.cornell.edu/constitution/tenth_amendment

Legal Information Institute. (n.d.b). Reasonable suspicion. https://www.law.cornell.edu/wex/reasonable_suspicion

Legal Information Institute. (n.d.c). Supremacy clause. https://www.law.cornell.edu/wex/supremacy_clause

Meeks, K. (2000). *Driving while black: highways, shopping malls, taxi cabs, sidewalks: How to fight back if you are a victim of racial.* Crown.

Merriam-Webster. (2015). Profiling. http://www.merriam-webster.com/dictionary/profiling

Morales, M. C., & Curry, T. R. (2021). Citizenship profiling and diminishing procedural justice: Local immigration enforcement and the reduction of police legitimacy among individuals and in Latina/o neighbourhoods. *Ethnic and Racial Studies, 44*(1), 134–153.

Oyez. (n.d.). *Whren v. United States.* https://www.oyez.org/cases/1995/95-5841.

Parascandola, R. (2015). NYPD officially debuts stop-and-frisk 'receipts' and new rules for cops. *New York Daily News.* http://www.nydailynews.com/new-york/nyc-crime/nypd-debuts-stop-and-frisk-receipts-new-rules-cops-article-1.2374455

Peyton, K., Sierra-Arevalo, M., & Rand, D. G. (2019). A field experiment on community policing and police legitimacy. *PNAS, 116*(40), 19894–19898.

Pickett, J. T., Graham, A., & Cullen, F. T. (2022). The American racial divide in fear of the police. *Criminology, 60*(2), 291–320.

Rice, S. K., Reitzel, J. D., & Piquero, A. (2005). Shades of brown: Perceptions of racial profiling and the intra-ethnic differential. *Journal of Ethnicity in Criminal Justice, 3*(1/2), 47–70.

Seghetti, L. M. (2009). Enforcing immigration law: The role of state and local law enforcement. Congressional Research Service. https://www.everycrsreport.com/files/20090311_RL32270_a7bbe8763684424b48f0d4b1d61c92412ac50d0c.pdf

Sotto, P. (2016). The French court: Police illegally checked three minority men. Associated Press. http://bigstory.ap.org/article/9a55dab8c4fa46878a9edad27901925d/french-top-court-rule-racial-profiling-first-time

Starr, T. J. (2015). Community policing is not the solution for police brutality. It makes it worse. *The Washington Post*. Retrieved from https://www.washingtonpost.com/posteverything/wp/2015/11/03/community-policing-is-not-the-solution-to-police-brutality-it-makes-it-worse/?utm_term=.940eb1c31279.

Tidball, J. (2012). Routine justice: Research shows how racial and gender profiling can affect outcome of traffic stops. Kansas State University. https://www.k-state.edu/media/newsreleases/jun12/racialprofiling62112.html

Tucker, E. (2014). White House issues guidelines to ban racial and religious profiling. PBS News Hour. http://www.pbs.org/newshour/rundown/white-house-issues-guidelines-ban-racial-religious-profiling/

U.S. v. Sokolow, 490 U.S. 1 (1989)

U.S. Immigration and Customs Enforcement (ICE). (n.d.). Secure Communities. https://www.ice.gov/secure-communities

Weitzer, R., & Tuch, S. A. (2002). Perceptions of racial profiling: Race, class, and personal experience. *Criminology, 404*, 435–456.

SEVEN

The Militarization of Law Enforcement and Protest Policing

Learning Objectives

1. Critically examine how the federal 1033 Program has led to the militarization of the police within the United States.
2. Gain knowledge on the relationship between militarization, protest policing, and community relations.
3. Understand how the militarization of the police has damaged police and community relations within many communities, making it more difficult for law enforcement to do their job, and invoking calls to defund the police.

This chapter will examine how local and state law enforcement has participated in federal programs that distribute excess military equipment. The intention of these programs was to help police officers be better equipped to engage in the War on Drugs and the War on Terror at the state and local level. However, much of this equipment has been used outside of its original intended scope and has created a police force that resembles the military in many communities. This has led to the unintended consequence of heavily damaged relationships between the police and the community, particularly in poorer communities where the majority population are people of color. Recent events have shed light on how militarized police respond to protests for social and racial justice. The protests in response to the deaths of Breonna Taylor and George Floyd provide a backdrop for examining the role of using military-grade equipment to police communities of color.

IN FOCUS

Breonna Taylor

In 2020, the militarization model was deployed across the country as protests erupted in the wake of the deaths of Breonna Taylor and George Floyd. The 2020 protests were marked with imagery and media depictions of violent riots and conflicting grassroots reports of peaceful protests. On March 13, 2020, using a **no-knock warrant**, the Louisville Metro Police Department (LMPD) entered the home of Breonna Taylor. A series of disturbing events led to her death and the arrest of her boyfriend, Kenneth Walker. The initial reports led the public to believe that Ms. Taylor was receiving drug-related mail for a former boyfriend. The protests began after the public became aware of the false narratives of the night.

A group of local residents called the 502 Live Streamers began documenting the daily occupation of a local park where protests were often organized. Eventually, the local police department began their own livestream to show their perspective of the protests. In addition, there were news stations who reported live incidences of militarized police, such as a reporter displaying press credentials was still pepper balled by a Louisville Metro Police Officer. On May 29, 2020, a local news crew was reporting on the protests in response to the killing of Breonna Taylor. On live television, the audience witnessed a local reporter, Kaitlin Rust, and her cameraperson, James Dobson, pepper balled by LMPD after clearly following police instructions, including standing behind the police, not obstructing law enforcement activities, and displaying press credentials while possessing professional-grade equipment (Fabrizio, 2020). The media depictions of the 2020 protests follow those of their predecessors. News coverage of Ferguson shows the media as an "agenda setter and agenda builder" (Arora et al., 2019). The blending of protesters as media in 2020, like the 502 Livestreamers, presented a new mechanism used in protests.

The Militarization of Police and the Increased Use of SWAT

In 1990, the Department of Defense created the *1033 Program* to assist local and state law enforcement in their fight against the War on Drugs. In 1996, this program was made permanent by the United States Congress, and after the 2001 terrorist attacks the program was expanded to include the War on Terror. When President Bill Clinton signed the National Defense Authorization Act of 1997 (H.R. 3230), it permitted the Secretary of Defense to transfer what are deemed to be excess military weapons from the United States military to local and state law enforcement to combat the War on Drugs and the War on Terror (Delehanty et al., 2017). The equipment is free, but local and state law enforcement must pay for the delivery and maintenance of the equipment. The 1033 Program originally was created to distribute property no longer being used by the military, but audits of the program have shown 36% of the property distributed is new (Dansky et al., 2014). Other research shows that 80% of all U.S. counties have received equipment, with a 1,414% program expansion between 2006 to 2013 (Radil et al., 2017).

Police militarization is the practice buying into and promoting a culture of using force as the solution to problems. The two forms of police militarization are direct and indirect. **Direct militarization** refers to the utilization of armed forces for domestic police work. This type of police militarization can be traced back to the 1903 National Guard Act, when the federal government allowed state militias to act in national defense. Indirect police militarization relies on police departments gearing themselves with military-grade equipment (Balko, 2014). **Indirect militarization** was encouraged through the 1033 Program. It is argued that both strategies are becoming more interconnected, and this was evident in the 2020 racial justice protests. For example, in Louisville, Kentucky, the national guard was called in to assist the Louisville Metro Police Department (LMPD) to manage protests erupting across the city. It is important to note that military leaders have not been historically supportive of "the use of the military to quell disruptions" (Balko, 2014, p. 36). On June 1, 2020, the Kentucky National Guard, in town to enforce a citywide protest curfew, shot and killed David McAtee, a local well-known barbeque cook. The aftermath of McAtee's killing reverberated in a city already reeling from the death of Breonna Taylor and further fractured the relationship between law enforcement and the community.

The 1033 Program has been widely utilized and continues to grow as more equipment has become available for distribution, due to the War on Terror abroad. In 1990, for example, 1 million dollars of property was transferred from the military to local and state police for the fight against drugs, with this number reaching $324 million in 1995. However, by 2013, the amount of equipment given to local and state law enforcement had grown to $450 million in one year. Overall, since 1990, $4.3 billion in property has been transferred to 17,000 federal and state law enforcement agencies within all 50 states (Dansky et al., 2014).

There are very few criteria in place for local and state law enforcement to meet in order to receive the military-grade weapons. First, the police department must be able to demonstrate on their application they plan to use the equipment to fight the War on Terror or the War on Drugs within their state, city, or town. Second, all local and state law enforcement agencies must have an equal chance to receive the equipment no matter their size or location. Third, once the equipment is received it must be used within one year to demonstrate need. Fourth, once an agency receives the property it can only be transferred to other law enforcement agencies within that state (Dansky et al., 2014).

Access to military weapons as well as the criteria that the equipment be used within one year has directly impacted how police officers engage the community when enforcing the law. For instance, the use of *SWAT* or Special Weapons and Tactics has increased significantly. SWAT was originally intended to be utilized for barricade situations, when hostages have been taken, or when there is an active shooter. However, due to the 1033 Program, more local law enforcement agencies have access to SWAT equipment, including flashbang grenades, battering rams, and armored personnel carriers, making it easier for them to create and deploy SWAT teams. In the 1980s, for example, only 20% of small towns had a SWAT team, but by the mid-2000s this number had grown to 80% of small towns and 90% of large cities. SWAT raids also became more common; for instance, in the 1980s there were approximately 3,000 SWAT raids nationally, but by the mid-2000s this number had grown to 45,000 raids a year (Kraska, 2007).

SWAT teams are incredibly intimidating when they conduct a raid, since they are often dressed in military fatigues and arrive with military-grade equipment. This is intended to create a psychological impact as well as help to protect the police officers during the raid. In a typical SWAT raid, the police officers arrive at the location in an armored personnel carrier with a search warrant to search the property. The armored personnel carrier is not armed with a gun on the roof as it would be in war; instead police officers use the vehicle as a shield to hide behind and as a place to regroup. If the police officers believe the suspect will destroy evidence or is a physical threat, they will enter the location using a battering ram to destroy doors or windows and gain entry without announcing their presence. Once inside, the officers may deploy flashbang grenades, which when detonated produce a blinding light and a deafening sound that can debilitate those inside for 5–10 seconds. The flashbang grenades are used to allow the SWAT team to enter the location safely by temporarily disabling those inside (Dansky et al., 2014).

IN FOCUS

War on Drugs

The War on Drugs and access to military equipment has increased the use of SWAT teams within smaller police departments. However, due to size and funding these smaller departments do not have access to the same training and dedicated personnel as larger police agencies (National Tactical Officers Association, 2008). This can be problematic; for example, in Georgia a county sheriff's SWAT team used a no-knock warrant to enter a home where a man was suspected of selling methamphetamines (Lynn & Gutman, 2014). After attempting to enter the home, the officers noticed something was blocking the door. They used a battering ram on the door to gain access to the house and threw a flashbang grenade through the door. The SWAT team found the home occupied by the mother of the man suspected of selling methamphetamines along with her brother, his wife, and their four chil-dren. The police later learned the door had been blocked by a playpen where a 19-month-old was sleeping. The flashbang grenade had landed in the baby's bed, severely injuring him so that he required weeks of hospitalization and care. How-ever, there were not any drugs or weapons found in the home, and the suspected drug dealer was later arrested at a home in the neighborhood without the use of a SWAT team or a no-knock warrant (Lynn & Gutman, 2014).

An investigation into the case later disclosed the judge who had signed the no-knock warrant had been told a confidential informant had purchased drugs at the house and had noticed weapons within the home (Channel 2, 2015). A no-knock warrant is used when the police have a reasonable suspicion that those inside the location might destroy physical evidence or be a physical threat (Dansky et al., 2014). However, one of the deputies involved later admitted that it was the friend of the confidential informant who had made the drug purchase and no one had observed any weapons on the premises. The judge concluded he would not have signed a warrant for this investigation if he had been presented with an accurate portrayal of the situation. The SWAT team also stated they were unaware there were children in the home, and they would have not used the flashbang grenade if they had known. A state grand jury decided not to indict the members of the SWAT team on any criminal charges, but did conclude the investigation was rushed and sloppy. The drug task force that provided the information was disbanded. The fed-eral government later investigated the case and indicted the deputy that present-ed the evidence to obtain the no-knock warrant with civil rights violations for vio-lating the Fourth Amendment rights of those within the house. The jury found the deputy not guilty on all charges, and she has since resigned (Channel 2, 2015). Nearly two years after the incident, the family received a monetary award of $3.65 million for the baby's injuries from the city and county (Penny, 2016).

SWAT teams were intended to be used during situations where the police need extra protection, for instance, if there is an active shooter, a hostage situation, or someone deemed a threat has barricaded himself into a location and refused to come out. However, we know very little about when SWAT teams are deployed because data on these tactics are not collected at the federal level, while local and state law enforce-ment agencies typically collect data internally or sometimes not at all. The state of Maryland is the only state to collect data on SWAT use and release it to the public. However, this measure was only put in place after a small-town mayor in Maryland was mistakenly targeted for suspicion of receiving marijuana shipped through the mail. During the SWAT raid, his family was held at gunpoint for hours, and their two family dogs were killed by the police. The mayor then created a public campaign to change how SWAT was used in Maryland, but at this point only data is being collected on their use. The data collected in Maryland on SWAT raids, from 2010 to 2012, concluded most SWAT teams were deployed for nonviolent misdemeanor and felony offenses, while forced entry was used for both standard warrants and no-knock warrants (Dansky et al., 2014).

Due to the lack of information on how SWAT teams were being deployed nationally, the American Civil Liberties Union (ACLU) decided to conduct a study to better understand where and how SWAT raids were being utilized. The ACLU used public record requests and asked law enforcement agencies to release their records on the use of SWAT teams. The ACLU were able to examine 818 records from 20 different local law enforcement agencies in 11 states spanning from 2010 to 2013. Based on these records, the ACLU was able to conclude that 79% of SWAT raids were used to search homes with 62% of these raids being conducted to search the home for drugs. Only 7% of all raids were used for hostage, barricade, or active shooter situations. Half of all raids also caused significant damage to the property being searched, due to the use of battering rams and flashbang grenades. The ACLU also discovered a racial component of who was the target of the SWAT raids; for example, 42% of those targeted were Black, with an additional 12% reporting their ethnicity as Latino. The percentage of minorities targeted for SWAT raids increases even further to 61% when examining just those raids conducted for drug searches. The ACLU also concluded that SWAT raids for drug searches were typically deployed where the suspect was a person of color, while in hostage, barricade, and active shooter situations the suspect was typically white (Dansky et al., 2014).

IN FOCUS

SWAT Raids

Since SWAT raids were typically being deployed during drug searches in low-income communities, many Americans were unaware local law enforcement had access to military-grade weapons. However, this changed as media outlets nationwide covered the protests in Ferguson, Missouri, that occurred after the shooting death of Michael Brown, an unarmed teenager, by a Ferguson police officer. During the first week of protests, the St. Louis County Police Department utilized many of their military weapons obtained through the 1033 Program to intimidate the protestors. For instance, the police dressed in military camouflage and carried riot gear as well as tear gas to meet the protestors. Several local law enforcement officers arrived in armored personnel carriers with a police officer on top aiming large guns at the crowds below, while other Ferguson officers were on top of buildings within the community armed with sniper guns pointed at the protestors (Shinkman, 2014).

The actions of the St. Louis County Police were heavily criticized as the media covered the scene of what looked more like an international war zone than a protest within a small city in America. The St. Louis County Police defended their actions by stating if they had not used the military equipment the police would have been forced to use their weapons against the crowd and by using the military equipment it created an atmosphere where protestors did not engage with the police in this manner. However, the national criticism regarding the militarization of local police continued, and during the second week of protests, the governor of Missouri ordered the state highway patrol to take over crowd control from the St. Louis County Police (Madhani, 2014).

Militarization and Protest Policing

In the nineteenth century, as the U.S. became more industrialized, there was an increase in social tensions caused by growing inequality and poor working conditions. Social problems were exacerbated. Rioting became the political strategy used to fight for equal rights. These riots were the early form of union strikes and were quelled by police who had the legal backing to use force for order maintenance. According to Potter:

> More than crime, modern police forces in the United States emerged as a response to "disorder." What constitutes social and public order depends largely on who is defining those terms, and in the cities of 19th century America they were defined by the mercantile interests, who through taxes and political influence supported the development of bureaucratic policing institutions. These economic interests had a greater interest in social control than crime control. (n.d.)

The activities described as needing control were disorder related and often included "public drunkenness, hooliganism, political protests and worker riots" (Potter, n.d.). These disorder offenses were blamed on biological inferiority, immortality, and the low-skilled working class. Using violence as a response to protests has a long history in the U.S. As such, **protest policing** is embedded in the fabric of policing as is the social construction of disorder. It is documented that early, urbanized police departments did not distinguish between social control and crime control (Potter, n.d.) and were focused on maintaining economic power. According to della Porta and colleagues (2006/2016):

> protest policing has been defined as: The control of protest which requires a difficult balance between the protection of legal order and defense of individu-

Figure 7.1. A police force maintaining order during a rally. © Adobe Stock/teksomolika

al freedom, and citizens' rights to political participation. Protest policing operates as an indicator of the quality of democracy[;] its implementation may affect the evolution of protest, [and it] is affected by activist tactics. (p. 3)

Protest policing involves the strategies used to maintain order during protest activities (Vitale, 2018). Protesting is an essential element for participation in a democracy, yet it is evident that protest activity is often interrupted and controlled through governmental actions and authority (Maguire, 2015). There are several protest policing strategies that have been deployed. The first, the *escalated force model*, was characterized by a mindset where police used the amount of force necessary to control the situation. This model assumes that if the police display dominance then protestors will be forced into compliance (Maguire, 2015). The escalated force model has five characteristics:

1. Lack of appreciation or respect for protesters' First Amendment rights;
2. An intolerance for community disruption and a tendency for police to equate civil disobedience with anarchy;
3. A minimal level of communication or negotiation between police and protestors;
4. The widespread use of arrest, often under tenuous or legally questionable circumstances; and
5. Over-reliance by the police on the use of force. (Maguire, 2015, p. 75)

The escalated force model has been criticized for its treatment of protests, even peaceful assemblies, as riots. This type of domination of force technique has been shown to escalate conflicts with protesters as seen in the "riots" of the 1960s.

In response to a number of commissioned reports, the 1970s ushered in a new model of protest policing. The ***negotiated management model*** was the prominent manner to address civil unrest from the late 1970s to the late 1990s. This model was based on the assumption that police and the protestors have to work together to achieve desired outcomes. It opened the communication between the police and protesters, allowing for a more collaborative approach while decreasing the need to use force (Maguire, 2015). In this model, both the police and the protesters appointed a representative who would have ongoing and open communication. This form of protest policing was prevalent until the late 1990s when the first "wired protest" happened.

The World Trade Organization Conference (WTO) in Seattle marked a new era in protest policing. The protest informed police that protesters were utilizing new technology to coordinate their efforts and some were not interested in negotiating. As a result, an era of more aggressive tactics ensued. These more invasive approaches are known as the strategic incapacitation model, the command and control model, or the Miami model (Maguire, 2015; Vitale, 2018). The ***Miami model*** is named after tactics used in 2003 by the Miami Police Department during the Free Trade Area of the Americas meetings (Vitale, 2018).

According to Vitale (2018), the Miami model is employed when the police feel certain groups must be controlled by "no protest zones, heavy use of lethal force weaponry, surveillance of protest organizations, negative advance publicity about protest groups, preemptive arrests, preventative detentions, and extensive restrictions on protest timing and locations" (p. 215). The Miami model is reminiscent of the escalated force model, acts as an extension of police militarization, and seriously limits the right to protest. He notes that "even when there is isolated criminal conduct within a demonstration, police have an obligation to target those engaged in illegal behavior without criminalizing or brutalizing the entire demonstration, as long as the primary character remains peaceful" (p. 216). He further suggests that using armored vehicles and snipers to manage protests is unnecessary and promotes the imbalance between officer protection, police legitimacy, and constitutional rights.

GLOBAL SPOTLIGHT

Police Militarization in Latin America

While there are certainly different conceptions of civil and human rights around the world, there are some common ideas around how communities should and should not be policed. For instance, most would argue that "extrajudicial executions, crime scene manipulation, warrantless searches, arbitrary arrests and enforced disappearances" would fall outside of global standards of decency and justice (Flores-Macias & Zarkin, 2019, p. 529). In contrast to the U.S., militarization of law enforcement in Latin America takes on different forms. Flores-Macias and Zarkin (2019) provide a continuum of the "degree of militarization in law enforcement" in Latin America. The continuum ranges from "non-militarized police" to "generalized constabularization of the military" (p. 525). Non militarized policing rarely exists in Latin America outside of very few organizations at the "subnational level." On the continuum, higher degrees of militarization include paramilitary police under civilian control and constabularized police where countries allow the militaries to engage in law enforcement activities under military law. Paramilitary police are those with limited access while constabularized police have "full access heavier weapons and equipment" (p. 521).

Colombia is an example of a "generalized constabularization of the military" (p. 526), where they have both a national police but allow their military to address criminal activity such as drug trafficking and organized crime. Flores-Macias and Zarkin (2019) reported that "300,000 members of the armed forces work in citizen security activities" across Colombia (p. 527). Since the 1950s, the Colombian National Police, which boasts 140,000 officers, has been one of the few in the Americas that are housed in the Ministry of Defense the same as their armed forces.

In 2021, Colombia made international news when the Colombia National Police disrupted protests for economic justice issues exacerbated by COVID-19. The Mobile Anti-Disturbance Cadron, or ESMAD, are national police who are trained to work with large crowds but do not carry deadly weapons. During the "National Strike" of 2021, ESMAD were unable to maintain control so National Police officers came in and reportedly beat, detained, and killed protestors (Turkawitz & Villamil, 2021). Amnesty International reported one incident, called "Operation Siloe," pulled together ESMAD and the Special Operations Group of the National Police of Colombia (GOES) to respond to protestors in the city of Cali. The operation included the use of deadly weapons that led to at least three protesters' deaths.

Figure 7.2. Black Lives Matter Memorial in Davis, CA. © Creative Commons / sdttds

Police Reform and Militarization

Police reform strategies tend to increase police budgets and technology utilization, rely on the idea that police increase public safety, and increase the scale of policing (Critical Resistance, n.d.). *Reformist strategies* include body cameras, community policing, diversity training, and civilian review boards. *Abolitionist strategies* focus on reducing budgets and the use of technology while striving to scale down the scope of policing (Critical Resistance, n.d.). Police abolitionists believe in suspending paid administrative leave, withholding pensions from officers who use excessive force, making officers responsible for their own misconduct settlements, and caps on overtime pay. In addition, abolitionist strategies also promote police demilitarization. More specifically, demilitarization would focus on reducing the scale of policing. This would require reallocating militarization funds to resources that increase community and grassroot organizational budgets and focus on other structural issues such as housing, health, and education.

The 2020 protests resulted in a mainstream awareness of the terminology "Defund the Police." The debate about militarizing the police is unextractable from arguments to defund. In addition to the 1033 Program, it is further evidenced that after the 9/11 attacks, the Department of Homeland Security (DHS) has liberally doled out anti-terrorism grants to the extent that many municipalities and towns are able to now buy military-grade weapons for law enforcement purposes (Balko, 2014). Between 2001 and 2011, DHS dispersed approximately $34 billion of anti-terrorism grants that supported municipalities that were unlikely terrorism targets.

It has been noted that the DHS grants overshadowed the 1033 Program's dissemination of military-grade equipment to law enforcement. In fact, in 2011 alone DHS awarded $2 billion in grants, which was four times more than that supplied by 1033 (Balko, 2014). With the funds, these towns purchased military-grade weaponry such as:

- Fargo, ND: $8 million for assault rifles, Kevlar helmets, an armored truck
- Augusta, ME: $1,500 in tactical vests
- Des Moines, IA: $180,000 for bomb disarming robots
- Montgomery County, TX: $300,000 pilotless surveillance drone (p. 256)

The concept of defunding the police is not just a response to the 2020 protests. In fact, it could probably better be described as an evolution of thought related to reimagining public safety and protection. The contemporary calls for defunding the police are rooted in the abolitionist perspectives that can be attributed to works such as Angela Davis's "Are Prisons Obsolete" (2003). Defunding the police is a process for reimagining how safety is defined and implemented in communities. Patrisse Cullors defines the notion of ***defund the police*** as "the act of reducing the ability for law enforcement to have resources that harm our communities. It's about reinvesting those dollars into Black communities, communities that have been deeply divested from" (Mosley, 2020). As such, the idea of defunding the police seems to sit along a continuum between reformist and abolitionist strategies and includes demilitarizing the police.

In the aftermath of Ferguson, President Barak Obama's Task Force for Twenty-First Century Policing was established. The task force consisted of stakeholders from across the country and was charged with exploring building community trust while maintaining strategies to reduce crime. The task force called for changes in the ways that police interact with communities. Through the establishment of six pillars, the task force recommended that police departments focus on building trust and legitimacy. Their suggestions include a focus on ***procedural justice***. There are two types of procedural justice: internal and external. Internal procedural justice relates to policies and practices inside the agency that guide officer behavior and organizational operations. External procedural justice refers to how officers relate to the community and how those interactions affect trust in the police. External procedural justice is particularly related to policing communities of color because an important feature of it requires the police to be fair and impartial. In order to do so, they must recognize and change where implicit and explicit biases exist. According to the ***21st Century Policing*** report, in order to employ procedural justice, police should make sure that they are: "treating people with dignity and respect, giving individuals voice during encounters, being neutral and transparent in decision making and conveying trustworthy motives" (President's Task Force, 2015, p. 10).

In addition, one of the underlying themes was to change the culture of policing by trading in a warrior mindset for a guardian mindset. The ***warrior mindset*** focuses on officer safety and crime fighting. It is associated with militarization and traditional policing. Warrior-minded police cultures pit officers against the public in order to

Figure 7.3. Protestors in Louisville Kentucky. © Creative Commons / J4TNG GSO

maintain a sense that officers know best and should not be questioned. In contrast, the ***guardian mindset*** focuses on protection and service. Through that lens, guardian-minded police embrace building community trust by engaging in positive interactions (McLean et al., 2019).

Although many communities have military-grade equipment, the communities that are most likely to experience these weapons are poorer communities, particularly communities of color. In Ferguson, Missouri, for example, 67% of the population reported their race as Black on the last census, and one in four residents lived below the poverty line (U.S. Census Bureau, 2015; Kneebone, 2014). SWAT teams also are most likely to be deployed for search warrants in drug searches, and since the War on Drugs is primarily being fought in urban communities of color, minorities are the most likely to experience the militarization of the police. This has directly impacted the working relations between the police and the community within many neighborhoods. This is problematic because if the police and the community do not work together it becomes increasingly difficult for law enforcement to do their jobs effectively. In addition, there is growing research on the impact of police violence on Black communities. Police violence is higher among men, people of color, and LGBTQ persons. Within those social identities, police violence triggering suicidal ideation/attempts and psychotic experiences are higher (DeVylder et al., 2018).

This issue also impacts people at an early age and may have long-lasting consequences beyond police–community relations. Policing in school is already a controversial issue, but coupled with police militarization it becomes increasingly problematic. Research has shown that young people who have contact with the police through school have the greatest level of emotional distress and post-traumatic stress symptoms (Jackson et al., 2019). Prior to intervention under the Obama administration, the Los Angeles Unified School District militarization policies provided police access to three grenade launchers, 61 automatic military rifles, and a Mine Resistant Ambush Protected armored vehicle, (Ceasar, 2014). Ultimately, the grenade launchers were returned due to community backlash though they retained the armored truck. In 2015, as a result of President Obama's new guidelines that limited the way in which police departments could obtain military grade equipment, K–12 schools were barred from receiving the 1033 Program equipment (Knefel, 2015).

Summary

The militarization of the police has created an us-versus-them mentality between local law enforcement and the community. Police are given military-grade equipment by the federal government to use while enforcing the law, specifically where drugs and terrorism are the focus. Now all 50 states have local law enforcement agencies that have access to and have been trained to use military equipment. Access to military equipment and the training that accompanies it further creates a divide between police and the community, as the police no longer view themselves as part of the community, but instead see the community as the enemy (Nolan, 2014). In Ferguson, for example, military equipment was used to control protests because there was fear that if law enforcement were on the ground in their normal attire using their everyday weapons, protestors would harm them. The highest-ranking police officer in the St. Louis County Department defended his actions by stating that using the military-grade equipment and dressing in camouflage made his officers safer by creating fear among the protestors (Madhani, 2014).

The citizens within these communities are aware the police view them as the enemy and see their communities as war zones when armored personnel carriers and battering rams are used for drug searches and to keep the peace at protests. This atmosphere creates a distrust between the police and the community, where the police do not feel safe completing their duties without the use of military equipment and the citizens fear having military equipment used against them. If the citizens do not trust the police, they are not likely to call the police for help when there is a crime being committed or testify in a case or help the police gather evidence to arrest a suspect. If citizens do not notify the police when a crime is occurring or help them to locate evidence or testify in court, the police are severely limited in their ability to do their job (Nolan, 2014).

There is a time and a place for local law enforcement to utilize military equipment, such as in instances where a person deemed a threat barricades themselves in and refuses to come out, hostages are taken, or active shooters are involved. In each of these situations, it is appropriate for law enforcement to utilize SWAT teams for their

Knefel, M. (2015). What Obama's new military-equipment rules mean for K–12 school police *Rolling Stone*. https://www.rollingstone.com/politics/politics-news/what -obamas-new-military-equipment-rules-mean-for-k-12-school-police-60065/

Kraska, P. B. (2007). Militarization and policing: Its relevance to 21st century police. *Policing*, 1–13. http://cjmasters.eku.edu/sites/cjmasters.eku.edu/files/21stmilitar ization.pdf

Lynn, A., & Gutman, M. (2014). Family of toddler injured by SWAT 'grenade' faces $1m in medical bills. ABC News. http://abcnews.go.com/US/family-toddler-in jured-swat-grenade-faces-1m-medical/story?id=27671521

Madhani, A. (2014). St. Louis County Chief defends militarization of police. *USA Today*. http://www.usatoday.com/story/news/nation/2014/09/16/ferguson-st-louis -county-michael-brown-militarization/15736907/

Maguire, E. R. (2015). New directions in protest policing. *Saint Louis Law Review*, *35*(1), 67–109

The Marshall Project. (2017). Trump budget draft targets cops, crime victims. https:// www.themarshallproject.org/2017/01/19/trump-budget-draft-targets-cops-crime -victims#.0xuwkhvkx

McLean, K., Wolfe, S. E., Rojek, J., Alpert, G. P., & Smith, M. R. (2019). Police officers as warriors or guardians: Empirical reality or intriguing rhetoric? *Justice Quarterly*, *37*(6), https://doi.org/10.1080/07418825.2018.1533031

Mosley, T. (2020, June 3). Defunding the police can achieve real accountability and justice, Black Lives Matter co-founder says. WBUR, Here and Now. https://www. wbur.org/hereandnow/2020/06/03/black-lives-matter-co-founder

National Tactical Officers Association. (2008). SWAT standards for law enforcement agencies. https://ntoa.org/massemail/swatstandards.pdf

Nolan, T. (2014). Stop arming the police like a military. Defense One. http://www. defenseone.com/ideas/2014/06/stop-arming-police-military/87163/?oref=defense one_today_nl

Penny, A. (2016). Parents of Baby Bou Bou awarded 3.65 million. Fox 5 Atlanta. http:// www.fox5atlanta.com/news/98040278-story

Potter, G. (n.d.). The history of policing in the United States. https://plsonline.eku. edu/insidelook/history-policing-united-states-part-2

President's Task Force on 21st Century Policing. (2015). *Final Report of the President's Task Force on 21st Century Policing*. Office of Community Oriented Policing Ser- vices.

Radil, S. M., Dezzani, R. J., & McAden L. D. (2017). Geographies of U.S. police mili- tarization and the role of the 1033 program. *The Professional Geographer*, *62*(2), 203–213.

Rezvani, A., Pupovac, J., Eads, D., & Fisher, T. (2014, September 2). MRAPs and bay- onets: What we know about the Pentagon's 1033 program. National Public Radio. http://www.npr.org/2014/09/02/342494225/mraps-and-bayonets-whatwe-know -about-the-pentagons-1033-program

Shinkman, P. D. (2014). Ferguson and the militarization of police. *US News and World Report*. http://www.usnews.com/news/articles/2014/08/14/ferguson-and-the-shocking-nature-of-us-police-militarization

Stemle, C. (2020, July 8). The revolution will be streamed: Livestreamers redefine journalism during protests. *LEO Weekly*. https://www.leoweekly.com/2020/07/revolution-will-streamed/

Sylvestri, S. (2020, May 29). LMPD officer fires pepper balls at WAVE 3 News reporter, photographer during Louisville protest. Wave 3 News. https://www.wave3.com/2020/05/29/lmpd-officer-fires-pepper-balls-wave-news-reporter-photographer-during-louisville-protest/

Turkewitz, J., & Villamil, S. (2021a, May 12). Colombia's police force, built for war, finds a new one. *The New York Times*. https://www.nytimes.com/2021/05/12/world/americas/colombia-protests-police-brutality.html

Turkewitz, J., & Villamil, S. (2021b, May 31). Colombia police respond to protests with bullets, and death toll mounts. *The New York Times*. https://www.nytimes.com/2021/05/05/world/americas/colombia-covid-protests-duque.html

U.S. Census Bureau. (2015). Ferguson (city), Missouri state and county quick facts. Data derived from population estimates, American Community Survey, Census of Population and Housing, County Business Patterns, Economic Census, Survey of Business Owners, Building Permits, Census of Governments. http://quickfacts.census.gov/qfd/states/29/2923986.html

Vitale, A. S. (2018). *The end of policing*. Verso.

Courts and Sentencing

EIGHT

Judges, Prosecutors, and Indigent Defense

Learning Objectives

1. Understand why and how sentencing discretion was removed from judges.
2. Critically examine how prosecutorial discretion impacts what defendants are charged with as well as their sentences.
3. Critically examine the indigent defense system by understanding the differences between privately hired attorneys, public defenders, and assigned counsel.

In the criminal justice system, everyone from the victim (who decides whether or not to report the crime) to the judge (who decides how to sentence a convicted defendant) exercises discretion. *Discretion* is defined as the decision to act or not to act and is necessary within the criminal justice system, because each criminal case tends to have unique characteristics, making it difficult to create a one-size-fits-all system. However, discretion also can be utilized in ways that promote discrimination based on race, ethnicity, class, and gender—often unknowingly. In this chapter, we will examine some of the attempts to make the criminal justice system equal and fair for all as well as the unintended consequences this has created. The chapter will conclude with a discussion of how the indigent defense system works as well as problems that occur within this system.

Figure 8.1. © Pexels/ Muhammad Ghazie

Indeterminate Sentencing, Determinate Sentencing, and Sentencing Guidelines

Prior to the 1970s, all states as well as the federal government relied on indeterminate sentencing. An *indeterminate sentence* is a criminal sentence that contains a range with a minimum and a maximum, for instance three to five years in prison. Once the person has served the minimum sentence they are eligible to apply for *parole*, where a parole board will determine whether or not they should be released from prison early. The parole board makes their determination based on whether they believe the person is remorseful, has behaved well during incarceration, and has been adequately rehabilitated to be able to reenter society successfully. Therefore, the goal of indeterminate sentencing is to encourage inmates to behave while incarcerated and to engage in rehabilitation programs within the prison system, which gives the inmate a better chance at early release on parole. If the offender meets the criteria set forth by the parole board and the parole board believes they are ready, the offender can be released back to their community under the supervision of a parole officer. The parole officer sets criteria the parolee must meet under supervision within the community, and as long as these criteria are met, the parolee is released from parole supervision after the minimum portion of the sentence has been met. However, if the parolee does not meet the parole expectations, they can be sent back to prison to serve the remainder of their sentence (Legal Information Institute, n.d.).

Indeterminate sentencing gave the primary discretion for sentencing to the judge who determined the sentence and to the parole board who determined release. Judges who utilized indeterminate sentencing were guided only by the maximum possible sentence set by the government for the crime. However, the actual sentence could vary widely from one person to the next based on the judge's discretion, as long as it did not exceed the maximum possible sentence. This was problematic, as sentencing and release were based on individual and group decisions that were unpredictable and could vary from one judge or parole board to the next, even in cases with similar circumstances. By the 1970s, there was concern that race, gender, and class biases were in part determining sentences and when offenders were released. Due to the belief they were less likely to reoffend, white individuals, females, and those who were employed received shorter sentences and were released on parole. Others worried that offenders were being released from prison too early and were not serving a long enough sentence to deter them from committing future crimes (Law Library, 2016).

These concerns led to major changes for sentencing in the United States, where there is no longer one system of sentencing. Approximately half of the states still utilize an indeterminate system, but other states and the federal government have moved to using determinate sentencing or a form of sentencing guidelines. Determinate sentencing is based on deterrence theory, or the idea that if the punishment outweighs any benefit one would receive from committing a crime, then one would rationally choose not to engage in the crime. *Determinate sentencing* occurs when an offender receives a set sentence for a crime, for instance a person serves three years. Determinate sentencing was implemented to decrease the discretion judges and parole boards had in determining a sentence and so the offender knew exactly when they would be released from prison. States with determinate sentencing structures also no longer utilized parole boards. However, in some states a person's sentence could be reduced by *good time credit*, where every day they served in prison and did not get into trouble could be applied towards an earlier release date (Law Library, 2016).

Some states and the federal government also implemented sentencing commissions to create specific sentencing guidelines that would be followed by judges to reduce their discretion in sentencing. These guidelines can be used in states with determinate or indeterminate sentencing, and there are two types. *Presumptive sentencing guidelines* provide a required base sentence for each crime that is determined by the seriousness of the offense as well as the offender's prior criminal history. Under presumptive sentencing guidelines, the judge still retains some discretion as they can take into consideration aggravating circumstances and increase the sentence or mitigating circumstances and decrease the sentence. However, if a judge departs from the required sentence under the sentencing guidelines, they have to provide written justification, and the judge's decision is later reviewed at the appellate level. Other states and the federal government rely on *voluntary advisory guidelines* or recommended sentences for each crime that also take into consideration the seriousness of the offense and prior criminal history as well as aggravating and mitigating circumstances. However, the main difference is that voluntary advisory guidelines are not required, but rather suggestions as to what the judge should follow. There also is not a review process in place for when a judge deviates from the recommended sentence (Austin et al., n.d.).

The research conducted on the use of determinate sentencing and sentencing guidelines at the state level has been mixed, with some research studies finding these measures to be less effective than indeterminate sentencing and other studies finding them to be more effective. An example of this is a study conducted by Zhang and colleagues (2014), where the authors examined the differences between mandatory release (determinate sentencing) and parole board release (indeterminate sentencing) in states that utilized both types of release, including New York, Maryland, Oregon, Texas, North Carolina, and Virginia. The authors analyzed differences in recidivism rates for the two types of release through data on the person's first arrest within three years of release from prison. Overall, when examining all six states together, those who reentered their communities under mandatory release were significantly more likely to be arrested more quickly than those released by a parole board. However, results differed when examining data for each state. Those released from prison in New York and North Carolina, for instance, were more likely to be arrested sooner when released on parole, while those in Virginia and Maryland were arrested more quickly when under mandatory release. However, in Oregon and Texas the differences between release types were not found to be significant. The authors concluded the differences between the states were likely due to how the parole programs were implemented within the community (Zang et al., 2014).

Another research study conducted by Bales and Miller (2012) compared inmates in Florida under indeterminate sentencing to inmates after the shift to determinate sentencing to better understand the impact of sentencing structure on inmate misconduct. The authors found that those sentenced under determinate sentencing were much more likely to get into trouble while incarcerated than those who had been sentenced under indeterminate structures. The authors concluded this was because the determinate sentenced offenders did not have the same set of incentives to behave while incarcerated as indeterminate sentenced offenders who had the possibility of being released by a parole board (Bales & Miller, 2012).

However, since 1988, the United States Sentencing Commission has consistently found that federal judges using the sentencing guidelines have sentenced Black men to significantly longer sentences than white men. For instance, between 2011 and 2016, Black men received sentences that were 19.1% longer than white men when controlling for multiple variables, such as criminal history, violence, and weapon used. Gender differences also have been consistently noted, as women from all racial and ethnic backgrounds were significantly more likely to receive shorter sentences than white men (Schmitt et al., 2017).

Prior to 2005, the differences in sentences for Black and white men at the federal level were largely attributed to sentencing disparities due to harsher sentences that were in place for crack cocaine. However, in 2005, the United States Supreme Court decided in the case **United States vs. Booker** that sentencing guidelines at the federal level would no longer be mandatory, but would instead be voluntary (*United States v.*

guilty after the prosecutor has agreed to recommend
committed, while *fact bargaining* is used when a defe
for certain facts being left out of the case. This is typ
would have received a mandatory minimum sentence
not to include the facts in the case that would have
mum sentence (Find Law, 2016).

There also are ethical concerns regarding the high
the United States criminal justice system. Some worr
ceive justice as the defendant does not have their day
the family. However, others worry those who are innc
a plea deal, due to the fear that if they do not plead g
sentence. For example, in cases where defendants were
deciding instead to take their case to trial, they recei
tence. This was particularly true for federal-level dru;
sentence was three times longer if the person refused
the prosecutor. Therefore, it is not surprising that only ;
go to trial (Fellner, 2014).

Bail Bondsman

After a suspect is arrested and charged with a felony
who will determine if the person will be released pr
person charged with the crime is determined to be a d
judge may decide to hold the person in jail until trial. I
released on personal recognizance (the belief the pe
community and will appear in court as required) or ba
ey that a person must pay to the court in order to be
trial date or a resolution, such as a plea bargain, oc
Policy Institute, 2012).

If a person is assigned a bail they cannot afford, in a
Illinois, Oregon, and Wisconsin) one can hire a bail b
requires the person who has been charged with a crim
them. The bail bondsman then pays the bond on beha
If the client shows for their court appearance, then th
is used to pay for the service. However, if the person f
their court date, the bondsman will lose the bond they
of the defendant. At that point the bondsman has th
recover the money or locate the person on their own c

Figure 8.2. United States Supreme Court Building. © Adobe Stock/W. Scott McGill.

Booker, n.d.). Then in 2007, the United States Supreme Court in the case ***Gall v. United States*** decided that federal judges could depart from the minimum sentence in the sentencing guidelines, if they were able to explain and justify the departure from the guideline (*Gall v. United States*, n.d.). These United States Supreme Court decisions had a huge impact on sentencing at the federal level, as much of the difference found in sentences between Black and white men now can be explained by examining ***variance***, or when the judge uses their discretion to depart from the guidelines, and ***downward departures***, where the judge goes below the minimum sentence suggested (Schmitt et al., 2017). For instance, between 2011 and 2016, Black men were 21.2% less likely to receive a downward departure or variance than white males; and even when Black males did receive a downward departure or discretion was used, their sentences were still 16.8% longer than white males. In comparison, when judges stayed within the guidelines Black males received a sentence that was 7.9% longer than white males, which seems to suggest that when federal judges stay within the guidelines they at least somewhat decrease the racial differences found in sentencing at the federal level (Schmitt et al., 2017).

Prosecutorial Discretion and Plea Bargains

The current mixture of sentencing policies and laws within the United States occurred due to the fear that judges and parole boards had too much discretion in the sentencing and release process. The implemented changes were intended to create more uniformity in sentencing across criminal acts as well as for individual characteristics, such as one's race, gender, and class background. However, many have argued these shifts in sentencing policies and laws have led to the unintended consequence of prosecutors having more discretion within the criminal justice system than

before, with some stating the prosecutor is n
sentencing process. This is cause for concern,
ances in place for prosecutors. This is because
review, and the public is largely unaware of how
not required to keep an official record or transc
cess (Shermer & Johnson, 2010). This can be pr
of control over the sentencing process, such a
charges and sentences through plea bargaining

Plea bargaining occurs when the prosecut
the offender admits guilt in return for being cha
a shorter sentence. Plea bargains are not lega
United States plea bargains are used in 90% of al
benefits for the judicial process. Plea bargains,
time and costs for the criminal court as well as
can focus on more serious offenders. Plea barga
ey by not having to pay an attorney throughout

GLOBAL SPOT

Plea Bargains in India

Plea bargains are a common practice in the l
countries. However, plea bargains are not u:
world. Although, some countries are starting t
within the United States and whether it can
tries. In 2005, for example, plea bargaining w
help alleviate the overburdened criminal cou
can only be used in criminal cases where the
tence of seven years and cannot be used in ca
ted against a woman or a child under the age
not a popular practice in India and was usec
criminal cases in 2015. Some critics worry de
when they should not, while others fear those
the sentence they truly deserve (Vishwanath,

There are three types of plea bargains. The n
gain is *charge bargaining*, where the defendar
convicted of a lesser charge. *Sentence bargair*

hunter. Once the former client has been located, the bondsman will take the person to jail in order to recoup their losses (Justice Policy Institute, 2012).

Across the United States, approximately 60% of those who are in jail have not been convicted of a crime and are waiting for their case to be resolved, which costs taxpayers 9 billion dollars a year (Justice Policy Institute, 2012). Although defendants can be released on personal recognizance, 70% of those who are charged with a felony are assigned bail. Black defendants also are less likely than white defendants to be released on personal recognizance, and young Black men between the ages of 18 and 29 are assigned higher bail amounts than any other race or ethnicity (Justice Policy Institute, 2012). The consequences of not being able to pay for one's bail can include losing one's job and housing and can cause emotional and financial strain on one's family as they are separated during this time period. The longer someone waits in jail, the more consequences they will face.

Prosecutors are aware of these negative consequences, and many use it to their advantage by offering a plea bargain to the person who is unable to pay their bail or a bail bondsman. If someone chooses to plead guilty, in many instances they will be released with a punishment of time served. However, this is a short-term solution because now this person has a conviction on their record, which will impact them for the long term. The pressure also causes some to plead guilty even when they have not committed a crime. For example, a research study found that more than half of those who had not committed a crime and were awaiting trial plead guilty out of fear of receiving the maximum sentence (Justice Policy Institute, 2012).

Prosecutors also have a lot of discretion and control over sentencing when it comes to charge bargaining because when one's charge is reduced, one is placed in a lower offense category and receives a shorter sentence. In order to better understand the impact of charge reductions, Shermer and Johnson (2010) conducted a study where they examined federal cases from initial charges through sentencing for 90 United States federal districts. The authors analyzed sentencing data to examine cases where charges were reduced from the maximum possible sentence.

The authors found that only 12% of all cases received charge reductions from the maximum sentence, but concluded this was most likely a conservative estimate since it was based only on those cases where the maximum sentence had been applied. In those cases where the charge was reduced, property offenders were two times more likely to receive a charge reduction than violent offenders, while those charged with immigration violations were the least likely to receive a charge reduction. Charge reductions also were impacted by gender, race, and ethnicity. Females, for example, were significantly more likely to receive a charge reduction when compared to males. The authors concluded this was based on males being perceived as more dangerous and more likely to reoffend as well as male offenders committing crimes that tended to be more serious. Overall, there were not charge reduction differences based on age or race, but Black and Hispanic offenders were less likely to receive a charge reduction than white offenders for crimes that included a weapon offense (Shermer & Johnson, 2010).

Another study conducted by Wooldredge and Griffin (2005) examined the impact of the implementation of Ohio's sentencing guidelines on prosecutorial discretion by examining cases prior to the implementation of the guidelines and after. Overall, charge reductions were 4% higher after the guidelines were implemented. The authors also noted those charged with first-degree felonies were more likely to have their charges dropped post guidelines, which supported the notion that discretion had moved from judges to prosecutors. There also were differences for charge reductions based on gender, where males were more likely to have their charges dropped after the guidelines were implemented (Wooldredge & Griffin, 2005).

IN FOCUS

Real Justice PAC

In 2017, the Real Justice PAC (political action committee) was formed to create change in the criminal justice system by supporting reform-minded district attorney candidates in their elections at the local and county level. This strategy was chosen after realizing that 84% of all county prosecutors ran unopposed in their elections in 2016. Real Justice endorses candidates based on their commitment to criminal justice reform and the elimination of cash bail, discriminatory policing practices, and policies that contribute to high rates of incarceration. Real Justice uses social media and grass roots organizing to raise awareness and funds to support their candidates. The PAC has had some success and between 2017 and 2020 endorsed thirty-five total candidates with eighteen of them winning their races (Real Justice, n.d.).

Another way federal prosecutors utilize their discretion is by using a *substantial assistance departure*. This tactic is used when the defendant cooperates with the prosecutor and provides information to assist with the prosecution of another offender. In exchange for the defendant's testimony, the prosecutor asks the judge for the defendant to be sentenced outside of the sentencing guidelines. The prosecutor then makes a sentencing recommendation, but the ultimate sentencing decision belongs to the judge. This tactic is particularly common in drug cases and is regularly used; for example, almost 20% of all federal offenders received a substantial assistance departure, resulting on average in a 50% reduction in sentence. However, how often this tactic is used varies from one region of the country to the next, and the sentence reduction is dependent upon the crime committed (Hartley et al., 2007).

Hartley and colleagues (2007) conducted a research study and examined what factors contributed to substantial assistance departures for federal crack and powder cocaine cases. The authors found that those charged with crack offenses were significantly less likely to be given a substantial assistance departure than those charged with powder cocaine offenses. Other findings included offenders who were charged with more serious crimes and those who were white being more likely to receive a substantial assistance departure than Black offenders and those charged with less serious offenses. Those who had a high school diploma also were more likely to receive a substantial assistance departure than those without a high school education (Hartley et al., 2007).

Gender, race, and ethnicity also mattered in regards to who received a substantial assistance departure when taking into consideration the type of drug and whether the crime could be charged as a mandatory minimum. Black male defendants, for instance, were less likely than white and Hispanic male defendants to receive a substantial assistance departure regardless of the drug and type of offense. However, Hispanic men were less likely than white men to receive a substantial assistance departure, unless the drug was crack cocaine and there was a mandatory minimum sentence. Conversely, females, regardless of race or ethnicity, were more likely than males to receive a substantial assistance departure, unless the drug was powder cocaine and there was a mandatory minimum sentence (Hartley et al., 2007).

Prosecutorial Discretion, Three Strikes, Mandatory Minimums, and the Death Penalty

Due to the get-tough-on-crime movement of the 1980s and 1990s, other measures also were put into place to ensure offenders were serving their full sentences and to decrease judicial and/or parole discretion. These measures were included in states that relied on indeterminate and determinate sentencing as well as sentencing guidelines, and all fifty states and the federal government have included one or more of these sentencing rules. The *three-strikes rule*, for example, was implemented to remove judicial and parole board discretion. This rule differs from one state to the next, but essentially requires a person who is convicted of a second felony sentence to serve a longer sentence than would typically be given and a life sentence or a significantly longer sentence than normal for a third felony conviction. Another sentencing policy passed to reduce parole board discretion is *truth-in-sentencing*, where an offender must serve 80% or more of a sentence before they can be considered for early release (Tonry, 1999).

As discussed earlier in the chapter, mandatory minimums also were created by legislators and required a specified sentence be given for certain crimes in order to remove judicial and parole board discretion. If a person is convicted or found guilty of a crime with a mandatory minimum, they are required to serve the full sentence set by the legislators, and factors such as mitigating circumstances as well as efforts towards rehabilitation and good behavior are not allowed to be considered for sentence reduction (Tonry, 1999). One of the unintended consequences of mandatory minimum sentencing is the concern that prosecutors will use a possible mandatory minimum sentence to coerce a defendant into pleading guilty. The majority of federal drug offenders (60%), for example, were charged with a crime that triggered a mandatory minimum sentence, and those who did not agree to the plea bargain were sentenced to 11 years longer on average than those who accepted the plea deal (Fellner, 2014).

Prosecutors also utilize mandatory minimum sentences to obtain guilty pleas at the state level. In Pennsylvania, for example, prosecutors have the ability to decide if the crime is eligible for a mandatory minimum. If a mandatory minimum is applied, the judge must sentence accordingly. However, if the person is not charged with a mandatory minimum, the sentencing guidelines will be utilized, requiring a shorter sentence. Therefore, prosecutors utilize a tactic referred to as ***de-mandatorize*** where the prosecutor does not reduce the charge, but instead does not add the mandatory minimum, allowing the offender to be sentenced under the sentencing guidelines (Ulmer et al., 2007).

Ulmer and colleagues (2007) conducted a study to better understand how mandatory minimum sentences were being applied to drug crimes and those who were eligible for three-strike sentences in Pennsylvania. The authors found that prosecutors did not utilize mandatory minimum sentences often, with only 18% of those who were eligible receiving one for drug crimes and three-strike policies. They also noted that if the mandatory minimum sentence was substantially more than the sentencing guideline then prosecutors tended not to use it. Also, those who pled guilty instead of going to trial were significantly more likely not to be charged with the mandatory minimum. This was particularly true for drug offenders who were 60% less likely to be charged with a mandatory minimum if they plead guilty (Ulmer et al., 2007).

The authors also found significant differences in who received mandatory minimum sentences based on gender, race, and ethnicity. Males, for example, were significantly more likely than females to be charged with a mandatory minimum, while Black offenders were not any more likely to be charged with mandatory minimums than white offenders. However, Hispanic offenders were significantly more likely to be charged with a mandatory minimum than white offenders. This was particularly true when examining those who were charged under the three-strike policies, where Hispanic offenders were 4.5 times more likely to be charged under this policy than white offenders (Ulmer et al., 2007).

The authors concluded by stating that race and ethnicity mattered when examining who was eligible for mandatory minimum sentencing. In Pennsylvania, for example, 70% of those who were eligible for mandatory minimum sentences were Black or

Hispanic, even though only 10% of all Pennsylvania residents were Black and only 4% were Hispanic. This suggests that even though mandatory minimum sentences appeared to promote equality on paper, when implemented there were serious racial and ethnic implications. This was because Black and Hispanic offenders were more likely to be arrested than white offenders for crimes that could trigger a mandatory minimum sentence. However, it should be noted that white offenders were just as likely to commit these crimes, even though Black and Hispanic offenders were more likely to be arrested, convicted, and sentenced because of the War on Drugs and get-tough-on-crime policies that tend to target urban communities (Ulmer et al., 2007). (See Chapter 5 for more detail.)

California is an example of a state where prosecutors have great discretion in who is charged under the three-strikes law. California's three-strikes law was implemented in 1994, at the height of the Get Tough on Crime movement, through direct democracy, where citizens drafted the policy and voted it in. The law requires a second felony conviction sentence be doubled, if the offender has already been convicted of a felony that is considered serious or violent. However, if one receives a third felony conviction, for a violent or nonviolent crime, the offender faces a sentence of 25 to life, where one must serve 80% of the sentence to be eligible for parole (Chen, 2014).

A judge or prosecutor can decide not to count a strike, so the law is not enacted. However, it is typically the prosecutor who exercises this discretion at the charging stage. The chief district attorney, who is elected, is given the power to create internal policies for how the law will be implemented by the prosecutors under their supervision. The policies can include discretion for the prosecutor not to count the second or third strike or petition the court to waive a strike. However, this is not a mandatory requirement, and how these policies are implemented varies from one county to the next depending upon the politics within the county. Conservative counties, for example, were more likely to implement the law to the fullest extent. However, predominately liberal counties tended not to implement the third strike, if the third felony conviction was nonviolent or not considered to be serious (Chen, 2014).

Chen (2014) conducted a study to better understand how the three-strikes law was being implemented in California and examined data on who was sentenced under these laws. The author found that Black offenders were 40% more likely than white offenders to be sentenced using the three-strikes law because a felony was not dismissed when deciding whether to implement the law. However, Hispanic offenders were not any more likely than white offenders to receive the three-strikes sentence. The author notes it was difficult to definitively conclude why this was happening, since there were not public records to indicate why or how the charging process occurred. The author also noted that counties with higher levels of unemployment also saw greater use of the three-strikes law (Chen, 2014).

Prosecutors also maintain a lot of discretion in deciding whether or not one receives the death penalty in cases where the offense is death penalty eligible. In most

Figure 8.3. © david_franklin/ Fotolia.

cases, the consequence of not utilizing a plea bargain is the fear of a longer sentence, while in a death penalty-eligible case the person could lose their life. This puts significantly more pressure on the defendant to plea bargain. In some instances, prosecutors charge a case as a capital offense because they believe the death sentence is warranted, but they may also do so to help increase their chances in gaining a guilty plea or a harsher sentence. Capital offense cases also are the most expensive to prosecute, and a plea bargain alleviates the cost of a trial (Ehrhard-Dietzel, 2012).

Vito and colleagues (2014) conducted a study to examine death penalty eligible cases in Kentucky from 2001 to 2010. The authors found the death penalty was sought in 70% of eligible cases and 69% of these cases were plea bargained to a lower offense. The authors also noted prosecutors were three times more likely to seek the death penalty if the victim was female. If the victim was white and the offender was Black, the prosecutor was 56% less likely to offer a plea deal (Vito et al., 2014). In addition, Black offenders who were charged with killing white victims and were not offered a plea were the most likely to be sentenced to life without parole (Vito et al., 2014, p. 762).

Indigent Defense in the United States

The Sixth Amendment of the United States Constitution states citizens have the right to counsel when facing criminal charges, but it was not until 1963 that this right was extended to **indigent defendants**, or those who are unable to afford an attorney. The United States Supreme Court case **Gideon v. Wainwright** concluded that those who are unable to afford an attorney will have one appointed, if charged with a felony crime. In 1972, this right was expanded under the United States Supreme Court case **Argersinger v. Hamlin**, which stated indigent defendants have the right to counsel for felony or misdemeanor charges when the defendant is facing imprisonment (Cohen, 2014).

IN FOCUS

Clarence Gideon

In 1961, Clarence Gideon broke into a bar to steal money from their vending machines. He was later arrested and charged with breaking and entering with the intent to commit a misdemeanor, which is a felony in the state of Florida. Gideon requested that he be appointed an attorney because he could not afford to hire one. However, the trial judge denied his request because at the time an indigent defendant was only appointed an attorney if they faced the death penalty as a possible sentence. Gideon, who had an eighth grade education and had spent his adulthood in and out of prison for nonviolent offenses, was then forced then to represent himself. He gave an opening statement to the jury, cross-examined the prosecutor's witnesses, and brought in witnesses to testify on his behalf. However, the jury found him guilty and sentenced him to five years in prison (McBride, 2006).

Gideon filed a writ of habeas corpus with the Florida Supreme Court, stating that his incarceration was unjust because the trial judge had refused him counsel. The court did not agree, because the law did not require it. Gideon then filed a handwritten petition with the United States Supreme Court asking for them to review the lower court's decision. The United States Supreme Court agreed to review the case and reversed the decision of the lower court. This decision guaranteed those who were indigent and charged with a felony the right to counsel under the Sixth Amendment (McBride, 2006).

American citizens now have the right to counsel when facing criminal charges that could lead to incarceration, but it is up to each state to decide how to provide counsel for those who are unable to pay. Most states rely on a combination of public defenders, assigned counsel, and contract attorneys to defend indigent clients. *Public defenders* are salaried and work for the government or a nonprofit organization to provide counsel to those who cannot afford it. They typically have investigators and staff that can assist them with their cases as well as experience in criminal cases. Public defenders also are in the courtroom on a regular basis, allowing them to create relationships with those working in the courtroom, which is helpful for plea negotiations. *Assigned counsel* is appointed by the judge and is picked from a list of private attorneys, while *contract attorneys* are utilized when the government secures a contract with an attorney for a period of time. Both are paid an hourly wage or a flat fee to represent the defendant, and those who are assigned criminal cases in this manner are often attempting to gain experience; for example, they are recent graduates of law school (Cohen, 2014).

In the United States, the court system annually spends 3.5 billion dollars less on public defenders than prosecutors, even though 80% of criminal defendants cannot afford an attorney. This is problematic, because the number of people processed through the criminal justice system has drastically increased. In 1963, when *Gideon* was decided, there were 217,000 Americans incarcerated. However, today there are 2.3 million incarcerated Americans. It has been estimated that the court system nationwide would need 6,900 more public defenders to meet this increase in caseload demand (Levintova et al., 2013).

Public defender caseloads also can be very high, because most states (60%) do not allow public defender offices to refuse cases, even when they are overburdened. This forces some public defender offices into a situation where they meet with their client for the first time anywhere from a few minutes to a few hours. The average amount of time spent on a case, for example, in New Orleans was seven minutes, while in Detroit it was 32 minutes, and in Atlanta it was 59 minutes. A public defender should be spending on average 1,500 hours per year total on their felony cases. However, the average total time spent with felony offenders nationwide is 1,000 hours. The lack of time results in some public defenders encouraging their clients to accept a plea deal as a way to cope with their large caseloads (Levintova et al., 2013).

States and the federal government utilize assigned counsel and contract attorneys as a way to alleviate the large caseloads of public defenders. Private attorney pay for indigent defendants is determined in one of three ways, including through a written law, judicial discretion on a case-by-case basis, or through a contract between the state and the attorney. In the federal court system, private attorneys are paid $125 per hour and up to $9,700 for felony criminal cases or up to $2,800 for misdemeanor criminal cases to defend indigent clients. However, at the state level these lawyers tend to be drastically underpaid, because most states have not increased their hourly wages since the 1980s and 1990s. In 30 states, for example, private attorneys for indigent defendants were paid an average hourly wage of $65, but this varied, with some states paying as low as $40 per hour (Gross, 2013).

Hourly rates also do not take into consideration overhead expenses, even though 50% of what the private attorney is paid goes towards overhead expenses. In New York City, for example, assigned counsel were paid $40 per hour when in court and $25 for work completed outside of the court. However, their hourly overhead cost was $42.88, which meant they lost money when working on cases with indigent clients. These low wages lead to only the most inexperienced and least skilled private attorneys being willing to take on these cases. There also is the concern that if you underpay assigned counsel, they will be tempted to take on larger caseloads than they can manage in order to make up for the lack of pay or make decisions based on pay. In Detroit, for example, assigned counsel were paid $200 more if their client plead guilty versus having the case dismissed (Gross, 2013).

Research on Private Attorneys, Public Defenders, and Assigned Counsel

Hoffman and colleagues (2005) conducted a study in Denver, Colorado, to better understand the differences between those who hired a private attorney (29%) and those who were assigned a public defender (65%). In all of the examined cases, the defendant had been charged with a felony offense. The authors found that public defenders and private attorneys had similar conviction rates, if they went to trial. However, clients of public defenders spent on average three years longer in prison than those who had a private attorney, even when charged with an equally serious offense. The authors noted the differences were due to the public defender system in Denver being drastically underfunded due to the rise in the number of indigent defendants. Prior to 1980, for example, 50% of criminal defendants were designated as indigent, but this number had increased to 80% by the time of the study. However, the rate of funding for public defender offices to did not match this increase in caseload (Hoffman et al., 2005).

In another study examining the differences between public defenders, assigned counsel, and privately hired attorneys, Cohen (2014) examined cases where the defendant was charged with a felony in the 75 most populated counties across the country. Overall, the majority had a public defender or assigned counsel (80%), while 20% hired a private attorney. The majority of those who did not hire an attorney relied on a public defender (75%), with 25% being assigned counsel. White defendants were more likely to hire a private attorney than Black defendants, and those who relied on assigned counsel or public defenders were more likely to have a criminal history. The author found those who were convicted and had obtained assigned counsel were more likely to be incarcerated and served longer sentences than those who were convicted and hired a private attorney or were allocated a public defender (Cohen, 2014).

In another study conducted by Anderson and Heaton (2011), the authors examined the Philadelphia indigent counsel system. In Philadelphia, those who are indigent are randomly allocated to a public defender or assigned counsel, with 20% of cases receiving a public defender. The authors only examined cases where the defendant had been charged with the crime of murder and found that 95% of defendants charged with murder were not able to afford to hire a private attorney. The authors also found that those who had a public defender were 19% less likely to be convicted, 62% less likely to receive a sentence of life and their sentences on average were 24% shorter than those who were assigned a private attorney by the court. Assigned counsel clients also were more likely to take their cases to trial and reject plea bargains than those with public defenders (Anderson & Heaton, 2011).

In order to better understand the differences between public defenders and assigned counsel, the authors interviewed assigned counsel, public defenders, and judges. They found that assigned counsel were poorly paid and received $1,333 if the case did not go to trial and $2,000 if the case did go to trial, which equated to about $2 per hour. Those interviewed believed these low rates of pay discouraged preparation and encouraged some assigned counsel to take cases to trial that should be plea bargained instead. Interviewees also noted that most assigned counsel worked solo, without the benefit of other attorneys around to offer a second pair of eyes, which could lead to mistakes. In comparison, public defenders were paid by salary, had manageable caseloads, had staff support, and spent more time with their clients (Anderson & Heaton, 2011).

Summary

The original intention of moving from indeterminate sentencing to determinate sentencing and sentencing guidelines was to reduce bias in sentencing by removing or reducing the discretion of judges and parole boards. However, an unintended consequence of this switch has been transferring discretion to prosecutors. Prosecutors now have a tremendous amount of power to negotiate sentences through the plea bargaining process, and the decisions they make are not recorded for later review or analysis as is the case with judges and parole boards. Despite the good intentions of the shift in sentencing, the research on prosecutorial discretion tends to support the idea that biases based on race, ethnicity, gender, and class still impact the decisions of prosecutors just as they had with judges and parole boards. It should also be noted that sentences in many instances have increased due to policies such as mandatory minimums, three strikes, and truth-in-sentencing.

A little over fifty years ago, indigent defense was established through United States Supreme Court cases that stated those who could not afford an attorney would be provided one. This was a step towards making the criminal justice system fairer for those who were poor. However, the research shows this system works for some, but not all. This is because the indigent defense system remains drastically underfunded in many states, even though the number of criminal defendants who rely on it has significantly increased.

Discussion Questions

1. Was sentencing better or worse when judges had more discretion?

2. Should the plea bargaining decision process be recorded for later review?

3. How would you convince your state legislators to put aside more money in the state budget for indigent counsel pay?

Key Terms

discretion

indeterminate sentencing

parole

determinate sentencing

good time credit

presumptive sentencing guidelines

voluntary advisory guidelines

United States v. Booker

Gall v. United States

variance

downward departure

plea bargaining

charge bargaining

sentence bargaining

fact bargaining

substantial assistance departure

three-strikes rule

truth-in-sentencing

de-mandatorize

indigent defendants

Gideon v. Wainwright

Argersinger v. Hamlin

public defenders

assigned counsel

contract attorneys

References

Anderson, J. M., & Heaton, P. (2011). How much difference does the lawyer make?: The effect of defense counsel on murder case outcomes. Social Science Research Network. http://ssrn.com/abstract=1884379

Austin, J., Jones, C., Kramer, J., & Renninger, P. (n.d.). National assessment of structured sentencing. Bureau of Justice Assistance. https://www.ncjrs.gov/pdffiles/strsent.pdf

Bales, W. D., & Miller, C. H. (2012). The impact of determinate sentencing on prisoner misconduct. *Journal of Criminal Justice, 40*(5), 394–403.

Chen, E. Y. (2014). In the furtherance of justice, injustice, or both? A multilevel analysis of courtroom context and the implementation of three strikes. *Justice Quarterly, 31*(2), 257–286.

Cohen, T. H. (2014). Who is better at defending criminals? Does type of defense attorney matter in terms of producing favorable case outcomes. *Criminal Justice Policy Review, 25*(1), 29–58.

Ehrhard-Dietzel, S. (2012). The use of life and death as tools in plea bargaining. *Criminal Justice Review, 37*(1), 89–109.

Fellner, J. (2014). An offer you can't refuse: How U.S. federal prosecutors force drug defendants to plead guilty. *Federal Sentencing Reporter, 26*(4), 276–281.

Find Law. (2016). Plea bargains: In depth. http://criminal.findlaw.com/criminal-procedure/plea-bargains-in-depth.html

Gall v. United States. (n.d.). Oyez. https://www.oyez.org/cases/2007/06-7949

Gross, J. P. (2013). Rationing justice: The underfunding of assigned counsel systems. *Gideon* at 50: A three-part examination of indigent defense in America. National Association of Criminal Defense Lawyers. Retrieved from https://www.nacdl.org/

getattachment/cf613fe0-8f46-4dc1-b747-82346328522e/gideon-at-50-rationing
-justice-the-underfunding-of-assigned-counsel-systems-part-1-.pdf

Hartley, R. D., Maddan, S., & Spohn, C. C. (2007). Prosecutorial discretion: An examination of substantial assistance departures in federal crack-cocaine and powder-
cocaine cases. *Justice Quarterly, 24*(3), 382–407.

Hoffman, M. B., Rubin, P. H., & Shepherd, J. M. (2005). An empirical study of public
defender effectiveness: "Self-selection" by the marginally indigent. *Ohio State Journal of Law, 3,* 223–255.

Justice Policy Institute. (2012). Bail fail: Why the U.S. should end the practice of using
money for bail. http://www.justicepolicy.org/uploads/justicepolicy/documents/
bailfail_executive_summary.pdf

Law Library. (2016). Sentencing: Sentence disparity and sentence reform. http://law.
jrank.org/pages/2052/Sentencing-Disparity-Sentencing-disparity-sentence-re
form.html

Legal Information Institute. (n.d.). Indeterminate sentence. https://www.law.cornell.
edu/wex/indeterminate_sentence

Levintova, H., Lee, J., & Brownell, B. (2013). Charts: Why you're in deep trouble if you
can't afford a lawyer. *Mother Jones.* http://www.motherjones.com/politics/2013/05/
public-defenders-gideon-supreme-court-charts

McBride, A. (2006). Landmark cases: *Gideon v. Wainwright.* PBS. http://www.pbs.org/
wnet/supremecourt/rights/landmark_gideon.html

Real Justice. (n.d.). The Strategy. https://realjusticepac.org/#the-strategy

Schmitt, G. R., Reedt, L., & Blackwell, K. (2017). Demographic differences in sentencing: An update to the 2012 Booker report. United States Sentencing Commission.
https://www.ussc.gov/sites/default/files/pdf/research-and-publications/research
-publications/2017/20171114_Demographics.pdf

Shermer, L. O., & Johnson, B. D. (2010). Criminal prosecutions: Examining prosecutorial discretion and charge reductions in U.S. Federal District Courts. *Justice
Quarterly, 27*(3), 394–430.

Tonry, M. (1999, September). Reconsidering indeterminate and structured sentencing. *Sentencing and Corrections: Issues for the 21st Century.* National Institute of
Justice. https://www.ncjrs.gov/pdffiles1/nij/175722.pdf

Ulmer, J. T., Kurlychek, M. C., & Kramer, J. H. (2007). Prosecutorial discretion and the
imposition of mandatory minimum sentences. *Journal of Research in Crime & Delinquency, 44*(4), 427–458.

United States v. Booker. (n.d.). Oyez. https://www.oyez.org/cases/2004/04-104

Vishwanath, A. (2016). Why hasn't plea bargaining taken off in India? Live Mint.
http://www.livemint.com/Politics/otm5XvV7DTZJ9KaKScbJ4H/Why-hasnt-plea
-bargaining-taken-off-in-India.html

Vito, G., Higgins, G., & Vito, A. (2014). Capital sentencing in Kentucky, 2000–2010.
American Journal of Criminal Justice, 39(4), 753–770.

Wooldredge, J., & Griffin, T. (2005). Displaced discretion under Ohio sentencing guidelines. *Journal of Criminal Justice, 33*(4), 301–316.

Zhang, Y., Zhang, L., & Vaughn, M. S. (2014). Indeterminate and determinate sentencing models: A state-specific analysis of their effects on recidivism. *Crime & Delinquency, 60*(5), 693–715.

NINE

Death Penalty

Learning Objectives

1. Understand how the death penalty has evolved in the United States since the colonial period.
2. Critically examine how concerns about violations of one's Eighth Amendment rights have been addressed as well as criticisms of the death penalty, such as racial differences, costs, and wrongful convictions, along with differences based on gender and class.

The *death penalty*, also referred to as capital punishment, has been used in the United States since the colonial period. In the United States, the death penalty occurs once someone has been convicted of the most serious crimes, including murder, and is sentenced to be executed by the state or the federal government within the correctional system. However, how this punishment is used varies from state to state, with some states having abolished it all together. Perhaps the most interesting thing about the death penalty in the United States is how the method of execution constantly evolves in the search for a more humane process. However, after each new method is implemented a new set of problems and barriers arise. In this chapter, we will examine the evolution of the death penalty as well as the decisions made by the United States Supreme Court, along with the criticisms regarding wrongful convictions, racial differences, deterrence, cost, and differences based on gender and class.

The History of the Death Penalty in the United States

In the mid-1700s, there were 225 crimes that could be punished by death in Great Britain. Those who emigrated from Great Britain to the American colonies brought the death penalty with them and, in 1776, most of the colonies utilized the death penalty for "arson, piracy, treason, murder, sodomy, burglary, robbery, rape, horse-stealing, slave rebellion, and counterfeiting" (Reggie, 1997, para. 9). However, some colonies, such as Rhode Island, implemented the death penalty for fewer crimes, while other colonies used it for additional crimes. In North Carolina, for example, the death penalty also was used for the crimes of "statutory rape, slave-stealing, stealing bank notes, highway robbery, castration, buggery, bestiality, dueling where death occurs, hiding a slave with intent to free him, taking a free Negro out of state to sell him, bigamy, inciting slaves to rebel, and circulating seditious literature among slaves" (Reggie, 1997, para 10). Therefore, what was included as a capital offense was dependent on what was occurring within that state politically and economically; for example, in Southern states there were several crimes that dealt with slaves since slavery played a large role in continuing the farm-based economy. These laws also were made by those who were in positions of power and favored those who were land and slave owners in the South.

Since the use of the death penalty during the colonial period, there have been those who have opposed it. However, the implementation of the death penalty changes based on what is occurring at that time within society. Once the states were formed, for example, some states abolished the death penalty, but then brought it back again years later. This has been true in modern times as well. For instance, in 1972, the United States Supreme Court decided in the case *Furman v. Georgia* that the death penalty violated the defendants' *Eighth Amendment* right against cruel and unusual punishment. A couple of the justices believed the death penalty itself was cruel and unusual, but the majority opinion was that the death penalty was applied arbitrarily or unfairly from one case to the next. This is because one of the defendants in the case under review had received the death penalty for accidentally killing his victim during a burglary, while another had been convicted of rape. However, defendants who had committed similar crimes, within the same state, had not received the death penalty. The only difference then appeared to be the race of the defendants, where those who were white did not receive the death penalty. Therefore, the justices concluded the death penalty violated the Eighth Amendment because there was not a set criterion for how the death penalty was applied. This case placed a *moratorium* on the death penalty in the United States, where the use of this punishment was temporarily stopped (Oyez, n.d.b).

Later, in 1976, the United States Supreme Court decided in the case *Gregg v. Georgia* that the death penalty did not violate one's Eighth Amendment right against cruel and unusual punishment nor one's Fourteenth Amendment right to ensure equal treatment under the law. In this case Gregg had murdered someone during the course of an armed robbery, so the death was intentional. The state of Georgia also had created criteria for how the death penalty process was applied, so it was no longer considered to be arbitrary (Oyez, n.d.d). After the decision of *Gregg v. Georgia* allowing the death penalty to be reinstated, there were 35 states who immediately implemented the punishment once again (Reggie, 1997).

The types of crime one can be punished for using the death penalty also have changed. By the 1970s, the punishment of death was only used for the crimes of rape and aggravated or first-degree murder, although some states also utilized the death penalty for crimes such as espionage or terrorism (Death Penalty Information Center, 2016). However, in 1977, the Supreme Court of the United States ruled in the case *Coker v. Georgia* that the crime of raping an adult could no longer be punished as a capital offense. The majority of the justices believed the death penalty for the crime of rape violated one's Eighth Amendment right against cruel and unusual punishment, because the punishment was excessive in comparison to the crime (Find Law, n.d.).

GLOBAL SPOTLIGHT

Countries That Have the Death Penalty

Approximately two-thirds of the countries in the world have abolished the death penalty for all crimes, or it is not carried out even though one can be sentenced to death. In 2021, there were only 18 countries that utilized the death penalty, executing a total of 579 people which is a 20% increase from the previous year. The number of people who are sentenced to death has also been on the rise. For example, in 2021, there were 2,052 people who were sentenced to death globally, which was a 39% increase over the previous year (Amnesty International, 2021). The following four countries account for 88% of worldwide death sentences (this list does not include China): Iran (246+), Egypt (107+), Iraq (45+), and Saudi Arabia (27) (Death Penalty Information Center, 2020).

In many countries, the numbers reported by Amnesty International (remove 2015) on death penalty statistics are conservative estimates. This is because there are a few countries, for example China, who will not report how many people are executed or sentenced to death because they believe this information is a state secret (Amnesty International, 2021). However, it is estimated that China executes more people than the rest of the world combined, or approximately 3,000 people per year. This high number of people being sentenced to death is in part due to the number of offenses for which one can receive the death penalty; for example, there are 55 crimes that carry capital punishment as a possible sentence, with 31 of these crimes being nonviolent offenses, such as drug trafficking (Lim, 2013).

The United States Supreme Court also ruled in ***Kennedy v. Louisiana*** (2008) that the death penalty was excessive for the crime of raping a child. In a 5–4 decision, the majority opinion concluded the punishment was excessive when the offender did not kill or intend to kill the victim (Oyez, n.d.e). At the time of the case, only six states listed the rape of a child as a crime punishable by death. However, it was rarely ever used, with only the state of Louisiana having sentenced two offenders to death, while no one had been executed for the crime (Death Penalty Information Center, 2016).

The 2002 case ***Atkins v. Virginia*** also informs us about how death penalty jurisprudence has evolved. The case addressed intellectual disabilities and the death penalty. In question was whether not Atkins' intellectual disability prohibited him for adequately developing the mens rea necessary to be sentenced to death. The Court ultimately ruled that defendants with intellectual disabilities may have a diminished capacity to develop mens rea, or criminal intent, and do not meet the constitutional standard for a death sentence. A few years later in ***Roper v. Simmons*** (2005), the Court ruled that juvenile defendants have a similar diminished capacity and therefore the death penalty would be cruel and unusual punishment. Due to an improved understanding of adolescent brain science and research about youth being more susceptible to external influences and lack of maturity, the Court in *Roper* struck down the juvenile death penalty.

IN FOCUS

Federal Executions Under Trump

In 2020, the Trump Administration oversaw an unprecedented number of federal executions, a number no other U.S. president in the twentieth or twenty-first century had authorized in a single calendar year. Prior to this execution binge, there had not been a federal execution in 17 years and only three since the federal death penalty was reinstated in 1988. Fifty-nine percent of those executed in 2020 were inmates on federal death row, which exceeded the total executed by all states combined and included the first woman, Lisa Montgomery, to be executed by the federal government in 70 years (Death Penalty Information Center, 2021a; BBC News, 2021). Even amidst criticism and concern, this execution trend continued as a global pandemic caused the largest dip in state executions in 37 years. For the most part, prisons were deemed as high risk for COVID-19 outbreaks, leading states to postpone or halt executions. However, the federal government continued with a remarkable 10 executions after July 2020. At the execution of Orlando Hall, the execution team failed to wear protective gear, leading to nine members, including the inmate's religious counsel, contracting COVID-19 (Death Penalty Information Center, 2020b). When President Trump failed to get reelected he continued to authorize executions, making him the first lame duck president to do so since 1836 (*The Guardian*, 2020).

Methods of Execution in the United States

There are currently five methods of execution employed in the U.S. Depending on state law, execution can be carried out via hanging, firing squad, lethal gas, electrocution, or lethal injection (Death Penalty Information Center, 2021c). Initially, capital punishment was carried out through the method of hanging. This was typically done in a public area within the town or city, where everyone would gather to watch. The belief was that those who saw the execution would be deterred from committing similar crimes. However, this public display typically created a party atmosphere, where people would drink

Figure 9.1. © iStockphoto.com/inhauscreative.

excessively and often fight. Therefore, by the 1830s, states began to do away with public executions and instead moved them indoors, because the chaos that ensued was often difficult to manage and only provided fuel for the anti-death penalty movement. Interestingly, ever since this time, states have been attempting to find the most humane way to execute a person, and the methods that followed were an attempt to make the process more efficient and less painful (Reggie, 1997).

In the 1880s, for example, the technique of electrocution was discovered because of two electric companies who were battling for their share of the market and the direction of how electricity would enter the home. The Edison Company had created direct current (DC), which was currently being used within homes and businesses. However, there was competition from a new company, Westinghouse, which was proposing a move towards the use of alternating current (AC). In order to dissuade the public from using AC, Edison employees started travelling around the country and providing demonstrations of the dangers of AC by electrocuting small animals. However, these demonstrations only piqued the curiosity of New York officials who were searching for a more humane way to implement the death penalty and, in 1888, the state of New York built the electric chair, with the first person being electrocuted two years later, in 1890 (Reggie, 1997).

However, the process of electrocution could be gruesome; for example, it might include the smell of burning flesh. Therefore, in 1924, the state of Nevada decided to try a new, more humane method by using cyanide gas to poison an inmate. Initially, the plan had been to secretly poison the inmate by pumping the gas directly into his cell, while he slept. However, there were logistical concerns regarding how the gas would disperse, and instead a gas chamber was built to provide a space for the execution to take place (Reggie, 1997).

By the 1930s, the majority of states were using either the electric chair or cyanide gas as their primary method of execution. This switch occurred after a botched hanging, in Arizona, where the executioner did not accurately measure the rope and the force of the body dropping ripped the female inmate's head from her body. This gruesome display made the case for the electric chair and cyanide gas as being the most humane method (Reggie, 1997). However, both of these methods had their problems, and the search for a more humane method continued until 1982, when the state of Texas executed the first inmate through lethal injection (Ford, 2014).

Lethal injection gives the appearance of a medical procedure, as it is conducted in a room within the prison where the inmate is strapped down to a medical gurney and given three separate drugs intravenously. The first drug, sodium thiopental, is used to anesthetize the inmate, so they do not feel the pain of the remaining two drugs. The second drug, pancuronium bromide, paralyzes the person, which ultimately stops their breathing, while the third drug, potassium chloride, stops the heart. Today, lethal injection has become the preferred method of execution for those states with the death penalty, because it is believed to be the most humane (Ford, 2014).

Lethal Injection, the American Medical Association, and the European Union

In 1980, the American Medical Association (AMA) made it a part of their professional ethical code that physicians could no longer participate in the execution of inmates because their role as a physician is to save lives, not take them. The AMA recognized that doctors can have their own personal opinions on the topic, but they could no longer "cause the death of the condemned," "assist, supervise, or contribute to the ability of another individual to directly cause the death of the condemned," or perform "an action which could automatically cause an execution to be carried out on a condemned prisoner" (AMA, 2016, para. 1). If a physician were to violate this policy and it was reported, the case would be brought before the AMA's Council on Ethical Judicial Affairs to decide whether the doctor's membership in the AMA should be revoked. The case also could be brought before the board of medical examiners within the state to decide whether the doctor's license should be revoked, but this step is dependent upon the state where the doctor is licensed and that state's medical board's policies (Brand & Chadwick, 2006).

The ban on physicians participating in the execution of inmates became problematic for correction officials as they were left on their own to administer the three drugs for lethal injection. This led to botched executions, where the drugs were not administered properly. For example, in Texas, during the execution of Raymond Landry, the needle came out of his vein a couple of minutes after being inserted, spraying drugs all over the room. The needle was then quickly reinserted into his vein to finish the execution (Radelet, 2014).

These botched executions led to the United States Supreme Court case ***Baze et al. v. Rees*** (2008), where the defendants argued the lethal injection process used in Kentucky and 30 other states violated their Eighth Amendment right against cruel and unusual punishment. The majority opinion (7–2) was that this process did not violate an inmate's Eighth Amendment right, if it was done correctly. The justices also concluded the defendants had not demonstrated that if the procedure was done incorrectly it would amount to cruel and unusual punishment. However, it was noted that this procedure could violate one's Eighth Amendment right, if there was an alternative execution method that was perceived to be more effective (Oyez, n.d.a).

The next hurdle for the process of lethal injection came in 2011, when the European Union banned the sale of the drug sodium thiopental, which is the first drug used in the lethal injection process. This ban came about because of the European Union's position that capital punishment is a human rights violation. Therefore, once European Union officials became aware this drug was primarily being purchased by prisons for the purpose of executions, the decision was made to ban the sale of the drug to the United States. This created a major barrier for the lethal injection process, even though the other two drugs used in this method were widely available within the United States because they are used in medical procedures. However, sodium thiopental is no longer manufactured in the United States because other anesthetics have been created that are more effective (Ford, 2014).

Lethal Injection and the Search for New Drugs

The European Union's ban on sodium thiopental has led to some states placing a moratorium on the death penalty until a replacement for the drug can be found. This drug sales ban has been credited with fewer states carrying out executions. In 2013, for example, only nine states executed an inmate, which is the lowest number of executions in the United States since the moratorium on the death penalty, in 1973 (Pilkington, 2013).

However, other states have begun to experiment with different drugs with the hopes of finding a drug replacement on their own. This has proven to be difficult since medical professionals are not allowed to participate or assist in the death penalty. Florida, for example, has begun using the drug midazolam in place of sodium thiopental, even though this drug had not been used before in the execution process (Pilkington, 2013). This is because midazolam is a drug used to relax patients before entering surgery and if given in a high enough dose can result in unconsciousness, but not at the same level as pentobarbital or sodium thiopental (Stern, 2015). However, those who witnessed the Florida execution stated the inmate reacted throughout the execution by shaking his head and opening his mouth (Stern, 2015).

Ohio then became the next state to use midazolam to execute an inmate. The inmate also had a bad reaction to the drug, and witnesses stated he clenched his fists and gasped for air for fifteen minutes before he died (Stern, 2015). After this execution, a federal judge placed a moratorium on the death penalty in the state of Ohio, until a more suitable drug could be found to carry out the lethal injection process (Pelzer, 2014).

After being unable to find another drug replacement for sodium thiopental, Oklahoma decided to use midazolam for the execution of Clayton Lockett. Lockett's death was particularly painful because the drug was administered incorrectly, going into the muscle instead of the vein. Lockett reacted by attempting to speak and move around throughout the execution process (Stern, 2015). After Lockett's botched execution, twenty Oklahoma death row inmates asked a federal judge for a stay on their executions because the lethal injection process using midazolam violated their Eighth Amendment right against cruel and unusual punishment. However, the federal judge denied the stay because the inmates had not proposed an alternative execution method. Next, the death row inmates took their case to the court of appeals, but the appellate court agreed with the judge's decision, and the next execution took place in Oklahoma as scheduled. The inmate's execution did not run into the same complications as Lockett's, although he did state his body was on fire during the process (Oyez, n.d.c).

Glossip and two other death row inmates in Oklahoma then took their case before the United States Supreme Court, arguing that the drug midazolam used in Oklahoma's lethal injection process violated their Eighth Amendment right against cruel and unusual punishment. The court was divided, and in a 5–4 decision the majority concluded there was not enough evidence to show the drug midazolam created severe pain in comparison to other drugs. This is because the death penalty itself has been found to be constitutional and is not meant to guarantee that there will not be any pain during the process. Therefore, the court agreed with the federal judge that until the inmates can find an alternative that is more effective, the current method is allowed to stand (Oyez, n.d.c).

Innocence, Eyewitness Misidentification, and Faulty Forensic Science

Since 1973, 185 wrongly convicted persons have been exonerated (Death Penalty Information Center, 2021b). DPIC adopted the term "*legal exoneration*" in an effort to objectively identify people who have been wrongly sentenced to death. In order to be considered a legal exoneration, the following criteria must be met:

- Subsequently acquitted of all charges related to the crime that placed them on death row, either at retrial or by an appellate court determination that the evidence presented at trial was insufficient to convict;

IN FOCUS

Firing Squads

Since the current most commonly used method of lethal injection is not accessible due to a lack of drugs, some states are considering alternative methods of execution. For example, in Alabama, a congressman proposed a bill that would allow inmates to request a firing squad in place of lethal injection. The firing squad would consist of five law enforcement officials each shooting the death row inmate simultaneously. This method is currently offered as an alternative in Utah and Oklahoma and has been used as recently as 2010, when Ronnie Lee Gardner was executed by a firing squad, in Utah (Lyman, 2016).

- Had all charges related to the crime that placed them on death row dismissed by the prosecution or had reprosecution barred by the court in circumstances implicating the reliability of the evidence of guilt; or
- Been granted a complete pardon based on evidence of innocence (Death Penalty Information Center, 2021b).

This means that for every ten people executed, one has been released due to their innocence (Equal Justice Initiative, 2014). The majority of those freed were non-white. Exonerated individuals reported their race or ethnicity as Black (53%), white (36%), or Latino (8%). In the majority of criminal cases where the person is exonerated, the person was sentenced to death. For example, death sentences make up less than 1% of all criminal convictions, but are 12% of all those convicted of crimes who were later found to be innocent. This is primarily because the person's life hangs in the balance, and more resources are put forth when examining claims of innocence for death penalty cases (Gross et al., 2014).

Most of the previous studies that had examined innocence and the death penalty had not taken into consideration those cases where the person had been removed from death row and instead was sentenced to life in prison. It is difficult to determine in what percentage of these cases the person was actually innocent, because those who have a death sentence removed are less likely to have someone fight for their innocence because their life is no longer in the balance. Gross and colleagues (2014) examined all of the cases (7,482) where the person had been sentenced to death between 1973 and 2004. The authors conducted the study to better understand the actual number of those who were sentenced to death, but are innocent. Of these cases, 12.6% had been executed, 4% had died on death row, 1.6% had been exonerated,

46.1% remained on death row, and an additional 35.8% had been released from death row, but remained in prison. The researchers found there was a 2.2% chance of being exonerated if one was still on death row and their life was at risk. However, once those who had been exonerated as well as those who were removed from death row and sentenced to life were included in the analysis, this number increased to 4.1% of all death row inmates sentenced to death row being exonerated (Gross et al., 2014).

The most common reason for wrongful convictions in criminal cases is eyewitness misidentification. For example, in 70% of convictions overturned due to DNA evidence, the person had been convicted due to eyewitness misidentification (Innocence Project, n.d.a). The death penalty case of Troy Davis is a good example of how faulty eyewitness testimony can convict an innocent person. In this case, Troy Davis and Sylvester Coles, both African American men, along with several other people, were standing around at a bus station late at night. Coles approached a man and asked him for a beer, but the man walked away, refusing Coles the beer. Coles then pistol whipped the man, and a white security guard who was an off-duty police officer was called to the scene for help. After the security guard arrived, he was shot and killed. The next day Coles went to the police station and said that Davis was the one who shot and killed the officer (NAACP, 2016).

Davis was arrested for the crime, and the case received significant news coverage that included his mug shot. The investigating police officers then took those who were witnesses back to the scene of the crime and laid out photographs of possible suspects, with one of the pictures being of Troy Davis. The witnesses were then asked to identify the shooter. However, none of the other pictures were of men who had been at the crime scene that night, and Coles was included in the investigation as a witness and not as a suspect. The majority of the witnesses stated that the same person who pistol whipped the man also was the same person who shot the security guard and identified that person as Troy Davis (NAACP, 2016).

During the trial, Coles admitted to being the one who assaulted the man over a beer and stated that he owned a gun that was the same model as the gun used to kill the officer. However, this gun was never confiscated or tested because Coles claimed it had been lost. Davis was then convicted for the murder and was sentenced to death (NAACP, 2016). After the trial, 7 of the 9 witnesses recanted or contradicted their statements. One witness admitted to being a jailhouse snitch who had lied about witnessing the crime. Two of the witnesses said the person who shot the officer was the same one who had attacked the man, and they believed this person was Coles. Two of the witnesses said they felt intimidated by the police to testify that Davis was the suspect. One witness admitted she had identified Davis, but that she had been standing across a tree-lined, four-lane road, and it was dark outside. Another witness later died, but had stated she believed the person who assaulted the man was the same one who shot the officer, and she believed this was Coles after seeing him at the trial because of his lighter skin. The only two witnesses who did not recant their testimony

Figure 9.2. Death Penalty Protest in Maryland, 2013. © iStockphoto.com/EyeJoy.

were Coles and another man who said he would not recognize the shooter if he saw him again. There also were two additional witnesses who came forward after the trial who implicated Coles. Both said they had not done so previously because they knew Coles and feared he would retaliate against them (NAACP, 2016).

Davis' case received an enormous amount of attention, and world leaders from the Pope to former United States President Jimmy Carter spoke on his behalf. However, Troy Davis' case was unsuccessfully appealed to the United States Supreme Court. In 2011, Davis was executed, after four stays of execution and over 22 years on death row (Curry & James, 2011).

The second leading cause of wrongful criminal convictions is the improper use of forensic science. DNA testing is a sound method of forensic science, but only 5–10% of all criminal cases contain biological evidence that could be used for DNA analysis. Therefore, other forensic science techniques, such as bite mark analysis, fire science, shoe print analysis, and hair analysis are used to gather evidence when DNA is not available. However, these other methods are not based on scientific proof, but rather the personal experiences of the person who is presenting the evidence. Those who testify about the evidence admitted under these types of situations often lead the jury to believe that their conclusions are scientific and based on fact, even though that is often not the case (Innocence Project, n.d.b).

Cameron Todd Willingham is an example of a person who was convicted and sentenced to death based on faulty forensic science. In this case, Willingham's house caught on fire while he was sleeping. He was able to escape the fire. However, his three young daughters all died. His wife had not been at home at the time, and Willingham was charged with arson and the murders of his three children. The prosecutor offered him a plea bargain in exchange for life in prison. However, Willingham refused the deal and went to trial declaring he was innocent of the crimes. At the trial, Willingham was convicted of arson and murder and was sentenced to death based on the testimony of the fire investigators and a jailhouse snitch. The fire investigator testified that Willingham had set the fire, while the jailhouse snitch testified Willingham had confessed his crimes to him when the two were in jail. Willingham's attorneys sent a report to the governor of Texas and the Board of Pardon and Parole that was written by a national expert on arson who concluded Willingham had not set the fire. Despite this evidence, Willingham was executed 13 years after being convicted for the murders (Innocence Project, 2010).

After Willingham was executed, the Innocence Project compiled a team of arson experts who released a report that concluded the fire science used in the case to convict Willingham was not valid. The Innocence Project then used the report to have the state of Texas open an investigation into the case. The Texas Forensic Science Commission reviewed the case. However, based on parameters set by the Texas attorney general, the commission was not allowed to use any of the reports written by outside experts who had stated the original fire investigators had been wrong. Therefore, the panel was unable to state there had been any misconduct that occurred in the case (Innocence Project, 2010).

Race, Class, Gender, and the Death Penalty

In 1983, David Baldus, along with his colleagues Charles Pulaski and George Woodward, published a study that later became known as the *Baldus Study*. The three researchers had examined 2,000 homicide cases in the state of Georgia since 1972 and found that race played a significant factor in whether one received the death penalty. They concluded that Black defendants were 1.7 times more likely to receive the death penalty than white defendants, and those who murdered white victims were 4.3 times more likely to receive the death penalty than those who murdered Black victims (Dow, 2011).

In 1987, the Baldus Study was used in the United States Supreme Court case *McKleskey v. Kemp*. In this case, McKleskey, an African American man, had murdered a white Atlanta police officer. McKleskey's defense argued that based on the findings from the Baldus Study, McKleskey's death sentence was racially biased and should be thrown out. However, in a 5–4 decision the United States Supreme Court ruled that the sentence was not racially biased because "general patterns of discrimination do not prove that racial discrimination operated in a particular case" (Dow, 2011, para. 3).

Nationally the majority of those who receive the death penalty are white (55.8%). However, African Americans (41.9%) are significantly overrepresented on death row because only about 12% of the United States population is Black. Since the reinstatement of the death penalty in 1976, Black defendants make up 43% of all those executed (Cokley, 2019). In 2022, the percentage of those on death row by race is nearly the same for white (42%) and Black (41%) inmates (NAACP Legal Defense and Educational Fund, Inc., 2022). Future researchers continued to build off of the Baldus Study and found similar results regarding race in other states and across the country. For example, the biggest predictor of whether someone will be charged with a death penalty eligible crime is the race of the victim, and when the victim is Black the offender is significantly less likely to be charged with a crime that carries the death penalty (Amnesty International, 2016). In Alabama, only 6% of murder cases involved a Black defendant and a white victim. However, more than 60% of those who are Black and on death row were sentenced for killing a white victim (Equal Justice Initiative, 2014). The American Bar Association also conducted a study on death row inmates, where the crime was committed in the city of Philadelphia. The authors concluded that one-third of the African American defendants who had been sentenced to death would have received a sentence of life, if they had not been Black (Amnesty International, 2016).

The sentence of death also is dependent upon your attorney and their abilities. The majority of those who commit a crime that is death penalty eligible are appointed an attorney because they cannot afford one. However, appointed attorneys are often underpaid and overworked. In Alabama, for example, half of those who faced a sentence of death and were appointed an attorney had attorneys whose out-of-court work was capped at $1,000. This leaves very little funding for bringing in expert witnesses or investigating leads or to pay for the paperwork the lawyer is also expected to complete (Equal Justice Initiative, 2014).

Gregory Wilson's case is an example of a defendant being sentenced to death, even though his two appointed attorneys were inexperienced and one was an alcoholic. In this case, the first chair attorney drank throughout the trial and only attended half of the days the case was heard in court, while the second chair attorney had never tried a felony case. Eventually, the defendant attempted to defend himself during the trial. Wilson's case was appealed based upon his attorneys' actions during the case. However, his appeal was denied, and he remained on death row until 2019 when then Kentucky Governor Matt Bevin commuted his sentence (Wolfson, 2019).

George McFarland's case is an example of a defendant being sentenced to death even though his two appointed attorneys were inexperienced and one slept through the case. In this case, the lead attorney in the case took naps throughout the trial and left the work of the case to the second attorney, who was inexperienced. McFarland's case was appealed based upon his lead attorney napping. The second attorney in the case testified that the lead attorney did indeed sleep during the trial. However, the appeal was denied, and the majority opinion of the appeals court even suggested that the naps were strategically used, so there would be a case for an appeal later. McFarland is still on death row (Bookman, 2013).

The case of Jack Carlton House is an example of a death penalty eligible defendant being appointed two attorneys who were inexperienced. In this case, the appointed attorneys were real estate lawyers who had never tried a criminal case. They had been assigned to the case two days before the trial started and did not visit the crime scene or interview any witnesses for the case. The attorneys also were unaware there would be a separate sentencing phase for the trial and were unprepared. The defendant was sentenced to death, but was successful on his appeal that his defense was inadequate. Later, he was appointed a new attorney who advised him to plead guilty in exchange for life in prison. He took the plea deal and is still incarcerated (Bookman, 2013).

Since 1976, when the death penalty was reinstated, there have been a total of 16 women executed in the United States, including 4 Black women and 12 white women (Death Penalty Information Center, 2017). Currently, only 51 of the over 3,000 people on death row are women, and the majority of those who are executed (98.9%) are men (Oliver, 2016). However, in contemporary times those who are executed in the United States are sentenced to death for the crime of murder, which is much more likely to be committed by men (90%) than women. Although women commit 10% of all homicides, they are still not as likely to receive the death penalty as men. This is in part because of who women kill. For example, women are more likely to murder a significant other or someone they knew, while men (80%) typically murder a stranger or someone they barely knew, making them more likely to receive the death penalty as their sentence. In South Carolina, for example, one study found that those who killed a stranger were six times more likely to receive the death penalty than those who killed someone they knew (Oliver, 2016). Although most of the 17 women who were executed killed someone they knew, often family, half of these cases involved the death of a husband or boyfriend who was murdered for financial gain and did not involve self-defense or mental illness (Death Penalty Information Center, 2021d). Further breakdown by race shows that white women are more inclined to murder someone they care about or are related to, while Black women were more likely to murder someone unrelated to them. Latina women more likely to murder associates. As it pertains to women offenders and their victims, white women tend to kill males while Black women are more likely to have a female victim (Greenlee & Greenlee, 2008). Since there are so few women sentenced to death it is challenging to make empirical inferences about women death row inmates (Greenlee & Greenlee, 2008).

Deterrence Theory and Cost

Some argue the death penalty should be utilized based on deterrence theory. This theory states that if the punishment outweighs any benefit one would receive from committing the crime, then one will rationally choose not to commit the crime. For example, if someone knows they could receive the death penalty for the crime of murder, then they will rationally choose not to commit the crime. There are three components of the deterrence theory that must be present in order for it to be considered to be effective. First, the punishment must follow as close to the crime as possible, so the offender is able to make the connection that they are being punished for the crime they committed. Second, the punishment must be certain, so the offender knows that they will indeed receive the penalty of death if they murder another human. Third, the punishment must be severe or outweigh any benefits one would receive from committing the murder (Onwudiwe et al., 2005).

However, the death penalty is not an effective deterrent because it only meets one of the three components of the deterrence theory—severity. The death penalty is the most severe punishment one can receive for committing a crime. However, the death penalty is not swift. Most death row inmates, for example, spend about 10 years on death row before being executed, while some remain on death row for 20 years or more. In 2012, death row inmates averaged 190 months from the time they received their sentence until the time they were executed. The length of time spent on death row has increased over the years, mainly due to the appeals process. However, there also are some states who use the death penalty as a sentence, but do not execute inmates very often (Death Penalty Information Center, 2016).

The death penalty also is not certain. For example, there are 24 states that do not have death penalty statutes (NAACP Legal Defense and Educational Fund, Inc, 2022). Therefore, if you commit a murder in a state, such as West Virginia, that does not use the death penalty, you cannot be sentenced to death. This means that whether you receive this penalty is dependent upon the state in which you committed the crime. Even in states that do have the death penalty, it is not certain that one will receive this punishment for the crime of murder. For example, the defendant may plea bargain to reduce their sentence to a lesser sentence than death (Death Penalty Information Center, 2016).

IN FOCUS

Death Penalty in California

In 2016, the state of California had two propositions on their state ballot that specifically dealt with the death penalty, but with very different outcomes. The first, Proposition 62, was an attempt to abolish the death penalty, while the second, Proposition 66, was an attempt to streamline the appeals process. Proposition 62 specifically proposed to abolish the death penalty, making life without parole the harshest sentence in the state. It also required those sentenced to life without parole to work while incarcerated and to give between 20 and 60 percent of their wages to the victims of their crimes. Proposition 66 also included a work requirement, where 70 percent of the inmate's wages are given to the victim's families, but the similarities end there. Proposition 66 would put the trial court that heard the original case in charge of the initial petitions challenging the conviction along with a specific time frame for this process. The state court of appeals would no longer be in charge of this procedure, which would shorten the appeals process. The vote count was close, but in the end Proposition 62 was defeated, with 47 percent of the votes in favor of ending the death penalty and 53 percent in favor of keeping it. However, Proposition 66 became law, with 51 percent of the votes in favor of streamlining the appeals process for the death penalty and 49 percent against (Ballotpedia, 2016).

Most of the cost of the death penalty occurs before and during the trial because of the need to be certain you are indeed convicting the correct person. Many people assume the major cost of these cases is due to the lengthy appeals process. However, if you removed the costs of the appeals process, the death penalty would still cost more than the trial and sentencing of a person to life without parole (Amnesty International, 2016). The investigation and the trial for a death penalty case are so expensive because everyone wants to ensure they are convicting the correct person, since the defendant's life is at stake. Research that has been conducted on the cost of the death penalty have found the death penalty costs more than sending the person to prison with a sentence of life without parole. For instance, in Kansas, from investigation to execution, a death sentence costs $1.26 million, while a comparable case where the person is sent to prison for life costs $740,000. In Tennessee, the death penalty was found to cost 48% more than a sentence of life without parole, while in Maryland a death penalty case costs three times more than a comparable case where the person was sentenced to life without parole (Amnesty International, 2016).

Intersectionality, Public Opinion, and the Death Penalty

Of all crime-related topics, the death penalty has arguably emerged as the dominant topic in public opinion research over time. Whether the research includes an entire survey or one survey question, attitudes toward capital punishment are of interest to a variety of stakeholders. Bohm's (1991) seminal examination of 50 years of Gallop Poll data resulted in a comprehensive compilation of the trends of views toward capital punishment (Longmire, 1996). In his analysis, he discovered that historically Americans have held a dominant supportive stance toward capital punishment (Bohm, 1991; Longmire, 1996). Upon analysis of 1936–1986 Gallup Poll data, Bohm found that an average of 59% of respondents held favorable attitudes toward the death penalty, while 33% were in opposition and 9% were described as "neutral" (Longmire, 1996). Demographic variables also appeared to be related to fluctuations between support and opposition. In sum, Bohm (1991) stated "whites, wealthier people, males, Republicans, and Westerners have tended to support the death penalty more than blacks, poorer people, females, Democrats, and Southerners" (p. 135; Longmire, 1996, p.93).

Contemporary research supports Bohm's findings. Oliphant (2018) reported that opinions about the death penalty remain delineated by social identities. For gender, the majority of men (61%) support while women are split, with 46% in support and 41% opposed to the death penalty (Oliphant, 2018). The intersection of religious affiliation and race appears to be related to death penalty opinions with support from 73% of white evangelical Protestants, 53% of Catholics, and 48% of religiously unaffiliated (Oliphant, 2018).

When it comes to race, 59% of white respondents favored the death penalty while 47% of Hispanics and 36% of Black respondents were in support (Oliphant, 2018). Reasons for the distinct racial differences in death penalty attitudes of demographic subgroups have also been the focus of public opinion studies. Young (1991) suggested that causes of crime explanations differ between African-Americans and whites. African-Americans tend to base their crime causation opinions on "trust in the police and perceptions of inequity," while whites develop opinions based on "responsibility attribution" (p. 95). This, he posits, may explicate differing death penalty attitudes by race. Other research found that white racism that was described as the belief that "Blacks are lazy, irresponsible, devoid of culture, and dangerous" explained one third of the study's racialized division in support for the death penalty (Trahan et al., 2019, p. 454).

Though race is a determining factor, other research has looked at the potential for public opinion toward capital punishment to also be influenced by experiences. Another example of capital punishment research was a survey conducted by Whitehead, Blankenship, and Wright (1999) who examined the views of Tennessee criminal justice officials versus the ideas of its citizens regarding the death penalty. The results reflect supportive attitudes toward capital punishment (state legislators: 95%; prosecutors: 91%; citizens: 75%) with the public defender group (21%) serving as the exception. Similar to previous research, Whitehead et al. (1999) chose to explore the effect of giving respondents the option of choosing the death penalty or life without parole for the sanction in a particular scenario. However, even with the life without parole option, a substantial number of respondents (40%) still supported the death penalty (Whitehead et al., 1999).

Summary

How the death penalty is carried out in the United States continues to evolve; for example, executions have been moved inside prisons and the methods of execution change as state officials continue to try and find the most effective and humane process. The United States Supreme Court also has changed who can receive the death penalty and for what crimes, but continues to uphold the states' right to decide whether or not to implement the death penalty as well as the manner in which the execution is carried out. The death penalty also faces scrutiny based on those cases where people have been exonerated as well as for racial differences, the sheer cost of it, and because the outcome of one's case is often dependent upon one's ability to afford a private attorney.

The death penalty has been abolished in many countries, even though it continues to be used in some states within the United States. However, the number of people sentenced to death in those states continues to decrease as well as the number of people executed each year. This is in part due to changing public opinion as well as the availability of drugs used in the execution process. In March 2020, Colorado became the twenty-second state to abolish the death penalty. While there is expected to be an uptick in executions due to pandemic postponements, support for the death penalty continues to decline, with 60% of Americans saying they favor the use of life without the possibility of parole for death-eligible offenses. A 2020 report found that a majority of Americans (54%) deemed the death penalty objectionable (Ndulue, 2020).

Discussion Questions

1. Explain the court cases *Baze v. Rees* and *Glossip v. Gross*. What are your thoughts? Does the execution method of lethal injection violate one's Eighth Amendment right against cruel and unusual punishment?

2. Can the death penalty be implemented in the United States in a manner where only those who have committed the crime are executed and there are not racial or class biases in who receives the punishment? Why or why not?

3. Define the theory of deterrence. Can the death penalty be implemented in a way that it serves as a deterrent?

Key Terms

death penalty	*Atkins v. Virginia*
Furman v. Georgia	*Roper v. Simmons*
Eighth Amendment	*Baze et al. v. Rees*
moratorium	legal exoneration
Gregg v. Georgia	Baldus Study
Coker v. Georgia	*McKleskey v. Kemp*
Kennedy v. Louisiana	

References

American Medical Association (AMA). (2016). Capital punishment. http://www.ama-assn.org/ama/pub/physician-resources/medical-ethics/code-medical-ethics/opinion206.page

Amnesty International. (2015). Death sentences and executions. https://www.amnesty.org/en/documents/act50/3487/2016/en/

Amnesty International. (2016). Death penalty cost. http://www.amnestyusa.org/our-work/issues/death-penalty/us-death-penalty-facts/death-penalty-cost

Ballotpedia. (2016). California Proposition 66, Death Penalty Procedures. Ballotpedia: The Encyclopedia of American Politics. https://ballotpedia.org/California_Proposition_66,_Death_Penalty_Procedures_(2016)

BBC News. (2021, January 13). Lisa Montgomery: US executes only woman on federal death row. https://www.bbc.com/news/world-us-canada-55642177

Bohm, R.M. (1991). American death penalty opinion, 1936–1986: A critical examination of the Gallup Polls. In R.M. Bohm (Ed.), *The Death Penalty in America: Current Research* (pp. 113–145). Anderson.

Bookman, M. (2013). 10 ways to blow a death penalty case. *Mother Jones.*http://www.motherjones.com/politics/2014/04/10-death-penalty-cases-bad-lawyering

Brand, M., & Chadwick, A. (2006). The medical ethics of the death penalty. NPR. http://www.npr.org/templates/story/story.php?storyId=5226605

Cokley, K.O. (2019, November 27). Why support for the death penalty is much higher among white Americans. The Conversation. https://theconversation.com/why-support-for-the-death-penalty-is-much-higher-among-white-americans-127853

Curry, C., & James, M. S. (2011). Troy Davis executed after stay denied by Supreme Court. ABC News.http://abcnews.go.com/US/troy-davis-executed-stay-denied-supreme-court/story?id=14571862

Death Penalty Information Center. (2016). Crimes punishable by the death penalty. http://www.deathpenaltyinfo.org/crimes-punishable-death-penalty

Death Penalty Information Center. (2017). Innocence and the death penalty. http://www.deathpenaltyinfo.org/innocence-and-death-penalty#race

Death Penalty Information Center, (2020a). Executions Around the World. https://deathpenaltyinfo.org/policy-issues/international/executions-around-the-world

Death Penalty Information Center. (2020b). ACLU: Documents show federal executions likely caused prison COVID-19 outbreak. https://deathpenaltyinfo.org/news/aclu-documents-show-federal-executions-likely-caused-prison-covid-19-outbreak

Death Penalty Information Center. (2021a). The death penalty in 2020: Year end report. https://reports.deathpenaltyinfo.org/year-end/YearEndReport2020.pdf

Death Penalty Information Center. (2021b). DPIC adds eleven cases to innocence list, bringing national death-row exoneration total to 185. https://deathpenaltyinfo.org/news/dpic-adds-eleven-cases-to-innocence-list-bringing-national-death-row-exoneration-total-to-185

Death Penalty Information Center. (2021c). Methods of execution. https://deathpenalty info.org/executions/methods-of-execution

Death Penalty Information Center. (2021d). Women and the death penalty. http://www.deathpenaltyinfo.org/women-and-death-penalty

Dow, D. R. (2011). Death penalty, still racist and arbitrary. *The New York Times*. http://www.nytimes.com/2011/07/09/opinion/09dow.html

Equal Justice Initiative. (2014). Innocence. https://eji.org/news/tag/innocence/

Find Law. (n.d.). *Coker v. Georgia*. http://caselaw.findlaw.com/us-supreme-court/433/584.html

Ford, M. (2014). Can Europe end the death penalty in America? *The Atlantic*. http://www.theatlantic.com/international/archive/2014/02/can-europe-end-the-death-penalty-in-america/283790/

Greenlee, H., & Greenlee, S. P. (2008). Women and the death penalty: Racial disparities and differences. *William & Mary Journal of Race, Gender and Social Justice, 14*(2), 319. https://scholarship.law.wm.edu/ wmjowl/vol14/iss2/7

Gross, S. R., O'Brien, B., Hu, C., & Kennedy, E. H. (2014). Rate of false convictions of criminal defendants who are sentenced to death. *Proceedings of the National Academy of Sciences of the United States of America, 111*(20), 7230–7235.

The Guardian. (2020, December 15). Trump administration has executed more Americans than all states combined, report finds. https://www.theguardian.com/us-news/2020/dec/15/trump-administration-us-death-penalty-executions

Innocence Project. (n.d.a). Eyewitness misidentification. http://www.innocenceproject.org/causes-wrongful-conviction/eyewitness-misidentification

Innocence Project. (n.d.b). Unvalidated or improper forensic science. http://www.innocenceproject.org/causes-wrongful-conviction/unvalidated-or-improper-forensic-science

Innocence Project. (2010). Cameron Todd Willingham: Wrongfully convicted and executed in Texas. http://www.innocenceproject.org/news-events-exonerations/levela-todd-willingham-wrongfully-convicted-and-executed-in-texas#summary

Lim, Z. H. (2013). Why China executes so many people. *The Atlantic*. http://www.theatlantic.com/china/archive/2013/05/why-china-executes-so-many-people/275695/

Longmire, D.R. (1996). "Americans attitudes about the ultimate weapon: Capital punishment." In T.J. Flanagan & D.M. Longmire (Eds.), *Americans View Crime and Justice: A National Public Opinion Survey*. Thousand Oaks, CA: Sage.

Lyman, B. (2016). Bill would bring firing squad executions to Alabama. *Montgomery Advertiser*. http://www.montgomeryadvertiser.com/story/news/politics/southunionstreet/2016/11/07/bill-would-bring-firing-squad-executions-alabama/93427800/

NAACP. (2016). Significant doubt about Troy Davis' guilt: A case for clemency. http://www.naacp.org/pages/troy-davis-a-case-for-clemency

NAACP Legal Defense and Educational Fund, Inc. (2022). DEATH ROW U.S.A. Winter 2022. https://www.naacpldf.org/wp-content/uploads/DRUSAWinter2022.pdf

Ndulue, N. (2020). *Enduring injustice: The persistence of racial discrimination in the US death penalty*. Death Penalty Information Center. https://documents.deathpenalty info.org/pdf/Enduring-Injustice-Race-and-the-Death-Penalty-2020.pdf

Oliphant, J.B. (2018). Public support for the death penalty ticks up. Pew Research Center. https://www.pewresearch.org/fact-tank/2018/06/11/us-support-for-death -penalty-ticks-up-2018/

Oliver, A. (2016). The death penalty has a gender bias. *The Huffington Post*. http:// www.huffingtonpost.com/amanda-oliver/are-women-getting-away-wi_b_8227690 .html

Onwudiwe, I. D., Odo, J., & Onyeozili, E. C. (2005). Deterrence theory. In M. Bo-sworth, (Ed.), *Encyclopedia of prisons and correctional facilities*. Sage Publishing.

Oyez. (n.d.a). *Baze v. Rees*. https://www.oyez.org/cases/2007/07-5439

Oyez. (n.d.b). *Furman v. Georgia*. https://www.oyez.org/cases/1971/69-5030

Oyez. (n.d.c). *Glossip v. Gross*. https://www.oyez.org/cases/2014/14-7955

Oyez. (n.d.d). *Gregg v. Georgia*. https://www.oyez.org/cases/1975/74-6257

Oyez. (n.d.e). *Kennedy v. Louisiana*. https://www.oyez.org/cases/2007/07-343

Pelzer, J. (2014). Ohio's death penalty moratorium extended until next January. Cleve-land.com. http://www.cleveland.com/open/index.ssf/2014/08/ohios_execution_ moratorium_ext.html

Pilkington, E. (2013). European boycott of the death penalty drugs lowers rate of US executions. *The Guardian*. http://www.theguardian.com/world/2013/dec/19/death -penalty-boycott-drugs-execution-new-low

Radelet, M. L. (2014). Examples of botched executions post-*Furman*. Death Penalty Information Center. http://www.deathpenaltyinfo.org/some-examples-post-fur man-botched-executions

Reggie, M. H. (1997). History of the death penalty. PBS *Frontline*. http://www.pbs.org/ wgbh/pages/frontline/shows/execution/readings/history.html

Trahan, A., Andrekus , A., & Nodeland, B. (2019). Public opinion of capital punish-ment: An intersectional analysis of race, gender, and class effects. *Criminal Justice Review*, 44(4) 452–469.

Stern, J. E. (2015). The cruel and unusual execution of Clayton Lockett. *The Atlantic*. http://www.theatlantic.com/magazine/archive/2015/06/execution-clayton-lockett/ 392069/

Whitehead, J.T., Blankenship, M.B., & Wright, J.P. (1999). Elite versus citizen attitudes on capital punishment: Incongruity between the public and policymakers. *Journal of Criminal Justice,* 27 (3), 249–258.

Wolfson, A. (2019, December 10). He was sentenced to death after a scandalous trial. Matt Bevin commuted his sentence. *The Courier Journal*. https://www.courier-jour nal.com/story/news/crime/2019/12/10/matt-bevin-commutes-death-sentence -gregory-wilson/4384704002/

Young, R.L. (1991). Race, conceptions of crime and justice, and support for the death penalty. *Social Psychological Quarterly*, 54, 67–75.

Corrections

TEN

The Overuse of Incarceration and Possible Alternatives

Learning Objectives

1. Critically examine the use of imprisonment in the United States and how this impacts those from different race, gender, and class backgrounds.
2. Critically examine the attempt to alleviate overcrowding through the use of private prisons.
3. Explore possible alternatives to incarceration and current drug policies.

The War on Drugs had a major impact on the corrections system in the United States. Today, for example, there are more inmates incarcerated in America as a proportion of its population than in any other country in the world. However, this was not the case only a few decades ago. In this chapter, we will examine the impact of the incarceration binge on the corrections industry as well as possible alternatives to incarceration that can keep people out of the traditional criminal justice system and effectively offer treatment that reduces recidivism rates. Different types of drug policies also will be examined as possible alternatives to the current model of prohibition that is utilized in the War on Drugs.

The Incarceration Binge

Today, the United States incarcerates 655 people per 100,000, which is more than any other country in the world. The next highest rates of incarceration are found in El Salvador (618 per 100,000), Rwanda (464 per 100,000), and Russia (383 per 100,000). However, most countries are incarcerating their citizens at far lower rates, such as Canada (114 per 100,000), France (104 per 100,000), and Germany (77 per 100,000) (Sentencing Project, 2020). However, prior to the wars on drugs and crime there were very few people who were incarcerated across the United States. For instance, in 1980, there were 500,000 people sentenced to prisons and jails (Cahalan & Parsons, 1986). Nonetheless, by the late 1980s this number began to dramatically increase, and today there are approximately 2.3 million people in prisons and jails across the country, with 1 in every 110 adults incarcerated in a jail or prison (BBC, n.d.). If probation and parole are included, this number increases to 1 in 35 adults under correctional supervision (Sawyer & Wagner, 2020).

The War on Drugs has directly impacted people of color, who are only 37% of the total American population, but are 67% of those who are serving time (Sentencing Project, 2020). Over the last 20 years the number of Black offenders incarcerated for drug offenses increased by 550%, and African Americans are 10 times more likely to be incarcerated for a drug offense than a white person. The majority of Black offenders (53%) and Hispanic offenders (57%) who are serving time in federal prison are there for drug offenses (NAACP, 2016; Common Sense for Drug Policy, 2016).

The increase in Black and Hispanic drug offenders is not due to an increase in drug crime, but rather the amount of money spent on law enforcement and courts within Black and Hispanic neighborhoods. For example, those counties that spent the most on law enforcement and court proceedings also had the highest number of drug offender arrests (Common Sense for Drug Policy, 2016). Black individuals, for example, are not any more likely to state they use drugs than any other race, and only 12% of those who report using drugs on a monthly basis report their race as Black. However, African Americans are 32% of those who are arrested for a drug offense (NAACP, 2016).

Women also have been directly impacted by the War on Drugs, and their numbers have increased dramatically within the prison system since the start of this war in the mid-1980s (The Sentencing Project, 2015). For example, in 1980 there were 26,378 women who were incarcerated in jail as well as state and federal prisons, but by 2014 this number had increased to 215,332—a more than 700% increase. Women tend to become involved in the criminal justice system through nonviolent convictions, such as drug offenses (24%) and property offenses (28%). Both of these crimes are typically tied to substance abuse, as property offenses are often committed to support one's addiction. However, there are not more women using and abusing drugs today then there were in 1980, but the policies regarding illegal substances have changed drastically, bringing more women into the criminal justice system than ever before. The impact of poverty combined with race also has had a devastating impact on women of color. For example, in 2014, Black women were incarcerated at two times the rate of white women, while Hispanic women were imprisoned 1.2 times more often than white women (The Sentencing Project, 2015).

The number of people imprisoned has been directly impacted by the increased sentences offenders have faced over the last few decades. For instance, in 1990, the

Figure 10.1. Sign for privately owned Core Civic Detention Center in Otay Mesa, where San Diego County's illegal immigrants are held as they go through the legal process. © Adobe Stock/Simone.

average sentence for both violent and nonviolent offenders was 36% shorter than the average sentence in 2009 (Families Against Mandatory Minimums, 2014). Policies such as mandatory minimums also have increased sentences. In 1981, for example, the sentence one received for a first-time drug offense was, on average, thirteen months (Cahalan & Parsons, 1986). However, today the majority of those sentenced under mandatory minimum laws are for drug offenses, with six years being the average sentence for a federal drug offender (Families Against Mandatory Minimums, 2014).

The increase in the number of imprisoned offenders and longer periods of time spent in prison also has increased the cost of corrections for the state and thus the taxpayer. Over the last twenty years, the cost of prisons has increased at the state level by 300%, with the average annual cost to house an inmate in a state prison being $33,274 (Families Against Mandatory Minimums, 2014; Mai & Subramanian, 2017). The increase in incarceration costs taxpayers more than $43 billion for state prisons each year. These costs include housing, securing, and treating the inmates as well as salary, benefits, retirement, and healthcare for staff (Mai & Subramanian, 2017).

Private Prisons

As the number of people incarcerated continued to rise throughout the 1990s, so did the need for space to house the inmates. In order to fill this gap, many states turned to the *private prison industry* or for-profit institutions that house inmates based on a contract between the company and the government. Private prison corporations argued they could build prisons more quickly and house inmates more cheaply than the government-run institutions, and between 1990 and 2009, the number of private prisons increased by 1,600% (Shapiro, 2011). In 2017, there were 127,718 inmates housed in state and federal private prisons (Sentencing Project, 2019).

Private prisons often assert that they can run a prison more efficiently than the government, making their services cheaper. However, most research shows that private prisons either cost the same or slightly more than government-run facilities (Shapiro, 2011). Research studies that did find savings concluded this was due to private prisons taking on low-level, nonviolent offenders and leaving state facilities with those inmates who are higher risk and in need of more care (Mason, 2012). Corrections Corporation of America, now known as CoreCivic, for example, has 14 criteria they use to exclude potential inmates, including HIV-positive status, the elderly, and those with other serious health diagnoses (Canon, 2015).

Another cost-saving measure is the lack of physical and mental healthcare within the private prison industry. Research studies have found instances where health diagnoses have been changed in order not to offer services as well as cases where necessary prescriptions were not filled, leading to significant health problems and in some instances death (Mason, 2012). The majority of private prison contracts also required the government to keep the facility at an occupancy rate of 90%, and if they were unable to do so the government had to pay for the empty beds (Cohen, 2015). This measure ensured the private prison profited in cases where the government was not able to fulfill their end of the contract.

Private prisons also do not train their staff effectively, and because the staff is non-union, their wages tend to be lower than those of state employees, which leads to higher turnover rates (Mason, 2012). Staff in private prisons, for example, receive on average 58 hours less of training and are paid significantly less through salary and benefits than state employees (Mason, 2012). The lack of training also makes it difficult for staff to conduct their jobs. For example, inexperienced and poorly trained staff have a difficult time handling violent situations or emergencies (Shapiro, 2011). Therefore, assaults are twice as likely to occur within a private facility (Mason, 2012). Inmates held in private facilities also are more likely to receive infractions for behavior, which lengthen their sentences on average by two to three months at a cost of approximately $3,000 (Canon, 2015).

Today, twenty-eight states and the federal government utilize private prisons (Sentencing Project, 2019). Overall, private prisons house 8.2% of all state and federal inmates and 73% of all those sentenced for immigration violations (Sentencing Project, 2019). The private prison industry also is profiting and, in 2019, the two largest private prison companies claimed a total of more than 4.5 billion dollars in profit (Sanders, 2020). However, the continued financial success of private prisons is dependent on the continuation of tough sentencing laws. Therefore, the top two private prison companies spent $26.2 million between 2012 and 2017 in 16 states in order to lobby for policies that support tougher sentencing, such as three-strikes legislation (O'Neill, 2018).

Private Prisons

In August of 2016, the Justice Department released a memo stating the Federal Bureau of Prisons would begin to phase out their contracts with private prisons. This led to a downturn in stock prices for companies such as CoreCivic, formerly Corrections Corporation of America, whose shares fell 35% in one day. However, the majority of the contracts for private prisons were with Homeland Security on behalf of Immigration and Customs Enforcement (44%) or with the states; less than 16% of all private prison contracts were with the Federal Bureau of Prisons. However, on November 9, 2016, the stock prices for CoreCivic rose 43% with the news Donald Trump had been elected president. President Trump had run for office on a law-and-order platform and stated he planned to utilize private prisons, if he was elected. On November 10, 2016, Corrections Corporation of America announced it was rebranding and would now be known as CoreCivic. They also expanded their interests and offered private residential reentry centers in addition to detention facilities (Sommer, 2016).

Then, in 2018, private prisons began to receive a fair amount of negative press for how they were treating migrants held in their custody. The public backlash became severe as more and more news stories began to appear about children being separated from their parents and held in detention centers that resembled cages. This public awakening to private prisons provided an opportunity for prison reform advocates, who organized petitions and protests around social media hashtags such as #FamiliesBelongTogether and #BackersOfHate. These social media campaigns demanded that companies and states withdraw their financial support from the private prison industry (Sanders, 2020). By 2019, twenty-two states had banned contracts with private prisons and eight large banks, including JP Morgan Chase, Wells Fargo, Bank of America, BNP Paribas, Sun Trust, Barclay's, Fifth Third, and PNC, severed ties with private prisons (Simon, 2019).

Losing the support of some of the largest banks in the United States has taken a toll on the private prison industry. The two largest private prison companies, GEO Group and CoreCivic, lost a total of 2.35 billion in credit and loans, while their credit ratings dropped, making it more difficult for them to acquire new contracts, finance debt, and keep up with long-term costs. The three largest private prison companies, GEO Group, CoreCivic, and Management and Training Corporation, have joined together to form the Day 1 Alliance (D1A) to improve their public image (Sanders, 2020). However, this does not seem to be having the desired impact as stock prices for CoreCivic fell from a high of $17.25 a share in February of 2020 to a low of $5.26 a share in late October of the same year (Intercontinental Exchange, 2020).

In January of 2021, President Biden signed an executive order to phase out federal prisons as part of his campaign promise to address inequities within the criminal justice system. However, this action has been criticized by many as not going far enough, as it will only impact approximately 14,000 people held in private facilities and does not address the usage of private prisons at the state level (Adams, 2021).

Incarceration and the Lack of Drug and Mental Health Treatment

The increase in the number of prisoners also was impacted by the high number of nonviolent offenders, particularly drug offenders. For instance, 46% of the federal prison population as well as 26% of females and 13% of males in state prison are serving time for drug offenses (Carson, 2020). Drug addiction also is a major cause of crime, as 18% of federal inmates and 16% of state inmates stated they committed the crime they are incarcerated for to obtain money to buy drugs (Common Sense for Drug Policy, 2016). The majority of those incarcerated used drugs regularly prior to coming to prison, including 70% of state inmates and 64% of federal inmates (National Institute on Drug Abuse, 2014).

Drug offenders are the largest population within the federal prison system, but due to overcrowding and lack of staff there are not enough drug treatment programs. Therefore, only 15% of state and 17% of federal inmates were able to access drug treatment with a trained professional while incarcerated (National Institute on Drug Abuse, 2014). For example, the federal system had 31,803 inmates enrolled in a drug education program, but there were over 51,000 inmates on the waiting list, with many waiting for at least three months to enter the program because the prisons were 40% over capacity (Johnson, 2012). The Residential Drug Abuse Program reduces a participant's sentence by one year after successful completion. However, the waiting list is so long that only 25% of those who graduated from the program had enough time left on their sentence to benefit from the one-year reduction (Johnson, 2012).

The number of those with mental health diagnoses who are imprisoned also has increased dramatically over the past few decades. Prior to the 1970s, government-run mental health institutions housed those who had serious mental health problems and could not afford private insurance to pay for services on their own. However, these institutions were closed in the 1970s due to concerns about patient abuse and neglect. The plan had been to utilize community mental health services to fill the gap left by the state-run institutions. However, community mental health was not funded at the federal level and has been underfunded at the state level across the country ever since (DeMoss, 2015).

This major change in the mental health field has left a lot of people with serious mental health diagnoses without access to treatment and medication. Many of those who do not have insurance will attempt to treat themselves through self-medication by using drugs and/or alcohol, which for most eventually becomes addiction. The combination of drug addiction and mental health challenges makes those with these co-occurring disorders particularly vulnerable to getting caught up in the criminal justice system and eventually being imprisoned. However, prisons and jails are not set up for those who are mentally ill, and this population is more likely to get into trouble due to their difficulties in coping with the restrictive environment (DeMoss, 2015).

Today, 15% of those in state prison and 20% of those in jail have been diagnosed with a severe mental illness, and there are ten times more people in prisons and jails with severe mental illness than in state mental health hospitals (Treatment Advocacy Center, 2016). Jails rarely have treatment options for those who are mentally ill, and prisons offer some treatment, but many times inmates refuse treatment because they do not believe they need it. Prison staff also is not always trained to work with mentally ill inmates and use what measures they know, such as restraints and solitary confinement. These measures often make matters worse and the person's symptoms are only exacerbated (Treatment Advocacy Center, 2014). Therefore, those with mental illness are reincarcerated at higher rates (54%) than those without mental illness, while those who have been diagnosed with both mental illness and substance abuse are the most likely to experience reincarceration (68%) (Wilson et al., 2011).

Problem-Solving Courts as an Alternative to Incarceration

Problem-solving courts grew out of the recognition that the traditional criminal justice system could not address the needs of those whose behavior had been deemed criminal by society, but was often rooted in lack of community resources and/or treatment. *Problem-solving courts* are specialized courts that attempt to break the cycle of recidivism by working directly with the defendants to keep them from getting further involved in the criminal justice system and to help them reenter their community to be successful citizens. Problem-solving courts utilize an interdisciplinary approach, where all of the actors within the courtroom work together to provide due process, justice, and treatment in an effort to rehabilitate the offender and keep them from coming back to the criminal justice system. Those working within the courtroom, including judges, probation officers, case managers, and social service representatives, collaborate with community programs in order to provide a more holistic approach for the offenders' needs (Winick, 2002).

Problem-solving courts first took shape in the form of a drug court and, in 1989, the first drug court was created in Miami, Florida (National Institute of Justice, 2008).

Today, in the United States, there are over 3,400 problem-solving courts, and the majority of this total are drug courts or a variation of a drug court. *Drug courts* use a non-adversarial process, where the defendants have given up their right to have an attorney present. Instead, there is a multi-disciplinary team consisting of the judge, probation officers, treatment professionals, and social services all with the goal of helping the defendants to work through the underlying problems that have led them to the criminal justice system and ultimately helping them through rehabilitation. If the defendant successfully completes the program, the criminal charges or conviction against them will be dropped. However, if the person is unable to complete the program, the charges or conviction will remain in place and they will face the consequences of the traditional criminal court. Those who are eligible to participate in drug court programs have committed a nonviolent crime and have a verifiable substance addiction (National Institute of Justice, 2015).

The drug court consists of a judge who has been trained specifically to work with defendants who have a substance addiction. The judge serves the role of encouraging the participants and being the enforcer, if the participants do not follow the rules. The probation officers involved play a major role, as they are the ones who meet with the participants regularly, complete the random urine screens, assess the needs and risks of the participants, and help them to find employment, as well as enroll them in treatment and other needed programs offered within the community. The probation officer must create an individual plan for each participant, as not all participants will have the same needs and strengths. The probation officer also is responsible for reporting the progress of the participants to the drug court judge, both in the courtroom and through weekly reports (National Institute of Justice, 2015).

The drug court program is typically divided into phases. The first phase of the program is the most intensive and requires the greatest amount of supervision from both the probation officer and the judge. In this phase, the participant will receive more random urine screens and will be expected to check in with the probation officer and judge more frequently. This also is when the participant's needs will be assessed and treatment will begin. Once the participant successfully makes it through the first phase, the subsequent phases will be less intense, with fewer random urine screens as well as fewer meetings with the probation officer and the judge. In the final phase, the participant will begin to transition to life on their own; for example, there is an expectation that they will be employed and working on implementing a plan for when they are no longer under supervision. However, in the last phase there are still required supervision meetings with both the probation officer and the judge to continue monitoring progress and encouraging the participants throughout the process as well as ensuring they have the tools they need to be successful. Most drug court participants will make mistakes at some point in the process, for example, by using substances. If this happens, the probation officer reports the behavior to the judge, who acts as the enforcer. This behavior often is punished by the judge, who may send the person to jail for a few days to remind them what the consequences are if they do not succeed in the program. If the participant makes repeated mistakes and the probation officer and judge do not believe they are taking the program seriously, one can be removed from the drug court program and sent back to the traditional criminal court process (National Institute of Justice, 2015).

Drug courts increase program compliance through intensive supervision and the ability to rapidly provide treatment to participants on an individual basis (Superior Court of San Mateo Valley, 2016). A study in Pennsylvania found drug courts were more effective than any other criminal justice sanction for treating those with substance addictions (Huseman, 2010). The author noted participants were six times more likely to comply with the program than those in other criminal justice related drug programs. Those who had children also were more likely to complete a drug court program than other types of treatment programs (Huseman, 2010).

Drug courts also have been found to save money; for example, for every $1 invested in drug courts $2.21 in criminal justice costs is saved (White House, 2011). Drug courts also cost significantly less than incarceration and free up space in jails and prisons for those who are violent offenders. Nationally, treatment for drug court participants costs between $900 and $2,200 per person, but saves on average $5,000 per person in jail space. Drug courts also create taxpaying citizens, as most drug court participants are required to be employed as a criteria of the drug court program (Superior Court of San Mateo Valley, 2016).

Drug court programs help to reduce recidivism, because they target the root of the participant's criminal justice behavior and attempt to treat it. Nationwide, 84% of drug court graduates are not rearrested within the first year of program completion and 72% are not rearrested within two years (White House, 2011). Those who participate in drug court programs also are less likely to recidivate than those who are punished through traditional probation (National Institute of Justice, 2008).

Individual program evaluations also find that those who participate in drug court programs reduce their rates of recidivism. One study found that felony rearrest two years after completion of the program decreased to 12%, while prior to the drug court program being implemented the rearrest rate had been at 40% for the same population (National Institute of Justice, 2008). In Oregon, another research study found that, even 10 years later, those who participated in the drug court were less likely to be rearrested in comparison to nondrug court participants who had committed similar offenses (National Institute of Justice, 2008). Gallagher (2014) also conducted a research study to compare drug court program graduates to those who were dismissed from the program in order to examine recidivism rates. Those who were terminated were more likely to be rearrested (43.59%) than graduates (6.56%). Therefore, those who graduated from the drug court program were 11 times more likely to not recidivate than those who did not graduate. The authors also noted that those who did not receive a violation within the first 30 days of the drug court program were seven times less likely to recidivate when released from the program than those who received a violation (Gallagher, 2014).

Although drug courts have reduced recidivism rates, some argue these rates could be even further decreased by focusing more heavily on higher risk offenders. Drug courts often include those who are low risk because they meet the basic criteria of substance abuse, while those who are at a higher risk for reoffending may not be included for fear they may be more likely to recidivate. However, research conducted on criminal justice rehabilitation programs have concluded that those who are a higher risk for reoffending will have the largest decrease in recidivism rates, if they are placed in programs that target high-risk offenders (Koetzle et al., 2015).

Due to their structure and level of supervision, drug courts are a great fit for high-risk offenders. Researchers compared high-risk drug court participants to a sample of matched high-risk probationers and found that those in the drug court were significantly less likely to be charged with a new offense (34%) in comparison to those who were on probation (66%). Overall, for those who were rearrested the charge was typically drug related or a technical violation. The authors concluded drug courts should specifically target those who are at high risk for recidivism because it is more effective than traditional probation, due to the combination of intense supervision and treatment (Koetzle et al., 2015).

In the late 1990s, mental health courts started because of a need that grew out of the drug court movement to work with participants who have a *dual diagnosis*, or those with both a mental health diagnosis as well as a substance addiction. Therefore, those who are admitted to a *mental health court* usually have a serious mental health diagnosis, such as bipolar disorder, schizophrenia, or major depression, and have committed a nonviolent misdemeanor or felony, where their criminal behavior was connected to their mental illness (Castellano, 2011). There are still a limited number of mental health courts, which makes it difficult to serve all who need programming. Therefore, mental health court officials must carefully target participants for the program, ensuring there is a clear connection between the crime committed and the person's mental health diagnosis. Officials also need to be certain potential participants can access needed mental health services once in the program (Thompson et al., 2008).

Similar to the drug court, mental health courts also rely on a non-adversarial process, where participants typically plead guilty in exchange for participating in the program. If the participant successfully completes the program, the charges are dismissed or reduced. However, if someone does not complete the program they are sent back to the traditional court system (Ray & Dollar, 2013). Mental health courts also use a multi-disciplinary team who have knowledge of mental illness and the criminal justice system. This team includes judges, case managers, and service providers all working toward the goal of successful reintegration for the participant. Case managers supervise participants and ensure they receive needed treatment, including creating individual treatment plans to help the participants work towards graduating from the program and being productive citizens within their communities. The judge also takes on a leading role within the courtroom and engages in regular supervision, where participants are rewarded for good behavior and receive short-term sanctions for negative behavior (Thompson et al., 2008).

Research studies conducted on mental health courts have found that participation in the program reduces costs associated with incarceration for mentally ill defendants. One study found the mental health court program in Allegheny County, Pennsylvania (Pittsburgh), costs were higher than jail, due to $6,844 more being spent per person for mental health treatment in mental health court. However, there were significant savings when comparing the overall cost of participation and treatment in mental health court to the cost of one year in jail, with a savings of $5,532 per person (Ridgely et al., 2007). Another study, in Cook County, Illinois (Chicago), found those who participated in the mental health court on average had cost the criminal justice system $17,200 in the year prior to their participation in the program. However, while enrolled in the program the cost per year on average for each participant was $5,000. Over seven years, this saved taxpayers in Cook County a total of $4.2 million in the cost of incarceration for those who participated in the mental health court program. Other cost savings were due to reduced arrest rates, where mental health court participants decreased their overall rate of arrest by 81% when comparing pre- and post-program participation (Treatment Alternative Safety Committee, 2012).

IN FOCUS

Veterans Courts

Over the last 15 years, the wars in Iraq and Afghanistan have placed a heavy burden on those who are in the military as well as the National Guard and Reserve, with some experiencing multiple tours of duty in combat zones. These experiences have directly impacted veterans, with many having a hard time reintegrating back into civilian life after returning home from active duty. Today, there are a significant number of veterans struggling with depression, anxiety, unemployment, homelessness, and/or difficulties with relationships. In the United States, for example, 13% of the total homeless population are veterans along with 8% of those incarcerated in state and federal prisons (National Coalition for Homeless Veterans, 2022; Yezo, 2021).

Due to the lack of rehabilitation in prisons and jails, only 20% of veterans who needed treatment for illegal substance abuse have received it. However, 81% of veterans who were incarcerated reported substance addiction, and 25% were diagnosed with mental illness (Russell, 2009b). More than half of combat veterans who have been diagnosed with Post Traumatic Stress Disorder (PTSD) also have been arrested one or more times, and those who have PTSD are more likely to experience other mental health problems, such as thoughts of suicide (Slattery et al., 2013).

The needs of veterans within the criminal justice system led to the creation of the first veterans court, in 2008, in Buffalo, New York (National Center for State Courts, n.d.). Today, there are more than 220 veterans courts in the United States (Crawford, 2016). Veterans courts are a combination of drug courts and mental health courts that focus specifically on military veterans (National Center for State Courts, n.d.). A veterans court participant needs to be a veteran who has substance addiction and/or a mental health diagnosis and is involved in the criminal justice system. Most veterans courts accept those who have committed nonviolent misdemeanor and felony offenses (National Center for State Courts, n.d.).

Veterans courts are implemented in a similar manner to drug courts and mental health courts. However, one of the differences of the veterans court is the inclusion of mentors who also are members or veterans of the military from a variety of time periods. Research has shown that veterans are more likely to respond to treatment when they believe those involved can understand or empathize with their military experience (Russell, 2009a). Mentors support the participant during court hearings and keep in touch between court dates via phone, email, or in person. However, the amount and type of contact between court dates is dependent on each set of mentors and mentees (Moore, 2012).

Community Supervision Alternatives to Incarceration

Several states have started to divert nonviolent offenders out of the prison system and into community-supervised programs. In New York, for example, the state did away with mandatory minimum sentences for drug offenders and instead started sentencing them to drug courts and other community-supervised programs for treatment. The state has since diverted 1,700 offenders at a savings of $5,144 per offender. These savings are due to those in community treatment being less likely to recidivate as well as the lower cost of treating the offender within the community instead of in prison (Berman, 2013).

One type of a community supervision program is *long-term residential care*, where those under supervision live within the treatment center. This type of program typically takes the form of a *therapeutic community*, where the staff and patients work together in a treatment setting that is intended to help the participants work on their strengths as well as weaknesses both socially and emotionally. Enrollment in therapeutic communities lasts between 6 and 24 months depending upon the needs of the client and how the program has been implemented (National Institute on Drug Abuse, 2012).

In general, therapeutic communities are structured programs that assist the individual with counseling and getting to the root of why they are abusing substances, with an emphasis on personal responsibility. These programs also work with the individuals to ensure they have the skills they need to be successful upon release, such as education and employment skills. Participants are expected to comply with the program's strict guidelines, which are very intensive in the beginning of the program and then taper off as the individuals progress through the program in an attempt to prepare them for their return to the community. Long-term residential treatment programs also have been found to be successful. Those with substance abuse problems tend to stay in treatment longer and commit fewer crimes, in part because there is pressure from the criminal justice system in the form of sanctions (National Institute on Drug Abuse, 2012).

One example of a long-term residential program is the **Drug Treatment Alternative to Prison program** (DTAP), which is offered and supervised through the Brooklyn, New York, prosecutor's office. Participants who are eligible have been charged with a felony drug conviction, have at least one prior felony, and are addicted to substances. This program is a diversion program where participants are removed from the traditional criminal justice system. In exchange for being diverted, participants plead guilty to their crimes and are contractually obligated by the courts to complete the DTAP. Participants must enter a long-term residential treatment facility for anywhere from 15 to 24 months dependent upon the individual and their needs. This residential program is based on the therapeutic community model, where participants live together in a community setting to work on improving their coping skills. If one completes the program successfully, the conviction is removed from one's record (Crime Solutions, n.d.).

The DTAP progresses in three phases. The first phase lasts three months and is used as an orientation to the program and its policies. The second phase includes group and family counseling, and the participant takes on work assignments within the program to begin preparing for employment. Other programs also are available during this phase based upon the individual's needs, such as educational and vocational programming. In the third phase, the participant gradually starts to prepare for their reentry back into their home community by obtaining employment and beginning to examine how to maintain sobriety once on their own. The participants also receive aftercare in the form of case management, where an assigned case manager helps them to overcome any barriers they may face after release (Crime Solutions, n.d.).

Program evaluations have shown the DTAP to be successful. Three years after treatment completion, program participants were rearrested at a rate of 23% in comparison to 47% of those who did not participate. The DTAP also saved money due to lower recidivism rates and less time spent in prison. It was estimated the program saved $47,836 per participant in criminal justice costs, which amounted to $7.3 million over a period of six years (Crime Solutions, n.d.).

A second type of community-supervision program that has been shown to be effective is smart probation programs. These programs are based on *traditional probation*, where one is sentenced to community supervision instead of incarceration. Probation officers supervise the offender within the community, which allows the probationer to keep their ties within the community, for example, by staying connected with family and/or a job. Probation officers also provide assistance to those who are in need of drug treatment, counseling, or vocational training. However, if one violates one's probation by not complying with the conditions of supervision and treatment, then one can be required to fulfill the remaining sentence in prison or jail. However, those with substance abuse problems are likely to violate their conditions of probation, such as by not passing a urine screen due to drug use. After this happens on more than one occasion the probation officer is required to bring the probationer before the judge to decide whether or not to revoke the sentence of probation and replace it with imprisonment. However, in traditional probation programs, because jails and prisons are overcrowded and those with substance addictions are not likely to get the treatment they need, judges often do not do anything and the behavior is not punished (Office of National Drug Control Policy, 2011).

IN FOCUS

For-Profit Probation

Local courts are often financially reliant on fees paid by misdemeanants to fund court services (Human Rights Watch, 2014). However, these same courts are unable to afford to pay for staff to collect these fees. This has led over 1,000 courts across the United States to outsource the role of collection agency to for-profit probation companies. Therefore, those who are convicted of a misdemeanor offense and are unable to pay their fine are placed on community supervision through a for-profit probation company who is responsible for collecting the fees owed by the probationer to the court. In return for the services provided to the court by the for-profit probation company, the probationer is charged a monthly supervision fee, and the court requires the person to remain under the supervision of the for-profit probation company until the fines and fees are paid. In this agreement, the court does not have to pay to recoup their fines and the for-profit probation company makes money by charging supervision fees for each month the probationer is in debt. This is incredibly problematic for those who are poor and unable to pay their fines and supervision fees, because the debt is constantly accumulating as one attempts to pay off the fine in monthly installments (Human Rights Watch, 2014).

Several states are now trying a different approach to traditional probation, called smart probation, in order to keep offenders out of prison. When on *smart probation*, an offender is placed on probation, but when they are unable to comply with the conditions of probation they are placed in jail for a short term, usually a two- or three-day stay. This allows the probation officer as well as the judge to have a sanction that can be utilized without having to place the person in prison or jail for a longer period of time. Initial evaluations of these programs have found they do increase compliance and help to reduce recidivism (Office of National Drug Control Policy, 2011).

An example of smart probation is Hawaii's Opportunity Probation with Enforcement, or H.O.P.E. program. This program targets high-risk probationers, including violent offenders, sex offenders, and those with substance addictions. If a person continues to use substances while on probation, they will be sent to a drug treatment program. Probationers are supervised and provided with treatment, but also are given immediate sanctions any time they violate a condition of their probation. This helps to deter violating one's conditions of probation along with criminal behavior because the negative actions are dealt with immediately and the punishment is certain and serious, involving a short term of incarceration. If a probationer is employed, they are allowed to complete their short-term sentence on the weekends, so it does not interfere with their employment (Office of National Drug Control Policy, 2011).

Program evaluations have shown this probation strategy to be effective. For example, those who were in the program for one year were significantly less likely to be arrested for a new crime (55%), to use drugs (72%), and to have their probation revoked (53%) when compared to those on traditional probation. This program also costs significantly less than incarceration, with an average cost of $2,500 per probationer (Office of National Drug Control Policy, 2011). A long-term follow-up evaluation also found when comparing H.O.P.E. probationers to those on traditional probation that they were significantly less likely to have their probation revoked and return to prison, less likely to commit new crimes, and more likely to be released from probation supervision early due to successful completion (Myers, 2016).

Changes in Drug Policies as a Way to Reduce Incarceration

Currently, several states and the federal government along with many countries around the world participate in the United States-led model of the War on Drugs. This policy is based on *prohibition*, or making substances illegal, targeting these substances through law enforcement, and sentencing those who are convicted of the crimes with harsh punishments. The ultimate goal of prohibition is complete eradication of all drug use. In Texas, for example, one sentenced for marijuana possession of under two ounces or selling seven grams or less will receive a maximum sentence of 180 days in jail and up to a $2,000 fine. However, if one is caught selling 50 pounds or more the sentence can be up to 99 years in prison (Find Law, 2016).

GLOBAL SPOTLIGHT

Iran, the Death Penalty, and Drug Trafficking

Iran utilizes a drug policy of prohibition in order to stop substance use and trafficking within its country. This is because Iran experiences high levels of drug trafficking within their country due to its border with the country of Afghanistan, which is the biggest supplier of opiates in the world. Afghans are highly motivated to move opiates through Iran and into Turkey, where they will be shipped on to European countries. This is because there is a significant demand in the European market for the opiates along with financial opportunity for the trafficker. However, the price if one is caught trafficking illegal substances in Iran is death by hanging. In 2015, for instance, 600 people were hanged for drug offenses (Dearden, 2016).

However, Afghans continue to take the risk of moving large quantities of drugs through Iran, even though the punishment for drug trafficking is death. This is due to the extreme poverty in the war-torn country of Afghanistan, where there are very few opportunities to support oneself and one's family. Therefore, this serious punishment, even though incredibly harsh, is not enough to deter people from committing the crime. There has even been a case where all of the men within an Afghan village were executed for drug trafficking. An Iranian official later spoke out against this punishment and stated the punishment did not stop drug trafficking because the children left behind would be forced to continue trafficking drugs as a means of economic survival (Dearden, 2016).

In 2017, Iran executed 500 people for drug trafficking. This led European countries, who do not have the death penalty, to threaten to cut off financial assistance to help fight the Iranian War on Drugs, if Iran continued to execute drug traffickers. In response, in August of 2018, the Iranian government raised the amount of heroin, opium, and methamphetamine needed to trigger a death sentence. This law was implemented retroactively with the potential to commute death sentences for approximately 5,000 people on death row, most of whom were in their 20s (Dehghan, 2018).

The drug policy of prohibition has not been successful in eradicating drug use or sales through long prison sentences or the threat of the death penalty (see Global Spotlight), while many experts are starting to refer to the War on Drugs as a failure.

This has led some states and countries to try other types of drug policies in order to reduce incarceration and in some instances drug use. One type of drug policy that helps to reduce incarceration rates is **legalization**, where one or more substances are made legalized for consumption. This policy model allows the government to control how substances are taxed and sold along with their potency. In the United States, an example of a legal substance is alcohol, where the product is regulated at the state level, and each state is allowed to decide how the product will be consumed, sold, regulated, and taxed (Miller, 2016).

Several states also have moved towards legalizing other previously illegal substances, such as marijuana, even though this drug remains illegal at the federal level. In Colorado, in 2012, recreational marijuana was legalized at the state level through a constitutional amendment voted on by registered voters in the state. By 2014, marijuana was sold at stores for consumption by adults ages 21 or older. The drug is heavily regulated by the state; for example, those who are authorized to grow the plants must tag the plants so they can be tracked by the government from seedling until harvest. Marijuana products also are tested for potency and must be sold in child-resistant containers. Anyone who is a minimum of 21 years of age is allowed to purchase the products and can possess up to one ounce legally. Marijuana products also are taxed through regular state and local sales taxes as well as an additional state and local tax specifically for recreational marijuana products (Miller, 2016). Between 2014 and 2019, the state of Colorado brought in more than one billion in state revenue from marijuana sales; and since June of 2017, the state has made at a minimum $20 million in taxes and fees each month (Rosenbaum, 2019).

Another type of drug policy that helps to reduce incarceration rates is **decriminalization**, or when law enforcement no longer targets the use or possession of a drug. In instances of decriminalization, the drug is not legal. However, people are not incarcerated for possessing and in some cases selling the drug; rather, a fine or citation is issued (*Merriam-Webster*, 2015). Kentucky's policy is an example of decriminalization, where one can possess up to eight ounces of marijuana before receiving jail time, and first-time offenders are charged with misdemeanors. If one possesses more than eight ounces of marijuana, this is considered to be intent to sell and the penalties increase to a possibility of one to three years of incarceration and/or less than a $500 fine. However, if one is convicted of possessing more than five pounds of marijuana, one can be sentenced to up to ten years in prison and/or up to a $10,000 fine (Discovery Place, 2015).

Ohio is another example of a state that has decriminalized marijuana. If one is convicted of possession of less than 100 grams of marijuana one will receive a fine of $150, while if one possesses between 100 and 200 grams of marijuana one faces up to 30 days in jail and a $250 fine. Both of these offenses are considered to be misdemeanors. Just as in Kentucky, if one possesses enough marijuana to raise suspicion one is selling or trafficking, the penalties increase. For example, someone in possession of anywhere from 1,000 to 20,000 grams of marijuana will be charged with a felony, and, if convicted, will face between one and five years in prison along with a $10,000 fine (NORML, 2016).

There also are different types of drug policies or ways that governments can attempt to reduce addiction to and the use of substances, as well as the rate of people incarcerated for nonviolent offenses. One example of this is ***harm reduction***, which is defined as reducing the damage caused by drugs instead of attempting to eradicate drug use. Harm reduction recognizes that not all who use substances have a drug addiction, but those who are addicted need to receive treatment. Policies are then created to recognize addiction as a medical problem that assist in reducing social and emotional damage. For instance, syringe exchange programs, where intravenous drug users can receive clean needles to inject their drugs, help to decrease harm by reducing illnesses that are associated with intravenous drug use, such as HIV and Hepatitis C (Harm Reduction International, 2016).

Summary

The wars on drugs and crime have sentenced both violent and nonviolent offenders to terms of imprisonment and for longer periods of time. This shift in policy has had the most impact on poorer communities, where the War on Drugs is primarily being fought, bringing non-White people and women into the criminal justice system in large numbers. This increase in incarceration has dramatically impacted how correction facilities operate as the characteristics and needs of inmates have changed. For example, nonviolent offenders often bring with them substance abuse problems as well as mental and/or physical health issues, which can be challenging for corrections officials who have not been trained on how to effectively handle these problems. The sheer number of people imprisoned also has created a situation where the federal government and several state governments have turned to private prison industries to assist them in housing the overflow, even though contracting with these corporations has caused another set of problems.

However, as the cost of incarceration continues to grow along with the size of the inmate population, many officials are beginning to question what they are getting for the tax dollars they are spending. This has led to criminal justice officials being more willing to try different alternatives to incarceration that have been shown to be successful and cheaper than traditional criminal justice approaches, such as problem-solving courts, smart probation, and long-term residential programming. Some states as well as a few countries globally also are beginning to question the effectiveness of the War on Drugs and are changing how they process drug offenders by instead using drug policies that incorporate legalization, decriminalization, and harm reduction.

Discussion Questions

1. Should states and the federal government rely on private prisons to house their inmates?

2. How would you convince legislators within your state to provide more funding for programs such as drug courts, smart probation, and long-term residential treatment?

3. Which of the drug policies discussed in this chapter (prohibition, legalization, decriminalization, and/or harm reduction) do you think would be most effective in the United States? Would you choose one policy over another, or do you think a combination of policies would be more effective?

Key Terms

private prison industry
problem-solving courts
drug courts
dual diagnosis
mental health court
long-term residential care
therapeutic community
Drug Treatment Alternative to Prison
    program (DTAP)

traditional probation
smart probation
prohibition
legalization
decriminalization
harm reduction

References

ACLU. (2015). The prison crisis. https://www.aclu.org/prison-crisis

Adams, C. (2021). Biden's order terminates private federal prison contracts. Here's what that means. NBC News. https://www.nbcnews.com/news/nbcblk/biden-s-order-terminates-federal-private-prison-contracts-here-s-n1255776

BBC. (n.d.). World prison population. http://news.bbc.co.uk/2/shared/spl/hi/uk/06/prisons/html/nn2page1.stm

Berman, G. (2013). Alternatives to incarceration are cutting prison numbers, cost and crime. *The Guardian*. http://www.theguardian.com/commentisfree/2013/jul/04/alternatives-incarceration-prison-numbers

Cahalan, M. W., & Parsons, L. A. (1986). Historical corrections statistics in the United States, 1850–1994. Bureau of Justice Statistics. http://www.bjs.gov/content/pub/pdf/hcsus5084.pdf

Canon, G. (2015). Here's the latest evidence of how private prisons are exploiting inmates for profit. *Mother Jones*. http://www.motherjones.com/mojo/2015/06/private-prisons-profit

Carson, A. E. (2020). Prisoners in 2019. Bureau of Justice Statistics. https://www.bjs.gov/content/pub/pdf/p19.pdf

Castellano, U. (2011). Courting compliance: Case managers as 'double agents' in the mental health court. *Law & Social Inquiry*, 36(2), 484–514.

Cohen, M. (2015). How for-profit prisons have become the biggest lobby no one is talking about. *The Washington Post*. https://www.washingtonpost.com/posteverything/wp/2015/04/28/how-for-profit-prisons-have-become-the-biggest-lobby-no-one-is-talking-about/

Common Sense for Drug Policy. (2016). Prisons, jails and people arrested for drugs. http://www.drugwarfacts.org/cms/Prisons_and_Drugs#sthash.F0FAUEgX.dpbs

Crawford, G. (2016). Fighting for those who fought for us: Veterans treatment courts. *Corrections Today, Jan/Feb*, 14–28.

Crime Solutions. (n.d.). Drug treatment alternative to prison program (DTAP). National Institute of Justice. https://www.crimesolutions.gov/TopicDetails.aspx?ID=31

Dearden, L. (2016). Every man in Iranian village 'executed on drugs charges.' *The Guardian*. http://www.independent.co.uk/news/world/middle-east/every-man-in-iran-village-executed-on-drugs-charges-death-penalty-capital-punishment-human-rights-a6898036.html

Dehghan, S. K. (2018). Iran's easing of drug laws could halt execution of 5,000 prisoners. *The Guardian*. https://www.theguardian.com/world/2018/jan/10/iran-ease-drug-laws-could-halt-execution-5000-prisoners-death-row

DeMoss, D. (2015). The nightmare of prison for individuals with mental illness. *The Huffington Post*. http://www.huffingtonpost.com/dustin-demoss/prison-mental-illness_b_6867988.html

Discovery Place. (2015). Drug possession laws in Kentucky. http://www.discoveryplace.info/drug-possession-laws-kentucky

Families Against Mandatory Minimums. (2014). Quick facts. http://famm.org/the-facts-with-sources/

Find Law. (2016). Texas marijuana laws. http://statelaws.findlaw.com/texas-law/texas-marijuana-laws.html

Gallagher, J. R. (2014). Predicting criminal recidivism following drug court: Implications for drug court practice and policy advocacy. *Journal of Addictions & Offender Counseling*, 35(1), 15–29.

Harm Reduction International. (2016). What is harm reduction? http://www.ihra.net/what-is-harm-reduction

Human Rights Watch. (2014). Profiting from probation: America's "offender-funded" probation industry. https://www.hrw.org/sites/default/files/reports/us0214_ForUpload_0.pdf

Huseman, J. (2010). Do drug courts work? National Center for Policy Analysis. http://www.ncpa.org/pub/ba717

Ingraham, C. (2016). Marijuana wins big on election night. *The Washington Post.* https://www.washingtonpost.com/news/wonk/wp/2016/11/08/medical-marijuana -sails-to-victory-in-florida/

Intercontinental Exchange. (2020). CoreCivic Inc CXW. NYSE. https://www.nyse. com/quote/XNYS:CXW

Johnson, K. (2012). Prisoners face long wait for drug-rehab services. *USA Today.* http://www.usatoday.com/story/news/nation/2012/12/04/prisoner-drug-treat ment-delays/1739371/

Koetzle, D., Listwan, S. J., Guastaferro, W. P., & Kobus, K. (2015). Treating high-risk offenders in the community: The potential of drug courts. *International Journal of Offender Therapy & Comparative Criminology, 59*(5), 449–465.

Mai, C., & Subramanian, R. (2017). The price of prisons: Examining state spending trends 2010–2015. Vera. https://www.vera.org/publications/price-of-prisons-2015 -state-spending-trends/price-of-prisons-2015-state-spending-trends/price-of -prisons-2015-state-spending-trends-from-the-director

Mason, C. (2012). Too good to be true: Private prisons in America. The Sentencing Project. http://sentencingproject.org/doc/publications/inc_Too_Good_to_be_ True.pdf

Merriam-Webster. (2015). Decriminalize defined. http://www.merriam-webster.com/ dictionary/decriminalize

Miller, J. (2016). In Colo., a look at life after marijuana legalization. *The Boston Globe.* https://www.bostonglobe.com/metro/2016/02/21/from-colorado-glimpse-life-after -marijuana-legalization/rcccuzhMDWV74UC4IxXIYJ/story.html

Moore, E. C. (2012). A mentor in combat veterans court: Observations and challeng- es. National Center for State Courts. http://ncsc.contentdm.oclc.org/cdm/ref/col lection/spcts/id/233

Myers, D. L. (2016). Hawaii Opportunity Probation with Enforcement (H.O.P.E): Fur- ther evaluation of swift and certain sanctions. EBP Society. https://www.ebpsociety. org/blog/education/220-hawaii-opportunity-probation-enforcement-hope

NAACP. (2016). Criminal justice fact sheet. http://www.naacp.org/pages/criminal -justice-fact-sheet

National Center for State Courts. (n.d.). Veterans court: Resource guide. http://www. ncsc.org/Topics/Problem-Solving-Courts/Veterans-Court/Resource-Guide.aspx

National Coalition for Homeless Veterans. (2022). Veteran Homelessness. Retrieved from https://nchv.org/veteran-homelessness/

National Institute of Justice. (2008). Do drug courts work?: Findings from drug court research. Office of Justice Programs. http://www.nij.gov/topics/courts/drug-courts/ pages/work.aspx

National Institute of Justice. (2014). Recidivism. http://www.nij.gov/topics/correc tions/recidivism/pages/welcome.aspx

National Institute of Justice. (2015). Drug courts. Office of Justice Programs. http:// www.nij.gov/topics/courts/drug-courts/pages/welcome.aspx

National Institute on Drug Abuse. (2012). *Principles of drug addiction treatment: A research based guide* (3rd ed.). National Institute of Health. https://www.drugabuse.gov/publications/principles-drug-addiction-treatment-research-based-guide-third-edition/drug-addiction-treatment-in-united-states/types-treatment-programs

National Institute on Drug Abuse. (2014). Drug addiction treatment in the criminal justice system. National Institutes of Health. https://www.drugabuse.gov/related-topics/criminal-justice/drug-addiction-treatment-in-criminal-justice-system

NORML. (2016). Ohio laws and penalties. http://norml.org/laws/item/ohio-penalties-2?category_id=879

Office of National Drug Control Policy. (2011). Alternatives to incarceration: A smart approach to breaking the cycle of drug use and crime. Executive Office of the President. https://www.whitehouse.gov/sites/default/files/ondcp/Fact_Sheets/alternatives_to_incarceration_policy_brief_8-12-11.pdf

O'Neill, C. (2018). Private prisons pour millions into lobbying state law makers. Follow the money. https://www.followthemoney.org/research/blog/private-prisons-pour-millions-into-lobbying-state-lawmakers#:~:text=Since%202012%2C%20the%20private%20prison,nearly%20half%20of%20this%20sum

Ray, B., & Dollar, C. B. (2013). Examining mental health court completion: A focal concerns perspective. *Sociological Quarterly, 54*(4), 647–669.

Ridgely, S. M., Engberg, J., Greenburg, M. D., Turner, S., De Martini, C., & Dembosky, J. W. (2007). Justice, treatment and cost: An evaluation of the fiscal impact of the Allegheny mental health court. Rand Corporation. http://www.rand.org/content/dam/rand/pubs/technical_reports/2007/RAND_TR439.pdf

Rosenbaum, E. (2019). Colorado passes $1 billion in marijuana state revenue. CNBC. https://www.cnbc.com/2019/06/12/colorado-passes-1-billion-in-marijuana-state-revenue.html

Russell, R. T. (2009a). Veterans treatment courts developing throughout the nation. National Center for State Courts. http://cdm16501.contentdm.oclc.org/cdm/ref/collection/spcts/id/204

Russell, R. T. (2009b). Veterans treatment court: A proactive approach. *New England Journal on Criminal & Civil Confinement, 35*(2), 357–372.

Sanders, K. (2020). GEO Group and CoreCivic lose financial support. Prison Legal News. https://www.prisonlegalnews.org/news/2020/oct/1/geo-group-and-corecivic-lose-critical-financial-support/#:~:text=Within%20the%20private%20prison%20industry,%241.981%20billion%20in%202019%20revenues

Sawyer, W., & Wagner, P. (2020). Mass incarceration: The whole pie 2020. Prison Policy Initiative. https://www.prisonpolicy.org/reports/pie2020.html

The Sentencing Project. (2015). Incarcerated women and girls. http://www.sentencingproject.org/wp-content/uploads/2016/02/Incarcerated-Women-and-Girls.pdf

The Sentencing Project. (2019). Private prisons in the United States. https://www.sentencingproject.org/publications/private-prisons-united-states/

The Sentencing Project. (2020). Criminal justice facts. https://www.sentencingproject.org/criminal-justice-facts/

Shapiro, D. (2011). Banking on bondage: Private prisons and mass incarceration. ACLU. https://www.aclu.org/banking-bondage-private-prisons-and-mass-incarceration

Simon, M. (2019). GEO Group running out of banks as 100% of known banking partners say 'no' to private prison partners. *Forbes*. https://www.forbes.com/sites/morgansimon/2019/09/30/geo-group-runs-out-of-banks-as-100-of-banking-partners-say-no-to-the-private-prison-sector/?sh=237591b83298

Slattery, M., Dugger, M. T., Lamb, T. A., & Williams, L. (2013). Catch, treat, and release: Veteran treatment courts address the challenges of returning home. *Substance Use & Misuse*, *48*(10), 922–932.

Sommer, J. (2016). Trump's win gives stocks in private prison companies a reprieve. Your Money. *The New York Times*. http://www.nytimes.com/2016/12/03/your-money/trumps-win-gives-stocks-in-private-prison-companies-a-reprieve.html?_r=0

Superior Court of San Mateo Valley. (2016). Benefits of drug courts. https://www.sanmateocourt.org/court_divisions/criminal/drug_court/benefits.php

Thompson, M., Osher, F., & Tomasini-Joshi, D. (2008). Improving responses to people with mental illnesses: The essential elements of a mental health court. Bureau of Justice Association. https://csgjusticecenter.org/wp-content/uploads/2012/12/mhc-essential-elements.pdf

Treatment Advocacy Center. (2014). The treatment of persons with mental illness in prisons and jails: A state survey. http://www.tacreports.org/storage/documents/treatment-behind-bars/treatment-behind-bars-abridged.pdf

Treatment Advocacy Center. (2016). Prevalence of serious mental illness in prisons and jails. https://www.treatmentadvocacycenter.org/storage/documents/backgrounders/smi-in-jails-and-prisons.pdf

Treatment Alternative Safety Committee. (2012). Cook County mental health court program: Outcomes and cost savings. http://www2.centerforhealthandjustice.org/sites/www2.centerforhealthandjustice.org/files/publications/CCMHC-OutcomesandCostSavings.pdf

The White House. (2011). Drug courts: A smart approach to criminal justice. Executive Office of the President. https://www.whitehouse.gov/sites/default/files/ondcp/Fact_Sheets/drug_courts_fact_sheet_5-31-11.pdf

Wilson, A. B., Draineb, J., Hadley, T., Metraux, S., & Evans, A. (2011). Examining the impact of mental illness and substance use on recidivism in a county jail. *International Journal of Law and Psychiatry*, *34*(4), 264–268.

Winick, B. J. (2002). Therapeutic jurisprudence and problem-solving courts. *Fordham Urban Law Journal*, *30*(3), 1055–1103. http://ir.lawnet.fordham.edu/cgi/viewcontent.cgi?article=1866&context=ulj

Yezzo, D. (2021). Veterans incarcerated and in the justice system. Vietnam Veterans of America. Retrieved from https://vva.org/programs/veterans-incarcerated/veterans-incarcerated-and-in-the-justice-system-committee-update-mayjune-2021/

ELEVEN

Reentry

Learning Objectives

1. Define the term "reentry" and critically examine the barriers returning citizens face when attempting to successfully reenter their communities after being imprisoned, along with how these barriers can be different based on one's race, class, and gender.
2. Discuss the Second Chance Act and how this has provided grant money to implement programs to help returning citizens reenter their communities more successfully.

Reentry is defined as returning to the community after having been under criminal justice supervision. For the purposes of this chapter, we will be defining and discussing *reentry* as one's return from prison to one's community. The concept of reentry has become a hot topic over the last decade as we grapple with the problem of high numbers of citizens returning to their communities. The overwhelming majority of those incarcerated (95%), for example, will be released back to their community at some point in time, with over 70% of those released returning under parole supervision (Carson, 2020).

In 2019, there were 608,000 people released from state and federal prisons, or approximately 1,666 people per day (Carson, 2020). However, most returning citizens will return to neighborhoods that are impoverished, with high crime rates and few opportunities for employment and education (US Department of Justice, n.d.). Therefore, it is not surprising that a significant portion of those released will *recidivate* or once again become involved in the criminal justice system. In this chapter, we will discuss the barriers returning citizens face upon their return to their communities as well as programs that are working with this population in an effort to help them successfully reenter their communities.

Reentry Barrier: The Difficulty of Reuniting with Family

In the United States, more than five million children (7%) have experienced a parent they lived with being incarcerated in prison or jail at some point in time. Although this number is incredibly high it a conservative estimate as it only includes children who were living with the parent at the time of the parent's incarceration (Murphey & Cooper, 2015). Black and Hispanic children with incarcerated fathers have been particularly impacted, as 40% of incarcerated fathers are Black and an additional 20% of incarcerated fathers are Hispanic. Racial and ethnic differences also exist for incarcerated mothers, but have not been as pronounced. For example, nearly half (48%) of incarcerated mothers are white, 28% are Black, and 17% are Hispanic (Glaze & Maruschak, 2010).

The separation of parent and child can be particularly difficult, as most incarcerated parents reported having been the primary financial provider for their family (Feig, 2015). The majority of inmates with children also are nonviolent offenders and are imprisoned on average over 100 miles from their families, making it difficult for parents to maintain a relationship with their children beyond writing letters. This is because phone calls from prison tend to be expensive, and the distance between prison and home can make travel for face-to-face visits difficult (Feig, 2015). For example, 70% of incarcerated parents exchanged letters with their children, while only 53% were able to speak with their children over the phone, and 42% were visited by their children at the prison (Glaze & Maruschak, 2010).

IN FOCUS

Phone Calls from Jail

In November of 2015, the Federal Communications Commission (FCC) voted to enact cost caps for local and long-distance phone calls from state and federal prisons along with jails. This was after an investigation concluded there was a monopoly on phone services for inmates. Prison phone companies, for example, were charging higher rates per minute along with an average of 43% in fees that were passed on to the inmate. These costs, when added together, were causing some consumers to pay as much as $14 per minute to speak with friends and family (Goldman, 2016).

Two prison phone companies have sued the FCC, claiming the FCC has overstepped their boundaries with the caps placed on prison phone calls. The prison phone companies argued that the higher costs were necessary due to the additional services they must provide for jails and prisons, such as allowing corrections officers to monitor phone calls, blocking 800 and 900 numbers, and blocking calls to certain people, such as a witness or a victim of a crime. The FCC was set to implement their caps on calls coming from a correctional institution in 2017. However, the prison phone companies successfully stopped the implementation of the caps through a petition to the court of appeals asking for the FCC to hold off on the caps until the case can be heard in court (Goldman, 2016).

The FCC has continued to try and address the inequities experienced by families attempting to stay in touch with their loved ones who are incarcerated. However, the court of appeals has continued to side with the prison phone companies and have concluded the FCC does not have the right to regulate the cost of phone calls made within the state by inmates from a correctional facility. However, the FCC has been able to limit costs of phone calls between states and continues to work to decrease these costs, while encouraging state agencies to advocate for lower call rates for inmates calling home from a prison within the state (FCC, 2020).

The dramatic increase in the prison population has been particularly devastating for mothers with children. Since 1991, for example, the number of children with a mother in prison has increased by 131%, while children with a father in prison has risen by 77% (Glaze & Maruschak, 2010). Nearly half (41%) of mothers in state prison reported having more than one child, with half of these children being under the age of nine, and an additional 25% of female inmates had given birth in the last year or were pregnant when arrested (Glaze & Maruschak, 2010).

The impact of losing a mother to incarceration can be incredibly difficult for children, as more than half of all mothers in state prison were living with their child prior to their arrest, in comparison to 36% of fathers who reported living with their child. There also are differences in where the child resides after the parent is incarcerated, depending upon whether it is the mother or father who is imprisoned. For example, the majority (88%) of children with an incarcerated father lived with their mother during his incarceration, while only 37% of all children with a mother in prison lived with their father (Glaze & Maruschak, 2010). The majority of children with a mother in prison lived with their grandmother, typically the maternal grandmother, and if this option was not available the child was cared for by other relatives or in the foster care system (Glaze & Maruschak, 2010).

Once a parent is released from incarceration, one of their primary goals is to reunite with their children. However, for those children who were placed in foster care this can be a challenge. In 1996, the *Federal Adoption and Safe Families Act* was passed in an attempt to create a more stable environment for all children within the foster care system, who often faced multiple short-term placements. Therefore, the

Figure 11.1. © Adobe Stock/fizkes.

act stated that children in foster care must be placed in permanent care, if the child has been in foster care 15 of the last 22 months. However, once the child is placed in permanent care, the biological parents lose their parental rights to their child (Arkansas Educational Television Network, n.d.).

The Federal Adoption and Safe Families Act had a devastating impact on mothers who are incarcerated, as many are sentenced to short-term sentences that are just over the 15-month limit. Therefore, this act has been revised in many states in an attempt to keep families with incarcerated parents together. For example, social workers will actively work with the mother to help her reunite with her child upon release. This, though, can be difficult to accomplish, because the parent will need to provide a stable environment before the social worker can recommend the child be returned to the parent. However, 9% of parents in prison reported being homeless in the month prior to their incarceration, while 57% were diagnosed with a mental health problem and 67% were addicted to substances. Only 40% of those who were addicted to substances received treatment while incarcerated (Glaze & Maruschak, 2010).

Reentry Barrier: The Lack of Healthcare and Treatment in the Community

The state prison systems provide inmates with access to healthcare for chronic physical health conditions, but once released their healthcare is provided by the county in which they reside (Davis et al., 2009). The overwhelming majority of those returning home (90%) do not have health insurance, and very few state prisons have programs to help those who are eligible for state health insurance to enroll before leaving prison (The Council of State Governments Justice Center, 2014). This is incredibly problematic as citizens returning to their communities experience higher rates of HIV, tuberculosis, hepatitis B, and hepatitis C than the general population as well as mental health diagnoses and substance addiction (Davis et al., 2009).

Mental healthcare and treatment for substance addiction also are major barriers, as 37% of prison and 44% of jail inmates had been diagnosed with a mental health disorder prior to their incarceration, and 24% of prison inmates had been diagnosed with an alcohol use disorder with even more male (30%) and female (51%) inmates experiencing substance use disorders (Bronson & Berzofsky, 2017; Fazel et al., 2017). However, few received treatment during their imprisonment, with only 25% of inmates being treated for their substance addiction and half being treated for their mental health disorders. This creates a large burden for community mental health and substance abuse treatment programs due to the high number who are in need of treatment, with only some having had any treatment during incarceration (Davis et al., 2009; Fazel et al., 2017).

Those returning home also are often concentrated within communities that are already facing difficulties economically, with few opportunities for treatment and healthcare, which disproportionately impacts minorities. This is incredibly problematic, as relapse increases the chance one will be returned to prison for not meeting the condition of parole to remain sober or for committing a new crime. Therefore, a high percentage of those returning to prison for a new crime typically have committed a property or drug offense in order to support their drug addiction (Davis et al., 2009).

The lack of treatment for substance addiction also is particularly problematic for women who are more likely than men to become involved with the criminal justice system due to prior abuse, poverty, and substance addiction. Women who have experienced abuse and/or poverty and who lack problem-solving skills as well as a social support network are more likely to turn to substances to cope with these problems. Eventually, the substance use becomes substance addiction and a high percentage of women become involved in the criminal justice system because of their addiction (Salem et al., 2013). At the state level, for example, 26% of female inmates were sentenced for drug crimes in comparison to 13% of male inmates, while 59% of female and 46% of male federal inmates were serving time for a drug offense (Carson, 2020).

Most women who are returning citizens must rely on community treatment programs to address their substance abuse, although the few treatment programs available for returning citizens within the community often focus on men who are returning citizens, since they are the majority of those involved in the criminal justice system. However, this is problematic for women as the reasons for their substance addiction are often different than those of men, so the root of their problems may not be addressed in treatment, leading to higher recidivism rates. Due to a lack of community substance abuse programs, female parolees are very likely to return to prison within one year due to a drug violation (44%) (Salem et al., 2013).

Figure 11.2. Sign protesting treatment of homeless people. © iStockphoto.com/ellisonphoto.

Reentry Barrier: Inability to Access Government Assistance

In 1996, the federal *Housing Opportunity Program Extension Act* created the one-strike law for public housing. The law was put in place to protect the majority of those living in public housing who were not committing crime in order to create a safer environment by removing those who were participating in illegal behavior. For example, those who were found to be engaging in illegal drug activity, on or off the property, were evicted and not allowed to reapply for public housing for three years. However, one could be evicted for the illegal behavior of the person whose name was on the lease as well as a family member or a guest residing in the home. This policy had a direct impact on those who were eligible for public housing, and six months after the one-strike policy was implemented, the number of tenants evicted from public housing increased by 40% (Kaplan & Rossman, 2011).

In 2002, the Supreme Court of the United States heard the case *Department of Housing and Urban Development v. Rucker*, where tenants had been evicted based on the drug use of family members living with them even though the person whose name was on the lease did not condone the behavior and was not aware of the activity. In several instances, the illegal activity did not occur at the property but in the surrounding neighborhood. However, the Supreme Court of the United States ruled in favor of the Department of Housing and Urban Development and upheld their decision to evict those they felt were a negative influence on the public housing community (Kaplan & Rossman, 2011).

Today, the federal government has lifetime bans on public housing for those convicted of a sex offense that requires the person to register as a sex offender for life or if one has been caught cooking methamphetamines in public housing. There also are policies in place that state that if one is using illegal substances, one can be denied access to public housing and if one is already living in public housing and abusing alcohol or other drugs, one can be evicted. Admission to public housing also can be denied if the person has been convicted of a violent or drug-related crime and one can still be evicted for the criminal behavior of a family member or guest. However, it is up to each public housing authority location to determine the criteria for exclusion, and this differs from one location to the next, with some denying access to anyone convicted of a felony (McCarty et al., 2015).

In 1996, the federal government also passed the ***Personal Responsibility and Work Opportunity Reconciliation Act***, which was a major overhaul of the federal welfare system. As part of this act, those who had been convicted of a drug felony were given a lifetime ban on Temporary Assistance to Needy Families (TANF), or the cash assistance program also known as welfare, as well as Supplemental Nutrition Assistance Program (SNAP), formerly known as food stamps. Many states opted out of this ban or modified it in some way. For example, 18 states allow those with felony drug convictions to access cash assistance and/or food assistance if one has completed a variety of conditions. These conditions vary from state to state and could include conditions such as mandated completion of drug treatment, negative drug tests, and/or participation in a reentry program. Some states modified the law to only ban those who were caught trafficking or manufacturing drugs, while others allow access after a period of time without any new crimes committed. Currently, there are seven states who completely ban those with felony drug convictions from receiving TANF and only one state that completely bans SNAP (CLASP, 2022).

IN FOCUS

TANF and Drug Convictions

The overwhelming majority (85%) of those who receive TANF benefits are women, so female returning citizens have been tremendously impacted by the felony drug ban. For example, from 1996 to 2011, there were 180,100 women who had been banned from accessing TANF. Even though Black and Hispanic women were not any more likely than white women to use drugs, they were more likely to become involved in the criminal justice system due to their neighborhoods being targeted by law enforcement. Therefore, Black and Hispanic women also were more likely to be impacted by the felony drug conviction ban on TANF than white women (Mauer & McCalmont, 2013). However, children of those who had been convicted of a felony drug conviction were still eligible to receive TANF and SNAP benefits. Although, the amount of money they received was decreased; for example, if a woman with a felony drug conviction has two children instead of receiving benefits for a family of three she only received benefits for a family of two (Mauer & McCalmont, 2013).

Reentry Barrier: The Inability to Access Employment

Nearly half (40%) of federal and state inmates do not have a high school diploma or a GED, which leaves them at a major disadvantage when they are released from prison and attempt to find employment. Many employers also are reluctant to hire someone with a prior felony conviction, so when the lack of education is combined with one's prior felony conviction, employment becomes a difficult obstacle to overcome. Visher and colleagues (2008) conducted a study where they examined 740 male inmates from three states for up to eight months after release to better understand their ability to gain or not gain employment. Slightly more than two-thirds (68%) of those in the study held a job prior to incarceration, making approximately $9 per hour. After release, the majority of study participants reported spending time looking for a job, while 27% stated they had a job lined up for when they returned to their community. The majority (86%) also reported using a variety of strategies for finding a job, including friends/family, former employers, and the newspaper "help wanted" section (Visher et al., 2008).

However, two months after release less than half (43%) reported being employed at some point, with only 31% stating they were currently employed. Even those who stated they had employment prior to release were struggling, with only half of this group still employed. Those who were employed also were making little money and on average were bringing in $8 an hour. Therefore, two-thirds were relying on financial assistance from family and friends, while 20% were utilizing public assistance (Visher et al., 2008).

Eight months after release the employment rate and average wage had increased slightly, with 50% of study participants reporting being employed and making on average $9 an hour, although nearly half (47%) were supplementing their income through informal jobs, such as helping out friends and family by working on their cars. The authors also noted those who were younger and who had a stronger work history prior to incarceration were more likely to report being employed post release from prison, while those who had mental and physical health diagnoses were less likely to be employed. The most successful strategy for employment reported by study participants was contacting a previous employer. However, this strategy put those who did not have a strong work history at a disadvantage (Visher et al., 2008).

The authors also concluded that those who participated in employment programs were more likely to be employed eight months out, and most returning citizens reported being interested in participating in employment and skills training within their communities. However, half had not participated in any programs because they were unaware of what was available in their community and how to get involved. The authors also noted that those who had a form of state or federal identification before or immediately after release were more likely to be employed, and those who made $10 or more an hour were half as likely to return to prison as those who made $7 an hour. However, the most commonly reported income eight months later was $700 a month. Overall, the authors concluded that being employed was critical in helping returning citizens to successfully reenter their communities by providing a source of income as well as a schedule and stability (Visher et al., 2008).

Pogrebin and colleagues (2014) also conducted a study with 70 parolees from Colorado (48 males and 22 females) who were interviewed approximately 18 months after release to better understand the obstacles they faced regarding employment. The authors noted that in order to be successful upon reentry, one must be employed and be able to pay for one's living expenses. Employment, for example, is often a required condition of parole, and not being able to maintain employment can be enough to be returned to prison. However, there also are many fees and payments that are often required, such as drug testing and court fees as well as child support payments, making this more difficult. Those who were paroled to a halfway house also were required to pay on average $400 a month for rent, and if parolees were unable to pay they began to accrue a balance, which they started paying off as soon as they were employed. However, for many parolees the balance became so high that once they found employment their entire paycheck was sent to the halfway house to pay off their debt. Parole officers who were interviewed for the study stated it was not uncommon for parolees to quit showing up for appointments because they felt overwhelmed and were unable to make their payments. Therefore, it is not surprising that only one third of those released on parole in the study were able to successfully reenter their communities (Pogrebin et al., 2014).

IN FOCUS

Ban the Box

Today there are 65 million Americans who have a criminal record, and it is estimated that returning citizens cost the economy approximately 60 billion dollars annually in lost productivity and output for goods and services because of their inability to find employment (Julian, 2015). These numbers have led to a movement referred to as Ban the Box, where employers are encouraged not to ask if a potential employee has a criminal record until after they interview the applicant. If the employer is interested in hiring the applicant, this is when they would check criminal records and decide whether they are still interested. This allows job applicants to meet with a potential employer face to face, which increases their chances of being hired instead of being eliminated from the application pile immediately once the employer sees they have a criminal record. Currently, there are more than 30 states along with the federal government that have policies in place to ban the box for government jobs (Rodriguez & Avery, 2016; Korte, 2015; Barreiro, 2021). There also are 13 states and the District of Columbia that utilize ban the box for government as well as nongovernment or private employment (Barreiro, 2021).

Couloute and Kopf (2018) also conducted a study to better understand the employment trends for returning citizens across the country. The researchers found that returning citizens had an overall unemployment rate of 27%, which is significantly higher than the unemployment rate for those without a felony conviction, which has remained at less than 10% unemployment since 1945. However, the unemployment rate for returning citizens varies significantly based on race and gender. For example, Black women (44%) and Black men (35%) with a prior felony conviction were significantly more likely to be unemployed in comparison to white women (23%) and white men (18%). Returning citizens who did find work tended to work in the lowest paid jobs, with the majority living below the poverty line. There also were differences in full-time employment by race and gender. For instance, white men (87%) with a prior felony conviction were the most likely to be working full time, while Black women (33%), Hispanic women (30%), and white women (24%) were more likely to be working part time or only occasionally. Unemployment also tended to be the highest for returning citizens less than two years after release from prison (32%), but decreased over time so that after four years the unemployment rate for returning citizens was at 14%. This suggests that the best time to intervene for employment assistance is before release from prison with continued services provided in the community after release from prison (Couloute & Kopf, 2018).

Reentry and Recidivism

Prisoners are often housed many miles away from home for years, which makes it difficult for them to maintain relationships with family and friends for when they return to their communities. This can be emotionally devastating, but also makes it less likely one will reenter their communities successfully as so many are reliant on friends and family for housing and employment as well as financial assistance. Those who cannot rely on friends and family for financial support must utilize government programs, such as public housing, welfare, and food stamps, but those with felony convictions will often find those paths blocked. Many also will return to their communities with chronic physical and mental health problems and/or substance addictions, but there will be few treatment options available to them once they are released, along with a lack of health insurance to help pay for the cost of care.

GLOBAL SPOTLIGHT

Norwegian Prisons

Norway has one of the world's lowest recidivism rates, with only 20% of those who are released from prison returning to the criminal justice system. Norwegians believe that the loss of one's freedom is enough of a punishment, which causes them to take a much different approach to their prison system. In Holden, a maximum-security prison in Norway, there are no bars on the windows, and the cells and common spaces are set up to look more like a dormitory space. Inmates are expected to participate in chores around the prison in order to keep it running, such as cooking and cleaning, while also participating in rehabilitation and vocational programming. In Norway, the belief is that if one is taught how to take care of oneself and given the tools to obtain a profession one is not likely to come back (Sterbenz, 2014).

Once one considers the barriers stacked up against those who are attempting to reenter their communities it is not surprising that returning citizens have high recidivism rates or are likely to return to the criminal justice system. For example, within five years of being released to one's community, more than half of returning citizens will return to prison for a new crime or for violating the conditions of their parole, while the majority (76%) were rearrested with 43% having been rearrested within one year. Property offenders (82%) also were the most likely to be rearrested within five years, followed by drug offenders (76%) and violent offenders (71%) (James, 2015).

There are some small differences in recidivism rates based on gender, race, and ethnicity. For instance, males are somewhat more likely than females to recidivate; for example, a survey of state inmates found that males recidivated and were arrested at a 10% higher rate than females after their first year of release from state prison and this gap continued at 10% for five years after their release (Durose et al., 2014). There also were slight differences based on race and ethnicity when examining recidivism and arrest rates, where Hispanic offenders (46%) and Black offenders (46%) were slightly more likely to recidivate than white offenders (40%) after one year of release from state prison. However, after five years of release from state prison Hispanic offenders (75%) and white offenders (73%) were recidivating at similar rates, and Black offenders (81%) were recidivating at a slightly higher rate (Durose et al., 2014).

The Second Chance Act and Programs Helping Returning Citizens Reenter Their Communities

In 2008, the *Second Chance Act* was passed, which provides federal grants to government and nonprofit agencies in order to implement programs to assist returning citizens in their transition back into the community. The act specifically funds programs that address employment, housing, family programming, and mentoring as well as substance abuse and mental health treatment (National Institute of Justice, 2016). This act has helped to fund many programs through the millions of dollars of grant money that have been distributed. However, these programs also are relatively new and their results have been mixed, as practitioners and researchers attempt to figure out the most effective and efficient way to implement these programs.

An example of a reentry program that was created to tackle the issue of housing is the Reentry Housing Pilot Program, in Washington, which attempted to reduce the number of homeless returning citizens who were at high risk for recidivating and were under community supervision. Those who are homeless are an important population to target, as approximately 10% of inmates were homeless prior to incarceration, and the same number will experience homelessness upon their return to the community. Program participants received 12 months of secure housing in exchange for participating in programming and working towards financial independence by securing a job and permanent housing. The program was implemented within three counties with the same basic structure; for example, each county utilized case management and created partnerships with law enforcement and social services as well as secured housing within the community. However, each program also was allowed to implement the program based upon their finances and needs (Lutze et al., 2014).

Lutze and colleagues (2014) compared those who participated in the program to those who met the criteria for the program, but did not participate, to better understand recidivism rates. Those who participated in the program were significantly less likely than the comparison group to be convicted of a new crime and return to prison and were less likely to have their parole revoked, although this did not reach significance. However, nearly half (41%) of those who participated were removed from the program for technical violations, such as failing urine screens and not following the rules (Lutze et al., 2014).

Although those who participated in the program were less likely to experience homelessness, both groups did have participants who experienced periods of homelessness. Those who experienced periods of homelessness, in both the treatment and comparison groups, were significantly more likely to have their parole revoked, commit a new crime, and/or be returned to prison. Therefore, the authors suggested that homelessness be considered a fluid event and not something that can be addressed as a one-time thing (Lutze et al., 2014).

Another example of a reentry program is Project Reconnect, in St. Louis. This is a voluntary program for those who are not under community supervision (probation or parole) after release that lasts six months and provides case management and financial support to program participants. Case managers work with inmates prior to release to determine what their needs will be upon reentry, and financial assistance is provided to participants after release for food, bus passes, substance abuse treatment, housing, and job training (Wikoff et al., 2012).

Wikoff and colleagues (2012) compared those who participated in the program to those who were eligible, but did not participate, to better understand recidivism rates. Those who did not participate were significantly more likely to recidivate (20%) than those who participated in the program (7%). The authors also noted that those who recidivated were less likely to have a high school diploma or GED and were more likely to have a serious substance abuse problem.

Another example of a reentry program is one that has been implemented by the Minnesota Department of Corrections, referred to as EMPLOY. This program was designed to help returning citizens find employment upon release from prison by working with inmates during their last few months of imprisonment and during their first year after release. Program participants meet with job training specialists in small groups to determine their strengths and to prepare them for the job market, by, for example, learning interviewing skills and how to write a resume. The job training specialist then works with each participant to help them make connections to employment opportunities within the community. Immediately after the inmate is released to the community under parole supervision, a retention specialist works with the participant by providing him with job leads and a copy of the resume he created in prison. The retention specialist will work with the participant for up to one year, and if the participant fails to contact their assigned specialist then he will be dropped from the program (Duwe, 2015).

Duwe (2015) conducted a program evaluation to better understand if the EMPLOY program was effective in helping returning citizens to find employment and to lower the rates of those who had their parole revoked. The author matched 232 participants to 232 nonparticipants who met the eligibility criteria, but did not participate in the program, for 28 months following release. The author found that those who participated in the EMPLOY program were significantly more likely to be employed, work more hours, and earn higher wages than those who did not participate in the program. The author also found that program participants were significantly less likely to recidivate when examining rearrest, revocation, committing new crimes, and reimprisonment. Those who participated in the program also were 72% more likely to employed 12 months post release than those who did not participate and earned on average $5,400 more a year than those who did not participate. Those who participated in the program also were 63% less likely to have their parole revoked (Duwe, 2015).

A final example of a reentry program is the Serious and Violent Offender Reentry Initiative as implemented in two communities, Camden and Essex, which are New Jersey's largest cities as well as ranked in the top three cities in the state for high crime rates. The program was created for serious violent offenders, while incarcerated, when on parole, and once no longer under supervision. The programs were required to target those under the age of 35, as younger offenders are more likely to recidivate, so those who participated in the program were between the ages of 14 and 35 and had been incarcerated in medium- to high-security facilities. The majority had committed a violent crime against a person, while some had committed multiple property crimes, suggesting an increase in criminal behavior (Veysey et al., 2014).

Once released on parole, participants attended quarterly meetings where they were provided with opportunities for programming and treatment. These meetings were attended by parole officers, judges, and nonprofit organizations along with community leaders who provided the message that they were there to support the parolees and their families to help them successfully reintegrate. However, program participants also were informed that if they did not follow the conditions of their parole, they would be punished and possibly sent back to prison. If a participant was viewed to be struggling, individual meetings were held to address his specific needs and to reinforce that there would be consequences if he continued to be noncompliant. Employment help also was provided and financial assistance could be obtained for those who desired to learn a new trade or skill. Other services, such as counseling and classes in parenting skills and life skills also were made available, as well as help in finding housing and obtaining identification (Veysey et al., 2014).

Veysey and colleagues (2014) compared those who participated in the program to those who were on parole, but did not participate, as well as those who were released unconditionally to better understand rearrest rates. The authors concluded that those who participated in the program along with those on parole supervision were significantly less likely to be rearrested than those who were released without any supervision. Program participants also were significantly less likely to be rearrested for drug, violent, or other crimes than the two comparison groups. Those who participated in the program also were less likely to be rearrested and remained in the community for longer periods of time than the comparison groups. However, 40% of program participants were rearrested within three years of release, and those who participated in the program had high rates of revocation. For example, half of those returned to prison were sent back due to revocation of their parole, with the majority (66%) returning for technical violations or violating the conditions of their parole. The authors noted the high rates of parole revocation may have been due to the intensive supervision nature of the program and program participants being watched more closely than the comparison groups (Veysey et al., 2014).

Summary

It is often difficult to understand why so many returning citizens become involved again in the criminal justice system, because most of us view prison as a deterrent and do not participate in illegal behavior because we fear the consequences of the criminal justice system. However, once one stops and examines the barriers that have been put in the paths of those attempting to reenter society, it becomes painfully clear as to why so many become involved repeatedly in the criminal justice system, with a majority at some point returning to prison. Many of these obstacles were put in place as a deterrent with the belief that if one was aware that illegal behavior would deny one access to public assistance, such as housing and welfare, that one would not participate in the illegal behavior. However, this notion does not take into consideration the lack of opportunities found within many communities across the United States as well as other issues, such as mental health challenges and substance addiction.

Today, there are those who are beginning to recognize the barriers facing returning citizens reentering their communities and are fighting to remove them. Returning citizens are now finding support through movements such as Ban the Box and federal funding for reentry programming through the Second Chance Act. These programs are still in their beginning stages, but it is a step in the right direction. As these programs are created it is important for them to take into consideration the needs of participants from a variety of backgrounds. For example, recognizing that males and females have different needs when reentering their communities, such as females being more likely to be the primary caretaker of their children and being in need of childcare or residential treatment that also accepts children. Program evaluations also should examine whether there are differences in how program participants experience or benefit from a program based on race and ethnicity. These findings would allow for adjustments to be made, if needed, to ensure all benefit and have a positive experience.

As we continue to remove the barriers to successful reentry it is important to remember that these programs benefit all of us as we spend fewer tax dollars on reincarcerating returning citizens, which makes our communities safer with less crime. Returning citizens who are employed and contributing to their communities also are less likely to be reliant on social services. Additionally, they are paying taxes and taking care of their families, which improves the outcomes for all within their community.

Discussion Questions

1. How would you convince legislators within your state to provide financial support for programs that target returning citizens to help them successfully reenter their communities?

2. Should all employers participate in the Ban the Box movement or are there some jobs where applicants should have to tell their potential employer about their criminal history during the application process?

3. Which of the barriers discussed in this chapter do you think provides the biggest obstacle for the successful reentry of returning citizens and why? What do you think could be done to help remove this barrier?

4. What is the Federal Adoption and Safe Families Act? Should this act be applied to female inmates?

Key Terms

reentry

recidivate

Federal Adoption and Safe Families Act

Housing Opportunity Program Extensions Act

Department of Housing and Urban Development v. Rucker

Personal Responsibility and Work Opportunity Reconciliation Act

Second Chance Act

References

Arkansas Educational Television Network. (n.d.). Mothers in prison: Children in crisis. http://www.aetn.org/programs/mothersinprison/facts

Barreiro, S. (2021). What is Ban the Box law? NOLO. https://www.nolo.com/legal-encyclopedia/what-is-a-ban-the-box-law.html#:~:text=Currently%2C%20thirteen%20states%20(and%20the,Island%2C%20Vermont%2C%20and%20Washington

Bronson, J., & Berzofsky, M. (2017). Indicators of mental health problems reported by prisoners and jail inmates, 2011–2012. Bureau of Justice Statistics. https://www.bjs.gov/content/pub/pdf/imhprpji1112.pdf

Bureau of Justice Statistics. (2016). Reentry trends in the US. Office of Justice Programs. http://www.bjs.gov/content/rentry/reentry_contents.cfm#contents

Carson, A. E. (2020). Prisoners in 2019. Bureau of Justice Statistics. https://www.bjs.gov/content/pub/pdf/p19.pdf

CLASP. (2022). No more double punishments: Lifting the ban on SNAP and TANF for people with prior felony drug convictions. The Center for Law and Social Policy. Retrieved from https://www.clasp.org/publications/report/brief/no-more-double-punishments/

Couloute, L., & Kopf, D. (2018). Out of prison and out of work: Unemployment among formerly incarcerated people. Prison Policy Initiative. https://www.prisonpolicy.org/reports/outofwork.html

The Council of State Governments Justice Center. (2014). Health and criminal justice populations. https://csgjusticecenter.org/reentry/issue-areas/health/

Davis, L. M., Nicosia, N., Overton, A., Krause, L., Derose, K. P., Fain, T., Turner, S., Steinberg, P. S., & Williams, E. (2009). Understanding the public health implications of prisoner reentry in California: Phase I report. RAND Corporation. http://www.rand.org/pubs/technical_reports/TR687.html

Durose, M. R., Cooper, A. D., & Snyder, H. N. (2014). Recidivism of prisoners released in 30 states in 2005: Patterns from 2005–2010. Bureau of Justice Statistics. https://www.bjs.gov/content/pub/pdf/rprts05p0510.pdf

Duwe, G. (2015). The benefits of keeping idle hands busy: An outcome evaluation of a prisoner reentry employment program. *Crime & Delinquency*, *61*(4), 559–586.

Fazel, S., Yoon, I. A., & Hayes, A. (2017). Substance use disorders in prisoners: An updated systematic review and meta-regression analysis in recently incarcerated men and women. *Addiction*, *112*, 1725–1739. https://pubmed.ncbi.nlm.nih.gov/28543749/

Federal Communications Commission (FCC). (2020). FCC seeks to reduce rates and charges for inmate calling services. FCC News. https://docs.fcc.gov/public/attachments/DOC-366002A1.pdf

Feig, L. (2015). Breaking the cycle: A family-focused approach to criminal sentencing in Illinois. The Advocate's Forum. http://ssa.uchicago.edu/breaking-cycle-family-focused-approach-criminal-sentencing-illinois

Glaze, L. E., & Maruschak, L. M. (2010). Bureau of Justice Statistics special report: Parents in prison and their minor children. http://www.bjs.gov/content/pub/pdf/pptmc.pdf

Goldman, D. (2016). Government's plan to cut sky-high prison phone rates is put on hold. CNN Tech. http://money.cnn.com/2016/03/09/technology/prison-phones/

James, N. (2015). Offender reentry: Correctional statistics, reintegration into the community, and recidivism. Congressional Research Service. https://fas.org/sgp/crs/misc/RL34287.pdf

Julian, L. (2015). States ban the box: Removing barriers to work for people with criminal records. Justice Center. https://csgjusticecenter.org/reentry/posts/states-ban-the-box-removing-barriers-to-work-for-people-with-criminal-records-2/

Kaplan, W. J., & Rossman, D. (2011). Called out at home: The one strike eviction policy and juvenile court. *Duke Forum for Law and Social Change*, *3*, 109–138.

Korte, G. (2015). Obama tells federal agencies to ban the box on federal job applications. *USA Today*. http://www.usatoday.com/story/news/politics/2015/11/02/obama-tells-federal-agencies-ban-box-federal-job-applications/75050792/

Lutze, F. E., Rosky, J. W., & Hamilton, Z. K. (2014). Homelessness and reentry: A multisite outcome evaluation of Washington state's reentry housing program for high risk offenders. *Criminal Justice & Behavior*, *41*(4), 471–491.

Mauer, M., & McCalmont, V. (2013). A lifetime of punishment: The impact of the felony drug ban on welfare benefits. The Sentencing Project. http://sentencingproject.org/doc/publications/cc_A%20Lifetime%20of%20Punishment.pdf

McCarty, M., Falk, G., Aussenberg, R. A., & Carpenter, D. H. (2015). Drug testing and crime related restrictions in TANF, SNAP and housing assistance. Congressional Research Service. https://www.fas.org/sgp/crs/misc/R42394.pdf

Murphey, D., & Cooper, P. M. (2015). Parents behind bars: What happens to their children? Child Trends. https://www.childtrends.org/wp-content/uploads/2015/10/2015-42ParentsBehindBars.pdf

National Institute of Justice. (2015). Offender reentry. Office of Justice Programs. http://www.nij.gov/topics/corrections/reentry/pages/welcome.aspx#overview

National Institute of Justice. (2016). Evaluation of Second Chance Act demonstration projects. Office of Justice Programs. http://www.nij.gov/topics/corrections/reentry/pages/evaluation-second-chance.aspx

Pogrebin, M., West-Smith, M., Walker, A., & Unnithan, N. P. (2014). Employment isn't enough: Financial obstacles experienced by ex-prisoners during the reentry process. *Criminal Justice Review*, *39*(4), 394–410.

Reentry Council. (2010). Reentry myth buster. https://csgjusticecenter.org/documents/0000/1064/Reentry_Council_Mythbuster_TANF.pdf

Rodriguez, M. N., & Avery, B. (2016). Ban the box: U.S. cities, counties, states adopt fair hiring policies. National Employment Law Project. http://www.nelp.org/publication/ban-the-box-fair-chance-hiring-state-and-local-guide/

Salem, B. E., Nyamathi, A., Idemundia, F., Slaughter, R., & Ames, M. (2013). At a crossroads: Reentry challenges and healthcare needs among homeless female ex-offenders. *Journal of Forensic Nursing*, *9*(1), 14–22.

Sterbenz, C. (2014). Why Norway's prison system is so successful. *Business Insider*. Law and Order. http://www.businessinsider.com/why-norways-prison-system-is-so-successful-2014-12

U.S. Department of Justice. (n.d.). Prisoners and prisoner re-entry. https://www.justice.gov/archive/fbci/progmenu_reentry.html

Veysey, B. M., Ostermann, M., & Lanterman, J. L. (2014). The effectiveness of enhanced parole supervision and community services: New Jersey's serious and violent offender reentry initiative. *Prison Journal*, *94*(4), 435–453.

Visher, C., Debus, S., & Yahner, J. (2008). Employment after prison: A longitudinal study of releasees in three states. http://www.urban.org/sites/default/files/alfresco/publication-pdfs/411778-Employment-after-Prison-A-Longitudinal-Study-of-Releasees-in-Three-States.PDF

Wikoff, N., Linhorst, D. M., & Morani, N. (2012). Recidivism among participants of a reentry program for prisoners released without supervision. *Social Work Research*, *36*(4), 289–299.

Additional Issues

TWELVE

Juvenile Justice

Intersectionality and Social Constructions of Childhood

Learning Objectives

1. Understand the historical implications of racialized and gendered justice on contemporary issues.
2. Apply an intersectional lens to critically examine how young people experience the juvenile justice system and the way their experience varies by race, gender, and class.

This chapter discusses how one's social location can contribute to one's interactions with the justice system. ***Intersectionality theory*** was coined by Kimberle Crenshaw in 1981 to describe the ways multiple oppressions intersect to impact lives. This chapter will explore how childhood is constructed and what that means for race and gender in the juvenile justice system. It is argued that childhood is a social construct that applies to children of color unequally (Epstein et al., 2017). As it relates to juvenile justice, intersectionality as a framework has been used to study how not all girls share the same experiences. Cyntoia Brown Long (see In Focus) is an illustration of how experiences in the system vary by race, gender, and class (see Leiber et al., 2009).

The History of Juvenile Justice in the U.S.

The modern juvenile justice system finds its roots in the Progressive Era of modern thinking, which was roughly from 1880 to 1920. During this time, progressive thinkers called for a separate court for juveniles. They advocated for this separate court to be rooted in the parens patriae doctrine, which derived from English Common Law.

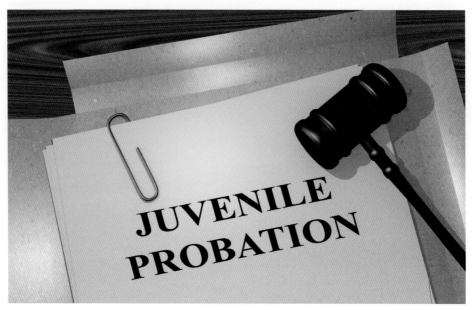

Figure 12.1. © Adobe Stock/hafakot

Parens patriae literally means "the state as the parent" and it is based on the premise that juveniles need the state to intervene in the best interest of a child if deemed necessary. Also referred to as the Child Saving Movement, this era marks the beginning of an informal, individualized system by which wayward children and youth who committed crimes could be treated rather than punished.

Before parens patriae became the prevailing philosophy, the care of children in need was guided by *in loco parentis*, which focused on family control and attempted to place troubled youth with other families (Mallet, 2018). Two pre-juvenile justice system cases that illustrate the court's treatment of juveniles are: *Ex Parte v. Crouse* (1839) and *People ex rel. O'Connell v. Turner* (1870). The *Crouse* case demonstrates the court's willingness to allow the state to exercise necessary restraints to protect children, even if that includes removing the child from their home. The *O'Connell* case dealt with just cause for placing a juvenile in a reform school. The court concluded that vagrancy is not a reasonable justification for commitment to a facility because it is based on misfortune, not criminality.

Almost thirty years after *O'Connell*, the first juvenile court was created in 1899 by the Illinois Juvenile Court Act. This was the catalyst that created what we now refer to as the juvenile justice system. Within 12 years of the Illinois Juvenile Court, twenty-two states had a separate juvenile court, and by 1945 all states had a separate court system for juveniles. Since that time, the juvenile justice system has evolved and now looks more like the formal and adversarial adult court, but there are still some major distinctions to keep in mind. Several core principles distinguish juvenile courts from adult criminal courts. They are:

- Juvenile courts have a limited jurisdiction.
- Juvenile courts are informal proceedings.
- Juvenile courts are individualized. In other words, they focus on offenders, not their crimes.
- Juvenile courts hand out indeterminate sentences.
- Juvenile courts usually remain confidential, although exceptions to this exist in many state statutes.

The shift towards a more formal, "criminalized" court is not always viewed as a bad thing. Since the mid-1960s, juveniles have acquired greater constitutional rights similar to those granted to adults in criminal courts. However, as juveniles obtain a greater range of constitutional rights, they become less subject to the influence of *parens patriae*. As the court became more formalized, there was increasing evidence that there was a different process for youth based on their intersectionality.

In 1974, the enactment of the Juvenile Justice Delinquency & Prevention Act (JJDPA) signaled that a change was on the horizon. The JJDPA was designed to provide resources to states and establish standards for how states treat juveniles. Ultimately, the act mandates four core requirements: (1) deinstitutionalization of status offenders (DSO); (2) sight and sound separation; (3) adult jail and lockup removal; and (4) disproportionate minority contact (DMC). It should be noted that the JJDPA was reauthorized in 2018 to include the Juvenile Justice Reform Act (JJRA). Among its many provisions, it substantially amended the approach to the DMC mandate and now requires states to "identify and reduce racial and ethnic disparities (R/ED) among youth who come into contact with the juvenile justice system."

IN FOCUS

Kentucky Court of Justice: Four-Step Agency Model to Reduce Racial and Ethnic Disparities

Racial and ethnic disparities in the juvenile justice system persist for many reasons. According to the Kentucky Court of Justice (KYCOJ), the strategies necessary to combat these disparities include "leadership, stakeholder collaboration, education, data analysis, strategic action planning and the ongoing evaluation of efforts and outcomes." Since 2014, the KYCOJ has worked to embed these principles into a four-step model that provides agency guidance for policy and procedural change that addresses racial and ethnic disparities. The four-step model for cultural change includes:

1. Identify. Identify disproportionality and disparities.
2. Construct. Construct strategies that will aggressively address the challenges and barriers to the desired equitable outcomes.

3. Institutionalize. Institutionalize the effective processes constructed.

4. Reevaluate. Reevaluate to measure progress and ensure continuous quality improvement. (Palmer et al., 2020)

IDENTIFY	CONSTRUCT	INSTITUTIONALIZE	REEVALUATE
• Understand Racial, Ethnic and Equity Disparities • Establish Contact Points • Conduct a Data Walk by Race	• Execute a Racial Equity Assessment • Establish a Strategic Plan and Reduction Goals • Provide Training • Engage Stakeholders • Develop Local Action Plans • Analyze Policies and Procedures	• Modify Policies and Procedures • Use an Individualized Approach • Apply a Racial Lens to Activities • Collaborate With Stakeholders	• Reassess Strategic Plan and Reduction Goals • Examine Performance Measures and Outcomes by Race • Review Policies and Procedures • Conduct Quarterly Review of Action Plans • Base Training on Equity Assessment Results • Provide Updates to Stakeholders

Racial Disparities and Juvenile Justice

Today, many researchers question the social construction of childhood as it applies to children of color. Tragedies such as the Tamir Rice case lend some credibility to such questioning. Tamir Rice was a 12-year-old Black boy playing with a toy gun in a park in Cleveland, Ohio. A 911 caller reported an 18- to 20-year-old armed Black man in the park. It took police less than 30 seconds at the scene to gun down Tamir and end his young life. While Tamir's story is tragic, it is reflective of a long-standing history of not applying child-like qualities to youth of color, particularly Black youth (Agyepong, 2018). This concept—*adultification*—refers to the unfair and unjustified application of adult-like characteristics and expectations on Black youth. A series of modern U.S. Supreme Court cases have solidified that children lack maturity, they are easily influenced by others, and their characters and personalities are still developing (see *Roper v. Simmons*, 2005). Epstein et al. (2017) suggest that adultification creates a false narrative that the transgressions of children of color are "intentional and malicious instead of immature decision-making" (p. 6). The justice system has accepted that young people are less culpable, or blameworthy, than adults. However, historical research reveals racial disparities in similarly situated incidences dating back to the 1800s. Ward (2012) contends that even the "child savers" were focused on the treatment of white youth and that Black youth were often enslaved and still subject to adult punishments, like capital punishment, convict leasing, and chain gangs. In direct contrast to the juvenile rehabilitative ideal, Black youth were still seen as more culpable and more criminal. Arguably, not much has changed today.

Jim Crow Juvenile Justice

There is clearly an omission of the role of race in the historical treatment of juveniles. Literature often race neutrally discusses the chronological development of juvenile justice, which dismisses the plight of minority youth in early juvenile justice. Recently, some scholars have introduced the importance of including race-conscious approaches to juvenile justice history. Mallett (2018) describes how "plantation discipline" contributed to early interpretations of justice for Black children (p. 232). This fed into the concept that Black children were unworthy of reformation and rehabilitation.

In *The Black Child Savers: Racial Democracy and Juvenile Justice*, Ward (2012) presents an unaccounted-for view of juvenile justice history. Deemed as "jim crow juvenile justice," he chronologically reveals that minority, particularly Black, youth were treated quite differently than their white counterparts (p. 4). Ward (2012) notes that as the juvenile justice system was being developed for white youth, Black youth were part of the convict leasing system, particularly in the Southern states. Convict leasing appeared as a post-Civil War tactic and served to provide public and private interests with cheap inmate labor (Blackmon, 2008; Ward, 2012). Reportedly, Black youth comprised over half the convict lease program in 1868 Louisiana. There are reports that some Black youth, as young as ten, were convicted and leased (Ward, 2012). These incidences provide examples that illustrate that minority youth have always encountered a parallel justice system in comparison to white youth.

Today's racial disparities follow a long tradition of differential treatment of Black youth by public institutions. According to Mallet (2018), Black youth make up approximately 15–16% of the youth population nationally, but comprise 26% of arrests, 31% of referrals to juvenile court, 44% of those held in juvenile detention, 34% of those formally processed by the juvenile court, and 32% of those adjudicated delinquent. (**Delinquency** is a violation of the law that would be a crime if not for the youthful age of the offender.)

Disproportionate Minority Contact

Disproportionate Minority Contact (DMC) refers to the overrepresentation of minority youth at critical decision points in the juvenile justice system. DMC as a concept has evolved over time. First referred to as "disproportionate minority confinement" in 1988, efforts to address DMC were codified in 1992 when it became a core requirement of the Juvenile Justice Delinquency and Prevention Act of 1974. In 2002, the definition expanded beyond confinement to contact and began to include

Figure 12.2. © Adobe Stock/LIGHTFIELD STUDIOS

other stages of the juvenile justice process. With the change from DMC to R/ED the original nine decision points for DMC data collection were reduced to the following five in 2019:

1. Arrest
2. Diversion (filing of charges)
3. Pre-trial detention (both secure and nonsecure)
4. Disposition commitments (secure and nonsecure)
5. Adult transfer (OJJDP, 2019)

Since 1992, states receiving JJDP Act Formula Grants have been charged with addressing DMC as a requirement of their funding. More specifically, the purpose of the JJDP Act's Part B Formula Grants program is to "address juvenile delinquency prevention efforts and system improvement efforts designed to reduce, without establishing or requiring numerical standards or quotas, the disproportionate number of juvenile members of minority groups, who come into contact with the juvenile justice system."

The 2009 OJJDP Technical Assistance Manual included a section outlining DMC Contributing Mechanisms, which are described as "social influences that increase the likelihood of a minority youth coming into contact with the juvenile justice system." There were eight contributing mechanisms that can accumulate throughout a youth's life and increase the likelihood of coming in contact with the juvenile justice system:

1. Differential Behavior
2. Mobility Effects: Importation/Displacement
3. Indirect Effects
4. Differential Opportunities for Prevention and Treatment
5. Justice by Geography
6. Legislation, Policies, and Legal Factors with Disproportionate Impact
7. Accumulated Disadvantage
8. Statistical Aberration

The disproportionate representation of minority youth in the juvenile justice system is well documented in criminal justice, as well as in adolescent development literature (Bishop, 2005; Kempf-Leonard, 2007; Pope & Leiber, 2005). Despite this recognition, however, there has been no clear consensus as to why DMC persists. There are two prevailing explanations for the cause of DMC: (1) the differential offending or differential behavior theory, which holds that youth are disproportionately represented because they commit a disproportionate amount of crime; and (2) the differential treatment theory, which attributes DMC to the unequal treatment of minorities in the juvenile justice process, whether it be inadvertent or intentional.

Most likely, however, a number of factors compatible with each theory contribute to the problem of DMC, including socioeconomic (Frazier & Bishop, 1995; Hawkins et al., 2000; Leiber, 2003), geographical (Feld, 1991; Sickmund, 2004), institutional/administrative (Kempf-Leonard et al., 1995), and educational factors (Marchbanks et al., 2018). Much scholarly literature acknowledges that, "the causes of DMC are complex, interrelated factors from multiple levels of influence involving the individual, family, communities, and systems of justice" (Kempf-Leonard, 2007, p. 82).

Increased attention has been directed to the problem of, as well as possible solutions to, DMC over the past decade. Because the JJDP Act requires that states investigate and mitigate the possible disproportionate representation of minority youth at every stage of the justice process, numerous federal and state-level studies have been conducted in order to determine the best ways in which DMC can be addressed at each decision point. As Kempf-Leonard (2007) asserts:

> Benevolent protection and personal accountability objectives must both be retained but uncoupled and each made explicit aims of juvenile justice procedures. The structural framework also must become more transparent, with consistency in application of procedures and more accountability of official decision making… although the solutions for DMC are nearly as complex, multilevel, and interrelated as the factors that give rise to the problems, the considerable benefits would be well worth the efforts. (p. 84)

The classification and assessment of juvenile justice decisions is an important tool in fighting DMC (Kempf-Leonard, 2007). In order to develop solutions to DMC, there must be a better understanding of the unique form it takes in each community; thus, the individualized assessment of the causes of DMC in various states, cities, or counties is important to the treatment of such problems. Jones (2016) suggests that DMC should be addressed at the local level for several reasons. First, community-level strategies are less likely to be bogged down by bureaucracy and political factors that persist at the state level. Second, stakeholders who live and work in these communities are more likely to develop realistic solutions that consider local nuances and practices. Finally, local-level DMC efforts are more likely to include community members and leaders who are familiar with the cultural diversity and relevant occurrences represented in those neighborhoods, and therefore maintain a distinct ability to offer resolutions that can address the problems currently relevant to DMC.

There are specific tools that have been shown to assist in the management of DMC: (1) accurate and timely information and analysis of data regarding the rate of incidence of DMC in a particular area (state, county, etc.) (Kempf-Leonard, 2007); (2) efforts to increase awareness and education concerning DMC (Mooradian, 2003); and (3) implementation of place-specific policies to address DMC (Bishop, 2005). While academics and practitioners alike commonly recognize that DMC exists, they do not all agree as to why this is a recurring problem. Some argue that DMC results from discriminatory decisions made by those within the justice system, while others argue it results from legally relevant factors such as variation in offense seriousness and prior record. Unfortunately, with any study, it can be difficult for researchers to examine white and non-white youth with similar situations when assessing the relationship between race and juvenile justice outcomes.

In the last few decades, DMC has been a well-documented aspect of the juvenile justice system with research consistently demonstrating that minority youth, particularly African American youth and Hispanic youth, are disproportionately represented in the juvenile justice system at every stage of the court process (Hawkins & Kempf-Leonard, 2005; Kempf-Leonard, 2007; Bishop, 2005). Minority youth are disproportionately petitioned to court (Leiber et al., 2011; Leiber & Stairs, 1999), held in pre-adjudication detention (Moak et al., 2012), adjudicated or determined delinquent (Hawkins & Kempf-Leonard, 2005; Kempf-Leonard, 2007; Leiber, 2015; Fix et al., 2015), confined to detention or correctional facilities following adjudication (Bishop, 2005; Bishop & Leiber, 2011; Davis & Sorensen, 2013), and transferred to criminal court (Bishop, 2005; Brown & Sorensen, 2013; Males & Macallair, 2000).

GLOBAL SPOTLIGHT

Youth Justice in New Zealand

The New Zealand youth justice system overhaul from the early 1990s illustrates how legislative mandates can transform whole systems. In 1989, the passage of the Children's and Young People's Well-being Act represents the first time a nation codified a shift from retributive to restorative justice (Maxwell & Morris, 2006). These changes were made in large part as a response to the mistreatment of Maori youth, who were six times more likely to enter the justice system than white youth (Goeman, 2018).

As such the New Zealand justice system has been seen as a relic of the British legal system that negated Maori culture. Their culture is rooted in their indigenous, Polynesian descent and how they have been oppressed since their colonization by Britain in the nineteenth century.

Traditionally, the Maori deal with offenses through a lens of "healing and problem solving" rather than punishment (p. 10). Overlooking these cultural traditions was viewed as institutionalized racism. Maxwell and Morris (2006) reported that:

> In Maori custom and law, *tikanga o nga hara*, the law of wrongdoing, was based on notions that responsibility was collective rather than individual and that redress was due not just to any victim but also to the victim's family. Understanding why an individual had offended was also linked to this notion of collective responsibility. The reasons were felt to lie not in the individual but in a lack of balance in the offender's social and family environment. The causes of this imbalance, therefore, had to be addressed in a collective way and, in particular, the imbalance between the offender and the victim's family had to be restored through mediation. (p. 244)

In an attempt to include Maori cultural traditions, the act's goals focused on "reducing youth involvement with the courts, promoting diversion, empowering victims, strengthening families and communities, and utilizing culturally appropriate practices" (Goemann, 2018, p. 1). In addition, it set forth a number of youth justice principles that provide guidance:

1. Criminal proceedings should not be used if there is an alternative means of dealing with the matter.
2. Criminal proceedings must not be used for welfare purposes.

3. Measures to deal with offending should strengthen the family, *whanau* (extended family), *hapu* (clan), *iwi* (tribe), and family group and foster their ability to deal with offending by their children and young people.
4. Young people should be kept in the community.
5. Age is a mitigating factor.
6. Sanctions should be the least restrictive possible and should promote the development of the child in the family.
7. Due regard should be given to the interests of the victim.
8. The child or young person is entitled to special protection during any investigations or proceedings. (Maxwell & Morris, 2006, p. 242)

While the 1989 legislation offered hope for a transformation, it quickly became apparent that its principles continued to privilege white youth while disproportionately and unfavorably impacting Maori youth. While it succeeded in shrinking the system, the disparities with Maori youth persist. Decades after the act, Maori youth are still overrepresented at every stage of the youth justice process (Goemann, 2018). As such, several remedies have been instituted since its enactment. One culturally responsive approach was the implementation of Rangathai Courts. This approach relates to aspects of the act that call for "strengthening of the "*whanau* (family), *hapu* (clan) and *iwi* (tribe)" (Goemann, 2018, p. 11). These courts infuse Maori principles within the current youth justice framework. Established as a way to address Maori youth disproportionate contact with the youth justice system, they have shown some success, with a reported 6% decreased incidence of reoffending compared to traditional youth courts.

Despite the promise of the act, unfortunately between 2008 and 2017 New Zealand saw a troubling trend with Maori youth accounting for 64% of youth in court (2017) compared to 49% in 2008 (Goemann, 2018). In 2017, several amendments were enacted that furthered the inclusion of Maori cultural traditions in New Zealand youth justice.

Research Studies on Disproportionate Minority Contact

Over the last 25 years, research examining DMC in the juvenile justice system has significantly increased (Fix et al., 2015), with some studies indicating mixed findings (McCoy et al., 2012). Prior research on DMC was often focused on one juvenile court and/or one stage of the court process. Further, research has not yet thoroughly examined whether DMC is prevalent for specific types of crimes when assessing the sentencing stage (Leiber, 2015; Fix et al., 2015). A number of studies have examined DMC concerning juveniles, with evidence consistently demonstrating that members of racial and ethnic minority groups are vastly overrepresented at numerous stages in the juvenile justice system (Claus et al., 2017).

Additionally, findings show that disparities exist in earlier stages of the justice system. Evidence indicates that Black and Hispanic/Latino adolescents are more likely than white adolescents to have had previous contact with the police and have been arrested, which increases the likelihood of further contact with the police in later adolescence (Crutchfield et al., 2009). Police officers are more likely to consider legal factors in their decision making because of their organizational role, which is to serve and protect the community. Further, they may also consider extralegal factors, such as race, sex, or age, based on personal experiences interacting with troubled youth (Leiber et al., 2010).

While OJJDP youth arrest data continues to show disparities based on gender and race, recent studies show that Black youth have higher probabilities of arrest (Tapia, 2010), while other studies report that even when controlling for delinquent behavior, Black youth were more likely to be arrested compared to white youth (Tapia, 2010). Huizinga and colleagues (2007) compared three different jurisdictions and found that Black youth are more likely to have contact/referrals regardless of reported offense type. In addition, Huizinga et al. (2007) reported that the effect of race on initial contact/referral was no longer significant when controlling for risk factors, which are referred to as indirect effects in DMC literature. Indirect effects refer to factors in a youth's life that are beyond their control, such as school performance, neighborhood variables, access to resources, and juvenile justice system decision-making factors. Huizinga and colleagues (2007) considered the indirect effects of type of neighborhood, family economic status, family structure, age of mother at first birth, and youth educational problems.

Over the years, there have been several meta-analyses demonstrating just how complex DMC is to study. As of 2018, there were five well-documented large-scale studies that attempted to examine the scope of research on DMC (Spinney et al., 2018). Spinney and colleagues (2018) found five extensive examinations of DMC literature. The first effort examined published studies from 1969 to 1989 (n=46), finding race effects on decision-making with few studies that could attribute that to discrimination. The second meta-analysis looked at 36 studies and discovered that in the years of 1989–2001, there were more mixed results in the findings on how race affects contact with the juvenile justice system. More importantly, evidence suggests that race effects appeared at certain decision points or were based on the offender or offense type. Engen and colleagues (2002) used theoretical framing (i.e., contributing mechanisms) to analyze 65 research studies and found no clear evidence supporting a particular framework. Leiber's 2002 study of DMC assessments (n= 40) required by federal law, found that the quality of the state assessment varied, yet not many states were held as non-compliant with the Juvenile Justice Delinquency and

Figure 12.3. © Adobe Stock/primipil

Prevention Act of 1974. In a recent study, Spinney et al. (2018) analyzed a much larger number compared to prior studies (n=107), which indicates a greater interest in DMC research.

Girls and the Juvenile Justice System

Historically, delinquency in girls has been intertwined with social constructions of propriety, or the proper way that girls should act. Early depictions of female delinquency were equated with promiscuity and a divergence from the feminine ideal (Pasko, 2010). Described as incorrigible and wayward, delinquent girls were socially constructed as problems due to perceived notions of how they should act, while overlooking and discounting why (Agyepong, 2018). The further away they deviated from the Victorian ideals of behavior, the more delinquent they were perceived to be. This focus on proper behavior elevated the numbers of girls involved in juvenile court while simultaneously disregarding the ways sexual assault victimization was socially constructed as the fault of the girls and perceived as a result of their sexual delinquency and poor decisions (Thomas, 1928; Pasko, 2010).

Houses of Refuge and Reform Schools touted the rehabilitative ideal by depicting adequate services and resources to reform "wayward" girls. These practices primarily focused on ensuring that white girls acquired the skills to comport with ideal perceptions of femininity. But even in the early days of reform, racialization occurred in conjunction with gendered justice. In reform schools, girls were segregated by race.

Black girls were often classified as more deviant than their white counterparts. At the Illinois Training School for Girls at Geneva, Black girls were immediately perceived as "more sexually promiscuous and diseased than their white counterparts" (Agyepong, 2018, p. 76).

These characteristics didn't necessarily have a proven basis or could perhaps be explained by the other social conditions that accompanied being Black in the U.S. at that time. According to Hartman (1997):

> Black lives are still imperiled and devalued by a racial calculus and a political arithmetic that were entrenched centuries ago. This is the afterlife of slavery—skewed life chances, limited access to health and education, premature death, incarceration, and impoverishment. (p. 6)

It is evident that the juvenile justice system has considered gender in its response to deviance. For girls, the leading reason for arrest is almost always a minor offense like a technical violation, misdemeanor, status offense, or outstanding warrant (Sadaa Sarr et al., 2015). According to the 2015 report *The Sex Abuse to Prison Pipeline*, "the decision to arrest and detain girls in these cases has been shown often to be based in part on the perception of girls' having violated conventional norms and stereotypes of feminine behavior even when that behavior is caused by trauma" (p. 7). The JJDPA of 1974 requirement that states deinstitutionalize status offenders was arguably most effective at changing the dominant way for dealing with delinquent girls. The use of incarceration for status offenses prohibited placing girls in confinement due to running away, truancy, and immoral behaviors. As a result, the rates of commitment to juvenile facilities significantly decreased following the enactment of the JJDPA.

Chesney-Lind (1997) suggested that a two-track system exists—one for white girls and one for Black girls. Agyepong's (2018) historical presentation of Black girls' experiences at the Illinois Training School Girls at Geneva in the early 1900s reflects a similar sentiment. At Geneva,

> African-American girls' intersecting racial and gender identities influenced both their experiences and the ways in which staff at Geneva perceived them. Staff members masculinized African-American girls and constructed them as the most violent and aggressive residents at the institution. In spite of the reality that African American girls were typically younger than white girls and the fact that a disproportionate number of them were sent to Geneva not because they had committed any crimes but because there were no available institutions for dependent African American children, staff members believed that they were the most violent, sexually deviant and uncontrollable girls at the institution. (Agyepong, 2018, pp. 79–80)

Evans-Winters (2009) speaks to this when she states that Black girls have been pathologized, meaning that their perceived problematic behavior is deemed a function of who they just are and not from societal constructions of them. Research continues to explore how Black and Brown girls are perceived. These perceptions seem to influence how Black and Brown girls are treated by public institutions, such as schools and the juvenile justice system. This could arguably be supported by research that historically shows Black girls are disproportionately punished by public systems. As Tonnesen (2013) wrote:

> School administrators, teachers, and people working for the criminal justice system often misidentify Black girls who physically defend themselves against their harassers as the aggressors, a phenomenon that can be linked to findings on implicit bias that Black girls and women are perceived as more masculine than girls and women of other races. (p. 5)

IN FOCUS

Cyntoia Brown-Long

In March 2004, Cyntoia Brown shot and killed a 43-year-old real estate agent who solicited sex from her. She was 16 years old. Her story is one rife with a social history most could not survive. Cyntoia's story began at conception. As the result of an unplanned (and unwanted) pregnancy of a white mother and Black father, Cyntoia was not welcomed by her maternal family in Georgia. Cyntoia's mother was sent away and told not to return home with the Black baby she bore (Hargrove, 2011). As a result, her mother became a drug-addicted sex worker who informally gave Cyntoia up for adoption. Throughout her childhood, Cyntoia experienced periods of familial instability, drug abuse, sex abuse, and prostitution. Her path to the adult criminal justice system began with time served for stealing $2,000 worth of jewelry from a family friend. Subsequently, she spent periods in mental health facilities and was possibly suffering from a dissociative personality disorder at age 16. Ultimately, her path ended with a murder conviction and a life sentence with the possibility of parole at 69 years old. Cyntoia's story made headlines in 2017 when celebrities, like Kim Kardashian West and Rihanna advocated for the commutation of her sentence. After 14 years in prison, she was released in August 2019 at the age of 31. In prison, she earned a GED and a bachelor's degree and served as a mentor to vulnerable youth. She is perhaps the ultimate illustration of the intersections of race, gender, class, and juvenile justice.

Leiber et al. (2009) posit that decision makers are influenced by both racial stereotyping and patriarchal notions and that beliefs that girls should be treated differently than boys are complicated by race. Wun (2016) asserts that U.S. institutional policies and practices perpetually punish Black girls. As it relates to juvenile justice, racialized and gendered justice results in harrowing statistics. Nationally, Black girls make up 14% of the female youth population but 33.2% of girls detained and committed. They constitute 43% of all girls arrested and are 31% of juvenile court referrals. These troubling outcomes for girls accompany other issues, such as greater risk for serious mental health problems. Additionally, adjudicated girls have higher incidences of physical, sexual, and emotional abuse than their male counterparts. When coupled with racial stereotyping, the negative outcomes for Black and Brown girls are exacerbated.

School to Prison Pipeline

A related and increasingly concerning topic is the *School-to-Prison Pipeline*, defined as "the collection of policies, practices, conditions, and prevailing consciousness that facilitate both the criminalization within educational environments and the processes by which this criminalization results in the incarceration of youth and young adults" (Morris, 2012, p. 2). The 1990s Get Tough on Crime policies in the justice system translated as zero-tolerance policies in schools and have left a legacy of punitive school discipline policies that have collateral consequences for students, their families, their classmates, and even their community. According to Perry and Morris (2014), these criminalized school discipline policies have led to increased suspensions, expulsions, alternate school placements, and uses of juvenile detention.

Nicholson-Crotty and colleagues (2009) argue that DMC in juvenile court referrals mirror the disproportionate discipline patterns of schools. It is increasingly apparent that troubled youth in both the education and juvenile systems tend to have similar risk factors. As such, more research is examining the idea that crossover youth (youth who fall both in the child welfare and juvenile justice system) are likely to fall into both the educational discipline track and the juvenile justice system (see Frabutt et al., 2008). While Black students only comprise 15% of the U.S. public school population, they make up 38% of those who are suspended one or more times and 31% of law enforcement referrals or arrests (U.S. Department of Education Office for Civil Rights, 2018).

As it relates to suspensions and expulsions, Black boys are still disproportionately overrepresented; however, Black girls follow American Indian and Hispanic boys in their rates of exclusionary discipline (Wallace et al., 2008). Furthermore, these trends in parallel systems are further evidence that an intersectional lens is important for examining the pervasiveness of disparities in juvenile justice outcomes.

Summary

Addressing intersectionality in the juvenile justice process is constantly evolving. While it is important to understand the historical treatment of youth in the U.S. as outlined in this chapter. It is increasingly important to understand the legacy of such history. Researchers and those on the front line are now examining the way race-based trauma impacts racial and ethnic disparities in the justice system. Racial trauma can be defined as:

> the mental and emotional injury caused by encounters with racial bias and ethnic discrimination, racism, and hate crime. Any individual that has experienced an emotionally painful, sudden, and uncontrollable racist encounter is at risk of suffering from a race-based traumatic stress injury (Mental Health America, n.d.; Carter et al., 2013; Helms et al., 2010).

This newer line of research and practice can contribute to understanding "differential treatment" as more broadly defined to include racialized encounters such as: racial profiling, verbal assault, denied access or service, etc. (Carter et al., 2013, p. 2), that can impact the lives of youth. Recent research has used this concept and studied the intersection of racial trauma with gender identity and victimization (Swan et al., 2022). The broadening of explanations is an encouraging new direction for understanding how young people experience the juvenile justice system and the way their experience varies by race, gender, and class.

Discussion Questions

1. In what ways do intersecting identities shape experiences in the juvenile justice system?

2. Compare and contrast the origins of the U.S. juvenile justice system with contemporary issues in juvenile justice.

3. How does DMC interplay with issues related to the School-to-Prison Pipeline?

Key Terms

Intersectionality theory

Parens Patriae

adultification

delinquency

Disproportionate Minority Contact

School-to-Prison Pipeline

Racial trauma

References

Agyepong, T. E. (2018). *The criminalization of Black children*. UNC Press.

Allyn, B. (2019, August 7). Cyntoia Brown released after 15 years in prison for murder. NPR. https://www.npr.org/2019/08/07/749025458/cyntoia-brown-released-after-15-years-in-prison-for-murder

Blackmon, D. (2008). *Slavery by another name: The re-enslavement of Black Americans from the Civil War to World War II*. Anchor Books.

Bishop, D. M. (2005). The role of race and ethnicity in juvenile justice processing. In D. F. Hawkins & K. Kempf-Leonard (Eds.), *Our children, their children: Confronting racial and ethnic differences in American juvenile justice* (pp. 23–82). University Press.

Bishop, D. M., & Leiber, M. J. (2011). Racial and ethnic differences in delinquency and justice system responses. In D. M. Bishop & B. C. Feld (Eds.), *The Oxford handbook of juvenile crime and juvenile justice* (pp. 446–484). The Oxford University Press.

Brown, J. M., & Sorensen, J. R. (2013). Race, ethnicity, gender, and waiver to adult court. *Journal of Ethnicity in Criminal Justice*, *11*, 181–195.

Carter, R. T., Mazzula, S., Victoria, R., Vazquez, R., Hall, S., Smith, S., & Williams, B. (2013).

Initial development of the Race-Based Traumatic Stress Symptom Scale: Assessing the emotional impact of racism. *Psychological Trauma: Theory, Research, Practice, and Policy*, 5(1), 1–9. Doi:10.1037/a0025911

Chesney-Lind, M. (1997). *The female offender*. Sage.

Claus, R. E., Vidal, S., & Harmon, M. (2017). *Racial and ethnic disparities in the police handling of juvenile arrests*. National Criminal Justice Reference Service, Office of Justice Programs. https://www.ncjrs.gov/pdffiles1/ojjdp/grants/250804.pdf

Collins, P. H. (2000). *Black feminist thought: Knowledge, consciousness, and the politics of empowerment* (2nd ed.). Routledge.

Crenshaw, K. (1991). De-marginalizing the intersection of race and sex: A Black feminist critique of antidiscrimination doctrine, feminist theory, and antiracist politics. In K. Bartlett & R. Kennedy (Eds.), *Feminist legal theory* (pp. 57–80). Westview.

Crutchfield, R. D., Skinner, M. Haggarty, K. P., McGlynn, A., & Catalano, R. F. (2009). Racial disparities in early criminal justice involvement. *Race & Social Problems*, *1*(4), 218–230. https://doi.org/10.1007/s12552-009-9018-y

Davis, J., & Sorensen, J. R. (2013). Disproportionate minority confinement of juveniles: A national examination of Black–White disparity in placements, 1997–2006. *Crime & Delinquency*, *59*, 115–139.

Engen, R. L., Steen, S., & Bridges, G. S. (2002). Racial disparities in the punishment of youth: A theoretical and empirical assessment of the literature. *Social Problems*, *49*, 194–220.

Epstein, R., Blake, J. J., & González, T. (2017). *Girlhood interrupted: The erasure of Black girls' childhood*. Georgetown Law, Center on Poverty and Inequality. https://

www.law.georgetown.edu/poverty-inequality-center/wpcontent/uploads/sites/14/2017/08/girlhood-interrupted.pdf

Evans-Winters, V. (2005). *Teaching Black girls: Resiliency in urban classrooms*. Peter Lang.

Fix, R. L., Cyperski, M. A., & Burkhart, B. R. (2015) Disproportionate minority contact: Comparisons across juveniles adjudicated for sexual and non-sexual offenses. *Sexual Abuse, 29*(3), 291–308.

Frabutt, J. M., Cabaniss, E. R., Kendrick, M. H., & Arbuckle, M. B. (2008). A community-academic collaboration to reduce disproportionate minority contact in the juvenile justice system. *Journal of Higher Education Outreach and Engagement, 12*(3), 5–21.

Feld, B. (1991). Justice by geography: Urban, suburban and rural variations in juvenile justice administration. *Journal of Criminal Law and Criminology, 82*(1). 156–210.

Frazier, C., & Bishop, D.M. (1995). Reflections on race efforts in juvenile justice. In K.K.

Leonard, C.E. Pope, & W. Feyerherm (Eds.), *Minorities in juvenile justice* (pp. 16–46). Thousand Oaks, CA: Sage.

Goemann, M. (2018). New Zealand's youth justice transformation: Lessons for the United States. The National Juvenile Justice Network.

Hanes, M. (2012). *OJJDP in focus factsheet: Disproportionate minority contact*. Office of Juvenile Justice and Delinquency Prevention, Office of Justice Programs, U.S. Department of Justice.

Hargrove, B. (2011, February 25). Life begins at sixteen: Teen prostitute, rape victim, murderer, inmate for life. Nashville Scene. https://www.nashvillescene.com/news/life-begins-at-sixteen-teen-prostitute-rape-victim-murderer-inmate-for-life/article_b49a54fa-bf53-5ae9-9512-fb90f4670381.html

Hartman, S. (1997). *Scenes of subjection: Terror, slavery, and self-making in nineteenth-century America*. Oxford University Press.

Hawkins, D.F., Laub, J., Lauritsen, J., & Cothern, L. (2000). *Race, ethnicity, and serious and violent juvenile offending* (NCJ 181202). OJJDP Juvenile Justice Bulletin. Washington, DC: U.S. Department of Justice.

Hawkins, D. F., & Kempf-Leonard, K. (2005). *Our children, their children: Confronting racial and ethnic differences in American juvenile justice*. University Press.

Helms, J. E., Nicolas, G., & Green, C. E. (2010). Racism and ethnoviolence as trauma: Enhancing professional training. *Traumatology, 16*(4), 53–62. Doi:10.1177/1534765610389595

Hirschfield, P. (2008). Preparing for prison? The criminalization of school discipline in the USA. *Theoretical Criminology, 12*(1), 79–101; 1362–4806.

Huizinga, D., Thornberry, T., Knight, K., & Lovegrove, P. (2007). *Disproportionate minority contact in the juvenile justice system: A study of differential minority arrest/referral to court in three cities* (Doc. No. 219743). Office of Juvenile Justice and Delinquency Prevention.

Jones, C. A. (2016). Is disproportionate minority contact improving? An exploratory analysis of the arrest, confinement, and transfer stages in rural and urban settings. *Journal of Ethnicity in Criminal Justice, 14,* 40–57. https://doi.org/10.1080/1537793 8.2015.1052172

Kempf-Leonard, K. (2007). Minority youths and juvenile justice: Disproportionate minority contact after nearly 20 years of reform efforts. *Youth Violence and Juvenile Justice, 5,* 71–87.

Kempf-Leonard, K. K., Pope, C. E., & Feyerherm, W. H. (Eds.). (1995). *Minorities in juvenile justice.* Sage Publications, Inc.

Leiber, M.J. (2003). *The context of juvenile justice decision making: When race matters.* State University of New York Press.

Leiber, M. J. (2015). Race, gender, crime severity, and decision making in the juvenile justice system. *Crime & Delinquency, 61*(6), 771–797. https://doi.org/10.1177/0011 128712446898

Leiber, M., Bishop, D., & Chamlin, M. (2011). Juvenile justice decision-making before and after the implementation of the disproportionate minority contact (DMC) mandate. *Justice Quarterly, 28*(3), 460–492.

Leiber, M. J., Brubaker, S. J., & Fox, K. C. (2009). A closer look at the individual and joint effects of gender and race on juvenile justice decision making. *Feminist Criminology, 4*(4), 333–358.

Leiber, M. J., & Stairs, J. M. (1999). Race, context and the use of intake diversion. *Journal of Research in Crime and Delinquency, 36*(1), 56–86.

Males, M., & Macallair, D. (2000). *The color of justice: An analysis of juvenile adult court transfers in California.* The Justice Policy Institute, Center on Juvenile and Criminal Justice.

Mallett, C. A. (2018) Disproportionate minority contact in juvenile justice: Today's, and yesterdays, problems, *Criminal Justice Studies, 31*(3), 230–248. https://doi.org/ 10.1080/1478601X.2018.1438276

Marchbanks, M. P., Peguero, A. A., Varela, K. S., Blake, J. J., & Eason, J. M. (2018). School strictness and disproportionate minority contact: Investigating racial and ethnic disparities with the school to prison pipeline. *Youth Violence and Juvenile Justice, 16*(2), 241–259.

Maxwell, G., & Morris, A. (2006). Youth justice in New Zealand: Restorative justice in practice? *Journal of Social Issues, 62*(2), 239–258.

McCoy, T., Walker, J. T., & Rodney, H. E. (2012). Predicting preadjudication detention decisions: An examination of family status and race. *Journal of Ethnicity in Criminal Justice, 10,* 87–107. https://doi.org/10.1080/15377938.2012.669652

Mental Health America. (nd). Racial Trauma. https://www.mhanational.org/racial -trauma

Moak, S., Thomas, S. A., Walker, J. T., & Gann, S. M. (2012). The influence of race and pre-adjudication detention: Applying the Symbolic Threat Hypothesis. *OJJDP Journal of Juvenile Justice,* 73–90.

Mooradian, J. K. (2003). Disproportionate minority confinement of African-American juvenile delinquency. LFB Scholarly Publishing, LLC.

Morris, M. (2012). *Race, gender and the school to prison pipeline: Expanding our discussion to include Black girls.* African American Policy Forum. http://schottfoundation.org/sites/default/files/resources/Morris-Race-Gender-and-the-School-to-Prison-Pipeline.pdf

Nicholson-Crotty, S., Birchmeier, Z., & Valentine, D. (2009). Exploring the impact of school discipline on racial disproportion in the juvenile justice system. *Social Science Quarterly*, *90*(4), 1003–1019.

Office of Juvenile Justice and Delinquency Prevention. (2009). *Disproportionate minority contact technical assistance manual* (4th ed.). U.S. Department of Justice, Office of Justice

Office of Juvenile Justice and Delinquency Prevention, US Dept. of Justice. (2019). *Racial/ethnic disparities.* https://ojjdp.ojp.gov/programs/racial-and-ethnic-disparities Programs, Office of Juvenile Justice and Delinquency Prevention.

Palmer, Sr., E. L., Bingham, R., Clark, D., Shepherd, R. I., & Carrington, P. (2020). *Kentucky Court of Justice response: A guide for identifying, addressing and reducing racial and ethnic disparities.* https://kycourts.gov/Court-Programs/Family-and-Juvenile-Services/Documents/RED_Guide_092220_web.pdf

Pasko, L. (2010). Damaged daughters: The history of girls' sexuality and the juvenile justice system. *The Journal of Criminal Law & Criminology*, *100*(3), 1099–1130.

Perry, B. L., & Morris, E. W. (2014). Suspending progress: Collateral consequences of exclusionary punishment in public schools. *American Sociological Review*, *79*(6), 1067–1087.

Pope, C. E., & Feyerherm, W. H. (1993). *Minorities and the juvenile justice system.* Department of Justice, Office of Juvenile Justice Delinquency Prevention.

Pope, C. E., & Leiber, M. (2005). Disproportionate minority contact (DMC): The federal initiative. In D. Hawkins & K. Kempf-Leonard (Eds.), *Our children, their children: Confronting racial and ethnic differences in American juvenile justice* (pp. 351–389). University of Chicago Press.

Pope, C. E., Lovell, R., & Hsia, H. M. (2002). *Disproportionate minority confinement: A review of the research literature from 1989–2001* (NCJ No. 198428). Office of Juvenile Justice and Delinquency Prevention.

Prison Policy Initiative. (2019). *Youth confinement: The whole pie 2019.* https://www.prisonpolicy.org/reports/youth2019.html

Roper v. Simmons, 543 U.S. 551 (2005).

Sadaa Sarr, M., Epstein, R., Rosenthal, L., & Vafa, Y. (2015). *The sex abuse to prison pipeline.* Center for Poverty and Inequality Georgetown University Law Center. https://www.law.georgetown.edu/poverty-inequality-center/wp-content/uploads/sites/14/2019/02/The-Sexual-Abuse-To-Prison-Pipeline-The-Girls%E2%80%99-Story.pdf

Sickmund, M. (2004). *Juveniles in corrections.* Juvenile and offenders national report series bulletin. Washington, DC: U.S. Department of Justice.

Spinney, E., Cohen, M., Feyerherm, W., Stephenson, R., Yeide, M., & Shreve, T. (2018). Disproportionate minority contact in the U.S. juvenile justice system: A review of the DMC literature, 2001–2014, Part I, *Journal of Crime and Justice*, *41*(5), 573–595. https://doi.org/10.1080/0735648X.2018.1516155

Swann, G., Dyar1, C., Baidoo, L., Crosby, S., Newcomb, M.E., Whitton, S.W. (2022). Intersectional minority stress and intimate partner violence: The effects of enacted stigma on racial minority youth assigned female at birth. *Archives of sexual behavior*, 51:1031–1043.

Tapia, M. (2010). Untangling race and class effects on juvenile arrests. *Journal of Criminal Justice*, *38*(3), 255–265.

Thomas, W. I. (1928). *The unadjusted girl* (pp. 109–112).

Tonnesen, S. C. (2013). Commentary: "Hit it and quit it": Responses to Black girls' victimization in school. *Berkeley Journal of Gender, Law & Justice*, 28.

U.S. Department of Education Office for Civil Rights. (2018). 2015–16 Civil Rights data Collection: School climate and safety. https://www2.ed.gov/about/offices/list/ocr/docs/school-climate-and-safety.pdf

Wadhwani, A., & Tamburin, A. (2019, January 15). Lawmakers to reexamine Tennessee's juvenile sentencing laws after Cyntoia Brown case. *The Tennessean*. https://www.tennessean.com/story/news/2019/01/15/prison-reform-juvenile-sentencing-laws-tennessee-cyntoia-brown/2546723002/

Wallace, J. M., Goodkind, S., Wallace, C. M., & Bachman, J. G. (2008). Racial, ethnic and gender differences in school discipline among U.S. high school students: 1991–2005. *Negro Educational Review*, 59(1–2), 47–62. https://www.ncbi.nlm.nih.gov/pmc/articles/PMC2678799/

Ward, G. K. (2012). *The Black child-savers: Racial democracy & juvenile justice.* The University of Chicago Press.

Wun, C. (2016). Against captivity: Black girls and school discipline policies in the afterlife of slavery. *Educational Policy*, *30*(1), 171–196.

THIRTEEN

Domestic Violence

Learning Objectives

1. Examine the definition of domestic violence in the United States and how it has changed over the years.
2. Understand the history of domestic violence laws and policies in the United States and how they have changed due to the influence of politics and social movements.

In the United States, ***domestic violence*** is defined as a pattern of abusive behavior with the goal of gaining control or power over one's intimate partner. Today, it is recognized that domestic violence can occur in married, cohabiting, heterosexual, or same-sex relationships. We also recognize that domestic violence can occur in any situation and is not limited to a particular class, race, ethnicity, or gender. In the United States, prior to the Women's Movement of the 1970s, domestic violence was defined as something that only occurred between two married people in a heterosexual relationship, where the husband was the perpetrator and the wife was the victim. However, today's definition of domestic violence has expanded to include both males and females as perpetrators and victims as well as those in intimate relationships outside of marriage, including same-sex relationships. More types of abuse are recognized as well, including physical (hitting or causing physical damage), emotional (constantly demeaning the person and destroying their self-worth), sexual (sexual contact without consent), financial (making the person financially dependent by taking control of finances), and psychological (threatening harm or damaging property or pets) (U.S. DOJ, 2015).

In this chapter, we will be exploring the changes in how domestic violence has been perceived by victims, perpetrators, the public, and the criminal justice system through the twentieth and twenty-first centuries. As we have done in previous chapters, we will utilize a social construction framework to better understand how politics and social movements have impacted changes in what is and is not acceptable within society for domestic violence laws. We will also look at the ever-evolving approaches to access help for victims as well as changes in policy for the arrest and prosecution of offenders.

Changes in Domestic Violence Laws and Services in the United States

Originally the definition of domestic violence only included those who were married in a heterosexual relationship, where the abuser was the husband and the victim was the wife. It was believed these types of incidents primarily occurred within economically disadvantaged homes and was personal family business that should not be discussed outside of the home. Despite this belief, some cases resulted in serious injuries and began to gain attention and concern outside of the home. In 1911, the first family court was established in Buffalo, New York, to handle domestic-related issues of child and spousal abuse. However, this court was separate from the criminal court, and criminal charges could not be filed against the abuser. The purpose of the family court was to intervene with social services in an effort to keep the family together and reduce the violence within the home. Shortly after the family court model was created in New York, other states began to adopt this model as well. It wasn't until 1945 that a criminal law passed at the state level, in California, stated that if a husband physically hurt his wife or child, causing serious damage, he could be charged with a felony and receive anywhere from 1 to 10 years in prison. However, later that same year this law was challenged with a case where a man was accused of killing his wife. A California Superior Court judge dismissed the murder charges, stating the law was written in a sexist manner and violated the defendant's Fourteenth Amendment rights of equal protection under the law, because the law did not apply to wives who caused serious damage to their husbands as well (Indiana Coalition against Domestic Violence, 2016).

By the 1960s, domestic violence was becoming more widely recognized as a problem by criminal justice agencies, and law enforcement began to receive training on how to mediate between spouses and refer them to social services. However, arrests were not made because domestic violence was still viewed as a problem that should be resolved within the home and not through the criminal justice system. It wasn't until the 1970s that real change began to occur in how domestic violence cases were handled, due to pressure from the Women's Movement. Born out of the Civil Right Movement of the 1960s, the Women's Movement was working towards equal rights for women, including recognizing domestic violence and treating it as criminal behavior through the criminal justice system. However, these advocates had their hands full, as domestic violence victims received very little support outside of the movement. Many cities, for instance, would not accept applications for social services, such as welfare, from married women who were being physically abused by their husbands and had left the relationship. This is because they were required to count their husband's income even though they no longer had access to it. Also, even though there were some shelters and hotlines for people to call to receive help, these services were organized by volunteers who had very little funding. Despite these odds, those involved in the fight against domestic violence were able to achieve many victories as the issue of domestic violence gained more recognition nationwide and social scientists began to conduct research to better understand the extent of the problem. By 1975, the majority of states allowed wives to file criminal charges against their husbands for physical violence (Indiana Coalition against Domestic Violence, 2016).

GLOBAL SPOTLIGHT

Domestic Violence in Iran

In Iran, it is difficult to know the true extent of domestic violence as it is not well documented by the government and is believed not to be a problem. One of the reasons suggested as to why the government is not interested in measuring domestic violence is because women face harsh, often violent punishments for what would be considered to be minor crimes in other countries. The crime of adultery, for example, or having sexual relations outside of marriage, can be punished by beatings, imprisonment, or even death for women. Men also face harsh punishments for adultery, but are typically not sentenced to as severe a punishment as women. In Iran, women also are still viewed as the property of their husband, making it difficult to prosecute domestic violence, even in severe instances. And even if a woman wants to leave a marriage due to abuse, it is very difficult for her to do so because children in the home over the age of seven will be awarded to her husband or his family for custody (Moradian, 2009).

Recently, there have been social scientists within Iran who have been conducting studies on domestic violence, but the results of their studies often are ignored by the government and are not widely distributed within the country, so awareness of the problem still remains low. However, the nationwide study found that two-thirds of women experienced some form of abuse in the first year of marriage by their spouse or in-law. Slightly over half of the women (52%) reported experiencing emotional abuse, but physical abuse also was high. The chief of police in Iran, for example, stated 40% of all murders in the country were domestic violence related and 50% of all women who were murdered were killed by a family member, typically within their own home. However, men are rarely prosecuted for these crimes, because they often justify their behavior by stating they suspected their wife of adultery (Moradian, 2009). Due to these cultural and criminal justice constraints, women in Iran report high rates of abuse, with 38% reporting physical abuse at some point in their marriage. However, there are some differences in domestic violence based on education and income, with women and men who are employed and have obtained higher education levels reporting less domestic violence within their homes (Rasoulian et al., 2014).

In 1976, research on domestic violence within the state of Pennsylvania concluded the police were unable to effectively intervene in domestic violence cases because the victims often did not want to press charges against their abuser. Victims were reluctant to press charges because in many cases they did not have anywhere to go, if they left their homes. This led to the state of Pennsylvania passing the *Protection from Abuse Act* that allowed women who were experiencing physical abuse or the threat of it to themselves or their children to file a restraining order, which would remove the husband from the house and allow the wife to gain temporary custody of the children as the case went to court. This was a huge step forward in recognizing domestic violence as a criminal issue and not something that should be left to domestic courts. This act was later amended to include criminal punishments for those who violated the restraining order of up to six months in jail and/or up to a $1,000 fine. This act also protected both married and divorced women, which was another step forward. The act allowed women and children to remain in the house, but there were still few alternatives outside of the home where women could receive assistance. It wasn't until 1980 that the state of Pennsylvania began to financially support shelters for women and children, allowing for services to expand within the state (Kelly-Dreis, 2015).

However, the lack of services and shelters for women was a problem nationwide; for instance, in 1983 there were only 700 shelters within the United States, servicing 91,000 women and 131,000 children per year. Surveys during this time showed 70% of women who wanted to go to a shelter were unable to do so because the shelter within their community was full. By 1992, the United States Surgeon General reported spousal abuse as the leading cause of injury for women between the ages of 15 and 44, which helped with the eventual passage in 1994 of the federal Violence Against Women Act. The *Violence Against Women Act* continues to fund services for victims of sexual assault and domestic violence at the state and federal level, training for police and court officials, and provisions for women to file civil charges against their perpetrators (Indiana Coalition against Domestic Violence, 2016).

IN FOCUS

Violence Against Women Act

The Violence Against Women Act is federal legislation that was originally passed in 1994 as part of the Violent Crime Control and Law Enforcement Act. It was the first time the federal government took a step towards ending violence against women by focusing on domestic violence. This act funded education, training, and prevention programs, as well as victims' services, and focused on evidence collection. It also encouraged states to recognize orders of protection from one state to the next. The passage of this act was a big victory for women's advocates, who had lobbied Congress to pass this act because the states were not adequately addressing the problem of violence against women. The act also created a shift in how law enforcement interacted with victims of violence as well as how victims' services were viewed within the community. The act was reauthorized and expanded in 2000 and 2005 to include victims of sexual assault and stalking and then again in 2013 to include same-sex couples and those who are undocumented (Legal Momentum, 2015).

Currently, the struggle for funding and providing adequate services to all those who need them continues across the United States. A survey conducted by the United States Census Bureau examined domestic violence programs nationwide over a 24-hour period to better understand what services were being provided and what needs went unmet. The survey included 89% of all domestic violence programs (1,697) offered across the country. Programs offered varied from one location to the next with the majority offering support services for adults (98%) and children (85%) along with emergency shelters (79%), transportation (55%), legal assistance (53%), and education (53%). On that one day, there were 67,646 adults and children who received services, including advocacy, housing, transportation, and assistance with completing paperwork for social benefits, such as welfare. However, there were an additional 10,871 clients who were unable to have their needs met due to a lack of funding because of decreases in government, private foundation, and individual donations, which also led to a reduction in staff. In that 24-hour time period, 40% of the clients who were turned away were seeking emergency shelter, and an additional 16% were in need of transitional housing (National Network to End Domestic Violence, 2015).

If domestic violence programs are able to house those seeking help, most emergency shelters can only house clients between 30 and 60 days, even though it can take anywhere from six to ten months to find permanent housing. This lack of adequate housing creates a need for transitional housing to fill that gap. Those turned away

Figure 13.1. Dramatic portrait of female victim of domestic violence. © iStockphoto.com/ pepifoto.

from emergency shelters and transitional housing face a very dangerous situation, as those who seek out services from domestic violence programs tend to do so as a last resort, after a particularly violent episode or when they feel their lives or the lives of their children are at stake. If victims are unable to secure safe housing, they are more likely to return to their abuser due to the fear of being homeless (National Network to End Domestic Violence, 2015).

Nearly all (98%) domestic violence victims experience financial abuse, where they do not have any control over the finances within their home, making it incredibly difficult for them to leave and lead independent lives. Financial abuse also makes those who want to leave a domestic violence environment heavily reliant on community services to assist them with transportation. Victims report the number one reason they return home is due to the lack of financial resources to support themselves and their children. Unfortunately, the fear of homelessness is real, with domestic violence being the third leading cause of homelessness for families. However, returning home is incredibly dangerous as well, because this is the time female victims are the most likely to be murdered by their partners. Women, for example, are 70 times more likely to be murdered in the few weeks following their leaving the home than at any other point in the relationship (Vaglanos, 2015).

There are programs that are providing innovative approaches to the financial and housing needs of those experiencing domestic violence. For example, the District Alliance for Safe Housing (DASH) in Washington, D.C., focuses on the individual, their specific needs, and how these needs can be addressed by removing barriers to assistance, such as requiring the client to meet specific program goals or conditions for housing. DASH provides Survivor Resilience Fund (SRF) grants to remove the barriers that threaten permanent housing through financial assistance. SRF grants are granted based on the needs of the individual applying for the grant, with most grants used to pay rent already owed or the deposit for a new place. However, the grants also have been used to assist with utility payments, home security, moving costs, childcare, car repair, or travel costs associated with child custody hearings. Throughout the grant process the applicant works with DASH to determine their individual needs and to create a safety plan for when they are in the community. Once the applicant is deemed eligible for the SRF grant, funds are distributed within 48 hours (Sullivan et al., 2019).

Sullivan and colleagues (2019) completed a longitudinal evaluation of the SRF grants and found the payments ranged from $275 to $8,508 with an average grant payment of $2,078. The overwhelming majority (94%) of SRF applicants who received a grant were living in permanent housing and felt safe six months later. All grant recipients reported their lives had improved since receiving the grant and 90% reported feeling hopeful about their future. The researchers concluded that SRF grants appeared to be a good way to address the housing and financial needs of those experiencing domestic violence whose cases are less complex and do not require long-term intervention (Sullivan et al., 2019).

The Domestic Violence Housing First (DVHF) program located in Washington State was created to address the barrier of housing for women who are experiencing more complex cases of domestic violence that require more in-depth intervention (Mbilinyi, 2015). This program specifically targets those who tend to face additional barriers to housing, such as those who live in rural areas or on tribal lands as well as immigrants. The program is based on the idea of housing first, where other problems cannot be addressed until participants are in stable housing. The program uses a three-prong approach to tackle domestic violence and housing. First, advocacy is addressed by connecting advocates and participants who have similar cultural backgrounds and life experiences. Advocates then work with participants to help them identify and address their needs. Next, the program provides flexible funding to assist with housing access and stability that is not limited to a one-time grant opportunity. Financial assistance can be used for a variety of needs, including "childcare cost, transportation, school supplies, uniforms, and permits requested for employment, as well as time-limited and flexible rental assistance" (Mbilinyi, 2015, p. 4). Finally, DVHF works with the community to improve access to housing by partnering with housing programs and landlords.

Mbilinyi (2015) conducted an evaluation of the DVHF program and found that over three years, the program had served 681 participants and nearly 1,000 children under the age of 18 with 40% of the children under the age of five. Program participants also were diverse with 67% representing women of color, including 35% who identified as Native American or Alaska Native. Overall, 22% of the women were immigrants, and this number increased to 69% when looking at only those living in an urban area. The majority of participants were defined as low income and had completed high school or a G.E.D. Half of those who entered the program had housing, but many did not feel safe or were about to become homeless. For example, when entering the program nearly 25% reported being spied on, 18% had been strangled, and 16% had received death threats. Participants faced multiple barriers when entering the program including unemployment, language barriers, eviction, criminal histories, and substance abuse. However, immigrant participants tended to experience the most barriers to housing, for instance, with the highest levels of unemployment when compared to nonimmigrant participants (Mbilinyi, 2015).

The DVHF program has shown promising results. After participating in the DVHF program for eighteen months, 96% were housed and 76% reported they only marginally continued to rely on the program for services. The majority of participants (84%) also strongly agreed the program had increased their safety as well as the safety of their children. Participants also noted they felt safe from the pressures of substance use and dangerous communities they had experienced prior to program participation. The overwhelming majority (99%) also "agreed that their advocate had helped to restore their sense of dignity" (Mbilinyi, 2015, p. 6).

Domestic Violence and Same-Sex Relationships

The discussion on domestic violence victims up until this point has primarily focused on female victims and their children in heterosexual relationships. This is because the majority of victims are women (85%) and many have children; 10,000,000 children witness some form of domestic violence within the home each year (Vaglanos, 2015). However, it is important to note those involved in same-sex relationships experience domestic violence at a similar rate as heterosexual couples, with one in four involved in a domestic violence incident at some point in their lives (Center for American Progress, n.d.). There also are additional challenges that arise in same-sex relationships for domestic violence victims. For example, the offender may threaten to out the victim's sexual preference to friends and family who may be unaware. Other challenges include law enforcement not recognizing the couple as being in a relationship and instead mistaking them as roommates who are fighting, which may cause the police officer to not intervene in the situation appropriately. Those in same-sex relationships also are more likely to fight back, which could lead to the victim being mistaken as the perpetrator and getting arrested (Center for American Progress, n.d.).

Other problems that arise in cases of domestic violence incidents between those of the same-sex are due to how domestic violence laws are defined. Not all states, for instance, specifically recognize same-sex relationships within their domestic violence laws. The majority of states have gender-neutral laws regarding domestic violence, which means the laws do not specifically mention they only protect heterosexual couples. This leaves the interpretation of the implementation and execution of these laws up to judges, who in some cases protect both heterosexual and same-sex couples and in other instances do not. There also are a few states (Florida, Maryland, and Mississippi) which have domestic violence laws that are gender neutral, but have been consistently interpreted by the courts to not include same-sex couples. Other states, such as Arizona, Delaware, Louisiana, Montana, New York, South Carolina, and Virginia, have domestic violence laws that specifically mention heterosexual couples, which then excludes same-sex couples from being protected by the law. Meanwhile, Hawaii, Illinois, Kentucky, and Ohio have domestic violence laws that do specifically mention they protect both heterosexual as well as same-sex couples (Johnston, 2015).

Not recognizing same-sex victims in domestic violence laws becomes problematic because domestic violence protection or restraining orders require an offender to leave the home, no matter if their name is on the lease or mortgage, and can prevent the offender from accessing joint finances. Domestic violence-specific restraining orders also are easier for a judge to implement due to the potential danger of the situation, which gives the judge more discretion to put one into effect. Unfortunately, a regular restraining order that is not domestic violence related can be much more difficult to obtain, which can leave a victim without the protection he or she needs (Johnston, 2015). There is a movement to expand domestic violence laws to protect both same-sex and heterosexual couples in states that do not recognize the rights of all victims. In South Carolina, for instance, the law used to not protect those who were in same-sex relationships and not married. However, this changed when the case Jane Doe v. State of South Carolina was brought to the South Carolina Supreme Court. In this case, the court found the definition of household had previously only included cohabitation between male and female partners, which violated same-sex couples' 14th amendment rights to due process and equal protection under the law (South Carolina Supreme Court, 2017).

IN FOCUS

Domestic Violence and LGBTQ Community

There are not enough organizations to assist those in abusive relationships, and most nonprofits focus on women in cis-gender relationships who often have children. There are only a few nonprofits organizations nationwide that work specifically with LGBT couples who are in domestic violence situations, for example the Los Angeles LGBT Center. The LGBT Center offers a wide range of services, including prevention, referrals, advocacy, crisis management, counseling, and support groups that are specifically tailored for the LGBT community. The center also offers assistance for both the offender and the victim (Los Angeles LGBT Center, n.d.).

Law Enforcement and Domestic Violence

From 1981 to 1982, in the city of Minneapolis, Lawrence Sherman and Richard Berk conducted a study to better understand the impact of arresting an offender for a misdemeanor domestic violence offense. At the time, there were two main ways police officers handled minor domestic violence offenses. They either separated the couple or they intervened by attempting to mediate, engaging the couple from a social work perspective. However, those involved in the Women's Movement were pushing to have minor domestic violence offenders arrested, since they were violent offenses. Sherman and Berk's study used an experimental design, where police officers were given a notepad with different colors that had been randomly organized. The color of the paper designated what should happen to the offender, with one color indicating the couple should be separated, another color meaning the two should receive mediation, and a third color specifying that the offender should be arrested. The police officers were supposed to implement this procedure for approximately one year until they had made contact with approximately 300 cases total. At that time, the researchers would conduct follow up interviews with victims to examine reoffending (Sherman & Berk, 1984).

The study concluded that those who were arrested were significantly less likely to reoffend. When comparing the official arrest data six months later, for example, only 10% of those arrested reoffended in comparison to 19% who received mediation and 24% who were separated. Interviews conducted with the victims six months after the study also found similar results with only 19% of those arrested reoffending, while 37% of those who received mediation and 33% of those who were separated reoffended. After the findings of this study were published, the Minneapolis police implemented an arrest policy where the preferred method was arrest, but the police officer could use their discretion not to make an arrest. However, if the officer chose not to make an arrest, they had to file a report explaining why (Sherman & Berk, 1984).

Sherman and Berk's research had a huge impact on police and domestic violence. Today, there are 22 states that have *mandatory arrest* policies, where the police are required to make an arrest when they are called to the scene of a domestic violence incident. Other states rely on a *preferred arrest* policy similar to what was implemented in Minneapolis, and the remaining states allow their officers to use their own discretion to decide whether to make an arrest or not. Recently, the use of mandatory arrest policies has been called into question as other studies have found they can have negative consequences for the victim. Peralta (2015), for instance, found when interviewing misdemeanor domestic violence victims that some victims may now fear calling the police when they experience abuse because there is a concern the offender may later retaliate for being arrested. Other victims reported they were worried they may be arrested along with the offender. Some victims also stated their decision to call for police assistance was based on their prior experience with law enforcement, with those who had negative past experiences being less likely to reach out for help (Peralta, 2015). Sherman also was unable to replicate his findings in other cities, such as Milwaukee, where the opposite was concluded, and those who were arrested were more likely to reoffend (Liscombe, 2014). The results also have been mixed when other cities have replicated the study, with some cities finding minor domestic violence reoffending decreasing after arrest and other cities concluding it increased (Hirschel et al., 2007).

GLOBAL SPOTLIGHT

India and Domestic Violence

In India, women experience barriers getting help for domestic abuse from the criminal justice system and their community because they are thought to be the property of their husband. There also are few studies conducted on the problem of domestic violence, and awareness of the problem within society is low. There have been women's groups and organizations within the government who have attempted to change the laws and bring about more awareness, but they have had very limited success, and domestic violence is still viewed as something that happens within the home and that should be resolved within the home (Bhat & Ullman, 2014).

In India, a large portion of families still participate in the use of dowries when their children are married. A dowry, or property given to the husband and his family by the wife's family before or immediately after marriage, symbolizes the family's wealth and status within the community. However, it also can lead to problems for the young bride, if the husband's family is not satisfied with the amount given. In some instances, the husband's family will attempt to extort more property or money from the bride's family by emotionally and/or physically abusing the wife. If the wife's family does not or is unable to pay the required amount, physical abuse can take the form of dowry burning, where the woman is covered in an accelerant and lit on fire. In these instances the husband is rarely prosecuted because it is reported as an accident within the kitchen. Burnt wife syndrome, where the husband pours acid on the wife's face to disfigure her or gives regular beatings that eventually lead to death, also occur when there is dissatisfaction with the wife's dowry. Dowry-related deaths are a major cause of death for young married women in India. Due to these dowry-related incidents, in 1961, the Dowry Prohibition Act was passed, making it illegal to exchange a dowry for marriage. However, many families still participate in the process as it is tradition, and those who violate the law are rarely prosecuted for doing so. In

1986, the Dowry Prohibition Act was amended to include legal ramifications for those who have a wife die within the first seven years of marriage and harassment was known to occur, but these crimes are rarely prosecuted, because they are viewed as family matters. The perpetrators of these crimes include both the husband and his family (Bhat & Ullman, 2014).

One study found that 43% of all crimes against women, in India, were perpetrated by the spouse or in-laws, with two-thirds of victims reporting their husband was the offender and an additional one-third of victims stating their mother-in-law was an accomplice. Overall, it was concluded that 40% of married women between the ages of 15 and 49 with at least one child living at home would experience physical abuse at some point within their marriage. Other research studies examining income and education level have found that women with more education and more financial means were less likely to report marital abuse, but they also were less likely to want to discuss the matter, perhaps masking the true number of incidents. There also was less abuse reported in homes where there was higher education level, unless the woman had less education than her husband (Bhat & Ullman, 2014).

To better understand how different arrest policies directly impacted arrests and reoffending for simple and aggravated domestic violence, Hirschel and colleagues (2007) conducted a study that examined nationwide data on arrests for domestic violence. The authors concluded that police officers in states that had mandatory and preferred arrest policies were much more likely to make an arrest than those states with a discretionary arrest policy. The researchers also noted that although *dual arrest*, where both the victim and offender were arrested, were low overall, they were more likely to occur when the state had a policy of mandatory arrest than those states that had preferred arrest policies. And although same-sex and heterosexual couples had an equal chance of being arrested for the crime of domestic violence, same-sex couples were more likely to experience dual arrests and were 30 times more likely to both be arrested than a heterosexual couple where the victim was a female and the offender a male. In heterosexual couples, dual arrest was more likely to occur when the victim was a male and the female was the offender (Hirschel et al., 2007).

Hirschel and colleagues' study also examined in more depth four states with different arrest policies, including Connecticut (mandatory arrest), Virginia (mandatory arrest), Tennessee (preferred arrest), and Idaho (discretionary arrest). Overall, 479 police departments within these four states were surveyed, covering a range in sizes of agencies. The authors concluded states with mandatory arrest policies that included the stipulation to arrest the primary aggressor had lower dual arrest rates. Those most likely to be arrested included an incident where the victim suffered injuries, where a minor was present, and/or the offender remained at the scene, but gender did

Figure 13.2 Woman beating up husband illustrating domestic violence. © Adobe Stock/pololia.

not impact whether one was arrested or not. Dual arrest rates also increased in larger cities and when the offender remained at the scene, but decreased if the police officer was aware of past violence within the home and when the primary offender was male. The author also noted those who had a prior record of domestic violence were seven times more likely to reoffend than first-time offenders, while males and those under the influence at the time of arrest also were more likely to reoffend. The authors concluded that to reduce dual arrest rates a policy of preferred arrest should be implemented as well as increased training and improved policies for domestic violence within police departments. This is because dual arrest rates increased when police officers were not sure how to determine who the primary aggressor was in the incident (Hirschel et al., 2007).

Although the use of mandatory arrest policies in the case of domestic violence became more popular after Sherman and Berk's study in Minneapolis, many have begun to question the effectiveness of these policies for misdemeanor domestic violence cases. This was the case in Charlotte, North Carolina, where there was a mandatory arrest policy in place, but research studies did not conclude the policy was reducing rearrest rates for low-level offenders. This led the city of Charlotte to implement *domestic violence police units* within their police departments. These units were specifically trained to work with domestic violence victims and community volunteers who assisted victims with social services, ensured policies were being followed, and escorted victims during court proceedings. Police officers within these units relied on preferred arrest policies and also worked directly with the victim by conducting follow-up interviews and by assisting victims when completing paperwork, such as restraining orders. All domestic violence arrests were forwarded on to the sergeant within the domestic violence unit, and they decided whether to keep the case within the domestic violence unit or send it on to regular patrol, based on a thorough review of the case. Police officers within this unit were the ones who decided what the offender would be arrested for and did not rely on the victim to make the decision of whether or not the offender should be arrested (Exum et al., 2014).

In Charlotte, social scientists were brought in to conduct a program evaluation to determine if those within the domestic violence unit had lower rates of reoffending for misdemeanor domestic violence offenders than those cases that were sent back to regular patrol. To complete this study, the researchers examined low-level domestic violence cases 18–30 months after the initial contact with law enforcement. When examining both those who had contact with standard patrol and the domestic violence unit, the most common original offense was simple assault, which was typically hitting, slapping, biting, or choking of the victim. Overall, 46% who committed misdemeanor domestic violence offenses were arrested and on average spent 11 days in jail. The authors concluded those who were sent to the domestic violence unit were significantly less likely to reoffend than those who were referred to standard patrol. However, the domestic violence unit was disbanded after 10 years of service, when a new police chief implemented different priorities (Exum et al., 2014).

Prosecutors and Domestic Violence

In the 1980s, the Women's Movement was successful in drawing attention to the lack of prosecutions in domestic violence cases. Even with police making more arrests, prosecutors and judges were still dismissing domestic violence cases because they were viewed as family matters and/or the victims in the case would ask for the charges be dropped. This led to what are known as *no-drop prosecution* policies, where the prosecutor is not allowed to dismiss the charges in a domestic violence case and must work to gain the cooperation of the victim to participate in the case. In some instances, what is referred to as soft no-drop policies are implemented, where the offender will be prosecuted, but the victim will not be forced to participate. However, other prosecutor offices rely on what are known as hard no-drop policies, where the offender is prosecuted, and if the victim refuses to participate they can be held in contempt of court and face possible jail time. Due to the hard no-drop policies, critics have argued the victim can experience trauma when they are not allowed to make their own decisions and point to research illustrating that victims who do not participate typically do so out of fear for retaliation and/or their financial dependence on the offender. Currently, most prosecutors' offices rely on some form of no-drop strategy and will move forward with prosecution as long as there is enough evidence to win a conviction (Nichols, 2014).

In interviews conducted with domestic violence advocates, Nichols (2014) found advocates recognized that not all victims will be able or willing to participate in the court proceedings. This led to most advocates working directly with law enforcement to help them understand what evidence should be collected at the crime scene to illustrate the abuse occurred, in case the victim decided to not participate in the prosecution. If a victim decided to not participate in the prosecution of the offender, prosecutors could then rely on the evidence gathered during the investigation to help them win their cases. Witnesses can be an excellent resource for the prosecutor, but are rarely available in domestic violence cases, because these crimes are more likely to occur behind closed doors. If there are witnesses present, they are usually the children of the victim and/or offender, and children are typically considered to be unreliable witnesses by prosecutors (Bechtel et al., 2012). The victim's statement taken by the police at the scene can be used as evidence of abuse, but only if the victim is willing to testify. This was decided in 2004 in a United States Supreme Court case, *Crawford v. Washington*, where it was decided a victim's statement cannot be entered as evidence if the victim does not testify, because this violates the defendant's Sixth Amendment right to face their accuser and cross-examine the witness. However, other evidence, such as medical records and 911 calls, can be used to demonstrate the abuse did occur (Flannigan, 2013).

The difficulty in obtaining evidence in domestic violence cases without the testimony of the victim has led to trying to find different ways to encourage the victim to participate, while at the same time giving the victim the sense they are in control of their own decisions. An example of this would be prosecutors working directly with victim advocates to help gain the cooperation of the victim in court. In a study conducted by Bechtel et al., (2012), 353 domestic violence cases that occurred between 1998 and 2001 were examined, to better understand what led to successful prosecution and conviction at the state level. In order for the crime to be considered for prosecution at the state level, the defendant had to be a repeat offender at the local level, a weapon had to be used in the crime, serious injury had to occur, or a restraining order had to be violated. A total of 302 of the 353 cases (86%) examined resulted in a conviction, so the researchers wanted to better understand what circumstances were most likely to lead to prosecution and conviction. All but five of the cases that resulted in conviction also had a victim who cooperated in the prosecution of the case. It was noted that the prosecutors' office worked directly with victim advocates to ensure they were receiving the help they needed and felt supported throughout the process. The victim advocates contacted the victim within 24 hours of the crime by phone and also followed up with mailings. Overall, 91% of the victims met with an advocate within one week of the crime, which was important because it was noted that 89% were connected with counseling, 82% received assistance with shelter, 53% were in need of social services, 44% needed assistance in the process of obtaining a restraining order, and 39% requested financial assistance. The victim advocates also worked with the victims throughout the process, which helped to empower them as they moved through the prosecutorial process. The authors concluded that by helping the victims to obtain and maintain their independence as well as to help them make decisions throughout the process, the victims were strengthened, making it more likely they would participate in the prosecution process (Bechtel et al., 2012).

IN FOCUS

The Duluth Model

The Duluth Model addresses domestic violence in the criminal justice system and the community by shifting the blame for the crime from the victim to the offender and stating that the victim's safety is the responsibility of the community (Domestic Abuse Intervention Programs, 2011). The model also addresses the problem of domestic violence by including the victims in the criminal justice and treatment process as well as listening to their needs. For example, program staff became aware that victims wanted their significant others to go through programming to address their violent behaviors after speaking with victims about their experiences. This led to a court-ordered men's program being created and implemented that works directly with domestic violence offenders to encourage them to take responsibility for their actions and to adopt strategies to prevent these violent behaviors in the future. Program evaluations have found the men's programming to be successful, with 68% of those who have been through the court-ordered programming staying out of the criminal justice system for domestic violence offenses eight years after program completion (Domestic Abuse Intervention Programs, 2011).

The assistance of victim advocates working directly with the victim is incredibly important because the victims were in need of immediate assistance to break free financially and emotionally from their abuser. This directly responds to the two main reasons why victims were reluctant to cooperate—fear of retaliation and concern about financial independence. The authors noted that if the victim was willing to cooperate with the prosecution the chance of winning a conviction against the defendant significantly increased, whether the victim testified or not. They also noted that victims were much more likely to participate if they were included in the decision making process during prosecution and were provided with resources for financial and emotional support. The authors concluded their study by recommending a strong relationship between victim advocates and the prosecutor for a better chance at winning a conviction (Bechtel et al., 2012).

Domestic Violence and Immigration Status

Once women's socioeconomic status is taken into account, women experience domestic violence at a similar rate across all racial and ethnic groups. However, domestic violence victims who also are undocumented immigrants face unique barriers in accessing assistance and services, due to their undocumented status. Surveys conducted with undocumented Latinas accessing domestic violence services found that abusers would threaten to reveal the victim's immigration status to police, if the victim reported the abuse to law enforcement. The victims stated they did not report the abuse to the police because they feared being deported and separated from their children who were legal citizens. Latinas with an undocumented status also faced language barriers that sometimes led to both the offender and the victim being arrested, resulting in double victimization. Language barriers also were noted to be problematic at domestic violence shelters, where only one in three shelters had someone on staff who spoke Spanish. The women who were surveyed also reported economic barriers as they and their children had been financially reliant on their husband's income, and less than 30% stated they were aware of the domestic violence services that were available to them (National Latina Network, n.d.).

Cultural differences also must be examined when delving into how and why services are accessed or not accessed by Latinas. For example, Latinas who experienced domestic violence were less likely as a group to access formal services, such as police or medical professionals, and more likely to seek out friends, family, or religious leaders for assistance. Latinas also reported they did not access domestic violence services because they feared this would be the first step towards a divorce, which did not align with their religious beliefs (National Latina Network, n.d.).

In an attempt to address many of these barriers, the Violence Against Women Act was expanded to include those who were undocumented immigrants and victims of domestic violence. For example, if the victim is an undocumented immigrant and the abuser is a citizen or permanent resident of the United States, the victim may qualify for a green card to obtain permanent residency without their abuser being notified of the application. There are three main groups of family members who are eligible to apply for a domestic violence-related green card—parents who reside with their son or daughter and are being abused by their child, children who are being abused by a parent they reside with, or a spouse who is being abused by their husband or wife as long as they were married within two years of filing the green card paperwork (U.S. Citizenship and Immigration Service, 2016).

Those who meet the criteria for the domestic violence-related green card complete *Form I-360, Petition for Amerasian, Widow(er), or Special Immigrant*. After filing the paperwork, if applicants are deemed eligible to apply for this special status, they will receive notification that they are temporarily eligible (for 150 days) for specific government benefits designated for domestic violence victims. If one's I-360 status is approved, one's deportation will be deferred, allowing one to stay in the country legally and work. If one's I-360 status is denied there may be the option to apply for a U visa. The *U visa* allows crime victims who have been physically and/or mentally abused to remain in the United States, if they are working with law enforcement to aid in the investigation or prosecution of their abuser (U.S. Citizenship and Immigration Service, 2016).

Summary

In the United States, the definition of domestic violence has expanded to include more variations of abuse as well as different types of intimate partner relationships. Domestic violence also is a problem we are continually trying to resolve within the criminal justice system by changing the process to assist the victim and gain convictions for those who are offenders. There have been significant changes and improvements within the criminal justice system over the last hundred years, but there is still much more that can be done to ensure all victims are protected. There also is a need to increase and fund programs that assist victims. Unfortunately, there are too many victims who are turned away from crucial services that could save their lives as well as the lives of their children. Due to a lack of funding from the federal and state governments as well as reductions in donations from foundations and individuals, fewer staff are employed at domestic violence programs, and there has been a decrease in available services. If we are truly serious about resolving the problem of domestic violence within the United States, we must fund the services and programs that directly impact victims by providing them with the opportunities to be independent financially and emotionally.

Discussion Questions

1. How have the laws against domestic violence in the United States changed over the last century? Who and what led to these changes? What could be done to make further improvements to domestic violence laws?

2. In the United States, what are some of the problems that domestic violence programs face today, and how do these problems directly impact victims of domestic violence? How would you convince legislators to increase funding for domestic violence programs in your community?

3. What are some of the barriers that undocumented Latinas who are victims of domestic violence face when attempting to gain access to services and assistance? How could these barriers be addressed at the community level?

Key Terms

domestic violence
Protection from Abuse Act
Violence Against Women Act
mandatory arrest
preferred arrest
dual arrest

domestic violence police units
no-drop prosecution
Crawford v. Washington
Form I-360, the Petition for Amerasian, Widow(er), or Special Immigrant
U-visa

References

Bechtel, K. A., Alarid, L. F., Holsinger, A., & Holsinger, K. (2012). Predictors of domestic violence prosecution in a state court. *Victims & Offenders, 7*, 143–160.

Bhat, M., & Ullman, S. E. (2014). Examining marital violence in India: Review and recommendations for future research and practice. *Trauma, Violence & Abuse, 15*(1), 57–74.

Center for American Progress. (n.d.). Domestic violence in the LGBT community: A fact sheet. https://www.americanprogress.org/issues/lgbt/news/2011/06/14/9850/domestic-violence-in-the-lgbt-community/

Domestic Abuse Intervention Programs. (2011). Why the Duluth Model works. http://www.theduluthmodel.org/about/why-works.html

Exum, M. L., Hartman, J. L., Friday, P. C., & Lord, V. B. (2014). Policing domestic violence in the post-SARP era: The impact of a domestic violence police unit. *Crime & Delinquency, 60*, 999–1032.

Flannigan, K. R. (2013). The importance of prosecution policies in domestic violence cases. *Criminology & Public Policy, 12*, 481–490.

Hirschel, D., Buzawa, E., Pattavina, A., & Faggiani, D. (2007). Domestic violence and mandatory arrest laws: To what extent do they influence police arrest decisions. *Journal Criminal Law & Criminology, 98*, 255.

Indiana Coalition against Domestic Violence. (2016). History of battered women's movement. http://www.icadvinc.org/what-is-domestic-violence/history-of-battered-womens-movement/

Johnston, K. (2015). Domestic violence protection for gay people. Legal Match. http://www.legalmatch.com/law-library/article/domestic-violence-protection-for-gay-people.html

Kelly-Dreis, S. (2015). A retrospective: The nation's landmark restraining order law and first state domestic violence coalition. *Family & Intimate Partner Violence Quarterly, 7*, 275–284.

Legal Momentum. (2015). History of the Violence Against Women Act. The Women's Legal Defense and Education Fund. https://www.legalmomentum.org/history-vawa

Liscombe, B. (2014). When not to arrest an abuser in a domestic violence case. *Time.* http://time.com/12682/when-not-to-arrest-an-abuser-in-a-domestic-violence-case/

Los Angeles LGBT Center. (n.d.). Mental health: Intimate partner violence/domestic violence. https://lalgbtcenter.org/health-services/mental-health/intimate-partner-domestic-violence

Mbilinyi, L. (2015). *The Washington State Domestic Violence Housing First Program. Cohort 2 agencies: Final evaluation report.* http://wscadv.org/wp-content/uploads/2015/05/DVHF_FinalEvaluation.pdf

Moradian, M. A. (2009). Domestic violence against single and married women in Iranian society: An overview of current Iranian research and possible underlying etiology. https://www.academia.edu/2435646/Domestic_Violence_against_Single _and_Married_Women_in_Iranian_Society

National Latina Network. (n.d.). Facts and statistics. http://www.nationallatinonet work.org/learn-more/facts-and-statistics

National Network to End Domestic Violence. (2015). Domestic violence counts 2014: A 24-hour census of domestic violence shelters and services. United States Census Bureau. http://nnedv.org/downloads/Census/DVCounts2014/DVCounts14_Natl Report_web.pdf

Nichols, A. J. (2014). No-drop prosecution in domestic violence cases: Survivor-defined and social change approaches to victim advocacy. *Journal of Interpersonal Violence, 29,* 2114–2142.

Peralta, R. (2015, March 26). Mandatory arrest laws may hurt domestic violence victims. *The University of Akron News.* http://www.uakron.edu/im/news/mandatory -arrest-laws-may-hurt-domestic-violence-victims

Pournaghash-Tehran, S. (2011). Domestic violence in Iran: A literature review. *Aggression & Violent Behavior, 16,* 1–5.

Rasoulian, M., Habib, S., Bolhani, J., Shooshtani, M., H., Nojomi, M., & Abedi, S. (2014). Risk factors of domestic violence in Iran. *Journal of Environmental and Public Health.* http://www.hindawi.com/journals/jeph/2014/352346/

Roldan, C. (2015). State high court to hear case expanding domestic violence law to unwed same-sex couples. *The Post and Courier.* http://www.postandcourier.com/ article/20151111/PC1603/151119837/

Sherman, L. W., & Berk, R. A. (1984). The Minneapolis domestic violence experiment. Police Foundation Reports. http://www.policefoundation.org/wp-content/uploads/ 2015/07/Sherman-et-al.-1984-The-Minneapolis-Domestic-Violence-Experiment.pdf

Sullivan, C. M., Bomsta, H. D., & Hacskaylo, M. A. (2019). Flexible funding as a promising strategy to prevent homelessness for survivors intimate partner violence. *Journal of Interpersonal Violence, 34,* 3017–3033.

U.S. Citizenship and Immigration Service. (2016). Battered spouse, children and parents. https://www.uscis.gov/humanitarian/battered-spouse-children-parents

U.S. Department of Justice (U.S. DOJ). (2015). What is domestic violence? http:// www.justice.gov/ovw/domestic-violence

Vaglanos, A. (2015). 30 shocking domestic violence statistics that remind us it's an epidemic. *Huffington Post.* http://www.huffingtonpost.com/2014/10/23/domestic -violence-statistics_n_5959776.html

FOURTEEN

Human Trafficking

Learning Objectives

1. Define the crime of human trafficking and understand how it occurs within the United States.
2. Understand and critically examine how the laws combatting human trafficking are enforced and prosecuted.

The United Nations has created a definition of human trafficking for the purpose of a universal definition to aid in the prevention, enforcement, and prosecution of human trafficking around the world. A single globally recognized definition is important because human trafficking occurs in every country around the world. There are three parts of the United Nations' definition for *human trafficking*. First, there is the criminal act itself, which can consist of recruiting a person, providing them with transportation or moving them from one place to another, and housing or receiving the person. The second part of the definition includes how the act occurs and can include, "threat or use of force, coercion, abduction, fraud, deception, abuse of power or vulnerability, or giving payments or benefits to the person in control" (United Nations Office on Drugs and Crime, 2016b, para 3). The third part of the definition is the purpose of the exploitation, which can include sexual acts, forced labor, slavery, or for the removal of organs (United Nations Office on Drugs and Crime, 2016b).

Human trafficking can happen to anyone, including men, women, and children. However, it most commonly occurs where the victim is a woman or a girl (United Nations Office on Drugs and Crime, 2016b). The trafficker also is typically from the

Figure 14.1 Raising awareness of the problem of human trafficking. © iStockphoto.com/rdegrie.

same country as the victim and generally is someone they trust, such as a friend or family member or someone who appears trustworthy because they are nice to them (United Nations Office on Drugs and Crime, 2016c).

Human trafficking is different from *migrant smuggling*, because smuggling always occurs across national borders, whereas trafficking can occur within a country as well as between borders. Migrant smuggling also is based on consent, where the person paid for someone to bring them into another country illegally. Migrant smuggling often occurs in awful conditions, but the person being smuggled paid for this service. In comparison, those who are trafficked did not consent and are making money for the person who trafficked them once they arrive at their destination. Sometimes a person may consent to being smuggled to another location, but once the person arrives at their destination they are not free to leave the smuggler. Once the person no longer consents to what is occurring to them these actions become criminal, and the consent the person had once given is no longer relevant. In some instances, the smuggler turned trafficker has confiscated the person's identification, threatening the migrant with deportation, or has placed them in *indentured service*, where the person must pay off a debt to their smuggler before they can be released. In these examples, the person who once was a smuggler is now a trafficker (United Nations Office on Drugs and Crime, 2016a).

In this chapter, we will examine how human trafficking occurs in the United States as well as the challenges faced by law enforcement and prosecutors in combatting this crime. We also will discuss what can be done to help combat and prevent the crime of human trafficking as well as the global scale of the problem.

Human Trafficking in the United States

It has only been very recently that human trafficking was identified as a crime at the federal and state level. In 2000, the United States passed the *Trafficking Victims Protection Act* (TVPA) at the federal level, which made human trafficking a criminal offense in the United States, increased the punishment for the crime of human trafficking, and assisted those who were brought into the country illegally with visas and the possibility of citizenship after three years (Dill, 2011). For example, *T visas* can now be granted to those who assist in the prosecution of human trafficking cases or are victims of trafficking under the age of eighteen (Farrell, 2014). Since the passage of the TVPA, all 50 states have passed laws making human trafficking a criminal act at the state level as well (McGough, 2013).

Due to a lack of data being collected at the local, state, and federal level on human trafficking, it is difficult to know the true extent of this crime within the United States. The lack of available data has caused disagreements as to how many people are being trafficked into the United States, with numbers varying from 14,000 to 50,000 victims being trafficked into the country each year and an additional 600,000 to 800,000 trafficked within the United States. These estimates have led some to believe the problem is much larger than what is being reported, while others believe the problem has been exaggerated. Unfortunately, as long as data remains inaccurate, it is difficult to know how and where to allocate resources to combat the problem (McGough, 2013).

The National Institute of Justice is working to fund research in the area of human trafficking to better understand the extent of the problem within the United States. However, human trafficking remains difficult to measure because victims are often hidden, for example, as domestic servants working in private homes. Those who are not United States citizens also often face language barriers and are threatened with deportation due to being in the country illegally. Human trafficking victims also do not come forward and identify themselves as such due to a fear of retaliation from their captor as well as concern for law enforcement and how they might react to their situation, possibly viewing them as a criminal instead of a victim (McGough, 2013). For example, those who engage in prostitution are viewed by some police departments to be victims of human trafficking, while other police departments may view those who are trafficked as an offender. This is because prostitution is still viewed by some as a crime due to the belief that the behavior is a choice and not something that one is forced into. However, the majority of those who engage in prostitution are forced or intimidated into the act and/or lack alternatives (Farley, n.d.).

One way to collect data on human trafficking within the United States is to examine calls received by nationwide hotlines set up specifically to assist victims and to help combat human trafficking. Between 2007 and 2020, the National Human Trafficking Hotline received reports of 73,946 cases of human trafficking across all 50 states, with the highest reported number of cases coming from California, Texas, Florida, New York and Georgia. These verified cases of human trafficking were discovered due to the more than 328,255 emails, phone calls, and tips reported to the hotline (National Human Trafficking Hotline, 2020).

IN FOCUS

Shared Hope International

Shared Hope International is a nonprofit organization that consists of Christian abolitionists who are working to end the sexual exploitation of women and girls in the United States and abroad. Shared Hope has three goals: to prevent, restore, and bring justice. Prevention efforts include training and educating the community on how to recognize trafficking as well as how to respond. Shared Hope also restores victims by supporting programs that work directly with victims of sexual exploitation to provide housing, education, and counseling, while the Shared Hope Center for Law and Policy works towards bringing justice to those who have been harmed. For example, the center influences and lobbies for policy and law at the state level to end the sexual exploitation of children, while mobilizing their constituency to contact state legislators to support laws and policies that support their cause (Shared Hope International, 2016).

Based on the resource center data, the three most common forms of sexual exploitation reported were being controlled by pimps, commercial stores that also had brothels in the back, and escort services. Of all who are sexually exploited, forty-two percent (42%) were prostituted by a pimp and were typically recruited by men who showed them affection and then later sold them for sex that was often advertised online. The traffickers were typically adult males with American citizenship who were exploiting young women or girls under the age of eighteen. The majority of sexually exploited victims (60%) also were American citizens. The most commonly reported type of forced labor occurred within domestic situations, restaurants, and through door-to-door sales. The majority of those who experienced forced labor were working in domestic situations, and 84% were not American citizens. Those who reported cases of forced labor stated the victims were working primarily within homes where they were being emotionally, physically, and/or sexually abused. The victims of domestic labor were from 74 different countries, with most being from the Philippines, Mexico, Ethiopia, India, or Kenya. Those under the age of eighteen made up 20% of those who were forced into labor exploitation. The most common request made by the survivors of forced labor and sexual exploitation was for shelter, but this was difficult to accommodate because there are very few shelters that assist victims of human trafficking specifically and even fewer shelters for men in general (Polaris Project, 2014).

Intersecting Identities and Human Trafficking

Gonzalez (2017) draws attention to the lack of focus on the intersectionality of human trafficking which is highly "raced, classed and gendered." Victim and offender interaction with the criminal legal system is manipulated by the U.S. sociopolitical structure. Violent crimes, such as sexual assault and human trafficking, are intertwined in this sociopolitical structure and nuanced by racism and sexism. As debates about human trafficking versus sex work continue to play out, it will be important to watch how "trafficking ideology" evolves. It is known that Black and Latinx women are overrepresented in human trafficking victim demographics nationally. For example, one study found that Black women represent 40% of all suspected human trafficking cases while 24% are Latinx women. Further, data shows that Indigenous women in South Dakota comprise 8% of the population but make up 40% of trafficking victims. Several other studies specific to certain locales have confirmed this national trend with a troubling revelation about the disproportionate impact it has on Black girls. For example, while they only comprise 1.1% of the population, Black girls make up 52% of sex trafficking victims in King County, Washington. In that same county, white men made up 80% of the sex buyers (Richey, 2017).

Butler (2015) highlights the failure to acknowledge the historical connections that help explain why these disproportionalities exist. Butler argues that "both racialized sexual fetish and racial animus fuel the market in which mostly white men purchase commercial sex with people of color, including minors" (p. 1483). Adultification and hypersexualization of children of color contributes to the inability of the public, lawmakers and law enforcement to view them as victims (more on this in Chapter 12). Multiple systems of oppression are involved in the long-standing exploitation of minoritized people through slavery and colonization. In the case of Latina women and girls, the "racialized sexual exploitation of people of color" can be traced back to perceptions and attitudes shaped by slavery and colonization:

> Sexual colonization has also been part of the systemic racial subordination of Latinos in the United States. In particular, Latina women have often been sexually exploited and forced into prostitution as part of their experience as exploited agricultural workers. For example, in the infamous "Reed Camps" of California, Mexican girls as young as seven were forced to provide sexual services to agricultural workers for over a decade. In the United States, Latina women have historically been made vulnerable to sexual exploitation and have been forced to work as prostitutes. (Butler, p. 1480)

Another group that shows up alarmingly in trafficking statistics are LBGT youth. The highest risk group for sexual trafficking are houseless LGBT youth, and they are more susceptible to trafficking than other houseless minors. While they only make up

20% of the houseless minors, 58.7% are exploited (Martinez & Kelle, 2013). The 2000 Victims of Trafficking and Violence Prevention Act includes "survival sex" in its conception of sex trafficking victimization, encouraging an evolution of language (e.g., moving away from using the term "child prostitution") on how vulnerable youth navigate and negotiate for their basic needs (Middleton et al., 2018).

It is difficult to create a profile for a human trafficking victim because as a group they are incredibly diverse and consist of those from all walks of life, including various socioeconomic backgrounds, races, ethnicities, sexual identities and genders as well as both adults and children. However, there are some characteristics that tend to make people more susceptible to becoming a human trafficking victim. For example, youth who run away and are houseless are particularly vulnerable to those who befriend them with the intention of later victimizing them. Traffickers also threaten those who are undocumented with the criminal justice system and deportation if they do not comply, and those who have experienced trauma and/or abuse are statistically more likely to become involved with someone who will exploit them again (National Human Trafficking Hotline, n.d.).

Law Enforcement and Human Trafficking

The involvement of state and law enforcement in human trafficking cases is of the utmost importance, as 32% of local and state law enforcement identified their victims while investigating other crimes (McGough, 2013). Training manuals have been created to help local and state police officers identify victims of human trafficking, since these victims often do not come forward on their own and may be mistaken as offenders rather than victims. The manual created by the International Association of Chiefs of Police (n.d.), for instance, makes several recommendations to help local law enforcement identify victims of trafficking. Police officers are encouraged to examine crimes, such as domestic violence, labor disagreements, and prostitution or pimp offenses, along with shoplifting and assault as possible scenarios where victims of trafficking could be found. Police officers also are encouraged to examine their surroundings differently, for example, looking to see if the security in a building is designed to keep people in rather than out and ensuring local businesses are not being used as a front. Police officers also are encouraged to critically examine working conditions for different clues, such as whether people move about freely, they live and work in the same place, their employer has their documentation or identification, and the workers owe a debt to their employers. Police officers also are asked to examine how the employees are treated, for instance, by looking for signs of neglect or trauma and to take notice if the employees are afraid to speak or being censored when they do speak (International Association of Chiefs of Police, n.d.).

The manual also reminds police officers to be careful when building their case against a trafficker in order to keep the trafficker from recognizing they are suspected of a crime. If the trafficker is unaware of the investigation, they are less likely to move from the area, and the police officer can continue to collect evidence. Local law enforcement also is encouraged to contact federal agencies with which they already have a working relationship to identify whether there is already a case being investigated or if their suspect is part of a larger network of organized crime (International Association of Chiefs of Police, n.d.).

However, investigating cases of human trafficking can be incredibly difficult for local and state law enforcement. For instance, it can be challenging for police officers to determine who is a victim and who is an offender when arrests are made, because those who are trafficked often are not willing to immediately identify themselves as victims. One way to gain the trust of the victims, especially in communities where the distrust of law enforcement is high, is to partner with community groups who have a proven track record of successfully working with the population (Anti-Human Trafficking Unit, 2008).

GLOBAL SPOTLIGHT

UNODC Database

United Nations Office on Drugs and Crime (UNODC) has been working to create tools to educate those working within the criminal justice system as well as policy makers to combat the crime of human trafficking. One example of this is a human trafficking database that allows public access to cases that have been prosecuted. The purpose of this database is for research or to see how other cases have been investigated, prosecuted, and convicted globally as well as to help identify global patterns and to raise awareness of the crime of human trafficking. The database contains approximately 1,100 cases to illustrate how victims are being exploited, routes of transportation, and how laws around the world are being used to prosecute these cases (UNODC, n.d.). The UNODC also works directly with law and policy makers to help them create laws to target and prevent the crime of trafficking, as well as working with law enforcement who are on the front line (UNODC, 2016c).

The UNODC also has been working to help prevent trafficking by educating those who could be exploited, community leaders, and non-government organizations (NGOs). For instance, the UNODC has placed public service announcements on the radio and television, which are broadcast all over the world to raise awareness on the topic of human trafficking with those who could potentially be exploited. They also work with NGOs to help distribute literature to their clients as well as those who are at risk or have been trafficked. The UNODC works directly with community leaders in particularly vulnerable communities by educating and helping them to work directly with potential victims and to provide resources to those who have been trafficked (UNODC, 2016c).

Prior to interviewing the victims, police officers also should work with victim advocates because of the trauma the victims are likely to have experienced. The victims' medical and emotional needs should be met first in order to help them gain the trust of those who are conducting the investigation and make them more credible witnesses for prosecution later. If the victim feels secure, they are more likely to cooperate and will feel more comfortable with the authorities. An effort also should be made to learn about the victims' family, because many victims are often threatened by their traffickers that their families will be harmed if they cooperate with law enforcement or escape their bondage. Ensuring the victims' families are safe will make the victim more likely to cooperate during the investigation and later prosecution by gaining their trust (Dill, 2011).

Law enforcement also must be sensitive to the needs of the victim when interviewing them and show compassion, so they are more likely to open up about their exploitation. This is especially important because many victims have a fear of law enforcement from their experiences in their own countries and communities. Trafficking victims also may fear they will be deported or treated as criminals if they cooperate, so it is important for law enforcement to gain their trust. In order to make the strongest case for criminal charges, law enforcement must consider asking about a variety of aspects of the victim's exploitation, such as what they were forced to do as well as how they were held captive. When interviews are conducted gender and language barriers should be considered, because victims are more likely to feel comfortable disclosing their traumatic experiences to those who are of the same gender. For instance, women and children will be more likely to open up to female investigators, and male victims will be more likely to open up to male investigators. The gender of the investigator should be taken into consideration from the beginning of the investigation to avoid the victim having to go through multiple interviews with different investigators. Language also can be a barrier and should be considered as well. The ideal situation would include an investigator who is the same ethnicity and speaks the same language as the victim (Anti-Human Trafficking Unit, 2008).

Throughout the case, it is crucial for local police officers to recognize the importance of victims in the investigation of traffickers as they are moved along the same routes as trafficked guns and drugs. If a victim can remember specifics about how they were transported, this can lead to arresting entire networks of those who are trafficking guns, drugs, and people. It is also important to assist and protect the victims, because if they are incarcerated or deported they are unable to assist with the prosecution as a witness. Therefore, police officers must begin to look at those who had been previously defined as offenders and treat them instead as victims (Dill, 2006). During the investigation, law enforcement also will need to gather corroborating evidence in order to help with the prosecution of the trafficker, for example, by examining trash and records or through surveillance (Anti-Human Trafficking Unit, 2008).

Although there are guidelines for how to identify, respond to, and investigate cases of human trafficking, the implementation of these practices and policies has been difficult for local law enforcement to manage. Since the passage of the TVPA, in 2000, over 64 million dollars have been given to state and local law enforcement to assist with training on how to handle human trafficking cases. Even though there is support from the federal government to enforce the laws against human trafficking, it is still up to each police department to do so, and if this is not a priority of the local community and the budget does not cover it, human trafficking investigations are likely to fall by the wayside. Due to the secrecy and trauma victims of human trafficking have experienced, police officers also may have a difficult time identifying them. And even if victims are identified, it can still be incredibly challenging to investigate these crimes, because the police officer needs to ensure they are not retraumatizing the victim throughout the investigation process. Unfortunately, these barriers have led the Department of Justice to rank human trafficking cases as the most time-intensive cases to investigate and prosecute because of the complexity of the crime and the level of trauma the victims have experienced, making it difficult to gain their trust (Farrell et al., 2010).

Research Studies on Law Enforcement and Human Trafficking

A research study conducted by Farrell and colleagues (2014) illustrates some of the difficulties law enforcement face when combatting the crime of human trafficking. In the study, human trafficking cases were typically (39%) identified by community members, victim advocates, and hotlines. In the cases examined, only 10% of the victims sought help directly from the police, with an additional 3% of victims' families contacting the police. Sex trafficking cases were most likely to be investigated by vice units as part of other criminal cases, where 45% of victims were identified in hotels, on the streets, or the internet, with an additional 42% of cases taking place in residences and 3% in massage parlors. The authors also noted law enforcement did not typically have units that specialized in labor violations, which most likely accounted for the low number of forced labor cases reported. The authors recommended police officers work and train with labor regulators in order to better understand the labor laws and be able to recognize the signs of forced labor (Farrell et al., 2014).

Figure 14.2. Visualizing human trafficking. © Adobe Stock/artit.

The researchers also noted victim services were lacking, and victims were either sent to a neighboring state for assistance, directed to programs that did not specialize in human trafficking, or were arrested (35%). The lack of local resources becomes problematic because law enforcement need the victim to stay close by to build their case, but the lack of available services makes this difficult unless they arrest them. However, arresting the victims also makes them less willing to cooperate. Therefore, programs are needed for human trafficking victims, where they can receive shelter and services as they assist law enforcement with the investigation (Farrell et al., 2014).

Farrell and colleagues (2010) also conducted a study to better understand the perception of law enforcement regarding human trafficking as well as their response to this crime. To do so, 3,189 surveys were sent to local, county, and state law enforcement agencies. In the end, 1,912 agencies participated in the survey. The highest ranking police officer within the agency was asked to complete the survey about their perceptions of sex and labor trafficking within their community; specifically, they were asked if there were residents within their community or being brought into their community who were being exploited either sexually or through forced labor. Interviews also were conducted with police officers working on federally funded task forces combatting human trafficking (Farrell et al., 2010).

The authors concluded that local law enforcement agencies had different levels of awareness and responses to the crime of human trafficking depending upon the size of the agency. Larger agencies, for instance, were more likely to report human trafficking was occurring within their communities than smaller agencies, but on average most police agencies still reported it as rare to occasional. Training and policies also were lacking, with slightly less than 20% of all agencies receiving some training for human trafficking and only 9% of all agencies having a policy in place to handle these cases. Again, the size of the agency mattered, as larger police agencies serving communities with 250,000 people or more were the most likely to report their police officers had received training on the crime of human trafficking. However, between 2000 and 2006, less than 10% of all agencies investigated human trafficking cases, resulting in a total of 2,397 suspected cases of human trafficking, but only 36% ended in an arrest (Farrell et al., 2010).

IN FOCUS

Sex Trafficking at Sporting Events Myths

The Super Bowl has been referred to as the largest sex trafficking event within the United States. Each year police specifically target the streets of the city hosting the Super Bowl, making large numbers of arrests for prostitution and declaring it a success. The media reinforces this story line by reporting on the increase in sex trafficking around sporting events and the police response. However, there is not any data to support the claim that large sporting events significantly increase prostitution in the host city. In fact, the research on the topic has concluded there is not an increase in sex trafficking for the Super Bowl or other sporting events, such as the World Cup or the Olympics. However, every year a law enforcement task force is formed in the host city and prostitution is heavily targeted for a few days with those being prostituted and their customers getting arrested. However, the traffickers are not targeted or arrested. Although this makes for a great story line on the news there are several negative unintended consequences. For example, a sting-style operation leads to double victimization for those being prostituted, as they experience sexual exploitation along with being processed through the criminal justice system. The money spent on these short-term police operations also could be better spent working towards long-term goals, such as training law enforcement how to recognize and assist victims or providing services for the victims. Another unintentional side effect of this myth is that it portrays to the public a picture where human trafficking is only a problem when there are certain circumstances in place, which allows the individual to overlook what is happening within their own community. Unfortunately, the reality is that sex trafficking is occurring across the country all year long, not just at large sporting events (Campbell, 2016).

Agencies that reported multiple cases of human trafficking were further examined to better understand if the cases they investigated were sexual or labor exploitation. Thirty-six percent of these agencies reported the cases they investigated involved only

sexual exploitation and an additional 34% of agencies reported the cases they investigated were for forced labor, while 30% of agencies reported investigating both cases
of forced sexual and labor trafficking. Half of the agencies (52%) also reported that at
least one of these cases resulted in charges being filed, and 42% of these cases ended
in conviction. The victims also were granted a T visa in 16% of the cases, but 20% of
the victims were deported. (Farrell et al., 2010).

Farrell (2014) also conducted a study to better understand why some police agencies were better at adapting to and implementing new policies for more recently acknowledged crimes, such as hate crimes and human trafficking, by examining police
agencies who served communities of 75,000 to 250,000. It was noted that police agencies who were able to rapidly adapt to and implement policies on hate crime laws also
were more likely to do the same with human trafficking laws. The author concluded
that police agencies who early on participated in training and adopted policies on
recently acknowledged crimes had created an environment where police officers were
more likely to be able to identify cases of human trafficking. The author also noted
that state and federal laws as well as news coverage of stories and victim advocacy
groups were not instrumental in change within the police agencies; rather, what happened within the agency internally, such as training and the adoption of policies, was
the most important for combatting the crime (Farrell, 2014).

Human Trafficking and Prosecution

The prosecution of human trafficking cases at the state level has been difficult because not many cases have been prosecuted to provide case law for clarification, and
there is an uncertainty as to whether you need to show force, fraud, and coercion were
all present to demonstrate the crime did occur. These uncertainties have led to human
trafficking cases oftentimes being prosecuted as other crimes, such as prostitution. In
other instances, human trafficking cases have been turned over to the federal court
system because there is concern about the lack of resources to handle the complexity
of these cases at the state and local level (Farrell et al., 2014).

To better understand the prosecution of human trafficking cases at the state level,
Farrell and colleagues (2014) conducted a study by examining 140 closed cases across
12 different sites in multiple states. Of the 140 cases, the majority involved sexual
exploitation (85%), while 11% involved forced labor, and an additional 4% involved
both labor and sexual exploitation. Half of the cases involved minors, and 25% of the
total victims were not American citizens (Farrell et al., 2014).

The most common elements within the 140 cases were an identified trafficker,
evidence money was made by the trafficker, and children under the age of 18 being
trafficked for sexual exploitation. The majority of the 140 cases (69%) ended in the
prosecution of at least one person with a criminal charge, although the criminal
charge was not typically for human trafficking. The most common criminal charge

was for promoting prostitution or transporting for the purposes of prostitution, with only 17% being charged with the crime of human trafficking. Slightly more than one-third (36%) of the cases were prosecuted at the federal level, while another one-third were prosecuted at the state level (Farrell et al., 2014).

The researchers also interviewed a total of 166 police officers, prosecutors, and victim advocates for a more in-depth understanding of human trafficking. The researchers noted that those who did move forward with prosecution sometimes faced barriers because of the lack of understanding from judges and juries as to what constituted the crime of human trafficking. One prosecutor, for example, stated the judge allowed the defense attorney to argue that it could only be human trafficking if the person was brought in from another country because the judge did not understand that human trafficking is defined as a crime that can also occur within a country, region, or city. Another theme that arose in the interviews with prosecutors was a fear they would not win a conviction for a forced labor case because they believed these to be more of a federal violation rather than a state violation. They also worried they would lose the case because most of the interviewees did not have any experience prosecuting cases where labor exploitation was involved (Farrell et al., 2014).

Another theme from the interviews with police and prosecutors was victims being viewed as less credible if they had engaged in illegal activity themselves, such as prostitution, drug use, or immigration violations. Unfortunately, these acts are typically a part of the larger crime of human trafficking. However, police and prosecutors were reluctant to view these witnesses as credible, and even if they did view them as credible there was a concern the judge or jury would blame the victims for their behavior. However, victim testimony is essential in prosecuting these cases because there are rarely other witnesses who are willing to come forward or who observe the crime. In two-thirds of the 140 cases that were examined, other evidence of human trafficking was gathered; for example, in sexual exploitation cases, items, such as condoms, clothing, ledgers, and pictures were discovered. However, this corroborating evidence was not enough for successful prosecution without the victim's testimony as well (Farrell et al., 2014).

The Global Reach of Human Trafficking

Human trafficking is a global phenomenon that is difficult to track, because victims are often afraid to come forward because they have been threatened or beaten by their traffickers. This makes it incredibly difficult to know exactly what is happening within this illegal industry, and what data has been gathered is based on those victims who are rescued and traffickers who are convicted. Human trafficking occurs worldwide, with those who have been recovered representing 152 different countries and being transported to or within 124 countries. Many victims are transported across national borders, with 60% of all victims crossing at least one national border, making

*Figure 14.3. Tourists and sex workers at night along Bangla road,
the main nightlife street in Patong, Thailand. © iStockphoto.com/ gionnixxx*

them an illegal immigrant in their country of destination. The majority of traffickers also are from the country they were convicted in (Me et al., 2014).

There have been 510 identified traffic patterns, with most of those who are trafficked being moved from poorer areas to more affluent ones. Wealthier countries in the Middle East, Western Europe, and North America attract mostly victims from other countries, while those who are trafficked regionally remain in areas with less wealth. Trafficking victims sent to North America are often from East Asia, South Asia, and Western and Central Europe. The type of exploitation that occurs tends to vary by region, with those from Africa and the Middle East (53%) as well as Europe and Central Asia (66%) being exploited for sexual purposes. A significant portion of trafficking victims from these regions also were exploited for labor; for example, 37% in Africa and the Middle East and 26% in Europe and Central Asia. Those in Latin America and the Caribbean were exploited for sexual purposes (48%) and labor (47%) nearly equally, while those in East Asia, South Asia, and the Pacific were typically exploited for labor (64%) followed by sexual purposes (26%) (Me et al., 2014).

There also has been an increase in the number of children, in particular girls, who have been trafficked. Most are sexually exploited, but the number of those exploited for labor has been increasing, with 40% of victims who were recovered reporting forced labor and an additional 53% reporting sexual exploitation. The majority of convicted traffickers were male (72%), but many also were female (28%). The majority of victims were adult women over the age of 18 (49%) followed by girls (21%), adult men over the age of 18 (18%) and boys (12%) (Me et al., 2014).

IN FOCUS

Airline Ambassadors

Airline Ambassadors International is a nonprofit organization that works specifically with the poorest and most vulnerable children in the world by providing transportation for sick children as well as delivering humanitarian aid (Airline Ambassadors International, 2015). In 2009, the organization also began to focus on human trafficking after discovering the living conditions of the homeless children of Cambodian women who had been trafficked and prostituted. This experience caused members of the nonprofit to become aware of the extent of the problem of human trafficking and to find ways the airline industry could get involved. The next month, airline employees who had been exposed to the problem of human trafficking were able to identify two cases of human trafficking on two separate airlines that led to 82 children being rescued by law enforcement in the Dominican Republic. The success of these tips in combatting human trafficking led to the creation of a course for those who work in the airline and travel industries to teach employees how to recognize a trafficking victim as well as how to report the crime. Since 2011, the nonprofit agency has provided 52 trainings to over 4,000 participants in the United States and internationally (Airline Ambassadors International, 2015).

Currently, 90% of countries have legislation that defines human trafficking as a crime. However, the laws are not always effective due to how they were written or implemented, leaving many victims, particularly women and children, still vulnerable. The number of convictions still remains very low, as 40% of 128 countries, between 2010 and 2012, reported 10 or fewer convictions per year, while 15% didn't report a single conviction. Due to the low conviction rates, the crime of human trafficking remains low risk and the profit margin remains high, making it an attractive crime (Me et al., 2014).

Human trafficking is a global problem, where people are often moved from one region or country to another. Therefore, in order to combat this problem, a global effort against trafficking must be deployed. Those who control trafficking locally are often a small group of people. However, the further one moves the victims the more likely they are to be highly organized. Moving people from one area to another, particularly if the region or country is affluent, means more profit as well as risk, requiring a more organized effort (Me et al., 2014). It also is important to recognize that those who are highly organized often participate in a variety of illegal activities, such as trafficking weapons and guns as well as smuggling migrants and laundering money. This means that even if there is not enough evidence to convict someone or a group of people for human trafficking, they could still be charged with organized crime and be effectively prosecuted (Anti-Human Trafficking Unit, 2008).

The United Nations has created the Organized Crime Convention to help countries develop strategies to fight organized crime and to work across borders with other countries. The Organized Crime Convention also has certain protocols set up to assist countries with specific issues, such as human trafficking and migrant smuggling. Countries can work together using *extradition* or sending a person of interest or who needs to be sentenced from one country to another. This strategy is important due to the global nature of the crime. For instance, the evidence to convict a person for trafficking could be gathered in one country, but the suspected offender is currently living in another country, making arrest and prosecution nearly impossible. If the two countries work together and allow for extradition, this person could be arrested and prosecuted in the country that has the ability and evidence to do so. Countries and regions also can work together across jurisdictions to enforce laws against trafficking and to gather evidence for prosecution by entering into treaties or mutual agreements. Traffickers are able to move from one area to the next easily, using advanced technology to help them to do so. If countries can work together to provide legal assistance they will have a better chance of combatting trafficking and keeping up with the offenders (Anti-Human Trafficking Unit, 2008).

Summary

Human trafficking is a global crime that can occur anywhere, even within the United States. It is modern-day slavery, where men, women, and children are being exploited for labor and sexual purposes without their consent. Awareness of this crime continues to grow. However, the crime itself also continues to thrive, as it is difficult to enforce laws against human trafficking, due to barriers faced by law enforcement and prosecutors at the state and local level. This makes human trafficking a highly profitable crime as the risk of being caught and punished is low, but the financial returns are high.

Discussion Questions

1. What are some of the barriers local law enforcement face when conducting their investigations with victims of human trafficking? What do you think could be done to help police officers investigate these crimes more effectively?

2. How would you convince state legislators to provide more funds to train law enforcement, prosecutors, and judges to combat the crime of human trafficking? What evidence would you use to support your statements?

3. How could the United States work with other countries around the world to help combat the crime of human trafficking?

Key Terms

human trafficking	Trafficking Victims Protection Act
migrant smuggling	T visas
indentured service	extradition

References

Airline Ambassadors International. (2015). Human trafficking. http://airlineamb.org/our-programs/human-trafficking-awareness/

Anti-Human Trafficking Unit. (2008). Toolkit to combat trafficking in persons. United Nations Office on Drugs and Crime. https://www.unodc.org/documents/human-trafficking/Toolkit-files/07-89375_Ebook [1].pdf

Butler, C. N. (2015, September 1). The racial roots of human trafficking. *UCLA Law Review*, 65, 1464–1514.

Campbell, A. (2016). Sex trafficking hype surrounding the Super Bowl does more harm than good. *Huffington Post*. http://www.huffingtonpost.com/entry/super-bowl-sex-trafficking-harmful_us_56b4e08be4b08069c7a7068b

Dill, S. (2006). Old crimes in new times human trafficking and the modern justice system. *Criminal Justice,* 21(1), 12–19.

Dill, S. E. (2011). Human trafficking. *Criminal Justice*, 26, 18–26.

Farley, M. (n.d.). Human trafficking and prostitution. Psychologists for Social Responsibility: Building Cultures of Peace for Social Justice. http://www.psysr.org/issues/trafficking/farley.php

Farrell, A. (2014). Environmental and institutional influences on police agency responses to human trafficking. *Police Quarterly*, 17, 3–29.

Farrell, A., McDevitt, J., & Fahy, S. (2010). Where are all the victims? *Criminology & Public Policy*, 9, 201–233.

Farrell, A., Owens, C., & McDevitt, J. (2014). New laws but few cases: Understanding the challenges to the investigation and prosecution of human trafficking cases. *Crime, Law & Social Change, 61*, 139–168.

Gonzalez, C. (2017). *Race, gender, and domestic human trafficking: An intersectional description of human trafficking cases at the state level* (Unpublished thesis). University of Colorado, Boulder.

International Association of Chiefs of Police. (n.d.). The crime of human trafficking: A law enforcement guide to identification and investigation. http://www.theiacp.org/portals/0/pdfs/CompleteHTGuide.pdf

Martinez, O., & Kelle, G. (2013). Sex trafficking of LGBT individuals: A call for service provision, research, and action. *International Law News, 42*(4). https://www.ncbi.nlm.nih.gov/pmc/articles/PMC4204396/pdf/nihms567983.pdf

McGough, M. Q. (2013). Ending modern-day slavery: Using research to inform U.S. anti-human trafficking efforts. *National Institute of Justice Journal, 271,* 26–32.

Me, A., Kangaspunta, K., Sarrica, F., & Johansen, R. (2014). *Global report on trafficking in persons.* United Nations Office on Drugs and Crime. https://www.unodc.org/documents/human-trafficking/2014/GLOTIP_2014_full_report.pdf

Middleton, J. S., Gattis, M. N., Frey, L. M., & RoeSepowitz, D. (2018). Youth Experiences Survey (YES): Exploring the scope and complexity of sex trafficking in a sample of youth experiencing homelessness. *Journal of Social Service Research, 44*(2), 141–157.

National Human Trafficking Hotline. (n.d.). The victims. https://humantraffickinghotline.org/what-human-trafficking/human-trafficking/victims

National Human Trafficking Hotline. (2020). Hotline Statistics. https://humantraffickinghotline.org/states

Richey, V. (2017, May 30). *Reducing demand for the commercial sexual exploitation of minors in your community* [Webinar]. OJJDP Online University.

Right4girls. (n.d.). Racial & gender disparities in the sex trade. https://rights4girls.org/wp-content/uploads/r4g/2018/09/Racial-Justice-fact-sheet-Sept-2018-Final.pdf

Shared Hope International. (2016). Our story. https://sharedhope.org/about-us/

United Nations Office on Drugs and Crime. (2016a). Frequently asked questions. https://www.unodc.org/unodc/en/human-trafficking/faqs.html

United Nations Office on Drugs and Crime. (2016b). Human trafficking. https://www.unodc.org/unodc/en/human-trafficking/what-is-human-trafficking.html

United Nations Office on Drugs and Crime. (2016c). Prevention. https://www.unodc.org/unodc/en/human-trafficking/prevention.html

United Nations Office on Drugs and Crime. (n.d.). Human trafficking case law database. https://www.unodc.org/documents/human-trafficking/leaflets/Infosheet_Jan_2015.pdf

Conclusion

FIFTEEN

Conclusion

Where Do We Go from Here?

Learning Objectives

1. Critically examine what it means to have a post-racial and post-sexist United States.
2. Discuss different examples of how to create change through hashtag activism and protest.

The Reality of a "Post-Racial" America

In 2008, there were many Americans who believed that Barack Obama winning the presidency proved America had moved beyond its racist past. This notion was supported with voting data that illustrated 43% of white voters voted for President Obama, garnering him the highest percentage of white votes for a democratic candidate in a two-person race since President Jimmy Carter, in 1976 (Kuhn, 2008). This belief was further supported with voting data that showed white voters, in particular rural and urban voters from working-class backgrounds, voted for President Barack Obama. TV pundits began to discuss how the country was entering into what they called a post-racial America, where the color of one's skin no longer was a barrier for opportunity and success. The proof of course was that a Black man had been elected to the highest office in the land—the presidency of the United States (Hannah-Jones, 2016).

Racism is often discussed in absolute terms; for example, you are a racist or are not. However, racism has always existed on a spectrum in the United States, and it depends on what is going on socially, economically, and politically as to where many Americans fall on this spectrum. For example, in 2008 the Great Recession impacted many Americans either through the loss of their retirement funds as the stock market began to plummet or their jobs as the national unemployment rate hit 10%. Those who voted in the 2008 presidential election did not forget that the turmoil they were experiencing had occurred under a Republican president. This led to many white voters voting for Barack Obama because they believed he was their best chance of improving the economy, and he had promised to go after those big bankers most believed were responsible for the recession. Therefore, many white voters who voted for President Obama were motivated by their economic situation and, at least for a period of time, the economy was viewed as more important than the color of one's skin (Hannah-Jones, 2016).

In the 2016 presidential election, race and ethnicity were mentioned repeatedly but in a very different way than had been discussed in recent elections. Trump supporters, for example, would chant "build the wall" as Trump discussed alleged crimes committed by undocumented immigrants and his proposal to build an impenetrable wall on the Mexico–United States border to stop immigration from Mexico (Dailymail.com, 2016). Trump also made multiple references to African Americans, the inner city, and the lack of education and jobs there, implying that African American and the inner city were synonymous (Semuels, 2016). However, many were offended by this notion, as only 13% of African Americans today live in an urban environment with concentrated poverty, and the overwhelming majority of Black Americans (73%) live above the poverty line. Then–Presidential candidate Trump also tweeted inaccurate statistics that exaggerated the amount of crime committed by Black people (Semuels, 2016).

These public comments did not go unnoticed, and white Nationalists, or those who want to maintain a white America, began to publicly support presidential candidate Trump (Berger, 2016). Former head of the Ku Klux Klan David Duke, for example, endorsed Donald Trump's campaign for presidency. Other prominent white Nationalists also began to support Donald Trump with the hope that if he was elected president, it would legitimize their beliefs and provide an avenue for those who were like-minded to run for political office (Berger, 2016). This support persisted during the Trump presidency and eventually led to the January 6, 2021, insurrection at the United States Capitol. With encouragement from Trump and false information from various media sources, disgruntled and dangerous Trump supporters felt like they needed to storm the Capitol and take their country back from an alleged stolen election. As a result of the *Capitol Riot*, an estimated 140 Capitol police officers were injured and five people were killed. Hundreds of accused rioters have charges that range from "entering or remaining in a restricted federal building or grounds" to "using a deadly or dangerous weapon or causing serious bodily injury to an officer" (Rubin, Mallin, & Steakin, 2022).

Unfortunately, it is going to take much more than one president's eight years in office to erode the hundreds of years of history of race in the United States. Today, it is difficult for most Americans to declare that we are in a post-racial period, as the nightly news covers example after example of Black Americans being verbally and physically harmed because of the color of their skin. Although there have been many advances in race relations within the United States over the years, it is important to remember there is still a long way to go. Ta-Nehisi Coates noted in a 2015 *Atlantic* article that "America's struggle is to become not post-racial, but post-racist. Put differently, we should seek not a world where the black race and the white race live in harmony, but a world in which the terms *black* and *white* have no real political meaning" (Coates, 2015, para. 1). Therefore, the true goal is a post-racist society, where the terms "Black" and "White" no longer contain power and impact people differently as they move through life (Coates, 2015).

Racial Injustice in a "Post-Racial" America

During President Obama's two terms in office, the issue of race did not disappear, and if anything, it became more visible. This was particularly true for the second term, where the deaths of Black men killed in police shootings began to grab national attention, bringing awareness to this problem. Police officers are tasked with protecting themselves and the community as well as resolving the problem when they fear themselves or the community is in grave danger. Therefore, a police officer can shoot to kill a civilian, if that person is a grave threat to the officer or the community. These deaths are referred to as ***justifiable homicides***, and occur when a police officer, during the course of their duty, kills a civilian without any ill intent or malice (Hill & Hill, 2005).

However, there have been a number of civilian deaths at the hands of police where it is difficult to clearly state that the killing was indeed justified. On July 15, 2014, Eric Garner was killed by a police officer in Staten Island after the police officer placed Garner in a prohibited choke hold. Garner's death was captured on video, and he was heard saying, "I can't breathe" before he died (Baker et al., 2015). On August 5, 2014, John Crawford III was shopping at a Wal-Mart in Ohio, where he was attempting to buy a toy pellet gun. The gun had been taken out of its package and left on the store's shelf. Crawford who was talking on the phone, picked up the gun, and continued to walk around the store carrying the toy gun with him. Another shopper called 911 and reported that a man was walking around the store waving a gun. The police responded and shouted at Crawford to drop the weapon. However, Crawford did not react immediately and the police officers shot and killed him. It was later confirmed on store video footage that Crawford had not been waving the gun around as stated by the person who reported the threat (Izadi, 2014).

A few days later, on August 9, 2014, Michael Brown, who was unarmed, was shot and killed by a police officer in Ferguson, Missouri, after an altercation with the police officer who confronted Brown for an alleged theft from a convenience store (Buchanan et al., 2017). A few months later, on November 22, 2014, Tamir Rice, a 12-year-old boy, was shot and killed by a police officer in Cleveland. Rice had been playing with a toy pellet gun outside of his home, when a man who saw him called 911 to report that someone was outside with a gun. The police officer, who was still in training, shot the 12-year-old boy almost immediately after arriving on the scene, because he believed the boy was about to aim the gun at him (Fantz et al., 2015).

Police-involved deaths continued into 2015, and on April 4, Walter Scott was shot and killed by a police officer in Charleston, South Carolina. Scott had been pulled over for a broken taillight, and after an altercation with the police officer he fled the scene on foot, unarmed. He was shot in the back as he ran away, with all of it being caught on video by a passerby on his way to work (Associated Press, 2016). A few days later, on April 12, 2015, Freddie Gray died in police custody in Baltimore. Gray had been arrested after a series of events, which began after he noticed police officers on the street. Gray took off running and was stopped and searched by a police officer, who found an illegal knife and arrested him (it was later determined the knife was not an illegal switchblade, but a pocketknife). After Gray was arrested and handcuffed, he was placed in the back of a police van, where he was not secured with safety restraints. Gray died from the trauma he encountered after experiencing what is referred to as a "rough ride," where the police officer driving purposefully creates a bumpy ride for their passengers in the back of the van. Gray suffered three broken vertebrae and an injured voice box. His injuries left him in a coma, and he later died (BBC News, 2016). A few months later, on July 9, 2015, Samuel DuBose was pulled over by a police officer in Cincinnati for missing a front license plate on his car. Dubose attempted to flee the scene in his car, and the police officer fired his gun into the car, shooting DuBose in the head and killing him instantly (Felton, 2016).

In recent years, the names of Black men, women, and children killed by the police continues to grow. Frustrations with injustices came to a head with the 2020 murder of *George Floyd* in Minneapolis. Minneapolis police officer Derek Chauvin was recorded pressing his knee on Floyd's neck for nine minutes and 29 seconds. As passersby and witnesses begged for him to get off an already restrained Floyd they watched as the officer stared, with his hands in pockets, at the crowd. Once EMS arrived, they had to ask the officer to get off of Floyd's neck. By the time they were able to assist him, Floyd was unconscious. The viral video, recorded by 17-year-old Darnella Frazier, was recognized as one of the most important pieces of evidence in the trial as it contradicted police statements about the incident. On Tuesday, April 20, 2021, Derek Chauvin was found guilty of murdering George Floyd. Chauvin is alleged only the second Minnesota officer to ever be convicted of an on-duty murder (Treisman, 2021)

The police officer-involved deaths mentioned above are not comprehensive but are an overview of some of the deaths that were covered extensively in the media. *The Washington Post* has been tracking police-involved deaths since 2015 and has concluded that there were 991 police-involved deaths in 2015 and an additional 963 in

Figure 15.1. Protect Black Women March to the Governor's Mansion in St. Paul Minnesota, 2020
© Creative Commons / Fibonacci Blue

2016 (Fatal Force, n.d.). The overwhelming majority of these deaths have been categorized as justifiable homicide, but it is clear that for some of these cases the designation of justifiable homicide is not always black and white. For instance, in the majority of cases covered in this chapter, the police officers were found to not be responsible for the death of the civilian because they either were not indicted or the trial ended in a mistrial due to a hung jury. However, in each of these cases there has been a multimillion-dollar lawsuit paid out to the family of the deceased. It should also be noted that in most of these cases the person was first approached by the police officer for a nonviolent crime, while in the two cases with toy guns the person was not even committing a crime, but the police officer believed he was about to commit a violent crime (Fatal Force, n.d.).

Seeking Racial Justice

An unfortunate trend continues in the U.S., serving as a collective reminder that the fight for racial justice continues. In 2020, the country was forced into a racial reckoning as protests erupted across the country in response to the tragic killings of Black people at the hands of the police. Ahmaud Arbery, George Floyd, and Breonna Taylor became household names as their deaths seemed to occur back-to-back. Situated and contextualized during a year of a record-breaking modern-day global pandemic, police violence against Black bodies required Americans to pause and reflect on the need for truth telling, healing, and racial reconciliation. Many have been forced to face the reality that the United States is not in a post-racial period. This realization is positive development because one must first recognize a problem exists before one can attempt to address it, and many are beginning to do just that.

The 2020 protests for racial justice represent a continuation of the ongoing work of activists who have showed up after the tragedies of Trayvon Martin, Tamir Rice, Michael Brown, Freddie Gray, Oscar Grant, Rekia Boyd, and many more. Most people will recall the Trayvon Martin case as a catalyst to the modern movement for racial justice. Black Lives Matter is phrase, with the accompanying hashtag #BLM, born from the acquittal of the George Zimmerman. Seventeen-year-old Trayvon Martin was killed on his way home from a convenience store by his neighbor, George Zimmerman, a Neighborhood Watch volunteer. Zimmerman stated his actions were in self-defense as he feared for his life. However, Zimmerman had been told by the 911 dispatcher not to engage Martin and that the police were on their way. Zimmerman was eventually found not guilty of the crime, and a debate ensued as to whether this would have happened if Trayvon had instead been a white high school student (CNN library, 2016). Shortly after Zimmerman's acquittal, Alicia Garza, Opal Tometi, and Patrisse Cullors came together to form the social movement Black Lives Matter. The three activists had been motivated by the result of Zimmerman's trial as well as by news coverage of Martin's death that often focused on Martin being suspended from school for having marijuana residue in his backpack, instead of how he died (Garza, 2014).

In July 2013 via Facebook, Garza penned a "love letter to Black people" for encouragement as Black people processed the decision which felt to many like confirmation that Black bodies were not safe and protected like those of white people. Garza wrote:

> the sad part is, there's a section of America who is cheering and celebrating right now. and that makes me sick to my stomach. we gotta *get it together y'all* … btw stop saying we are not surprised. that's a damn shame in itself. I continue to be surprised at how little Black lives matter. And I will continue that. stop giving up on black life … black people. I love you. I love us. Our lives matter.

Shortly after Garza's Facebook posts, her friend Patrisse Cullors added three words that would become the viral hashtag *#BlackLivesMatter* (Cobb, 2016). It has been stated that BLM has "pierced a big hole in the ideology of a post-racial America and exposed the deep and persistent patterns of racism in the United States" (Petersen-Smith, 2015). While these social media posts occurred in 2013, it wasn't until the death of Michael Brown in Ferguson, Missouri, in 2014 that the Black Lives Matter movement began to gain nationwide attention and support. Ilchi and Frank (2020) state that this is the point at which the BLM statement demanding equality transformed into a movement. The attention garnered has led to some positive outcomes.

For example, the Democratic candidates in the 2016 primaries were forced to discuss racial justice after protestors demanded it. Hillary Clinton apologized for the use of the term "superpredators" in the 1990s, where she had stated that juveniles who were committing crimes were a new breed of violent criminals that lacked a conscience, and Bernie Sanders began discussing mass incarceration and police-involved shootings (Capehart, 2016; Gass, 2015). However, sometimes this coverage also resulted in negative attention. For example, Micah Johnson, who killed five Dallas police officers and wounded several more, stated he had committed these crimes because he was tired of police shootings involving Black men and that he was inspired by the social movement Black Lives Matter (Li, 2016).

However, no matter where Americans stood on the issue of race at least they were discussing it. This was something that had not been done for years because the dominant belief had been that racism is only a problem when you talk about it. These discussions about race in America led to other discussions of how we can reduce the number of officer-involved shootings. Although we have a long way to go, there are people who are working towards creating and implementing solutions. For example, experts are looking into how body cameras can be used effectively to protect both the police officer and the public as well as how can we prosecute and convict those police officers who inappropriately use force, resulting in death or physical harm (National Institute of Justice, 2017; Kindy & Kelly, 2015). The FBI also is now collecting data on police-involved shootings, which had not been done before (Fatal Force, n.d.).

Black Lives Matter is now described as a grassroots organization that has moved from a hashtag to a network of chapters to a movement. Due to the loose structure and lack of core leadership, many struggle to completely understand who and what BLM actually is. As such, perceptions of BLM vary across demographics and levels of understanding. Contrary to popular conservative beliefs about the movement, BLM promotes nonviolent direct action to address police violence against Black people as well as a focus on "the needs of black queers, the black transgendered, the black undocumented, black incarcerated, and others" (Reynolds, 2015). Although that is what they purport to do, research shows that the strongest predictor of nonsupport for BLM are being white and possessing symbolic racist perceptions (Ilchi & Frank, 2020). They also found that those who do not support BLM also believe that BLM advances a "war on cops." Interestingly, these respondents also support BLM reform policies related to independent investigations and prosecutions for police shootings. This contradiction seems to show that a segment of Americans believe in some BLM messages but do not support the movement. More recently, while the levels of support remain lower than that of other racial groups, research has revealed that 67% of white Americans support BLM (Ilchi & Frank, 2020).

The Reality of a "Post-Sexist" America

Sexism is the belief that males are superior to females and should therefore be the dominate sex in making decisions regarding political, social, and economic matters (Dictionary.com, n.d.). Today, not everyone believes sexism exists, and whether you believe it occurs tends to be divided based on gender as well as political affiliation. One poll, for example, found most men (56%) believe that women no longer experience significant obstacles at work and outside of work, while 41% of women reported they believed these barriers still existed. The majority of women (63%) also reported they believed that women experienced sexism, but not all women agreed (31%) (Paquette, 2016). One's opinion on whether sexism exists also is divided based on political affiliation. For example, Republicans, both men (75%) and women (50%), were less likely to believe women experienced sexism, while male (60%) and female (74%) Democrats were more likely to believe that women do experience sexism (Paquette, 2016).

Today, there are not as many economic and social barriers for women to overcome within the workplace, and women are advancing and breaking glass ceilings. However, when you examine the top positions within the corporate world women's numbers are still small. For example, only 15% (74) of CEOs at the top 500 American companies are female (Buchholz, 2022). There also are very few women of color within these top corporate positions. Currently, there are two Black female CEOs leading Fortune 500 companies (Hinchliffe, 2021). The increase in diversity of Fortune 500 leadership has been attributed to cultural shifts during the COVID-19 pandemic. It has been argued that companies are seeking more "adaptable" and "empathetic" leadership, which is illustrated in the fact that in the first half of 2021 women made up 13% of newly appointed CEOs (Leech, 2022).

Although women represent half of the population within the United States they are still grossly underrepresented in Congress. For example, women make up only 27% of the United States House of Representatives and 24% of the United States Senate (Blazina & Desilver, 2021). Throughout history, a total of 397 women have served in Congress (Congressional Research Service, 2022). Women of color are even more vastly underrepresented within the United States Congress, as there have only been 94 women of color who have served or are serving Congress, including former Senator Kamala Harris, who was elected as the first vice president woman and woman of color in 2020 (Congressional Research Service, 2022). The overwhelming majority of women of color have served their term in office in the United States House of Representatives. Today, women of color represent 9.2% of Congress (Blazina & Desilver, 2021). There are 28 Black women, 16 Hispanic women, 11 women of Asian-Pacific descent, and 2 American Indian women serving in the 117th Congress (Congressional Research Service, 2022).

Misogyny in a "Post-Sexist" America

Misogyny is defined as when one does not like or trust women or harbors bias against them (Misogyny, n.d.). Misogyny is often referred to as the enforcer of gender norms and rules that uphold sexism, while sexism is used to justify this behavior as everyday conduct (Manne, 2016). During the 2016 presidential election, for example, a decade-old video of former President Trump surfaced, where he remarked that he could grab women "by the pussy" due to his star status. This remark was part of a larger private discussion between him and a television host who were both unaware they were being recorded. In this conversation Donald Trump discussed making sexual advances towards women he thought were beautiful. This story erupted into a media firestorm, and the discussion of whether grabbing someone by their intimate body parts is sexual assault or not was debated, even though this action fits the very definition of the crime. However, there were those who attempted to deflect criticism of this behavior by stating that this was just "locker room talk" between two men (Filipovic, 2016).

The dismissal of a hypersexual environment as boys and men letting off steam can also be seen in the case of Brock Turner. Turner was a young white college student who was a star swimmer at Stanford University who also was convicted of sexually assaulting a young woman behind a dumpster while she was unconscious. The act itself was never disputed because although the victim was unable to recall all of the events, there were two young men who happened to be riding their bikes by where the crime was taking place that intervened on behalf of the victim. However, a judge only sentenced Turner to six months in jail and three years of probation even though the prosecutor had recommended a sentence of six years. In the end, Turner only spent three months in jail after being released for good behavior. The judge who handed down the sentence, a Stanford University graduate, justified the sentence by stating that Turner should not spend a lengthy amount of time behind bars for the violent crime because it would not undo the harm suffered by the victim and would only serve to undeservedly harm him (Grinberg & Shoichet, 2016).

The dismissal of these behaviors is problematic because it helps to promote and normalize an environment where women are responsible for their offender's behavior because they were beautiful or because of how they were dressed, and not because the offender committed a crime. This situation reinforces stereotypical gender roles where women do not have autonomy over their bodies and must be careful about how they present themselves in public, so as not to attract the wrong kind of attention (Filipovic, 2016).

Seeking Social Justice for All

After the 2016 presidential election we also saw women and men from all backgrounds come together to protest for equality in what is now being called the largest one-day protest in U.S. history. Hundreds of thousands marched in Washington, D.C., the day after the presidential inauguration, while thousands marched in cities across the country in solidarity (Easley, 2017). The **Women's March** was created as a way for women and men all across the country to come together to protest publicly after what had been a very divisive presidential election. After the election, for example, there were many who expressed fear that they would be ostracized or possibly harmed due to statements that were made by presidential candidate Trump as well as his staff. For example, Muslim Americans were concerned there would be a registry

Figure 15.2. Women's March in San Francisco © Creative Commons / Fabrice Florin

created to track their whereabouts, documented and undocumented immigrants began to worry about themselves or family members being deported, and members of the LGBT community feared that many of the advances they had made in recent years would be reversed, while others were concerned about reproductive rights and the environment (Women's March, n.d.a).

The stated mission for the Women's March was to "stand together in solidarity with our partners and children for the protection of our rights, our safety, our health, and our families—recognizing that our vibrant and diverse communities are the strength of our country" (Women's March, n.d.a, para 1). The march that had originally started with one woman creating a Facebook event page eventually became an example of *intersectional feminism*, or where the perspectives of all women no matter their race, ethnicity, class, gender identity, or disability are taken into consideration when fighting for women's rights. For example, the Women's March took on not only traditional feminist causes of unequal pay and reproductive rights, but also mass incarceration, LGBT rights, racial profiling, police violence, the need for unions, civil rights, disability rights, immigrant rights, and environmental justice. The Women's March website states:

> We believe that Women's Rights are Human Rights and Human Rights are Women's Rights. We must create a society in which women—including Black women, Native women, poor women, immigrant women, disabled women, Muslim women, and lesbian, queer, and trans women—are free and able to care for and nurture their families, however they are formed, in safe and healthy environments free from structural impediments. (Women's March, n.d.b, para 1)

The **#*MeToo*** movement is another example of intersectional feminism. In 2006, Tarana Burke created the phrase "Me Too" to amplify the voices of marginalized girls and women who had experienced sexual violence (Pelligrini, 2018). The phrase became a viral hashtag in October 2017 when actress Alyssa Milano asked her followers to tweet #METOO if they've been sexually assaulted or harassed (Sayej, 2017). The #MeToo movement supports girls and women speaking up, but now it also emphasizes holding perpetrators accountable (Murphy, 2019). However, Burke reports that was not the original intent of her Me Too phrase, which centered marginalized people and communities (Warfield, 2018).

These intersectional movements showcase that there has been a reckoning whereby large swaths of Americans will no longer tolerate systems and structures of white supremacy and oppression. **#*stopAsianhate***, a more recent intersectional movement, became visible after months of protesting for social justice and experiencing the COVID-19 pandemic beginning in 2020. On March 16, 2021, the massacre of six persons of Asian descent as well as two white victims in the Atlanta, Georgia, area prompted another racial reckoning. As the nation reeled from this senseless act of racialized violence and the deadliest attack against Asians in recent U.S. history, more information came out on how violent rhetoric and historically racist dog whistles have a real impact on people's lives. Much of the anti-Asian violence has been attributed to former President Trump's descriptions of COVID-19 as the "Chinese Virus" and other virulent terms. The attribution of disease on Asian bodies is a long-standing trope amplifying white supremacy and confirming the perception that Asians in the U.S., regardless of immigration naturalization status, remain "perpetual foreigners" (Tessler et al., 2020). While much attention is given to them under the "model minority" characterization, not enough awareness surrounds their feelings of being "trapped in an American tragedy while being denied the legitimacy of being American" (Fan, 2021).

Not only does this anti-Asian violence represent an ongoing problem of racism in this country, but it also showed the dehumanization of Asian women. Six of the victims in the Atlanta area massacre were women of Asian descent. The perpetrator of the murders was described as just having a "really bad day" and suffering from a sex addiction who viewed his act as an elimination of a temptation that massage parlors represent. Fan (2021) discusses her experiences with how in a "split second […] a smidgen of sexual interest transmutes into racist scorn." Since the increasing tensions of 2020, it is more apparent than ever that intersectional justice is necessary. In 1969, Asian-American activist Uyematsu (1971) stated:

> Asian Americans can no longer afford to watch the black and white struggle from the sidelines. They have their own cause to fight since they are also victims—with less visible scars—of the white institutionalized racism. A yellow movement has been set into motion by the black power movement. Addressing itself to the unique problems of Asian Americans, this "yellow power" move-

Figure 15.3. © Adobe / blvdone

ment is relevant to the black power movement in that both are part of the Third World struggle to liberate all colored people.

Intersectionality requires us to unite social justice movements across places and spaces. Many have called for this type of collective action for decades.

Where Do We Go from Here?

Hashtag activism continues to be a form of social action and change for many. Using social media to uplift the causes you care about fall under "Advocacy and Raising Awareness" on the *Social Change Wheel* (Campus Compact Minnesota, 2020). The Social Change Wheel was designed by the Minnesota Campus Compact. It has a specific focus on getting college students to understand how they can be a part of social change. In a 2020 update, additional components were added to the wheel to indicate the need for centering anti-racism, co-creation and equity.

There are many causes to fight for, and sometimes it can be hard to know where to start and not feel overwhelmed by all that is occurring around you. However, there are lots of ways to get involved to make change for the causes that matter the most to you. First and foremost, practice your rights as a citizen and be sure to vote in elections at the local, state, and federal level. This falls under "Voting and Formal Political Activities" on the Social Change Wheel. It might sound like a simple action and it is, but there are far too few Americans who are participating in the political process. For example, in the 2016 presidential election only 55% of the population who was eligible to vote did so, which made it one of the lowest voter turnouts in two decades for a presidential election (Wallace, 2016). An example of voting as social change occurred in the Georgia Senate races of 2020. Record numbers of Black voters turned out for the January 2021 Georgia Senate runoff election. As a result, Black Georgians flipped two important Senate seats from Republican incumbents to Democrats who ran on platforms of justice and equity. The large Black voter turnout is attributed to Stacy Abrams, a former Georgia gubernatorial candidate and organizer with Black Votes Matter and a number of other Black grassroots organizations (Evelyn, 2021). The work of Abrams and her counterparts is an example of "Community Organizing" and "Community Building." Community organizing refers to "bringing people together to act collectively in their shared interest or toward a common goal." Community building means "strengthening the capacity of local residents and associations to work together by supporting opportunities for interpersonal connection."

Actively engage those who represent you at the local, state, and federal level. You can always write or email your representatives. However, phone calls or rather the volume of phone calls are more likely to make a staffer who works for the politician take notice and pass along your concerns and/or support. You also can make your voice heard by attending town hall meetings and directly engaging your representatives in a forum that is specifically set up for you to ask questions or raise concerns. Representatives notice numbers, and large crowds are much more likely to have their voice heard and are difficult to ignore, so do not to forget to bring your friends (Amatull, 2016).

Consider engaging in "Fundraising, Giving, and Philanthropy" or "Volunteering and Direct Service" by giving your time and/or money to causes that mean the most to you. Many of us do not give money to organizations because we believe that the small amount we are able to contribute would not have an impact. However, many small donations add up and can be used to lobby and make big changes—if 1,000 people each make a $25 donation to one organization, that organization now has $25,000 to further their mission. In the summer of 2014, for example, the Ice Bucket Challenge created awareness for the disease ALS and raised $220 million globally to help fight this disease. Those who participated in the fundraising effort created a video of themselves dumping a bucket of ice water over their heads and challenging a friend or family member to do the same along with making a donation to the ALS Association. The videos became a viral phenomenon and the many small donations that poured in began to add up (ALS Association, 2015).

Another way to make a change is engage in "Socially Responsible Daily Behaviors" by becoming aware of our own actions and implicit biases. When we discuss issues such as sexism and racism, we often make reference to *explicit bias* or when someone consciously acts in a biased manner towards another person due to their beliefs about that particular group. However, *implicit bias*, or when we engage those who are different from ourselves based on stereotypes or what we learn from media, can be just as problematic, if not more. This is because the person who engages in implicit bias is often unaware they are even doing it, which can make it difficult to change. As human beings we are all flawed, so it is incredibly important to remember that no matter who you are, or your background, you are most likely participating in implicit bias on some level. However, this can be addressed by taking the time to recognize our biases and then becoming more aware of our behaviors and how we treat those who are different from ourselves. For example, the Kirwan Institute for the Study of Race and Ethnicity at The Ohio State University has created what they call the seven-day bias cleanse. This program is intended to help make the participant aware of their biases regarding race and gender and provides strategies for how to reconcile with them (Kirwan Institute for the Study of Race and Ethnicity, 2015).

Discussion Questions

1. Is it possible for the United States to become post-racist and post-sexist or will there always be an element of discrimination regarding one's race and sex?

2. Briefly explain a social issue that is important to you. How could you work towards making change regarding this social problem?

Key Terms

Capitol Riot	intersectional feminism
justifiable homicides	#MeToo
George Floyd	#stopAsianhate
#BlackLivesMatter	hashtag activism
sexism	Social Change Wheel
misogyny	explicit bias
Women's March	implicit bias

References

ALS Association. (2015). Impact of the ice bucket challenge. http://www.alsa.org/news/archive/impact-of-ice-bucket-challenge.html

Amatull, J. (2016). Here's how to make sure Congress hears you. *The Huffington Post*. http://www.huffingtonpost.com/entry/contacting-your-congressional-representative_us_582a0965e4b060adb56f8e95

Associated Press. (2016). Walter Scott shooting: Officer Michael Slager's trial begins in South Carolina. *The Guardian*. https://www.theguardian.com/us-news/2016/oct/31/walter-scott-shooting-murder-trial-michael-slager-south-carolina

Baker, A., Goodman, J. D., & Mueller, B. (2015). Beyond the chokehold: The path to Eric Garner's death. *The New York Times*. https://www.nytimes.com/2015/06/14/nyregion/eric-garner-police-chokehold-staten-island.html

BBC News. (2016). Freddie Gray's death in police custody—What we know. http://www.bbc.com/news/world-us-canada-32400497

Berger, J. M. (2016). How White Nationalists learned to love Donald Trump. *Politico Magazine*. http://www.politico.com/magazine/story/2016/10/donald-trump-2016-white-nationalists-alt-right-214388

Blazina, C., & Desilver, D. (2021, January 15). A record number of women are serving in the 117th Congress. Pew Research Center. https://www.pewresearch.org/fact-tank/2021/01/15/a-record-number-of-women-are-serving-in-the-117th-congress/

Buchanan, L., Fessenden, F., Lai, K. K. R., Park, H., Parlapiano, A., Tse, A., Wallace, T., Watkins, D., & Yourish, K. (2017). What happened in Ferguson. *The New York Times*. https://www.nytimes.com/interactive/2014/08/13/us/ferguson-missouri-town-under-siege-after-police-shooting.html

Buchholz, K. (2022, March 10). How has the number of female CEOs in Fortune 500 companies changed over the last 20 years? *World Economic Forum*. https://www.weforum.org/agenda/2022/03/ceos-fortune-500-companies-female/

Brown, M., Ray, R., Summers, E., & Fraistat, N. (2017) #SayHerName: A case study of intersectional social media activism. *Ethnic and Racial Studies*, *40*(11), 1831–1846. https://doi.org/10.1080/01419870.2017.1334934

Campus Compact Minnesota (2020). Social change wheel 2.0 toolkit. https://mncampuscompact.org/resource-posts/social-change-wheel-2-0-toolkit/).

Capehart, J. (2016). Hillary Clinton on 'super predator' remarks: 'I shouldn't have used those words.' *The Washington Post*. https://www.washingtonpost.com/blogs/post-partisan/wp/2016/02/25/hillary-clinton-responds-to-activist-who-demanded-apology-for-superpredator-remarks/

Center for American Women in Politics. (n.d.). History of women of color in U.S. politics. Rutgers Eagleton Institute of Politics. https://cawp.rutgers.edu/history-women-color-us-politics

Clayton, D. (2018). Black Lives Matter and the Civil Rights Movement: A comparative analysis of two social movements in the United States. *Journal of Black Studies*, *49*(5), 448–480.

CNN Library. (2016). Trayvon Martin shooting fast facts. CNN. http://www.cnn.com/2013/06/05/us/trayvon-martin-shooting-fast-facts/

Coates, T.-N. (2015). There is no post-racial America. *The Atlantic*. https://www.theatlantic.com/magazine/archive/2015/07/post-racial-society-ditant-dream/395255/

Cobb, J. (2016, March 14). The matter of Black lives: A new kind of movement found its moment. What will its future be? *The New Yorker*. https://www.newyorker.com/magazine/2016/03/14/where-is-black-lives-matter-headed

Cobbina, J. (2019). *Hands up, don't shoot: Why the protests in Ferguson and Baltimore matter, and how they changed America*. New York University Press.

Congressional Research Service. (2022).Women in Congress: Statistics and brief overview. https://sgp.fas.org/crs/misc/R43244.pdf

Cumberbatch, P., & Trujillo-Pagan, N. (2016). Hashtag activism and why #BlackLives Matter in (and to) the classroom. *The Radical Teacher*, *106*, 78–86.

Dailymail.com. (2016). Trump gets mobbed by screaming fans at Ohio fair as they lay on the rock star treatment for him and Pence. http://www.dailymail.co.uk/news/article-3775181/Supporters-chant-Build-wall-Donald-Trump-arrives-greet-fans-Ohio-fair.html

Dictionary.com. (n.d.). Sexism. *The American heritage new dictionary of cultural literacy* (3rd ed.). http://www.dictionary.com/browse/sexism

Easley, J. (2017). Women's march is the biggest protest in US history as an estimated 2.9 million march. Politicus USA. http://www.politicususa.com/2017/01/21/womens-march-biggest-protest-history-estimated-2-4-million-march.html

Evelyn, K. (2021, January 7). How Black voters lifted Georgia Democrats to Senate runoff victories. *The Guardian.* https://www.theguardian.com/us-news/2021/jan/07/georgia-senate-runoff-black-voters-stacey-abrams

Fan, J. (2021, March 19). The Atlanta shooting and the dehumanizing of Asian women. *The New Yorker.* https://www.newyorker.com/news/daily-comment/the-atlanta-shooting-and-the-dehumanizing-of-asian-women

Fantz, A., Almasy, S., & Shoichet, C. E. (2015). Tamir Rice shooting: No charges for officers. CNN. http://www.cnn.com/2015/12/28/us/tamir-rice-shooting/

Fatal Force. (n.d.). *The Washington Post.* https://www.washingtonpost.com/graphics/national/police-shootings-2016/

Felton, R. (2016). Samuel DuBose shooting: University police officer to be retried for murder. *The Guardian.* https://www.theguardian.com/us-news/2016/nov/22/samuel-dubose-shooting-ray-tensing-retried-murder-unarmed

Filipovic, J. (2016). Donald Trump's 'p—y' comment is the root of sexual violence. *Time.* http://time.com/4523972/donald-trumps-comment-root-sexual-violence/

Garza, A. (2014). A herstory of the #BlackLivesMatter movement. https://www.thefeministwire.com/2014/10/blacklivesmatter-2/

Gass, H. (2015). Bernie Sanders on race: Did Black Lives Matter protest force his hand? *The Christian Science Monitor.* http://www.csmonitor.com/USA/Politics/2015/0817/Bernie-Sanders-on-race-Did-Black-Lives-Matter-protest-force-his-hand

Grinberg, E., & Shoichet, C. E. (2016). Brock Turner released from jail after serving 3 months for sexual assault. CNN. http://www.cnn.com/2016/09/02/us/brock-turner-release-jail/

Hannah-Jones, N. (2016). Iowa: The end of the post-racial myth. *The New York Times Magazine.* https://www.nytimes.com/interactive/2016/11/20/magazine/donald-trumps-america-iowa-race.html?_r=2

Hill, G. N., & Hill, K. T. (2005). Justifiable homicide. The Free Dictionary. http://legal-dictionary.thefreedictionary.com/Justifiable+homicide

Hinchliffe, E. (2021, June 2). The female CEOs on this year's Fortune 500 just broke three all-time records. *Fortune.* https://fortune.com/2021/06/02/female-ceos-fortune-500-2021-women-ceo-list-roz-brewer-walgreens-karen-lynch-cvs-thasunda-brown-duckett-tiaa/

Ilchi, O. S., & Frank, J. (2020). Supporting the message, not the messenger: The correlates of attitudes towards Black Lives Matter. *American Journal of Criminal Justice*, *46*, 377–398.

Izadi, E. (2014). Ohio Wal-Mart surveillance video shows police shooting and killing John Crawford III. *The Washington Post*. https://www.washingtonpost.com/news/post-nation/wp/2014/09/25/ohio-wal-mart-surveillance-video-shows-police-shooting-and-killing-john-crawford-iii/

Kindy, K., & Kelly, K. (2015). Thousands dead, few prosecuted. *The Washington Post*. http://www.washingtonpost.com/sf/investigative/2015/04/11/thousands-dead-few-prosecuted/

Kirwan Institute for the Study of Race and Ethnicity. (2015). Understanding implicit bias. The Ohio State University. http://kirwaninstitute.osu.edu/research/understanding-implicit-bias/

Kuhn, D. P. (2008). Exit polls: How Obama won. *Politico*. http://www.politico.com/story/2008/11/exit-polls-how-obama-won-015297

Leech, M. (2022, January 4). In pandemic, women at the top exhibited more empathetic and adaptable leadership. *Bizjournal*. https://www.bizjournals.com/bizwomen/news/latest-news/2022/01/number-of-female-ceos-doubles-during-first-half-of.html?page=all

Li, D. K. (2016). Dallas sniper's parents break their silence. *The New York Post*. http://nypost.com/2016/07/11/parents-of-dallas-sniper-hate-what-he-did/

Manne, K. (2016). The logic of misogyny. *Boston Review*. http://bostonreview.net/forum/kate-manne-logic-misogyny

Misogyny. (n.d.). Dictionary.com. http://www.dictionary.com/browse/misogyny

Murphy, M. (2019). Introduction to #MeToo movement. *Journal of Feminist Family Therapy*, *31*(2–3).

National Institute of Justice. (2017). Research on body-worn cameras and law enforcement. https://www.nij.gov/topics/law-enforcement/technology/pages/body-worn-cameras.aspx

Paquette, D. (2016). Sexism is over, according to most men. *The Washington Post*. https://www.washingtonpost.com/news/wonk/wp/2016/08/22/sexism-is-over-according-to-most-men/

Pelligrini, A. (2018). #MeToo: Before and after. *Studies in Gender & Sexuality*, *19*(4), 262–264.

Petersen-Smith, K. (2015). Black lives matter: A new movement takes shape. *International Socialist Review*, 96. http://isreview.org/issue/96/black-lives-matter

Reynolds, B. (2015, August 24). I was a civil rights activist in the 1960s. But it's hard for me to get behind Black Lives Matter. *The Washington Post*. https://www.washingtonpost.com/posteverything/wp/2015/08/24/i-wasa-civil-rights-activist-in-the-1960s-but-its-hard-for-me-to-get-behind-blacklives-matter

Rubin, O., Mallin, A. Steakin, W. (2022, January 4). By the numbers: How the Jan. 6 investigation is shaping up 1 year later. *ABC NEWS*. https://abcnews.go.com/US/numbers-jan-investigation-shaping-year/story?id=82057743

Sayej, N. (2017). Alyssa Milano on the #METOO movement: 'We're not going to stand for it anymore'. *The Guardian*. https://www.theguardian.com/culture/2017/dec/01/alyssa-milano-mee-too-sexual-harassment-abuse

Semuels, A. (2016). No, most Black people don't live in poverty—or inner cities. *The Atlantic*. http://www.theatlantic.com/business/archive/2016/10/trump-african-american-inner-city/503744/

Tessler, H., Choi, M., & Kaom, G. (2020). The anxiety of being Asian American: Hate crimes and negative biases during the COVID-19 pandemic. *American Journal of Criminal Justice, 45*, 636–646.

Treisman, R. (2021, April 20). Where the Chauvin verdict fits in the recent history of high profile police killings. NPR. https://www.npr.org/sections/trial-over-killing-of-george-floyd/2021/04/20/989292294/where-the-chauvin-verdict-fits-in-the-recent-history-of-high-profile-police-kill

Uyematsu, A. (1971). The emergence of yellow power in America (reprinted from *Gidra*, October 1969). In A. Tachiki, E. Wong, F. Odo, & B. Wong (Eds.), *Roots: An Asian American Reader* (pp. 9–13). UCLA Asian American Studies Center.

Wallace, G. (2016). Voter turnout at 20-year low in 2016. CNN Politics. http://www.cnn.com/2016/11/11/politics/popular-vote-turnout-2016/

Warfield, Z. J. (2018). Me Too creator Tarana Burke reminds us this is about Black and Brown survivors. Yes! Solutions Journalism. https://www.yesmagazine.org/democracy/2018/01/04/me-too-creator-tarana-burke-reminds-us-this-is-about-black-and-brown-survivors

Women's March. (n.d.a). Mission. https://www.womensmarch.com/mission/

Women's March. (n.d.b). Principles. https://www.womensmarch.com/mission/

Glossary

#MeToo: A phrase coined by Tarana Burke that became a viral hashtag in October 2017 when actress Alyssa Milano asked her followers to tweet #METOO if they've been sexually assaulted or harassed.

#StopAsianHate: A more recent intersectional movement condemning violence against Asian-Americans and Pacific Islanders (AAPI) that became visible after months of protesting for social justice and experiencing the COVID-19 pandemic beginning in 2020.

100:1 ratio: This legislation stated the penalty for crack cocaine would be 100 times harsher than powder cocaine to reflect the belief that crack cocaine was far more dangerous than powder cocaine.

1033 Program: This program transfers excess military weapons and equipment from the United States military to local and state law enforcement to combat the War on Drugs and the War on Terror.

21st Century Policing: Best practices or strategies developed to assist law enforcement agencies in effectively reducing crime while also considering public trust and protecting the well-being of officers.

abolitionist strategies: Strategies that focus on reducing budgets and the use of technology while striving to scale down the scope of policing, ultimately leading to reimagined ways to ensure community safety and support.

ace: An umbrella term for those who do not feel sexually attracted to others and a synonym for asexual.

actus reus: An act that causes harm.

adultification: Refers to the unfair and unjustified application of adult-like characteristics and expectations on Black youth.

agender: When one does not identify with a specific gender identity.

akoiromantic: May experience romantic attraction to another person, but loses interest once the person reciprocates the romantic feelings.

akoisexual: May experience sexual attraction to another person, but loses interest once the person reciprocates the sexual feelings.

alienation: This occurs when the colonized begin to dislike themselves and those who look like them, due to their experiences with the colonizers. This results in people attempting to distance themselves from their own cultural traditions, values, and the larger group.

American Dream: The belief that many Americans hold, that if one works hard enough one can achieve success.

American GI Forum: This organization advocated for the rights of Mexican American veterans and was the only veteran organization that accepted Mexican Americans. They addressed social service needs in the community and were active in fighting against discrimination at the polls.

American Indian Movement (AIM): A social movement that focused on Indigenous civil rights.

Anti-Drug Abuse Act: This act was passed during the Reagan administration and is the basis for the War on Drugs as we know it today. This act was the beginning of an attempt to rid the United States completely of illegal drugs.

anti-racist: One who is supporting an anti-racist policy through their actions or expressing an anti-racist idea.

Argersinger v. Hamlin: This US Supreme Court case concluded that indigent defendants have the right to counsel for felony or misdemeanor charges when the defendant is facing imprisonment.

Arizona v. U.S.: This U.S. Supreme Court case ruled that immigration is a federal issue and one that should not be taken up by the states.

aro: Synonym for aromantic.

aromantic: Person who does not experience romantic attraction to others.

asexual: This refers to one who does not feel sexually attracted to any particular group of people, although they are not necessarily celibate.

assigned counsel: Those who are appointed by a judge and picked from a list of private attorneys to defend indigent clients.

Atkins v. Virginia: A U.S. Supreme Court case that held a defendant's intellectual disability prohibited him from adequately developing the criminal intent necessary to be sentenced to death.

Atlacatl Battalion: An elite military unit created and trained by the United States military and led by Colonel Domingo Monterossa.

Baldus Study: Three researchers examined 2,000 homicide cases in the state of Georgia since 1972 and found that race played a significant factor in whether one received the death penalty. They concluded that Black defendants were 1.7 times more likely to receive the death penalty than White defendants and those who murdered White victims were 4.3 times more likely to receive the death penalty than those who murdered Black victims.

Barrio 18: During the El Salvador Civil War Salvadorans fled to the United States and lived in impoverished neighborhoods where they often experience gang violence. This led to the creation of the Barrio 18 gang as a form of self-defense.

Battle of Blair Mountain: Largest armed insurrection in the United States since the Civil War, it included miners wanting to form an union, the sheriff's office, and the federal government.

Baze et al. v. Rees: In this United States Supreme Court case the defendants argued that the lethal injection process used in Kentucky and 30 other states violated their Eighth Amendment right against cruel and unusual punishment. The majority opinion (7–2) was that this process did not violate an inmate's Eighth Amendment right, if it was done correctly. The justices also concluded the defendants had not demonstrated that if the procedure was done incorrectly it would amount to cruel and unusual punishment. However, it was noted that this procedure could violate one's Eighth Amendment right, if there was an alternative execution method that was perceived to be more effective.

beyond a reasonable doubt: The level of evidence needed to convict someone of a crime. The judge or jury must not have any reasonable doubt the person committed the crime in order to come to the conclusion that the person is guilty.

bigender: When one has two distinct gender identities that can occur at the same time or independently.

The Birmingham Campaigns: Nonviolent civil rights protestors organized and participated in a series of protests, including lunch counter sit-ins as well as marches and targeted store boycotts, in Birmingham, Alabama, which led to the city of Birmingham agreeing to desegregate the city.

bisexual: A sexual orientation where one is sexually attracted to those of one's own gender as well as those of another gender.

#BlackLivesMatter: A social movement that was formed after the death of Trayvon Martin and the trial of George Zimmerman for the crime. It gained national prominence during the protests that occurred in Ferguson, Missouri, after Michael Brown was shot and killed by a police officer.

Bostock v. Clayton County, Georgia: On June 15, 2020, the United States Supreme Court, in a 6–3 decision, concluded that sexual orientation and being transgender were included under the Civil Rights Act and that one cannot be fired from one's job because one is gay or transgender.

Brown v. Board of Education: Thurgood Marshall argued that segregation in education was unconstitutional due to the unequal environments of segregated schools, and this violated the Fourteenth Amendment by denying an entire race equal protection under the law. The Supreme Court unanimously voted schools should no longer be segregated.

Capitol Riot: The January 6, 2021, insurrection in which disgruntled and dangerous Trump supporters stormed the Capitol to "take back their country" from an alleged stolen election.

Chapultepec Peace Accords: On January 16, 1992, an agreement was reached and the El Salvador Civil War officially ended. The agreement ended the war, reduced the size of the military, established a civilian police force, overhauled the electoral system, and reformed the judicial system. The agreement also reintegrated FMLN members back into social and political life by making the FMLN a legal political party.

charge bargaining: This is the most common type of plea bargain, where the defendant pleads guilty in exchange for being convicted of a lesser charge.

cis-gender: This category of gender refers to those whose biological makeup matches their gender identity.

citizenship profiling: Occurs when stops, searches, and inquiries by the police are related to immigration status.

civil case: The plaintiff brings a complaint against another person or organization because they believe the person or organization wronged them. The punishment in a civil case is a fine, where if the person is believed to have committed the act, they are required to pay the complainant an amount of money decided by the court to compensate them for the wrong.

Civil Rights Act of 1866: This act declared that one could not be discriminated against based on race for jobs or housing and all citizens are equally protected by the law.

Civil Rights Act of 1875: This act declared that one could not discriminate based on race for public accommodations or public transportation.

Civil Rights Act of 1964: This act prohibited segregation in public spaces, businesses, and schools along with the prohibition of discrimination in employment.

The Civil Rights Cases: This U.S. Supreme Court case declared the Civil Rights Act Of 1875 unconstitutional because one cannot force private individuals to abide by the law, only state agencies. The U.S. Supreme Court also concluded the Thirteenth Amendment eliminated slavery, but did not prohibit one from being discriminated against.

Coker v. Georgia: This United States Supreme Court case ruled the crime of rape could no longer be punished as a capital offense. The majority of the justices believed the death penalty for the crime of rape violated one's Eighth Amendment right against cruel and unusual punishment, because the punishment was excessive in comparison to the crime.

colonial model: This model examines the colonization of an area and the impact this experience has on the native population and their identity as well as their opportunities.

community-oriented policing: This policing strategy allows law enforcement to work together with the community to create an atmosphere of trust, where the community also has a stake in their own safety. By working with the community, the police can better understand the needs of the community and enforce the laws in a preventative manner by working together.

community partnership: This is the first step in implementing a community-oriented policing approach and occurs when the police work with stakeholders within the community to determine their needs and to create solutions.

concurrence: When the actus reus (action) and the mens rea (intent) occur together, creating a crime.

conflict theory: Those in power make the laws the rest of us abide by. The conflict occurs because those in power are not likely to make laws that will directly impact them or those who help them to get elected to office, such as campaign contributors.

contract attorneys: Defense attorneys who are utilized when the government secures a contract with an attorney for a period of time to defend indigent clients.

corporate crime: A crime committed by a corporation or their executives in an attempt to meet the goals of the corporation.

Crawford v. Washington: This case ruled that a victim's statement cannot be entered as evidence if the victim does not testify, because this violates the defendant's Sixth Amendment right to face their accuser and cross-examine the witness. However, other evidence such as medical records and 911 calls can be used to demonstrate the abuse did occur.

crime: A behavior that is deemed to be illegal or against the law by the majority of the population.

crimmigration: Where criminal and immigration law merge, encouraging local law enforcement to address immigration issues.

criminal case: The state or federal government brings charges against the accused because it is believed he or she has broken the law and caused harm. The accused must be found guilty beyond a reasonable doubt. The punishment in a criminal case is dependent upon the crime and can range from a fine to imprisonment.

CSI effect: The belief that crimes should be resolved quickly and there is always DNA at the scene that can be tested to verify the suspected offender committed the crime, due to the public's consumption of crime-based television shows.

cultural disintegration: This occurs when the native populations are no longer allowed to express their identity and culture and are punished for doing so.

cultural imposition: This is the notion that the colonizers' culture and values are superior to those of the indigenous population.

cultural recreation: This occurs when the colonizers replace the culture and values of the indigenous population with their own.

death penalty: This is a sentence of death for one who has committed a heinous crime, typically reserved for those who have committed the crime of murder.

death squads: Unmarked security forces that consist of military and police intelligence agencies.

decriminalization: This drug policy occurs when law enforcement no longer targets the use or possession of a drug. In instances of decriminalization, the drug is not legal. However, people are not incarcerated for possessing and in some cases selling the drug; rather, a fine or citation is issued.

defund the police: The act of reducing the ability for law enforcement to have resources that harm communities and reinvesting those dollars into communities of color.

delinquency: A violation of the law that would be a crime if not for the youthful age of the offender.

de-mandatorize: This occurs when the prosecutor does not reduce the charge, but instead does not add the mandatory minimum, allowing the offender to be sentenced under the sentencing guidelines.

demiromantic: Those who are only interested in forming a romantic relationship with others after a bond has been developed over time.

demisexual: Those who are only sexually attracted to others after a bond has been developed over time.

Department of Housing and Urban Development v. Rucker: This United States Supreme Court case examined a situation where tenants had been evicted based on the drug use of family members living with them even though the person whose name was on the lease did not condone the behavior and was not aware of the activity. In several instances, the illegal activity did not occur at the property, but in the surrounding neighborhood. However, the Supreme Court ruled in favor of the Department of Housing and Urban Development and upheld their decision to evict those they felt were a negative influence on the public housing community.

determinate sentencing: This occurs when an offender receives a set sentence for a crime; for instance, a person serves three years. Determinate sentencing was implemented to decrease the discretion judges and parole boards had in determining a sentence and so the offender knew exactly when they would be released from prison.

deterrence theory: A theory that states if you make the punishment outweigh any benefit one would receive from committing the crime, people will rationally choose not to commit the crime.

Differences of Sex Development (DSD): These diagnoses could occur for a variety of reasons and are typically genetic or related to chromosomal or hormonal production in utero. The end result could be over- or underdeveloped sex organs as well as the absence of the sex organ, depending upon the diagnosis.

direct militarization: The utilization of armed forces for domestic police work.

discretion: The decision to act or not to act based on one's professional experience and the circumstances that are occurring at the time.

disenfranchise: This occurs when one is denied the right to vote through legislation or intimidation.

Disproportionate Minority Contact: Refers to the overrepresentation of minority youth at critical decision points in the juvenile justice system.

domestic violence: A pattern of abusive behavior with the goal of gaining control or power over one's intimate partner.

domestic violence police units: Police officers who are specifically trained to work with domestic violence victims and community volunteers who assist victims with social services.

downward departure: When the judge decides to sentence below the minimum sentence suggested in the sentencing guidelines.

"driving while Black": This is used to describe the phenomena of Black drivers being pulled over by the police and searched on suspicion of a crime based solely upon the color of their skin.

drug courts: This is a type of problem-solving court that specifically focuses on defendants who have nonviolent drug charges or have committed a nonviolent crime due to their drug addiction.

Drug Treatment Alternative to Prison program (DTAP): This is a type of long-term residential program which is offered and supervised through the prosecutor's office. Participants who are eligible have been charged with a felony drug conviction, have at least one prior felony, and are addicted to substances. This program is a diversion program where participants are removed from the traditional criminal justice system.

dual arrest: This occurs in a domestic violence situation, where both the victim and offender are arrested.

dual diagnosis: This occurs when one has been diagnosed with both a mental health condition as well as a substance addiction.

economic subordination: This occurs when the colonized are not provided the same opportunities to improve their economic conditions, such as lack of employment within one's community or failing schools.

Eighth Amendment: This amendment protects citizens from receiving a cruel and unusual punishment for their criminal behavior.

El Mozote Massacre: This massacre occurred over four days in December of 1981 and is the largest massacre in modern Latin American history.

Emancipation Proclamation: This act freed slaves living in states fighting against the Union.

Enforcement Acts: If a state fails to recognize a Black man's right to be on a jury, vote, hold office, or be treated with equal protection under law then the federal government can step in to address the violation.

escalated force model: Protest policing strategy characterized by a mindset where police use the amount of force necessary to control the situation.

ethnicity: A way to categorize a group of people based on shared cultural meaning, for example, speaking the same language, living in the same country/region, and/or shared cultural traditions and holidays.

explicit bias: This occurs when someone consciously acts in a biased manner towards another person due to their beliefs about that particular group.

external colonialism: This occurs when one group invades the land of another and sets up a colony in order to maintain their presence.

extradition: This occurs when a country sends a person of interest or a person who needs to be sentenced to the country making the request.

fact bargaining: This type of plea bargain is used when a defendant pleads guilty in exchange for certain facts being left out of the case.

Families First Coronavirus Response Act: Gave working parents with children who were at home due to childcare or school closure 12 weeks of guaranteed paid leave. However, there were a lot of restrictions placed on this paid leave, such as working at a company that employed fewer than 500 employees.

family detention centers: Detention center where women and children are housed while they seek asylum.

Family Medical Leave Act (FMLA): This act entitles caretakers to take 90 days off from work without losing their jobs upon return, but it is up to the employer to decide whether this time is paid or not, and most employers do not provide paid leave.

Federal Adoption and Safe Families Act: This act was passed in an attempt to create a more stable environment for all children within the foster care system who often faced multiple short-term placements. Therefore, the act stated that children in foster care must be placed in permanent care, if the child has been in foster care 15 of the last 22 months.

Fifteenth Amendment: Amendment to the Constitution that stated all men despite, color, race, or if one had been previously enslaved, have the right to vote.

Flores Settlement Agreement: Migrant children must be released without delay from detention to their parents, relatives, or a licensed program, for instance a foster care program. During detention, children must be provided with food, water, medical assistance, toilet and sink, temperature-controlled environment, supervision, and separation from unrelated adults.

FMLN: The Farabundo Marti Front for National Liberation consisted of students, farm labor, factory workers, teachers, and those who had been involved in the government in El Salvador. They were inspired by the 1950s Cuban revolutionaries who were able to overthrow their government through armed resistance.

Form I-360, Petition for Amerasian, Widow(er), or Special Immigrant: This form can be used by victims of domestic violence who are not documented and have been abused by a family member with whom they reside to request a green card or permanent resident status.

Fourth Amendment: This amendment protects citizens against unreasonable searches and seizures.

Fourteenth Amendment: An amendment to the Constitution passed in 1868 that stated that all men, regardless of race, had access to due process and equal protection under the law.

Furman v. Georgia: This United States Supreme Court case examined whether the death penalty violated the defendants' Eighth Amendment right against cruel and unusual punishment. A couple of the justices believed the death penalty itself was cruel and unusual, but the majority opinion was that the death penalty was applied arbitrarily or unfairly from one case to the next.

Gaines v. Canada: Gaines, a Black student, was denied admission to the all-White Missouri State Law School. The court upheld the *Plessey* decision and concluded the state of Missouri had to pay for Gaines to attend school out of state or build a law school for Black students. This began the dismantling of "Separate but Equal," because it was now more expensive and logistically difficult to uphold segregation.

Gall v. United States: The Supreme Court of the United States decided that federal judges could depart from the minimum sentence in the sentencing guidelines, if they were able to explain and justify the departure from the guideline.

gay: This is defined as being sexually attracted to members of the same sex, for example, males who are sexually attracted to males or females who are sexually attracted to females, although this term is more commonly used to refer to men who are sexually attracted to other men.

gender: This concept is defined by how one identifies within society as either masculine or feminine.

gender fluid: One who moves between two gender identities.

gender queer: Synonym for nonbinary.

George Floyd: A Black man murdered by Minneapolis police officer Derek Chauvin. Floyd's recorded death in 2020 sparked social justice protests across the world.

Ghost Dance: A dance performed by Native Americans in the nineteenth century. The dancers would dance in a circle for hours on end as a form of prayer and meditation asking for help from their ancestors. After dancing for hours, sometimes they would fall over and die from exhaustion and starvation. The Ghost Dance did not harm anyone, but it scared the White people who were living in the area.

Gideon v. Wainwright: This United States Supreme Court case concluded those who are unable to afford an attorney will have one appointed, if charged with a felony crime.

good time credit: This is a form of early release where every day one serves in prison and doesn't get into trouble can be applied towards an earlier release date.

The Great Chain of Being: Monarchies relied on this concept to impart the belief to their subjects that if they offended against the crown, they would be offending directly against God. This is because God is the highest on the chain followed by the king, people, animals, and plants.

The Great Migration: As part of Operation Bootstrap the United States actively recruited Puerto Ricans living on the island to immigrate to the United States for seasonal and full-time work to reduce unemployment. This mass exodus led to 25% (500,000) of the Puerto Rican population leaving for the mainland between 1950 and 1970.

Gregg v. Georgia: This United States Supreme Court case removed the moratorium placed on the death penalty by the case *Furman v. Georgia*.

grey-asexual: Someone who is somewhere between asexual and sexual who may experience sexual attraction sometimes.

greyromantic: One who falls between aromatic and romantic who experiences romantic attraction in some circumstances and none in others.

guardian mindset: A law enforcement mindset that focuses on protection and service and embraces building community trust by engaging in positive interactions.

harm reduction: This type of drug policy is defined as reducing the damage caused by drugs instead of attempting to eradicate drug use. Harm reduction recognizes that not all who use substances have a drug addiction, but those who are addicted need to receive treatment. Policies are then created to recognize addiction as a medical problem and that assist in reducing social and emotional damage.

hashtag activism: A form of internet activism that uses hashtags to unite social media users on social or political issues and create a space where conversations can span across the world.

Hernandez v. Texas: Mexican Americans, although categorized as White, were not treated as such and were segregated and discriminated against as though they were a special class in violation of the Fourteenth Amendment. The United States Supreme Court voted unanimously that Mexican Americans, as well as other ethnicities and races beyond Black and White, did have the right to be recognized under the Fourteenth Amendment.

heterosexual: This sexual orientation is defined as being attracted only to those of the opposite sex, for example, males who are sexually attracted to females and females who are sexually attracted to males.

Hispanic: Those who can trace their origin to Spain or Spanish-speaking countries.

homosexual: This is the clinical term for being attracted to members of the same sex and is viewed by some to have a negative connotation.

Housing Opportunity Program Extension Act: This act created the one-strike law for public housing. The law was put in place to protect the majority of those living in public housing who were not committing crime in order to create a safer environment by removing those who were participating in illegal behavior.

Human Genome Project: Researchers mapped the human genome and concluded there were not separate species of humans.

human trafficking: The United Nation's definition includes three parts. First, there is the criminal act itself, which can consist of recruiting a person, providing them with transportation or moving them from one place to another, housing them, or receiving the person. The second part of the definition includes how the act occurs and can include, "threat or use of force, coercion, abduction, fraud, deception, abuse of power or vulnerability, or giving payments or benefits to person in control" (United Nations Office on Drugs and Crime, 2016a, para 3). The third part of the definition is the purpose of the exploitation, which can include sexual acts, forced labor, slavery, or for the removal of organs (United Nations Office on Drugs and Crime, 2016a).

Hurricane Maria: This hurricane was the third most expensive hurricane in United States' history, with 94 billion dollars in damage and 80% of Puerto Rico's crops destroyed (Mercy Corps, 2020). Over the next couple of years, nearly 200,000 Puerto Ricans would leave the island due to the slow recovery and the lack of power on the island for nearly a year (Acevedo, 2020).

Immigration and Nationality Act: This act gave the federal government control over immigration regulations, allowing the United States Congress to define immigration policy and the White House to enforce immigration laws.

implicit bias: This occurs when we engage those who are different from ourselves based on stereotypes or what we learn from media. This can be problematic, because the person who engages in implicit bias is often unaware they are even doing it, which can make it difficult to change.

income inequality: The variety of ways one has money coming into one's home and how these resources are distributed within a population.

indentured servitude: The contract between an employer and a laborer where the laborer is brought to the United States and in exchange the laborer works off the debt for a set number of years with the promise of eventual freedom.

indeterminate sentence: This is a criminal sentence that contains a range with a minimum and a maximum, for instance three to five years. Once the person has served the minimum sentence they are eligible to apply for parole, where a parole board will determine whether or not they should be released from prison early.

indigent defendants: Those who are unable to afford an attorney.

indirect militarization: Police departments gearing themselves with military-grade equipment.

institutional racism: This occurs when the policies and procedures of an institution, public or private, treat people differently or provide different services based upon race.

internal colonialism: This ensues when the colonized are subjected to a subordinate position within the larger community and occurs through political, economic, and social subordination.

intersectional feminism: This occurs when the perspectives of all women no matter their race, ethnicity, class, gender identity, or disability are taken into consideration when fighting for women's rights.

intersectionality: A term coined by Kimberle Crenshaw in 1981 to describe the ways multiple oppressions intersect to impact lives.

intersex: Replaced the term hermaphrodite and is defined as between sexes. This term has been replaced by Differences of Sex Development (DSD).

investigatory stops: Occur when safety stops shift towards a focus on decreasing the incidence of violent crime and drug trafficking.

Jim Crow laws: These social laws segregated Black people and White people in public and social spaces within the South, for example, by providing separate bathrooms for White people and Black people as well as separate restaurants and stores.

Jones-Shafroth Act: The passage of this act gave United States citizenship to all who lived in Puerto Rico.

justifiable homicide: This occurs when a police officer, during the course of their duty, kills a civilian without any ill intent or malice.

Kennedy v. Louisiana: This United States Supreme Court case ruled the death penalty was excessive for the crime of raping a child. In a 5– 4 decision, the majority opinion concluded the punishment was excessive when the offender did not kill or intend to kill the victim.

Latino: Those who can trace their roots to Latin America.

Latinx: Describes those of Hispanic and Latino descent and is used to be more gender and LGBTQ inclusive, as Spanish is a Romance language that is gender-based.

legal exoneration: A way to objectively identify people who have been wrongly sentenced to death using criteria adopted by the Death Penalty Information Center.

legalization: This drug policy occurs when one or more substances are legalized for consumption. This policy model allows the government to control how substances are taxed and sold along with their potency.

lesbian: A sexual orientation where women are sexually attracted to other women.

long-term residential care: This is a type of community supervision program where those under supervision live within the treatment center.

lower-middle class: Defined as those making between $46,000 and $75,000 per year.

lower-upper class: Defined as making millions of dollars per year.

mandatory arrest: A policy that says the police are required to make an arrest when they are called to the scene of a domestic violence incident.

mandatory minimum sentences: These sentences are enacted by legislators and declare that if one is convicted (found guilty) of a particular crime then they will serve the entire required sentence set forth by the legislation.

Manifest Destiny: The belief that it was the duty of the United States to go west and acquire land to spread its ideas of freedom and democracy.

Matewan Massacre: Private police had been sent to Mingo County to remove people from their coal company housing who were involved in union organizing. Instead they were met at the train station by the sheriff, the mayor, and miners, which led to a gun fight where ten people died.

McKleskey v. Kemp: McKleskey, an African American man, had murdered a White Atlanta police officer. McKleskey's defense argued that, based on the findings from the Baldus Study, McKleskey's death sentence was racially biased and should be thrown out. However, in a 5–4 decision the United States Supreme Court ruled that the sentence was not racially biased because "general patterns of discrimination do not prove that racial discrimination operated in a particular case."

mens rea: The intent to commit a crime.

mental health court: This is a type of problem-solving court, where the participants usually have a serious mental health diagnosis, such as bipolar disorder, schizophrenia, or major depression, and have committed a nonviolent misdemeanor or felony, where their criminal behavior was connected to their mental illness.

Miami model: Protest policing strategy reminiscent of the escalated force model, which acts as an extension of police militarization and seriously limits the right to protest. Named after tactics used in 2003 by the Miami Police Department during the Free Trade Area of the Americas meetings.

migrant caravans: These are formed to help protect those making the dangerous journey north as it is common for migrants to experience violent crimes along their journey, such as murder, rape, and robbery.

migrant smuggling: This occurs when a person is hidden from view and taken across national borders.

misogyny: This occurs when one does not like or trust women or harbors bias against them.

monogenism: The belief that there is only one human race.

moratorium: This is defined as temporarily stopping something.

MS-13: During the El Salvador Civil War Salvadorans fled to the United States and lived in impoverished neighborhoods where they often experienced gang violence. This led to the creation of the MS-13 gang as a form of self-defense.

National Association for the Advancement of Colored People (NAACP): This organization brought Black and White civil rights leaders together to fight for racial justice through the media, protests, investigating acts of lynching, and advocating for defendants of court cases.

negotiated management model: Prominent manner of protest policing strategy used to address civil unrest from the late 1970s to the late 1990s. This model was based on the assumption that police and the protestors have to work together to achieve desired outcomes.

no-drop prosecution: The prosecutor is not allowed to dismiss the charges in a domestic violence case and must work to gain the cooperation of the victim to participate in the case.

no-knock warrant: This type of warrant specifically states that the police do not have to knock or announce their presence. These warrants can be utilized if the police have reasonable suspicion, prior to attaining the warrant, that those inside the location might destroy physical evidence or be a physical threat.

nonbinary: an umbrella term used to describe those who do not fit into the traditional categories of male and female.

open-air drug markets: This occurs when one sells drugs outside on street corners, waiting for customers to approach.

Operation Bootstrap: Attracted American manufacturing companies to Puerto Rico by offering them cheap labor and eliminating the Puerto Rican corporate tax.

organizational component: This is the second step in implementing a community-oriented policing approach and occurs when the law enforcement agency's management, police officers, and technology must come together to support the mission of community-oriented policing.

pansexual: A sexual orientation that refers to one who self-identifies as being attracted to members of all gender identities.

parens patriae: Means "the state as the parent" and it is based on the premise that juveniles need the state to intervene in the best interest of a child if deemed necessary.

parole: This is supervised release from prison within the community. The parole officer sets criteria the parolee must meet under supervision within the community, and as long as these criteria are met, the parolee is released from parole supervision after the maximum portion of the sentence has been met. However, if the parolee does not meet the parole expectations, they can be sent back to prison to serve the remainder of their sentence.

Personal Responsibility and Work Opportunity Reconciliation Act: This act was a major overhaul of the federal welfare system. As part of this act, those who had been convicted of a drug felony were given a lifetime ban on Temporary Assistance to Needy Families (TANF), or the cash assistance program also known as welfare, as well as the Supplemental Nutrition Assistance Program (SNAP), formerly known as food stamps. Many states opted out of this ban or modified it in some way.

plea bargain: This occurs when the prosecutor and defense attorney negotiate and the offender admits guilt in return for being charged with a lower-level offense and/or a shorter sentence.

Plessey v. Ferguson: This United States Supreme Court case ruled that racially separated social and public spaces were constitutional as long as the spaces were equal.

police militarization: The practice of buying into and promoting a culture of using force as the solution to problems.

political subordination: This occurs when one is kept from being able to participate in the political process.

poll taxes: This policy was used to disenfranchise minority voters by requiring one to pay a tax prior to voting.

polygenism: The belief that humans fall into different species and are not one race.

preferred arrest: Police officers use their own discretion to decide whether to make an arrest or not when called to the scene for a domestic violence incident.

preponderance of the evidence: The level of evidence required for a civil case. The court only has to determine it is reasonably likely the person committed the act against the complainant.

presumptive sentencing guidelines: This provides a required base sentence for each crime that is determined by the seriousness of the offense as well as the offender's prior criminal history. The judge still retains some discretion, as they can take into consideration aggravating circumstances and increase the sentence or mitigating circumstances and decrease the sentence. However, if a judge departs from the required sentence under the sentencing guidelines, they have to provide written justification, and the judge's decision is later reviewable at the appellate level.

Priority Enforcement Program (PEP): This program replaced Secure Communities. ICE has to determine if the person who has been arrested and is in the country illegally fits one of the priorities set forth by the DHS for removal. If the person does not fit a priority for removal, they are not to be placed in the custody of ICE. This allows ICE to question and possibly deport those who meet the priorities for re-moval prior to their release from local police custody.

private prison industry: These are for-profit institutions that house inmates based on a contract between the company and the government.

privilege: This advantage is often not acknowledged by the group who holds it and can be difficult to notice unless you are the one being excluded. You can be privileged in one area of your life and not in another. For example, you could experience advantages due to your race being White, but face disadvantages in other situations because you identify as gay.

probable cause: This is the belief a crime has been or is about to be committed.

problem-solving courts: These are specialized courts that attempt to break the cycle of recidivism by working directly with the defendants to keep them from getting further involved in the criminal justice system and to help them reenter their community to be successful citizens.

procedural justice: Centers fairness and involves police officers treating community members with dignity and respect.

profiling: This is a practical tool used by law enforcement to help an officer narrow down potential suspects, where an officer uses observed behavior to determine if there is reasonable suspicion the person may be committing a crime.

prohibition: This drug policy is based on making substances illegal, targeting these substances through law enforcement, and sentencing those who are convicted of the crimes with harsh punishments. The ultimate goal of prohibition is complete eradication of all drug use.

PROMESA: In 2016, the United States Congress passed the Puerto Rico Oversight Management and Economic Stability Act. This act created an eight-member oversight board tasked with restructuring Puerto Rico's debt, and which limited debt collection through lawsuits for a period of time, lowered the federal minimum wage on the island for those 24 years of age and younger from $7.75/hour to $4.25/hour, and cut pension payments by 10%.

Protection from Abuse Act: This allowed women who were experiencing physical abuse or the threat of it to themselves or their children to file a restraining order, which would remove the husband from the house and allow the wife to gain temporary custody of the children as the case went to court.

protest policing: The control of protests, which requires a difficult balance between the protection of legal order and defense of individual freedom, and citizens' rights to political participation.

public defenders: Those who are salaried and work for the government or a nonprofit organization to provide legal counsel to those who cannot afford it.

race: A way to categorize a group of people based on common physical characteristics, such as skin color or hair texture.

racial profiling: This occurs when a police officer targets or suspects someone of a crime based on their race, ethnicity, national origin, or religion.

racial terror lynchings: Often taking place on the "courthouse lawn," these acts of terrorism bypassed existing state-sanctioned justice processes and instead used the heinous murders of Black people to terrorize whole communities while never holding the perpetrators accountable (see: https://eji.org/wp-content/uploads/2005/11/lynching-in-america-3d-ed-110121.pdf).

recidivate: When one is released from supervision by the criminal justice system and then becomes involved in the criminal justice system again.

recipromantic: Are not attracted to a person romantically until they know that person is attracted to them.

reciprosexual: Are not attracted to a person sexually until they know that person is attracted to them.

reentry: This occurs when one returns from prison to one's community.

reformist strategies: Strategies that typically increase police budgets and include body cameras, community policing, diversity training, and civilian review boards.

remittance: This occurs when family living abroad sends money back to their home country to help support their families.

replacement effect: This occurs when those who are arrested and removed from the street corners are easily replaced by another drug dealer waiting to take their place.

Roper v. Simmons: A U.S. Supreme Court case that eliminated the death penalty for juvenile defendants.

school-to-prison pipeline: The collection of policies, practices, conditions, and prevailing consciousness that facilitate both criminalization within educational environments and the processes by which this criminalization results in the incarceration of youth and young adults.

scrip: How coal company paid coal miners for their labor. It could only be spent in the coal town.

Second Chance Act: This act provides federal grants to government and nonprofit agencies in order to implement programs to assist ex-offenders in their transition back into the community. The act specifically funds programs that address employment, housing, family programming, and mentoring, as well as substance abuse and mental health treatment.

Secure Communities: This program was created in an effort to manage the issue of immigration at the federal level in order to remove those who were violent and/or felony offenders who also were undocumented and in the United States illegally, with an ultimate goal of removing up to 400,000 people per year.

Senate Bill 1070: This bill has been recognized as the toughest state immigration law and was an attempt to make coming into the state of Arizona illegally so difficult that one would be deterred from doing so.

sentence bargaining: This type of plea bargain occurs when a defendant pleads guilty after the prosecutor has agreed to recommend a lower sentence for the crime committed.

sex: This concept is typically categorized into the two categories of male and female and is determined by one's biological makeup, such as chromosomes and hormones along with external and internal sex organs.

sexism: This is the belief that males are superior to females and should therefore be the dominate sex in making decisions regarding political, social, and economic matters.

sexuality: This is defined as who you are attracted to sexually, who you choose to engage in sexual activity with, and how you identify your behavior.

sexual orientation: This is defined as the sexual attraction one feels towards others.

"show me your papers": This section of Arizona's Senate Bill 1070 refers to the police in Arizona having the power to stop and question, arrest, or detain anyone they believe to be undocumented.

Slaughter House Cases: The U.S. Supreme Court concluded the Fourteenth Amendment only applied to an American citizen's federal rights and not their state rights.

smart probation: This occurs when someone is placed on probation, but when they are unable to comply with the conditions of probation and are placed in jail for a short-term, usually two- or three-day, stay. This allows the probation officer as well as the judge to have a sanction that can be utilized without having to place the person in prison or jail for a longer period of time.

Social Change Wheel: Designed by the Minnesota Campus Compact, it has a specific focus on getting college students to understand how they can be a part of social change.

social construction: Concepts that are perceived as the norm and have a commonly accepted meaning to society or a group.

social subordination: This occurs when people are segregated from the larger society.

socioeconomic status (SES): This is determined by measuring an individual's or group's education, income, and employment. One's SES directly impacts one's quality of life, including development across the lifespan as well as physical and mental health. SES also is a powerful measurement, because it provides insight into inequalities regarding access to resources, while also examining how privilege, power, and control impact these opportunities.

Southern Christian Leadership Conference (SCLC): The civil rights group founded by Dr. Martin Luther King that used nonviolent protest as a mechanism to bring awareness to the issue of segregation in the South.

Spanish-Cuban-American War: United States invaded Cuba and the Philippines in support of the revolutionaries in both countries who were trying to overthrow their Spanish governments for their independence

stop and frisk: This occurs when the police officer is unable to form probable cause, but has a reasonable suspicion a crime is about to take place. The officer in this situation has the right to stop this person, question them, and frisk or pat them down on the outer layers of their clothing in order to look for guns or drugs. If the officer believes they have detected a gun or drugs based on the frisk, the officer can conduct a more invasive search of the person and their property.

stop, question, and frisk: A law enforcement policy implemented in New York City, where officer were encouraged to stop and frisk those they believed were carrying weapons or drugs. The policy was eventually found to be unconstitutional because it differentially impacted people based on race and ethnicity.

street crime: This is what we typically think of when the term "crime" is used; for example, assault (physically harming another), robbery (taking property by force or the threat of force), murder (taking the life of another with the intent to cause harm), drug sales (selling illegal drugs), and theft (taking the property of another) would all be categorized as street crimes.

substantial assistance departure: This tactic is used by federal prosecutors when the defendant cooperates with the prosecutor and provides information to assist with the prosecution of another offender. In exchange for the defendant's testimony, the prosecutor asks the judge for the defendant to be sentenced outside of the sentencing guidelines. The prosecutor then makes a sentencing recommendation, but the ultimate sentencing decision belongs to the judge.

SWAT: Special Weapons and Tactics units within police departments that were originally intended to be used in hostage and barricade situations, but have in recent years also been used in cases where the person is suspected of selling illegal drugs.

Tax code section 936: In 1976, the United States federal government implemented this tax code to allow companies doing business in United States' territories tax breaks on income generated there.

Temporary Protected Status (TPS): This allowed Salvadorans who had fled the violence of the civil war to legally live and work in the United States.

Terry v. Ohio: Terry appealed his case to the United States Supreme Court and stated that his Fourth Amendment rights were violated, because the officer searched him without probable cause because it is not illegal to look into a store window. The court upheld the verdict and stated the officer could use reasonable suspicion in a case such as this, where the officer had a reasonable belief that either he or the community was in danger.

therapeutic community: This is a type of long-term residential care program where the staff and patients work together in a treatment setting that is intended to help the participant work on their strengths as well as weaknesses, both socially and emotionally.

third gender: A category of gender that refers to those who do not identify with a specific gender or take on multiple gender identities, as well as cultures that recognize three or more gender categories.

Thirteenth Amendment: Amendment to the Constitution passed in 1865 that abolished the practice of slavery throughout the United States.

three-strikes rule: This rule differs from one state to the next, but essentially requires a person who is convicted of a second felony sentence to serve a longer sentence than would typically be given and a life sentence or a significantly longer sentence than normal for a third felony conviction.

traditional probation: This occurs where one is sentenced to community supervision instead of incarceration. Probation officers supervise the offender within the community, which allows the probationer to keep their ties within the community, for example, to stay connected with family and/or a job. Probation officers also provide assistance to those who have specific needs, such as for drug treatment, counseling, or vocational training.

Trafficking Victims Protection Act (TVPA): A federal act which made human trafficking a criminal offense in the United States, increased the punishment for the crime of human trafficking, and assisted those who were brought into the country illegally with visas and the possibility of citizenship after three years.

transgender: A category of gender, where one's biological sex does not match their gender identity or how they present themselves to the world.

Treaty of Guadalupe Hidalgo: This treaty ended the Mexican-American War and gave 500,000 square miles of land— approximately half of the country of Mexico—to the United States for what is now known as the state of Texas.

Treaty of Paris: This treaty ended the Spanish-Cuban-American War and gave Cuba its independence from Spain. It also gave the islands of Puerto Rico and Guam to the United States and required Spain to sell the Philippines to the United States.

truth-in-sentencing: This occurs when an offender must serve 80% or more of a sentence.

T visas: A visa that can be granted to those who assist in the prosecution of human trafficking cases or are victims of trafficking under the age of eighteen.

two spirit: The two spirit feminine man is a biological male who fulfills traditional feminine roles within the community, while a two spirit masculine woman is a biological female who fulfills traditional male roles within the community. However, the Navajo would not consider the two spirit person to be transgender, because this is not something the two spirit person decides, but it is rather a decision made by the elders within the community.

unaccompanied minors: Children without a legal guardian present who have crossed the border into the United States from Central America and Mexico.

underclass: Those making less than $9,000 per year.

United States v. Booker: The Supreme Court of the United States decided that sentencing guidelines at the federal level would no longer be mandatory, but would instead be voluntary.

upper-middle class: Those grossing $76,000 or more.

upper-upper class: Those earning hundreds of millions up to billions of dollars per year.

U.S. v. Sokolow: The United States Supreme Court ruled a police officer could stop and frisk someone who was reasonably suspected to be involved in illegal drugs.

U visa: A visa one can apply for if one has been mentally or physically abused and is willing and able to help the police investigate and prosecute the case.

variance: When judges use their discretion to depart from the sentencing guidelines.

Violence Against Women Act: This act funds services for victims of sexual assault and domestic violence at the state and federal level, training for police and court officials as well as provisions for women to file civil charges against their perpetrator.

voluntary advisory guidelines: These are recommended sentences for each crime that also take into consideration the seriousness of the offense and prior criminal history as well as aggravating and mitigating circumstances.

Voting Rights Act 1965: This act made literacy tests illegal and assigned federal monitors to states that had participated in discriminatory practices related to voting.

warrior mindset: A law enforcement mindset that focuses on officer safety and crime fighting, including militarization and traditional policing.

wealth: This is measured by taking one's assets or what one owns (for example—house, stock, retirement, and savings) and subtracting one's liabilities or debt (for example— mortgage, credit card balance, or student loans).

wealth inequality: The unequal distribution of assets within a country.

white supremacy: A doctrine of White superiority and non-White inferiority that justifies domination and prejudicial treatment of minority groups.

whiteness: Refers to the way that White cultural traditions (customs and beliefs) serve as a basis of normality by which all other groups are compared. (see: https://nmaahc.si.edu/learn/talking-about-race/topics/whiteness)

Whren v. United States: This United States Supreme Court case questioned whether it violated one's Fourth Amendment right against unreasonable search and seizure to have one's car searched after a traffic stop for a minor traffic violation when there was no probable cause or suspicion of a crime. Ultimately, the Supreme Court ruled the law enforcement strategy did not violate one's Fourth Amendment rights because the Fourth Amendment only applies to unusually harmful searches and seizures.

Wilkins v. Maryland State Police: Wilkins was pulled over and his car was searched by the Maryland State Police. The police did not find any drugs on Wilkins or in his car, and he was not issued a ticket for any traffic violations. After this incident, Wilkins sued the Maryland State Police, stating that he was targeted by the police solely because of the color of his skin. The Maryland State Police settled the case and as part of the settlement were ordered to keep records on the demographics of those pulled over and searched in an effort to determine if there were larger racial patterns.

Women's March: This protest march has been called the largest one-day protest in American history. The day after President Trump's inauguration, men and women from all backgrounds marched in Washington, D.C., and in cities across the country, for equal rights for all.

working class: Those making between $19,000 and $45,000 per year.

working poor: Those grossing $9,000 to $18,000 per year.

Wounded Knee Massacre: U.S. army was sent to control the Lakota population who were protesting their living conditions on the reservation. The military rounded up members of Chief Big Foot's band and took away their weapons. The soldiers lined up above the encampment and after a lot of tension and confusion began to shoot the Lakota below with rifles and a rapid fire Hotchkiss gun, killing over 300 people, including mostly women, children, and elderly.

zero-tolerance immigration policy: This policy was put in place to serve as a deterrent to those considering crossing the border and separated parents from their children as they crossed the border into the United States.

Index